"Thomas Kidd's *American History* is a unique and significant contribution to the field. The author is especially masterful in his ability to highlight the intellectual and religious threads running through the tapestry of American history. Written in lucid prose, and interspersing narrative and commentary, these two volumes will captivate the imagination of a generation of students."

—**Bruce Ashford**, provost and dean of faculty,
Southeastern Baptist Theological Seminary, Wake Forest, NC

"Every teacher knows the frustration of trying to find a good textbook. The annual ritual makes them doubt any textbook exists that engages students, balances coverage with detail, and avoids the dreariness of ideological fashions. American history textbooks are among the worst offenders. Thomas Kidd has taken on the challenge and has written a survey of American history that goes beyond solving the problem. He highlights the experiences of ordinary people whose lives intersected with great events, brings religion back in from the margins of national life, and equips students to understand the often confusing world into which they were born."

—**Richard Gamble**, professor of history, Anna Margaret Ross Alexander Chair
of History and Politics, Hillsdale College, Hillsdale, MI

"This American history textbook sets a new standard for balanced treatment of political and cultural issues. Brisk and readable, it gives coverage of American history all the way through the 9/11 terrorist attacks and the election of Donald Trump, which so many textbooks don't reach. This new narrative is particularly valuable for balancing attention to minority groups and events crucial to the shaping and development of Christian culture and its impact on the main events of American history. It is about time that an American history textbook took notice of figures such as C. S. Lewis and Pope John Paul II and their transformative influence on American religion."

—**Susan Hanssen**, associate professor of history,
history department chair, University of Dallas, Dallas, TX

"Kudos to Thomas Kidd for returning Christianity to the narrative of American history. At the same time, he has conveyed in his measured, balanced, and accessible style, the multiethnic and multicultural tapestry that American history is, and always has been."

—**H. Paul Thompson Jr.**, dean of humanities,
history department chair, North Greenville University, Tigerville, SC

AMERICAN HISTORY

VOLUME 2 1877–PRESENT

THOMAS S. KIDD

B&H ACADEMIC
NASHVILLE, TENNESSEE

American History, Volume 2
Copyright © 2019 by Thomas S. Kidd

Published by B&H Academic
Nashville, Tennessee

ISBN: 978-1-4336-4443-6

Dewey Decimal Classification: 973
Subject Heading: UNITED STATES—HISTORY / UNITED STATES—
CIVILIZATION / UNITED STATES—RELIGION

Scripture quotations are taken from the Holy Bible, King James Version
(public domain).

The web addresses referenced in this book were live and correct at the time of the
publication of the book but may be subject to change.

Cover design by Darren Welch. "Once Upon a Time in Manhattan" painting
© Charles Santarpia.

Printed in the United States of America

1 2 3 4 5 6 7 8 9 10 • 24 23 22 21 20 19
VP

To Jonathan and Joshua Kidd

CONTENTS

Volume 2: American History, 1877–present

ACKNOWLEDGMENTS

Thanks to my wonderful, supportive colleagues at Baylor, including History Department chair Barry Hankins and Byron Johnson, director of Baylor's Institute for Studies of Religion. Thanks to my Baylor research assistants, including Kristina Benham, Matt Millsap, and Paul Gutacker; to my agent and friend, Giles Anderson; and to the great staff at B&H Academic, including Jim Baird, Chris Thompson, and Sarah Landers. As always, I am so thankful for my wife, Ruby, and my sons, Jonathan and Josh.

INTRODUCTION

Writing an overview of American history—or of any nation's history—is a daunting task. There's so much to cover, yet so much has to be left out. Most people who have ever lived left us little to no surviving records of their lives. Historical overviews usually focus on luminaries such as presidents, tycoons, inventors, and celebrities. And they focus on great events such as battles, economic disasters, and presidential elections. My overview of American history focuses a great deal on such characters and events too. But I have tried where possible to weave in anecdotes of regular people as well. Often my justification for weaving in such stories is their utter typicality, or the way they illuminate people's everyday experiences and struggles.

Focusing on great events also risks giving the impression that those events had the same significance for everyone in America, but that has rarely been the case. Take the Revolutionary War journal of Baptist chaplain Hezekiah Smith, for example. The July 1776 weekend that the Declaration of Independence was signed, Smith wrote one line in his journal: "Something unwell, tho' kept about." He was sick and did not know about events transpiring in Philadelphia that weekend. What seems inordinately significant in retrospect may not have seemed so important at the time. Conversely, events and people that seem momentous at the time may not appear that way in retrospect.

To narrow the focus of this book and make it manageable, I have emphasized certain major themes in American history. Some of the focus emerges from my own interests and perspective. Readers should know that I am a Christian, and a Baptist in particular. I identify with the historic evangelical tradition and the faith of figures such as the Baptist champions of revival and religious liberty in the eighteenth century. This commitment profoundly shapes my view of history. Therefore, I give a lot of attention to religion. I admittedly think that religious people (which in America has mostly meant Christians), for all their faults, have generally been a force for good in American history. I also illustrate that America's best ideas and most stirring speeches have often been rooted in the language and concepts of faith.

Another major theme of this book is racial and ethnic conflict. From the coming of the first colonizers, and the first shipments of slaves, racial tension and violence have been enduring themes in American history. They remain so today. There are obvious signs of progress in race relations in American history such as the end of slavery and the civil rights movement. But just when we think we've entered a "post-racial" America, racial controversies and racial violence roil American society again. These themes, both valuable and painful to consider, are ones to which Christian historians should give special attention.

A final major theme is the state of American culture, especially with regard to issues such as virtue, traditional moral norms, mass media, and entertainment. These issues are in the background of the whole book. Beginning in the late nineteenth century, however, entertainment and mass media have become progressively central to everyday American life. In an indirectly related development, our most basic cultural institutions, such as family and marriage, have come under increasing duress. Especially since the 1960s, Americans have been jettisoning some of our most basic assumptions about a good society and a wholesome life. We have simultaneously been "amusing ourselves to death," in the words of scholar Neil Postman, as mass media, sports, entertainment, and marketing have become increasingly paramount in our daily lives. I tend to observe and describe rather than excoriate and prescribe in this book. But the accelerating pace of social change, and Americans' concomitant obsession with entertainment, will be obvious.

A book on American history is something like national autobiography. It tells us how we got where we are. It cautions us about mistakes and sins we have committed in the past and urges us not to go there again. It encourages us to understand why the past is often pertinent to the present. It inspires us by the courage of historical heroes and stiffens our resolve as we try to honor their legacies. Christians believe the kingdom of God is our ultimate commitment, and we should confuse no temporal nation with that kingdom. But we are also thankful for the ways God has moved in American history, redeeming untold millions of people and building his church in each generation. I hope that readers will grow in their appreciation for the role faith played in the American past and discern the ways in which America has been (or has not been) a congenial place for people of faith to flourish.

Reforging the Nation

Out of the wreckage of the Civil War, the American nation began to emerge as a fully continental power with new ambitions that extended to the world stage. The war-torn South would languish for decades, hamstrung by bitter racial strife and the destruction unleashed by the war on its infrastructure and its young men. But immigration, massive capitalist businesses, and urban centers would all boom during the post-Reconstruction era. White settlers would also pour onto the Great Plains and surge out to the Pacific coast, making America a more unified continent than it had ever been before.

For individual settlers, forging a new life in the West was often difficult, full of daily struggles and drudgery. In 1875, a nineteen-year-old woman named Luna Kellie went ahead with her father into Nebraska while her husband stayed behind in Missouri to accumulate more cash for their new farm. She also brought her five-month-old son with her. A few hundred miles northwest of Kansas City, they came to the village of Hastings, Nebraska, which Kellie regarded as a "mudhole" and the "worst looking little town I had ever seen." On the bleak prairie no trees or any other notable structures broke up the monotonous landscape. All she saw were occasional sod houses. She had not expected them to be so dirty. Her father reminded her that sod houses were dirty because they were made of dirt. Her family would live not in a sod house but in a dug-out, or a cave excavated into the side of a riverbank. It had the great advantage that its roof did not leak, unlike most pioneer structures.

Only a year before Kellie moved, the Great Plains were struck by an invasion of grasshoppers that reminded many of the plagues that beset Pharaoh in the book of Exodus. Everywhere they stepped, they crushed grasshoppers underfoot. The insects

Figure 16.1. J. C. Cram sod house, Loup County, Nebraska.

ate all vegetation in sight and reportedly even gnawed on green-colored clothing. They consumed root crops such as carrots and onions down into the ground. Laura Ingalls Wilder, author of the enduringly popular Little House books about frontier life, wrote that the grasshoppers were the one thing that nearly vanquished her mother's indomitable will. Wilder remembered listening to the incessant "whirring and snipping and chewing" of the innumerable grasshoppers as she lay in bed. Everywhere the grasshoppers went, they laid eggs, ensuring that their progeny would be back the next growing season.

Indian Wars

As people like the Kellie and Wilder families moved into the West, they were not entering an unpopulated wilderness. Continuing an American story that went back to Columbus, the geographic expansion of people of European ancestry put increasing pressure on Native Americans' territory, cultures, and livelihood. At the end of the Civil War, about 250,000 Native Americans lived in the West, in an area that composed about half of the United States' territory. These areas had been absorbed by measures such as the Louisiana Purchase and the surrender of northern Mexico at the end of the Mexican War in the 1840s. But the Indians who lived there had an uncertain and often hostile relationship with the American nation. Some of them, such as the Cherokees, had been forced into the West by Indian removal policies. Others, including the Comanches and the Lakotas, had long lived in the West and experienced less pressure from whites than the Indian groups in the East had before the Civil War.

The West became easier for whites to access because of government forts built to protect settlers and because of growing national railroad networks. The first transcontinental railroad was completed in 1869, when the Central Pacific and Union Pacific lines joined in a ceremony at Promontory Point, Utah. Soon four more transcontinental lines would be completed, and towns spread out around railroad depots throughout the West.

Figure 16.2. Eastern approach to Dale Creek Bridge, 1869. The great West was illustrated in a series of photographic views across the continent taken along the line of the Union Pacific Railroad west from Omaha, Nebraska.

As settlement spread, so did fights, murders, and battles between whites and Indians across the Great Plains and Rocky Mountain region. In the late 1850s, gold was discovered in the area around Pikes Peak in Colorado, leading to a massive influx of whites and conflict with local Arapaho and Cheyenne tribes. Cheyenne chief Black Kettle eventually sought to negotiate peace with the US Army and took hundreds of his followers to an encampment at Sand Creek, Colorado. But Black Kettle's people were attacked in November 1864 by forces under the command of Colonel John Chivington. Chivington had declared, "I have come [to Colorado] to kill Indians, and I believe it is right and honorable to use any means under God's heaven to kill Indians." When recruiting for his militia, Chivington displayed the bodies of a white family that had been murdered by Indians.

Chivington told the soldiers to "kill and scalp all, big and little. Nits make lice"— he wanted even the Indian children exterminated. When Chivington's force attacked, Black Kettle sought to display an American flag and a white flag of truce to declare their peaceful intentions, but to no avail. Chivington's militia bombarded Sand Creek with artillery and rifle fire and then moved in to individually butcher the elderly, women, and children. (Only a few dozen fighting-age Indians were at the camp.) Some whites were disgusted by the Sand Creek massacre. Frontiersman and soldier Kit Carson wrote that Chivington's "men shot down squaws, and blew the brains out of little innocent children. You call such soldiers Christians, do ye? And Indians savages? What do you suppose our Heavenly Father, who made both them and us, thinks of these things?" Black Kettle and his wife survived the massacre, only to be killed when they were trying to flee US forces under the command of George A. Custer in 1868.

The Oglala leader, Red Cloud, launched one of the most effective offensives ever against US forces from 1866 to 1868, in what became known as "Red Cloud's War." Once again the hostilities resulted from an enormous influx of white prospectors and settlers, this time in response to the discovery of gold in Montana in the early 1860s. The US Army sought to protect white travelers along the Bozeman Trail into the region. They built Fort Philip Kearny in present-day northern Wyoming in 1866, but in late 1866 Red Cloud tricked army forces into pursuing his warriors outside the fort and led them into an ambush in which eighty-one US soldiers were killed. The attack was widely treated as a massacre in the national media, but it forced the army to temporarily reconsider its approach to the Great Plains Indians. Red Cloud agreed to the Treaty of Laramie (1868), with the provision that the Oglala and other Lakota peoples be given fairly large reservation lands, where the United States promised to ban white settlement. The army withdrew from forts, including Fort Philip Kearny, which Indians burned when the soldiers left.

In the southern Great Plains, Comanche and Kiowa Indians rose up in the 1870s against the incursions of white buffalo hunters, who were decimating the vast herds of buffaloes (American bison) upon which so many Native Americans of the southern plains depended. Whites killed the buffalo for a number of reasons; the value of their hides was only one. Another was clearing out ranchland for cattle raisers. But many saw killing the buffalo as an assault on the Indian way of life. "Every buffalo dead is an Indian gone," explained one white officer. The effect of the campaign against the buffalo was stunning: the herds went from a total of perhaps 13 million bison in 1850, to only a few hundred left alive in the 1880s. (In America today there are more than 500,000 American bison, most of them held by ranchers.)

The Comanches had long ruled the southern plains as a kind of Indian empire, but by the 1870s they were under severe duress because of the dwindling buffalo herds and pressure from US forces. The Comanches took new inspiration from the prophecies of a medicine man named Isatai, who urged them to return to traditional native rituals for spiritual and military power. In June 1874, Isatai and Quanah Parker, the Comanche leader whose Anglo mother, Cynthia Ann, had been stolen away from her family almost forty years earlier, led an attack on the buffalo hunter outpost of Adobe Walls, in the Texas panhandle. The battle was inconclusive, but it helped precipitate the Red River War of 1874–1875.

Philip Sheridan, a celebrated Union commander in the Civil War, vowed to root out the Comanches from the Texas panhandle once and for all. The decisive battle of the Red River War came at Palo Duro Canyon in September 1874, when US forces trapped a group of Comanches who were known to be leaders in the cattle-rustling trade across the Texas border with Mexico. Many of the Comanches escaped, but they had to leave behind their vast herd of ponies. The soldiers, realizing the ponies' value to the Comanches (and the likelihood that they would steal them back if possible), slaughtered more than a thousand of the animals. Some Comanches and other southern plains Indians continued to fight. But in June 1875, Quanah Parker decided to surrender and take his family and many followers to a reservation at Fort Sill, Oklahoma.

Little Bighorn and Wounded Knee

The 1868 Treaty of Laramie did not end the violence between the Lakota people and the US Army. Again, the discovery of gold in the Black Hills region (in what would become South Dakota) in the mid-1870s enticed thousands of white prospectors into Lakota territory. Conflict erupted, and the US Army sent in forces to protect white settlers and to convince the Lakotas to go to ever-smaller reservations. One of the army's commanders in the campaign against the Lakotas was George A. Custer, who overextended his detachment to attack an Indian camp on the Little Bighorn River in Montana in June 1876. (It was the week before the centennial of American independence.) Custer assumed it would be an easy victory, but his 260 soldiers stumbled into an encampment of at least 1,500 Lakota and Cheyenne warriors. The warriors under Lakota medicine man Sitting Bull and war leader Crazy Horse were flummoxed by the sight of the small American force attacking the vastly superior native army. Custer's soldiers were utterly decimated. The only ones left alive on Custer's side were his Crow and Arikara Indian scouts and allies. The national media was appalled at "Custer's last stand" and demanded the Lakota resistance be crushed. Most of the Lakotas surrendered to the American army by the end of 1876. Crazy Horse was bayonetted under mysterious circumstances at a Nebraska army fort in 1877. Sitting Bull held out until 1881, when he agreed to retire to a reservation.

Figure 16.3. Pueblo Indian farmers, one holding a hoe, one holding an ox yoke; possibly Pueblo of Isleta, New Mexico.

The US government sought to reduce the size of the reservations and to get Native Americans to possess land as individuals and families, not tribes. This was the motivation behind the Dawes Severalty Act (1887). This law provided for the breakup of the reservations into 160-acre plots, designed for purchase by heads of Indian families. (This followed a logic similar to that of the Homestead Act of 1862.) Taking the government's offer of a homestead would also make the Indian farmers citizens of the United States. Indians had not been considered citizens before, and section 2 of the Fourteenth Amendment had specifically excluded Native Americans from representation. The remaining reservation lands not designated as homestead allotments would become available for purchase by whites.

The Dawes Act tied Indian citizenship to the "civilized" pursuit of family life and sedentary farming. Even Buffalo Bill Cody, the popular Wild West entertainer, endorsed the Dawes Act. "Giving a tribe an immense tract to roam over, and feeding and clothing them until they learned to support themselves . . . is foolish," Cody said. "It would ruin white men if it should be applied to them." Some Native Americans took up the government's offer in the Dawes Act, but they often struggled to provide for their families, as they ended up on lands poorly suited even to subsistence farming. The Indian Reorganization Act of 1934, part of Franklin D. Roosevelt's New Deal, sought to reverse the failed policies of the Dawes Act, but the federal government continued to struggle to find effective policies to alleviate the endemic poverty found among many Native American groups.

Meanwhile, episodes of Indian resistance against the United States continued. In 1890, a nativist revival movement centered around the ritual of the "Ghost Dance" gave some of the Lakotas hope of a return of Indian power. The visions of a Paiute Indian leader in Nevada started the Ghost Dance movement, and it filtered up through the Great Plains and Rocky Mountains. The revelations, said to be from Native Americans' ancestors, urged them to give up alcohol and to turn back to traditional native practices and rites. If they did, the white people's power would falter and the buffalo herds would once again thrive, the prophecies said. When the Ghost Dance movement came to Sitting Bull's reservation, authorities worried that he would encourage the native revival. Lakota policemen came to arrest him in late 1890, and in the ensuing clash, more than a dozen people died, including Sitting Bull.

On December 29, 1890, US soldiers of the Seventh Cavalry, George Custer's old unit, confronted hundreds of Lakotas associated with the Ghost Dance movement. They were camped at the snowy Wounded Knee creek in southern South Dakota. A Lakota medicine man reportedly called on the Indians to resist the soldiers, believing the Ghost Dancers' ceremonial garb would deflect bullets. In the struggle a gun discharged, and the soldiers began shelling the encampment with cannon fire. When the shooting stopped, twenty-five soldiers and 146 Indians, including forty-four women and eighteen children, lay dead. Wounded Knee became symbolic for many Native Americans of their treatment by the American government. Eight decades after the massacre, in 1973, an internal dispute among Oglala Lakotas turned into a confrontation with federal law enforcement officials as Lakotas associated with the American Indian Movement occupied the town of Wounded Knee. The U.S. Marshals Service and the Federal Bureau of Investigation laid siege to Wounded Knee for seventy-one days before the protestors finally surrendered.

Figure 16.4. "Burial of the dead at the battle of Wounded Knee, South Dakota. US soldiers putting Indians in a common grave; some corpses are frozen in different positions." 1891.

New Lands and New Opportunities in the West

The decimation of Native American societies west of the Mississippi River opened the door for a massive migration of whites, including new European immigrants, onto the Indians' former lands. Smaller numbers of Asians also migrated into the new Pacific-coast states and territories. Almost 200,000 Chinese people came to the United States between the 1840s and 1880s. By 1870, Chinese people represented about one-tenth of California's population, playing a key role as laborers in the mining and railroad industries. Resentment among native-born and European workers prompted the national government to pass the Chinese Exclusion Act in 1882, which ended immigration from China for a decade.

Hispanics also moved across the Rio Grande into the American Southwest. As the United States came into possession of much of the former Mexican-controlled Southwest in the 1840s, the descendants of the original Spanish colonizers began to lose their hold on the land there. But the Spanish-speaking population continued to grow. Perhaps one-fourth of the population of Los Angeles County was Spanish-speaking as of 1880. (Los Angeles was founded in 1781, with the Catholic parish church of Our Lady the Queen of Angels [1784] serving as a focal point in the city's life for much of its first 150 years of existence.) The city of Los Angeles was growing fast, as was its Mexican population. Some 5,000 Mexicans lived in the city in 1910, but that number soared to 30,000 in 1920, when Los Angeles's total population was about 570,000. Federal authorities created the Border Patrol in 1924, in part to monitor the US–Mexico border.

African Americans from the South also migrated in ever-greater numbers to Los Angeles and other parts of the West in the early twentieth century, attracted by the prospect of greater economic and social opportunities. One of those migrants was an African American Pentecostal preacher named William Seymour, who in 1906 would lead one of the most significant events in twentieth-century religious history, the Azusa Street revival in Los Angeles. That revival attracted crowds of whites, blacks, Latinos, and Asians, many of whom said they received the spiritual gift of speaking in tongues. The gift of tongues was frequently mentioned in the New Testament, but until 1906 it had appeared only infrequently in American revivalist movements. Azusa Street birthed a new "charismatic" movement in America. Pentecostal missionaries from America would soon travel around the world. Many regard Seymour's revival as the beginning of the modern Pentecostal Christian movement, which has hundreds of millions of adherents worldwide today.

The national government had a vested interest in seeing the vast West settled by farmers to secure the land and integrate the territories and states into the American republic. The federal government "owned" hundreds of millions of western acres by the 1860s, but it needed homesteaders and railroad companies to build out the infrastructure there. Laws such as the Homestead Act of 1862 offered generous terms to those farmers who would take up the challenge. It supplied 160 acres for a modest fee to any farmer who promised to work the land for five years. The program was wildly successful as over four decades some 600,000 families took western homesteads under the act's provisions. Speculators took advantage of the law to buy up the best well-watered land available, however—160 acres was not worth much if it was in the middle of a desert.

In areas of the Great Plains not suited to agriculture, cattle ranching became common. At first ranchers kept their herds on open ranges on vast stretches of land running from Texas to the Dakotas. The "cowboys" who worked the ranches were a mix of Anglos, blacks, and Mexicans. Cowboys learned most of their cattle-ranching techniques from precedents developed by earlier Mexican ranch workers called *vaqueros*. Many of the cows themselves were Texas longhorns, which originally came from

Mexico as well. Although the longhorns' meat was not the best quality, the cows thrived with little supervision in south Texas. The King Ranch of south Texas, founded in 1853, came to encompass a mind-boggling 1.2 million acres. Even in its "scaled down" modern form, the King Ranch is larger than the state of Rhode Island.

The primary inefficiency in the ranching system in the 1860s was bringing the cattle to market, which involved lengthy cattle drives on north-south routes such as the Chisholm Trail, which ran from the Rio Grande in south Texas all the way to Kansas. There the railroads could take the cattle to points east, especially to Chicago and its vast network of meatpacking plants. Two developments undercut the golden age of the American cowboy and his cattle drives, however. One factor was the widespread fencing of ranch lands, which made the cattle much easier to restrain and manage.

The other factor signaling the end of the cowboys' golden age was the growing reach of the railroads into Texas. The coming of the railroad to Dallas in 1872 signaled the city's emergence as a key center of trade. In just over a year, its population spiked from 1,200 to 7,000. By the 1880s, much of the traditional work of the cowboys had been rendered irrelevant. White ranchers often turned more exclusively to Mexican cowboys after the 1880s because they could pay them less. Many of the former cowboys themselves turned to seasonal agricultural labor, or, ironically, to working for the railroads. One white railroad builder disparagingly observed a "rolling village" of workers laying down track, noting that it was composed of about 400 laborers, "a most conglomerate and strange population, white, negro, and for a short while a few Greeks, with the slow plodding Mexican predominating."

Farmers Organize

Ranchers, cowboys, and farmers of all kinds often found themselves at odds with corporations such as the railroads, which sometimes charged hefty prices to transport their crops. In the late 1860s, farmers began to establish societies called the "National Grange of the Patrons of Husbandry," or simply the Grange. Originally apolitical, the Grange intended to support farmers with social activities and educational opportunities. The Grange illustrated the typical American penchant for joining clubs and societies to address perceived common needs. It represented a critical organization standing between the individual farmer and the government or mammoth corporations. The Grange caught on quickly, with thousands of chapters nationally, especially in the South and the Midwest. A farmers' picnic in Mount Pleasant, Iowa, in 1873 drew 10,000 attendees, more than double the size of the town itself.

Grangers called for cooperative action to benefit the economic interests of farmers, setting prices that fellow Grangers agreed not to undercut and limiting the amount of harvested crops going to market. They used storehouses to preserve grain until prices rose to a profitable level. They lamented the influence of railroad lobbyists, "whose pockets are well filled with money, who want special legislation to replenish their own coffers." Pro-business leaders scoffed at the Grangers. The *Chicago Tribune* lambasted the "spirit of Grangerism, Workingmanism, Communism, Grievanceism, or by whatever name the present fever among those who assume to themselves the title of the 'industrial and producing classes.'" Railroad magnate Leland Stanford, the founder of Stanford University (1885), similarly said that Grange-inspired regulations on national corporations were "pure communism." In spite of farmers' efforts to organize their efforts, it remained difficult for many farmers to compete on the national market and to make a living. Droughts in the 1880s and '90s forced many farmers to quit and go back East. From the 1890s forward, American farming gradually turned more commercial and corporate rather than focusing on the efforts of the individual farmer.

To cite just one example, James Irvine, patriarch of the Irvine family of California, was a Scots-Irish immigrant who made a fortune in the California Gold Rush and the subsequent San Francisco real estate boom of the 1850s. The Irvines, who would give their name to a Los Angeles suburb, acquired major property holdings in Southern California, renting farmland to sharecroppers and tenants. Over time the Irvines would expand their company into a host of agricultural, ranching, and mining businesses. By 1910, the Irvine Ranch had become one of the state's most bountiful and lucrative farms, producing a dizzying array of crops, including avocados, oranges, and sugar beets. The Irvine Ranch would supply a significant share of the army's sugar rations during World War I.

The settlement of Oklahoma in 1889 represented the last great homesteading rush in American history. The land was initially reserved for Native Americans, especially those who had been forced to leave their tribal lands east of the Mississippi in the early 1800s. However, the American government secured the opening of 2 million acres in the "Unassigned Lands" formerly held by Creeks and Seminoles. In a remarkable episode the administration of President Benjamin Harrison scheduled the opening of the lands for noon on April 22, 1889. Tens of thousands of white and black settlers crouched on the edge of the territory. The government rounded up and evicted the "Sooners" who had established squatter settlements before the scheduled opening. In "Harrison's Horse Race," the teeming settlers raced across the Oklahoma plains to capture the best possible homesteads. Towns such as Oklahoma City sprang up overnight, surging from an initial population of 4,000, to 64,000 by 1910.

Figure 16.5. *Picking and Packing Oranges in the Orchards, Near Los Angeles, California.* Stereograph showing workers in an orange grove.

Oklahoma became a state in 1907. In 1912, New Mexico and Arizona became the last two of the contiguous forty-eight states to join the Union. Although the Compromise of 1850 had contemplated statehood for New Mexico six decades earlier, some in Congress were reluctant to admit it as a state because some perceived it as being too culturally Hispanic. A House committee in 1892 worried that the "people of New Mexico are not Americans. . . . They speak a foreign language and . . . they have no affinity with American institutions." Senator Albert Beveridge of Indiana, who chaired the Senate's committee on territories, also opposed the admission of New Mexico because of its Hispanic characteristics. He and other senators contrasted the "Mexican" population of New Mexico with the majority white "American" population of Arizona. Even Beveridge admitted in 1906, however, that some whites viewed New Mexico as a haven of Mexicans and "greasers" (an anti-Mexican epithet) simply because of its name. Beveridge noted hopefully that a majority of the "Mexicans" in New Mexico were actually descended from pure Spanish ancestry and "draw their blood for four hundred years from the very proudest nation on this globe." He proposed that if admission were handled properly, the United States could create "a situation ideal for the Americanizing within a few years every drop of the blood of Spain." Many white Americans were less confident about the successful assimilation of people of indigenous American ancestry, whether they were of mixed blood or not.

In 1893, historian Frederick Jackson Turner delivered one of the most influential papers in the annals of American historical scholarship, arguing that the settlement of Oklahoma and the rest of the West represented the closing of the frontier era of American history. In some obvious senses this was true, as only Hawaii and Alaska remained to be added to the American union. But economic "rushes" were not over, nor were massive shifts of population due to internal migration or the arrival of new immigrants from Europe, Asia, or Central America. Still, the end of the frontier immediately produced an enduring nostalgia in American culture for the "Wild West." Edison Studios, an early movie company founded by inventor and entrepreneur Thomas Edison, began to produce western-themed films by the late 1890s. Most importantly, in 1903, Edison Studios made a major mark on the history of filmmaking with *The Great Train Robbery*, the "first Western with a recognizable form" and one of the world's first action films. The twelve-minute movie followed what became the classic western and action-film script, with "crime, pursuit, showdown, and justice." The western genre has been an endless source for entertainment and literature in America, from the films of John Wayne and Clint Eastwood to TV shows such as *Gunsmoke* and *Little House on the Prairie*, to the books of authors such as Cormac McCarthy and Larry McMurtry.

Coming to America's Cities

In spite of the romance of the West, between 1860 and 1920, America became profoundly urban. On the eve of the Civil War, only about one-sixth of Americans lived in towns of 8,000 people or more. By 1920, half of all Americans lived in towns that size. In tandem with the closing of the frontier, America was also transforming from a rural, agrarian, farming nation to one of cities, businesses, and factories.

The sources of the new urban populations were varied. Some were internal sources. Many African Americans sought to move out of the former slave states as opportunity allowed. Thousands of African Americans went to northern and western cities starting in the 1880s. Then, beginning in the 1910s, millions more African Americans left the South. All told, some six million blacks left the southern states between 1910 and 1970, a mass exodus historians call the "Great Migration."

Another major source of urban growth in the late 1800s was immigration from overseas, especially central and eastern Europe. Improvements in steamship technology made the transatlantic journey cheaper and quicker for Europeans seeking employment, freedom from persecution, or just a new life in America. Ships traversing the Atlantic switched from sail to steam propulsion and from wooden hulls to iron and finally to steel, which came to dominate ship construction by the 1890s. Crossing the ocean under wind power could take months; by steam it generally took ten days.

By the late 1870s, the tide of immigration, mostly from Europe, became a flood. Between 1877 and 1890 alone, 6.3 million new arrivals entered the United States. Even more would arrive before World War I. This influx rapidly changed the character of the American population, particularly in cities. By 1890, some 15 percent of the national population had not been born in the United States. Cities such as Chicago and New York were utterly transformed. By 1890 and 1900, respectively, four-fifths of these cities' populations were foreign born, or at least had parents who were not born in the United States.

Russian Jewish Immigration

Sometimes economic and political instability prompted the immigrants' decisions to leave their homeland. In the 1840s, from opposite sides of the globe, the Irish potato famine and China's Taiping Rebellion (1848) sent hundreds of thousands of migrants to the East and West Coasts, respectively. In the 1880s, farmers under economic distress in countries such as Italy looked for better opportunity in the United States. Vast numbers of Russian Jews fled persecution beginning in the 1870s. Anti-Jewish hatred had exploded in major Russian cities and in small Russian towns. Tens of thousands of Jews were expelled from Moscow, St. Petersburg, and Kiev. In 1881–1882, more than 200 Russian towns saw the outbreak of anti-Semitic pogroms, or riots. Many displaced Jews ended up in American cities: between 1880 and 1900, 500,000 Russian Jews arrived in the United States. Another 1.5 million came between 1900 and 1914, with 125,000 Russian Jews arriving in America in 1906 alone.

Rose Cohen was just one of these millions of Russian Jewish immigrants. She had grown up in a tiny Russian village in Belarus, and her family lived in a log house with a thatched roof. Her home had few books other than the Hebrew Bible (the Old Testament), but once she learned to read, she read the Hebrew Bible through again and again. Suffering under the persecution of Russian authorities, Rose's father went to America first. Then in 1892, when Rose was twelve, she and her aunt traveled by train to Hamburg, Germany, where they took a steamship to New York City. She reunited with her father and began working at a clothes-making sweatshop. Dismayed by the terrible working conditions at the sweatshop, Rose was relieved to encounter a representative

Figure 16.6. Jews in New York City
praying on Brooklyn Bridge.

of a workers' union. He lamented how the girls had to work: "Fourteen hours with your back bent, your eyes close to your work you sit stitching in a dull room often by gas light. . . . The black cloth dust eats into your very pores. You are breathing the air that all the other bent and sweating bodies in the shop are throwing off, and the air that comes in from the yard heavy and disgusting with filth and the odor of the open toilets." He insisted that by themselves they could do nothing to combat their ill treatment, but together they could. Rose immediately announced, "I want to join the union."

Cohen also encountered a series of Christian missionaries in New York as well as Jews who had become Christians. When she realized that the missionaries wanted to convert her, she stuck her fingers in her ears, thinking it might be sinful even to listen. But soon she did begin to read the Christian Bible, with the New Testament, improving her English as she pored over the unfamiliar words. But she kept Christianity itself at bay. For her family, "a Jew who forsook his own religion, his own people, was worse than a Gentile, worse than a heathen." She found Christianity intriguing, but she ultimately could not countenance betraying her family by converting.

Immigrants most commonly arrived in New York City, which made Ellis Island its chief immigration inspection station starting in 1892. But many other ports received immigrants too. For example, tens of thousands of European immigrants, including many Russian Jews, arrived at Galveston, Texas, between 1906 and the beginning of World War I. By the early 1900s, Jewish leaders had already begun to worry about over-crowding in New York City's Jewish neighborhoods, so they directed immigrants else-where. Gershom Geifman was one of those newer immigrants. Geifman left Ukraine in 1911, fleeing anti-Jewish persecution. He shipped out of the German port of Bremen. When he came to Galveston, he was welcomed by a prominent local rabbi and other Jews helping the new arrivals get their bearings. Right away Geifman took a train north to Rock Island, Iowa, where he got a job as a custodian at a John Deere factory, which made farming equipment. (Five of Geifman's brothers also settled in the "Quad Cities" area of Iowa.) He soon lost that job because he could not speak English, and he became a door-to-door broom salesman. Geifman eventually made enough money to own a chain of grocery stores as well as various real estate ventures.

Chicago and the New Urban Pattern

New York's growth is well-known because of the city's role in receiving immigrants such as Rose Cohen. But Chicago's story was perhaps the epitome of urban growth in the late nineteenth and early twentieth centuries, with all of the grandeur and squalor that came with that expansion. Chicago had only been incorporated in 1837, but it quickly grew into one of the nation's key railroad hubs. On the eve of the devastating Chicago fire of 1871, the city already had about 300,000 residents. But with floods of immigrants coming to the city from Poland, Italy, and other central and eastern European locations, the city's population exploded tenfold to 3 million by the mid-1920s. As a new Chicago rose out of the ruins of the Great Fire, architects erected new skyscrapers that reflected the primacy of business. Steel building materials and the advent of elevators permit-ted these buildings to reach much higher than ever before. One of the key builders in Chicago said that the skyscraper office building reflected the "ideas of modern busi-ness life: simplicity, stability, breadth, dignity." Where church steeples once dominated the skylines of pre–Civil War cities, now office buildings immediately caught one's eye. Chicago's 1885 Home Insurance Company Building, while only ten stories tall, served as a prototype for much larger skyscrapers across the country.

Cities also developed distinctive downtown areas in this era, facilitated by streetcars, elevated trains, and eventually subways. The Chicago "L," or elevated train network, began service in 1892. The urban train systems soon made possible the development of suburbs farther away from the crowded urban core. Housing distant from the downtown area was often reserved for middle- and upper-class whites, while immigrants and native-born poor people stayed in the city center. Some of the tall buildings erected in downtown areas became apartment buildings, or tenements. These often packed vast numbers of people into small areas, with as many as sixteen families sharing just two toilets per floor. By 1890, almost half of New York City's residences were in tenement buildings.

The cities had terrible difficulties keeping up with the pace of growth and the teeming masses of people. There were few systematic efforts at waste disposal, and the rules cities made regarding dumping and disposal were often ignored. This prob-

Figure 16.7. The Chicago Building of the Home Insurance Company of New York. Poster showing America's first "skyscraper," 1885, by architect William LeBaron Jenney.

lem became especially acute as cities such as Chicago developed large-scale industries, including meat processing and the massive quantity of carcasses and bones it left behind. Chicago, which became the hub for processing the cattle of the Great Plains, developed the "Packingtown" district, one of the most active and lucrative industrial sites in the world in the early 1900s. More than 75,000 people lived in Packingtown's six square miles by 1920. Many of them were foreign-born and Roman Catholic. The majority of Packingtown's residents worked for the great meatpacking factories, especially those of Gustavus Swift and Philip Armour. Infant mortality, disease, and workplace injuries were all epidemic. Union organizing in the late 1910s helped alleviate some of the worst problems, but workers often divided among themselves along racial lines. Companies could play on tensions between European immigrants and African Americans, who composed about a third of Chicago's meatpacking workforce by the early 1920s.

Chicago struggled to maintain basic sanitary conditions in the city, especially in and around Packingtown. Leaders found it impossible to keep an uncontaminated water supply, no matter how far out into Lake Michigan they put the intake pipes. Already by

Figure 16.8. Row of tenements, 260 to 268 Elizabeth St., New York, in which a great deal of finishing of clothes was done.

the middle of the Civil War, before the meatpacking boom set in, empty fields around the processing factories were littered with the decaying skin and bones of sheep, cattle, and other animals, with accompanying swarms of flies and rats and intolerable odors. The Chicago River, likewise, became an open sewer, with trash, industrial waste, and human excrement.

Late nineteenth-century American cities smelled horrible, especially in the summers. Horses and horse-drawn carriages remained common modes of transportation, and the horses left countless tons of undisposed-of manure in the streets. Many homes and tenements also had outhouses. The *Chicago Times* in 1880 expressed revulsion at the "solid stink" that had enveloped the city. "The river stinks, the air stinks. People's clothing, permeated by the foul atmosphere, stinks." The *Times* was so disgusted that it waxed philosophical. "No other word expresses it so well as stink. A stench means something finite. Stink reaches the infinite and becomes sublime in the magnitude of odiousness."

The writer H. L. Mencken recalled how his childhood home in Baltimore had an outhouse with a foul-smelling sewage pit. African American workers would come every spring with a disposal wagon to pump it out and then fumigate the pit by burning buckets of tar in it. The Baltimore sewers emptied into the city's Back Basin. Mencken lamented that the Basin was relatively stagnant, so it "began to acquire a powerful aroma every Spring, and by August smelled like a billion polecats."

Ministering to the Needs of the City and the World

The plight of the cities led many churches and social reformers to experiment with new means of ministering to the needs of the urban poor. Many of these efforts led to "settlement houses" that catered especially to young women. The most famous settlement was Chicago's Hull House, founded in 1889 by Jane Addams and Ellen Gates Starr. Addams and Starr's experiment was based on moral principles but was also relatively secular in focus. It offered classes for neighborhood residents as well as day care and assistance for fair employment. Addams described Hull House's animating principles as "close cooperation with the neighborhood people, scientific study of the causes of poverty and dependence, communication of these facts to the public, and persistent pressure for reform."

Jews, Catholics, and most major Protestant denominations also opened settlement houses in American cities, many of them inspired by the ideals of the "Social Gospel," or the idea that Christian principles were better lived out in practice than merely discussed. (More conservative Christians worried that the Social Gospel was more "social" than "gospel," however.) For example, Baptists in Orange, New Jersey, near Newark, opened a missionary outreach chapel ("a sort of Settlement House") for Catholic Italian immigrants and their families in 1908. In addition to Sunday morning and evening services, the new building hosted a Sunday school and weeknight lectures that drew hundreds of attendees, even those "indifferent or hostile to religion." Other classes taught cooking and "industrial arts" to girls. The leaders of the Baptist mission all believed "in the value of preaching the Gospel," the church noted, but "they felt that they must first of all open the minds, instruct, educate these people [the Italians] to adjust themselves to life in this strange country, and help them to see and lay hold of what is best in American life, to truly Americanize so that they may become good and intelligent citizens." A Baptist periodical commended the church for not forgetting the "strangers within the gates."

As suggested by the Baptist church's concern to "Americanize" the immigrants, the flood of immigration in the period prompted anti-immigrant political organizing. Leaders of these groups worried that the immigrants would dilute the traditionally white and Protestant character of dominant American institutions. The Immigration Restriction League was founded in Boston in 1894. It was especially focused on

population control and eugenics, or the idea that superior races should protect themselves from the genetic qualities of inferior races, especially by protecting against inter-
marriage. One of the founders of the Immigration Restriction League explained that
the crisis of immigration was "a race question, pure and simple. . . . It is fundamentally
a question as to what kind of babies shall be born; it is a question as to what races shall
dominate in this country." Some critics worried that so many of the new immigrants
were Roman Catholics while others worried that some of the newcomers adhered to
radical political philosophies such as socialism (government ownership of businesses)
and communism, which emphasized class conflict and the abolition of private property. The Immigration Restriction League successfully convinced Congress to adopt a
literacy test requirement before admitting new immigrants from eastern and southern
Europe. But President Grover Cleveland vetoed the literacy test law, believing it violated America's historic commitment to welcoming immigrants. Such an immigration
test did finally become law in 1917, however, as Congress overrode a veto of President
Woodrow Wilson.

Christian evangelists such as Dwight Moody and Billy Sunday focused primarily
on the spiritual rather than social needs of the city. Whatever trouble a city dweller
was having was likely a result of poor personal choices and a lack of dependence on
God, the evangelists preached. Sunday was a former professional baseball player who
had experienced conversion in Chicago in the late 1880s. In the early 1890s, he began
working with the Chicago Young Men's Christian Association (YMCA) before launching his own itinerant preaching career. Sunday's flamboyant style complemented his
message of faith in Christ, hard work, and personal decency, much in the tradition
of the great revivalist Charles Finney. Many leading businessmen of the day, including Philip Armour, John D. Rockefeller, Andrew Carnegie, and J. P. Morgan, donated
to Sunday's ministry. Sunday often spoke in the rhetoric of business too: "Keep your
account straight so when the Great Bookkeeper calls for a statement, your account will
show a balance in your favor," he preached. Critics painted Sunday as a tool of big business, distracting from their abuse of workers with an overly spiritual emphasis.

Aside from evangelism in America, Moody and his associates kept promoting the
interests of overseas missions too. The most dynamic Protestant missionary movement of
the late nineteenth and early twentieth centuries was the Student Volunteer Movement
(SVM), which began in 1886 at a conference at Moody's Mount Hermon School in
Northfield, Massachusetts. The watchword of the SVM was "the evangelization of the
world in this generation." The missionaries believed that rapid improvements in transportation and communication made it possible for the Christian gospel to be preached
to "all nations, and kindreds, and people, and tongues," as the book of Revelation

put it. Doing so might set the stage for the return of Christ. Prominent missions advocate John R. Mott wrote in his popular book *The Evangelization of the World in This Generation* that "hundreds of millions are today living in ignorance and darkness, steeped in idolatry, superstition, degradation and corruption. . . . The burning question for every Christian then is, shall hundreds of millions of men now living, who need Christ and are capable of receiving help from Him, pass away without having even the opportunity to know Him?"

The SVM inspired thousands of students and other Americans to go on the mission field. One of them was Samuel Zwemer, who was born in 1867 in Michigan to Dutch immigrant parents. He joined the SVM when he was a student at Hope College. In

Figure 16.9. Billy Sunday.

seminary Zwemer studied Arabic and believed God was leading him to become a missionary to Arabia, the home of Islam's sacred sites. Zwemer would serve for decades in Arabia and Egypt before becoming a professor of missions at Princeton Theological Seminary in 1929. Like many American Christian missionaries in the Muslim world, Zwemer saw relatively few Muslim conversions to Christianity during his ministry. But he became the era's most influential Christian author on Islam, writing and editing almost fifty books about Muslims and missions.

Big Business and the American Economy

The new business titans such as J. P. Morgan in banking, Andrew Carnegie in steel, and John D. Rockefeller in oil revolutionized and exercised unprecedented dominance in their fields. Morgan made his fortune in helping finance the phenomenal growth in industry and transportation after the Civil War, especially in the railroad business. Another financial disruption in America in 1893 devastated many of the leading railroads, opening an unprecedented opportunity for consolidation in the industry. When the nation's gold reserves became dangerously low in 1895, Morgan personally assured President Cleveland that he would stabilize the US currency through action in international financial markets. His plan worked. By 1900, Morgan had become the key player in American finance and transportation networks, ending the speculative era of American railroads and reducing the number of railroad companies to a relatively small number, many of them controlled by Morgan's company.

Andrew Carnegie's impoverished family immigrated from Scotland to Pittsburgh, Pennsylvania, in the late 1840s. An incredible drive to succeed plus an uncanny sense of timing would turn Carnegie into one of the richest men in the world and make Pittsburgh one of the world's key centers of steel manufacturing until the 1970s. Along with oil, steel (an alloy of iron and carbon) became one of the essential new products of the global industrial economy of the post–Civil War era. In construction and transportation sectors, steel's toughness and durability made it ideal to use in everything from skyscrapers to railroad tracks and steamboats.

The Bessemer process of producing steel helped factories produce higher-grade and more uniform steel products. Although the process was pioneered in England in the late 1850s, America emerged as the dominant steel producer in the world by the late nineteenth century. This also energized an expansion in the mining of iron ore and coal, which fueled the steel furnaces. Although industrial expansion was often rooted in the Northeast and Midwest, Alabama saw a great rise in steel production and ore mining in the late nineteenth century. This was one of the few nonagricultural sectors where poor white and black southerners could find work. African Americans dominated the ranks of the iron ore miners in Alabama and composed a near majority of steel workers there by the 1910s.

But the center of the steel industry was Carnegie's Pittsburgh. Carnegie took his first job in a cotton mill, where he made $1.20 a week. But by his early twenties, he was climbing the ladder in the railroad business. As he began to make more money, he showed a great knack for management and investing, putting money into all the industries served by the railroads, including coal, lumber, and iron. In the early 1870s, the US government placed a protective tariff on steel imports, so Carnegie decided to move into the steel business, opening a factory outside of Pittsburgh. When the depression of 1873 began, Carnegie solidified his commitment to steel by selling all his other businesses. Carnegie rightly predicted that when the dust settled from the depression, the steel business and all the others it served would enter a boom phase, and he was ready for it when it came. Pittsburgh was the perfect site for the expansion of Carnegie's steel empire. In addition to good railroads, the city stood at the confluence of the two rivers that formed the Ohio River. It was also close to abundant coal mines and had a ready supply of new immigrant labor from southern and eastern Europe.

Carnegie came to dominate the steel industry through efficiency and "vertical integration" of the industry—in other words, controlling all aspects of steelmaking from the ore mines to sales, distribution, and construction. Carnegie's steel frames would go into making new structures, including the Brooklyn Bridge, a number of the early skyscrapers, and the Washington Monument in Washington, DC. The efficiency and scale of production took a toll on workers, however. Labor unions had demanded and often secured an eight-hour workday, but Carnegie insisted that having two twelve-hour shifts was better for productivity. When the steel mills also cut wages in the early 1890s, workers tried to strike. When the factory managers sought to break the strike, a gun battle broke out at Carnegie's Homestead factory in July 1892. Eight people were killed in the firefight. The protesting workers occupied the steel plant until Pennsylvania sent in the National Guard to break up the strike.

The clash at the Homestead factory damaged the public reputation of Carnegie's steel business, but in practice it signaled the victory of the management over union organizers. Wages continued to fall, and the twelve-hour day became standard. As efficiency spiked, the mills laid more workers off. Within five years of the Homestead incident, the factory's number of employees had dropped by 25 percent. For those who remained, working conditions were dangerous. One study discovered that in 1907, 250 out of every 1,000 men who worked a full year were injured on the job in the steel industry. Those suspected of trying to reorganize the unions were monitored and often fired. One worker at the Homestead factory complained that "they own us body and soul; our bread and butter depends on our silence" about working conditions or organized protests.

By 1900, Andrew Carnegie had built Carnegie Steel into the world's largest industrial company. Shockingly, in 1901 he decided to sell the business. J. P. Morgan was one of the only people in the world who could possibly pay the price required. In a legendary exchange Morgan dispatched an associate to go to Carnegie and "find his price." When Carnegie proposed selling out for almost a half a billion dollars, Morgan accepted, creating the U.S. Steel Corporation out of Carnegie's business and his other steel holdings. It was the first company worth more than a billion dollars.

Just as steel undergirded the era, the rise of oil lubricated the age of industrial expansion. Mechanization and turbines required oil for greasing, and oil-derived kerosene became the most common way to fuel lamps in American homes in the days before electrification. (The mass production of gasoline awaited the advent of the gasoline-powered automobile.) Oilmen began drilling in Pennsylvania in 1859, and in 1867 John

D. Rockefeller opened Standard Oil Company in Ohio. Rockefeller relentlessly consolidated the oil business, using Carnegie's principle of vertical integration but also employing "horizontal" integration by trying to establish a monopoly over petroleum refining. Rockefeller became so powerful that he could dictate transportation terms to the railroads, and his company paid politicians for favorable treatment. By the early 1880s, Standard Oil controlled the vast majority of the oil refinement business in America. Its reach was global, shipping oil and kerosene to South America, Africa, and Asia. In China, Standard Oil engaged in cutthroat competition with British, Dutch, and French firms, which imported oil products from places such as Russia and the Dutch East Indies.

In 1882, Standard Oil consolidated its far-flung companies and properties into the Standard Oil Trust, one of the first major efforts to establish a legal and financial monopoly of a business sector, controlled by a small board of trustees. "Trust" became common parlance for a monopoly that sought to eliminate competition, which was often bad for consumers and for workers. The invention of the trust precipitated a political backlash, and Congress overwhelmingly passed the Sherman Antitrust Act in 1890, designed to require sprawling multistate and multinational trusts like Standard Oil to dissolve.

It took decades of legal challenges to bring down the Standard Oil Trust, however. In the meantime, Ida Tarbell, a reformist, "muckraking" journalist who had seen her father's small oil business gobbled up by Standard Oil, emerged as one of Rockefeller's most relentless critics. "It takes time to crush men who are pursuing legitimate trade," Tarbell wrote. "But one of Mr. Rockefeller's most impressive characteristics is patience. . . . He was like a general who, besieging a city surrounded by fortified hills, views from a balloon the whole great field, and sees how, this point taken, that must fall; this hill reached, that fort is commanded. And nothing was too small: the corner grocery in Browntown, the humble refining still on Oil Creek, the shortest private pipe line. Nothing, for little things grow." In 1911, the Supreme Court finally decided that the Standard Oil Trust violated the Sherman Antitrust Act and ordered that it be broken up into its state-based components. These new, smaller companies included Mobil, Chevron, and Exxon Oil. These companies would themselves become global behemoths in time, but the American government had taken a stance against monopolies, especially ones that used coercive tactics to suppress competition.

An Age of Invention

The rise of large-scale industrial capitalism did not focus just on the mass production of basic materials such as oil and steel but also on new inventions that revolutionized home life and communication. Some of these, like the Bessemer process in steel, vastly streamlined the production or use of existing technologies. Steady improvements in telegraph cables meant that many of the world's cities, even beyond the United States and Europe, were connected by cable by the end of the nineteenth century. This meant that agents of global companies such as Standard Oil could use the telegraph to communicate quickly about developments on the other side of the world.

Although the telegraph remained one of the most transformative inventions in human history, the late 1800s saw the advent of the device that would replace it: the telephone. Alexander Graham Bell, a Scottish immigrant living in Boston, invented the telephone in 1876. It could convert sound waves into electrical impulses, and then back to sound on the receiving phone. Bell's company, American Telephone and Telegraph, came to dominate the market for phones and phone services for more than a century. (In 1982, the AT&T company, under antitrust pressure from the government, agreed to let go of its regional phone service companies, setting the stage for a flowering of new telecommunications companies and technologies in the late twentieth and early twenty-first centuries.) By 1905, there were 10 million phones in service in the United States. Household telephones remained a luxury, however, and telephones often came last to homes of the rural South and to impoverished sections of major cities.

Thomas Edison is rightly known as one of America's greatest inventors. Perhaps his most transformative invention was the electric lightbulb, or incandescent lamp. He also developed a sophisticated system for delivering electrical current to homes and businesses, to make lights and other electric-powered goods usable. Edison's company opened the coal-fired Pearl Street power station in New York City in 1882, the same year he opened a hydroelectric station in Appleton, Wisconsin. By 1900, thousands of power stations were illuminating about 2 million electric lights across the nation. Electrical power and light revolutionized everything from the urban environment, especially at night, to the working capacity of factories.

Electrification came first to the homes of wealthy urbanites; by 1907, only 8 percent of homes were running on electricity. But that number went up steadily to 68 percent of American homes in 1930. As part of the New Deal in the 1930s, President Franklin Roosevelt established initiatives promoting rural electrification. As was so often the case, the poor and those in rural areas were the last to benefit from these technological changes. The electrification of homes created a new market not only for lightbulbs, but for domestic appliances, such as irons, toasters, electric clocks, vacuum cleaners, and washing machines. Later came refrigerators, stoves, and electrical heaters.

Even places such as Luna Kellie's Nebraska were transformed by electrification. Just twenty-five miles north of Hastings, Nebraska, the town of Grand Island got its first electrical company in the mid-1880s, only ten years after Kellie's family had arrived on the Nebraska frontier. Then, in the mid-1890s, Grand Island got a power plant. It could only supply enough power to illuminate 900 light bulbs, but the threshold had been passed. America was swiftly entering the era of electricity. Electrical power would bring a whole range of changes and new technologies, the implications of which continue to unfold today.

■ SELECTED BIBLIOGRAPHY ■

Carlson, Paul H. *The Plains Indians*. College Station: Texas A&M University Press, 1998.

Daniels, Roger. *Coming to America: A History of Immigration and Ethnicity in American Life*. 2nd ed. New York: Harper Perennial, 2002.

Fink, Deborah. *Agrarian Women: Wives and Mothers in Rural Nebraska, 1880–1940*. Chapel Hill: University of North Carolina Press, 1992.

Gómez, Laura E. *Manifest Destinies: The Making of the Mexican American Race*. New York: NYU Press, 2007.

Hahn, Steven. *A Nation without Borders: The United States and Its World in an Age of Civil Wars, 1830–1919*. New York: Viking, 2016.

Hardwick, Susan Wiley. *Mythic Galveston: Reinventing America's Third Coast*. Baltimore: Johns Hopkins University Press, 2002.

Hinshaw, John. *Steel and Steelworkers: Race and Class Struggle in Twentieth-Century Pittsburgh*. Albany: State University of New York Press, 2002.

Montejano, David. *Anglos and Mexicans in the Making of Texas, 1836–1986*. Austin: University of Texas Press, 1987.

Moses, L. G. *Wild West Shows and the Images of American Indians, 1883–1933*. Albuquerque: University of New Mexico Press, 1996.

Pisani, Donald J. *From the Family Farm to Agribusiness: The Irrigation Crusade in California, 1850–1931*. Berkeley: University of California Press, 1984.

Richardson, Heather Cox. *West from Appomattox: The Reconstruction of America after the Civil War*. New Haven, CT: Yale University Press, 2007.

Weeks, Philip. *"Farewell, My Nation": American Indians and the United States in the Nineteenth Century*. 3rd ed. Malden, MA: Wiley-Blackwell, 2016.

17

The Gilded Age

The phenomenal changes wrought in America by mass immigration, industrial growth, and technological change made the "Gilded Age" (roughly 1870–1900) a troubled time for many Americans. Some wondered if the cohesion and virtue they remembered about pre–Civil War America was slipping away. Many Christians worried that the decades after the Civil War had seen a flood of salacious and even pornographic literature saturating the cities and threatening America's youth. Anthony Comstock, head of New York's Society for the Suppression of Vice, insisted that everywhere young people turned, there were enticements to sin. "Youth has to contend against great odds," he wrote. "Inherited tendencies to wrong-doing render the young oftentimes open to ever-present seductions. Inherited appetites and passions are secretly fed by artificial means, until they exert a well-nigh irresistible mastery over their victim. The weeds of sin, thus planted in weak human nature, are forced to a rapid growth, choking virtue and truth, and stunting all the higher and holier instincts."

In 1873, Congress affirmed Comstock's goal of limiting the availability of immoral literature when they passed the Comstock Law. The law made it illegal for the postal system to carry and distribute any "obscene, lewd, or lascivious book, pamphlet, picture, paper, print, or other publication of an indecent character." Comstock gave special attention to restricting information or supplies related to contraception or abortion, believing that detaching sex from the marital responsibility for children only encouraged promiscuity. The postmaster general also appointed Comstock as a special agent in charge of enforcing the laws and confiscating obscene materials. Comstock secured thousands of convictions for violators.

Many critics argued that Comstock was violating free speech and free press rights, as well as injecting undue moral influence into American law. Margaret Sanger, an early advocate of sex education, contraception, and birth rate restriction, tested the law by circulating articles on "birth control" (a term she coined) and sexually transmitted disease. Sanger fled to Europe when she was charged with publishing obscene material. Later she was arrested for opening a birth control clinic in Brooklyn. Beyond her rivalry with Comstock, Sanger had her own concerns about changes in American society, especially about the high birth rates among the poor immigrant classes. "Those least fit to carry on the race are increasing most rapidly," she wrote. "The most urgent problem today is how to limit and discourage the overfertility of the mentally and physically defective." Sanger went on to found the American Birth Control League (1921), which became the Planned Parenthood Federation of America in 1946.

Concern about the moral character of society was a much older theme in America, dating back to the colonial era. But the urbanization and diversification of American society in the late nineteenth century brought this concern for virtue to new heights. The anonymity of the city and numerous opportunities for "entertainment" presented unprecedented temptations. For example, Comstock wrote of the gambling houses "in some of the lowest dens in our large cities," where he had seen women and children waiting "while the atmosphere about them was poisoned with the fumes of whiskey and tobacco, and filled with the foulest language. . . . Into such influences, after once the torch of gambling is lighted in the human breast, the bright boy or clerk is easily led." Comstock and legions of reformers like him intended to wage a culture war against the forces of obscenity and addiction to preserve a decent American society for their children.

The New Culture of Entertainment

Pre–Civil War America had entertainment outlets such as P. T. Barnum's traveling circus, which took America by storm in the 1840s and '50s. But an overwhelmingly agrarian society could support few entertainment businesses. Church attendance and reading newspapers and books were among the most common ways of breaking up the routines of farm life. City life was different, especially for the white middle class, which had more disposable income and time off from work. The entertainment culture of the late nineteenth and early twentieth centuries grew more and more central to Americans' lives. The most popular forms of entertainment focused on the sensational or the nostalgic.

We have already seen that nostalgia for the Wild West pervaded live shows, books, and other popular art forms of the period, even as white settlement of the frontier and the seizure of Indians' lands was coming to a conclusion. "Buffalo Bill" Cody had opened his fabulously successful Wild West show in 1883. In 1885, Cody's show reached new heights of fame as he recruited Annie Oakley to the show, who in turn helped Cody convince the Native American leader Sitting Bull to join the tour. Oakley had no actual western experience whatsoever. She grew up in a troubled family in Ohio, where she learned to hunt and developed an uncanny skill for marksmanship. Sitting Bull dubbed her "Little Sure Shot." Oakley, Cody, and their troupe entranced eager audiences in American cities as well as across Europe through the 1890s.

The artist Frederic Remington was arguably the most important figure in helping middle-class Americans imagine what the West looked like before the closing of the frontier. Like Oakley,

Figure 17.1. Annie Oakley—famous rifle shot.

Remington lived most of his life in the East, but he did visit the Great Plains and dabbled in sheep ranching. After playing football at Yale, Remington showed aptitude for painting and illustrations and making key connections in the publishing world. He became one of the most sought-after illustrators for popular magazines such as *Harper's* and *Scribner's*. He also illustrated prominent books, including Henry Wadsworth Longfellow's *Song of Hiawatha* and future president Theodore Roosevelt's *Ranch Life and the Hunting Trail*. Remington produced thousands of paintings of frontier life, emphasizing the bravery of both Native American warriors and their cowboy adversaries.

Although black and Hispanic cowboys were common in real-life frontier culture, the Wild West shows and western-themed art tended to feature only white characters facing off against Native Americans. The most common entertainment venue that represented African Americans was the minstrel show. Pre–Civil War minstrel shows often used white actors in blackface, but after the Civil War some African Americans became popular actors in the shows. (Even the African American actors frequently performed in blackface, however.) The minstrels promised to reveal life as it really was on the old plantations. African American performer Billy Kersands became the most popular

Figure 17.2. *A Dash for the Timber*, Frederic S. Remington (1861–1909), 1889.

black entertainer of the late nineteenth century as part of the nationally known troupe Callender's Georgia Minstrels.

The black minstrel shows commonly added "Negro spirituals" to their repertoire, playing off of the popularity of singing groups such as the Fisk University Jubilee Singers. Among the most oft-sung songs were "Swing Low, Sweet Chariot" and "Go Down, Moses," which recounted the Israelites' struggle for freedom from captivity in Egypt.

When Israel was in Egypt's land:
Let my people go,
Oppress'd so hard they could not stand,
Let my people go.

Go down, Moses,
Way down in Egypt's land,
Tell old Pharaoh,
Let my people go.

Although these public performances—usually for white audiences—did not re-create the "real" tradition of the Negro spirituals sung by the slaves in secret church meetings on the plantations, they were nevertheless preserving a critical oral remnant of antebellum slave culture. The great African American writer W. E. B. Du Bois called the spirituals "the most beautiful expression of human experience born this side of the sea."

The popularity of the minstrel show transferred to the use of blackface characters and African Americans in advertising, which soon became a professional enterprise accompanying the expansion of consumer culture in the late nineteenth century. Most obviously, advertisers promoted the minstrel shows themselves. But product makers also used stereotyped images of blacks, as well as Indians and Asian Americans, to promote their commercial products. Among the most common were those caricaturing black characters who tried but comically failed to mimic white consumers. One cigarette ad, for instance, mocked a black woman who tried to play croquet but hit her foot with the mallet. Minstrel advertisements and outright racial epithets became associated with products from breakfast cereals to soap to chewing tobacco.

One of the most famous of the nostalgic racial images in American advertising was Aunt Jemima, debuted in 1893 and later used by the Quaker Oats Company of Chicago. Her character originated in a minstrel song and act, "Old Aunt Jemima," first performed by Billy Kersands and his troupe in the 1870s. (Sometimes a white man in blackface would perform the role of Aunt Jemima.) At the 1893 Columbian Exhibition in Chicago, a company that had invented the first ready-made pancake mix used a woman named Nancy Green to play Aunt Jemima at their exhibit. Green was a former slave now working as a household servant in Chicago. Aunt Jemima's promotion of pancakes was one of the only ways African Americans were allowed to appear at the Columbian Exhibition. Their exclusion as planners or serious exhibitors led African American reformers Ida B. Wells and Frederick Douglass to publish *The Reason Why the Colored American Is Not in the World's Columbian Exhibition* (1893). "We have long had in this country, a system of iniquity which possessed the power of blinding the moral perception, stifling the voice of conscience, blunting all human sensibilities and perverting the plainest teaching of the religion we have here professed," they explained. "That system was American slavery. Though it is now gone, its asserted spirit remains."

Musical performances became an enduring entertainment outlet for Americans, as did sporting events. Sports such as horseracing, boxing, and cockfighting had a much older history in American and European culture. But the post–Civil War era saw a boom in sports entertainment, as well as the promotion of playing sports as a healthful, Christian activity. Many in Britain and America promoted the idea of "muscular Christianity," or a Christianity that was vigorous and active, rather than weak and passive. Prominent Social Gospel pastor Washington Gladden spoke for many when he endorsed "sport, glee, fun" of the "real hilarious, exuberant sort" as an important

Figure 17.3. Advertisement for Thatcher, Primrose & West's Minstrels. 1889.

aspect of the full Christian life. The Young Men's Christian Association (YMCA) and its counterpart, the Young Women's Christian Association (YWCA), were among the key organizational manifestations of the new zeal for blending Christianity and sports. The YMCA and YWCA offered wholesome venues for sports, as well as addressing attendees' spiritual needs.

Participation in sports often went hand in hand with an interest in sports as entertainment. Baseball had secured its place as the national pastime by the late 1800s. The Cincinnati Red Stockings became the first professional baseball club in 1869, traveling nationally to play teams from New York to California, before thousands of spectators. In 1876, teams from eight cities combined to form the National League of Professional Base Ball Clubs, or just the National League. Here sports, entertainment, and big business overlapped, as the National League sought to establish a monopoly over professional baseball in America, to control players' rights to switch teams and to keep competing baseball clubs from challenging the National League's supremacy. National

League owners also tried to present its games as wholesome environments, banning games on the Sabbath and prohibiting on-site gambling.

Many of the early baseball players came from working-class Irish or German backgrounds. Arguably the most popular player of the era was Mike "King" Kelly, the child of Irish immigrants. In spite of attempts to make baseball a family-friendly game, Kelly and other players smoked and sometimes even drank alcohol during games. Kelly was such a huge draw that in 1887 the Boston "Beaneaters" club paid $10,000 to acquire his services, a mind-boggling figure for the time. Some African Americans played professional baseball too, but the Jim Crow system infected professional sports. By 1900, blacks were generally banned from professional baseball, prompting the formation of the Negro Leagues. As baseball became more popular in Latin America, Hispanic players occasionally appeared in the US major leagues starting in the 1910s. Darker-skinned Latinos had to play in the Negro Leagues.

Baseball exploited many commercial connections to the sport. Tobacco companies, for example, routinely used baseball cards printed on cardboard stock as an incentive to buy their products. Cigarette makers, such as the Duke company, later the American Tobacco Company, developed improved mechanical processes for the mass production of rolled cigarettes in the 1880s. (A $40 million gift from the Duke family would revolutionize the former Trinity College in Durham, North Carolina, which subsequently renamed itself Duke University.) Baseball cards became a way to improve packs of cigarettes so they would not be crushed in transport. But baseball cards also became so popular that they were identified with particular cigarette brands, as well as types of candy and

Figure 17.4. King Kelly, Chicago White Stockings, baseball card portrait. Goodwin & Co., 1887–1890.

chewing gum. Later, baseball and other sports cards came in their own packs, sometimes still packaged with a stick of gum.

Sports accessories also became a big business. Albert Spalding, a former player, established a sporting goods company in 1876 that aspired to dominate the American market in baseball paraphernalia as well as the tools of other popular sports. Spalding vertically integrated parts of the industry by acquiring a lumber mill and negotiating contracts with the professional leagues as their sole supplier of balls and bats. The balls and other implements of professional sports became common consumer goods and gifts, accessible even to rural Americans through the wildly popular Sears, Roebuck mail-order catalog. In its 1895 edition, Sears, Roebuck devoted eighty pages to the sale of sporting goods.

Advertising and media coverage also transformed boxing into a popular commercial enterprise. Irish immigrant and editor Richard Kyle Fox was not a boxer himself, but the *National Police Gazette*, his sensationalist newspaper, helped make boxing among the most-covered and discussed sports of the late nineteenth century. Because it was full of lurid, provocative "news" stories, Anthony Comstock sought unsuccessfully to shut down Fox's paper, which only made it more successful, especially among working-class readers. The media turned boxers into superstars. As Fox promoted prize fights, he insisted that they follow established rules and be real contests rather than the shady or vicious fights that characterized earlier eras of American boxing. The boxer John L. Sullivan (another child of Irish immigrants) was arguably the most famous sports celebrity of the era. Early in his career, Sullivan sometimes still participated in marathon, bloody, bare-knuckle fights, but his most famous clash came in 1892 against "Gentleman" Jim Corbett. In a gloved bout they competed for a stunning $50,000 prize before 10,000 spectators at a New Orleans arena. Corbett shocked the nation by defeating the "Boston Boy" Sullivan.

Figure 17.5. *John L. Sullivan, Champion Pugilist of the World.* Born in Boston, October 15, 1858.

White fighters such as Sullivan generally declined to box against African Americans, even though black fighters such as Jack Johnson of Galveston, Texas, were clearly emerging as major contenders. Johnson dominated the Negro boxing associations and eventually secured his first match against a major white boxer in Philadelphia in 1907. Then in 1908, Johnson defeated the reigning heavyweight champion, sending promoters into a frenzy to find the "Great White Hope" who could vanquish Johnson. Johnson relished engaging in provocative behavior that would stoke whites' fears, wearing flashy clothes and openly consorting with a number of white girlfriends. Johnson's match against former champion Jim Jeffries in Reno, Nevada, in

Figure 17.6. Jack Johnson and his wife, Etta.

1910, drew 20,000 people to watch the bout for a $101,000 prize. Johnson's triumph prompted race riots in American cities. When federal officials convicted Johnson on trumped-up charges of transporting a white woman (who was his wife and a former prostitute) across state lines for immoral reasons, he left the United States for exhibitions and matches in Canada, Europe, and Cuba. Johnson finally lost to a white fighter in a match in Cuba in 1915. President Donald Trump posthumously pardoned Johnson for his alleged crimes in 2018. African American admirers would have to wait until 1937 before another black fighter, Joe Louis, won the heavyweight title.

Wrestlers also became stars through the promotions of the *National Police Gazette* and other media outlets. Some wrestling matches followed fairly strict Greco-Roman rules while others became known as "catch" matches, which allowed most any tactics, save perhaps for chokeholds. Gilded Age wrestling matches, like some of Sullivan's bare-knuckle boxing contests, went on for hours. They were often not scripted, with no preordained outcome. Perhaps the greatest wrestler of the era was Frank Gotch, the son of German immigrant farmers in Iowa. In 1911, Gotch wrestled to submission the famous European wrestler George Hackenschmidt before an audience of 30,000 at the newly built Comiskey Park in Chicago, the home of baseball's White Sox. In future decades, promoters tended to "fix" the outcome of professional wrestling matches, cutting down on the time the matches required and enabling wrestling leagues to follow longer-term storylines about rivalries between wrestlers. The predetermined nature of wrestling matches has often led critics to say that modern professional wrestling is not a "real" sport, yet it has remained enormously popular through the present day across a range of American classes and ethnicities.

Wrestling and boxing tended to appeal especially to working-class Americans, particularly immigrants and African Americans, who celebrated their ethnic champions, such as John L. Sullivan and Jack Johnson. But college sports also emerged as a major force in the late nineteenth century, catering more to the children of elite families and the alumni of prestigious colleges, especially Ivy League schools such as Harvard and Yale. Competitions between college rowing and baseball clubs became major news stories. Baseball was the national pastime during the Gilded Age, but football came to the fore as the dominant college sport. This trend has remained true through present-day America, although the Ivy League's national prominence in most sports declined over the course of the twentieth century. Rutgers and the College of New Jersey (Princeton) met in 1869 in what is considered the first college football game ever. Yale and Harvard met in football for the first time in 1875. These football clubs were student organized, and formal rules and tactics only developed over time. The early games were more like

Figure 17.7. *Gotch-Hackenschmidt Wrestling Match for World's Championship.* Stereograph showing wrestlers in outdoor ring and spectators in grandstand, September 4, 1911, Chicago.

rugby than today's American football, and they were gruesomely violent. With little to no protective gear, it was not unusual for players to suffer crippling injuries or even to die. By the 1890s, annual Thanksgiving championship football games held in New York City were drawing up to 40,000 attendees.

Walter Camp of Yale emerged as the dominant figure in early college football. A former Yale player, Camp ruled the Yale football program with an iron fist even as he became chairman of the New Haven Clock Company. Camp codified a number of foundational football rules, such as the concept of a line of scrimmage. He also resisted appeals, including those from President Theodore Roosevelt, to cut down on the egregious violence of the game. Camp insisted that the savagery of football was an ideal incubator of manly virtue and business tactics. He declared that football had become "the best school for instilling into the young man those attributes which business desires." Camp was one of the leading advocates for the idea that college sports could serve as a practical education for participants. To the dismay of many faculty members, the traditional model of education was coming under increasing pressure, as sports and socializing became key aspects of the college experience. Princeton leader and future US president Woodrow Wilson worried that undergraduate social and sporting activities had "become the vital, spontaneous, absorbing realities for nine out of every ten men who go to college."

College, and college football clubs, remained inaccessible to most Americans. The invention of basketball had much broader significance in the short term for American sports. James Naismith, a Canadian child of Scottish immigrants, developed the game in 1891 at a YMCA training school in Springfield, Massachusetts. Naismith was a major advocate of "muscular Christianity" and its ideals of the person who is fit in body and soul. Later Naismith would become the athletics director and the chapel director at the University of Kansas, positions he held for four decades. Basketball was relatively simple to stage—all you needed was a ball and "baskets" of some kind (Naismith had tacked up peach baskets in a gym). The sport became a key way the YMCA and YWCA recruited children and teenagers, as it was especially appropriate to the urban centers of the North and their millions of new immigrants.

From its founding in Springfield, many women gravitated toward basketball, which became the most popular female team sport. Smith College, a women's school in Massachusetts, had already begun teaching basketball by 1892. Shortly after men's college basketball teams began playing one another, the first recorded intercollegiate women's basketball game was played in 1896 between the University of California–Berkeley and Stanford. Men were prohibited from viewing the game, even though the participants wore heavy woolen uniforms that showed little skin.

Education and the University

In 1900 most Americans still did not go to college. But more widespread secondary education and growing numbers of colleges and universities made college education increasingly accessible. The "common school" movement had spread the ideal of state-sponsored education based on a standard curriculum, but mandatory education for young children remained inconsistent throughout the states until after the Civil War. After 1870, there was a broad trend toward requiring education for teenagers. Even then, the states generally did not force children to stay in school after they turned fourteen. It remained rare for adults to complete high school. Only 14 percent of American adults had finished twelve years of formal schooling in 1900. A century later, more than 80 percent of American adults had done so.

As education became more "democratic," the focus of education gradually turned away from the classical model of education based on the study of Latin and other traditional liberal arts subjects. It moved toward "practical" and vocational education, preparing students for particular jobs. Religion remained a common subject in the public

Figure 17.8. *1913–1914 Basketball Game, Vassar College, May 1913.* Women of Vassar College playing outdoor game of basketball with a few spectators in attendance.

schools. Most states did not mandate Bible reading until the 1910s and 1920s, when a perceived attack on the biblical tradition from evolutionists and others prompted a number of states to require that the King James Bible be part of the curriculum. Voluntary Bible reading was a frequent part of the curriculum in the nineteenth century, however, prompting occasional complaints from non-Protestants, especially Catholics. Until the 1960s, American courts typically approved of Bible reading, contending that simple reading of the text was educational and nonsectarian. Some Catholics disagreed since they did not use the King James Version, instead preferring Catholic editions of the Bible, such as the Douay-Rheims translation. Controversy over the use of a Protestant Bible was one of the reasons American Catholics developed a robust parochial school system for Catholic students.

Aside from tension over the religious character of education, race was a major limiting factor in the democratic nature of American education. Many southern states legally required the segregation of schools for white and black students. Black education lagged behind that of whites, and public education in the southern states was generally poor for both whites and African Americans. Elsewhere, many local forms of de facto segregation were put in place by local school districts and superintendents. In southwestern states with growing Latino populations, school districts routinely sent Latino children to "Mexican" schools instead of allowing them to go to white children's schools. Officials often justified this practice by citing Latino students' need for better English-language skills. When Latino parents challenged these segregationist practices, courts issued contradictory decisions starting in the 1930s. Sometimes judges gave school districts latitude to separate white and Latino students. Sometimes the courts cited schools for ethnic discrimination.

In a case out of Lemon Grove, California, in 1931, Mexican Americans successfully challenged the local school board's plan to build a separate school for Latino students, as a California judge ruled that the scheme was discriminatory. But it would be four decades before the US Supreme Court would rule in the case of *Cisneros v. Corpus Christi Independent School District* (1970) that Hispanics were protected from public school discrimination just as African Americans were under the principles of the landmark case *Brown v. Board of Education* (1954).

The opening of education to more Americans extended to colleges and universities, which became more numerous in the post–Civil War era. Women's colleges such as Mount Holyoke (Massachusetts) and coeducational institutions such as Oberlin (Ohio) had already begun to appear before the Civil War. The Morrill Acts of 1862 and 1890 made federal funds available for the establishment of agricultural and mechanical public colleges to supplement the traditional liberal arts focus of older American universities.

The Morrill Acts created dozens of new "land-grant" universities, such as Kansas State (1863) and the University of California (whose Berkeley campus opened in 1868). Many of these new universities were coeducational, admitting both women and men from the outset. By 1900, about 40 percent of college students in America were female. Southern states commonly used land-grant funds to open separate colleges for whites and blacks, such as Texas A&M ("Agricultural and Mechanical") and the traditionally black Prairie View A&M, both of which originated in Texas in the 1870s.

Business magnates looking for philanthropic outlets often founded colleges in these years too. Leland Stanford founded his university in California in 1885 with a $24 million gift. John D. Rockefeller did likewise with $34 million to establish the University of Chicago in 1890. (Chicago was incorporated by the American Baptist Educational Society. But aside from the Divinity School, the university's first professional school, the University of Chicago speedily turned away from a Christian emphasis, aside from touting the generic ideal of service.) A gift from philanthropist Johns Hopkins established the university of the same name in Baltimore in 1876. Johns Hopkins was one of the first modern "research" universities in America. Johns Hopkins split its faculty into different departments and encouraged specialized research by professors as much as it focused on undergraduate liberal arts instruction.

Major philanthropists founded other key private southern universities, such as Vanderbilt (1873), Tulane (1884), and Rice, the coeducational university in Houston, where students first began classes in 1912. As with primary and secondary schools, universities were often segregated informally if not by rule. Rice dictated in its founding charter that it was meant for the education of the "white inhabitants of Houston, and the state of Texas." Like many universities in the South, Rice did not admit black students until the 1960s.

African Americans and Gilded Age Education

The brilliant writer and sociologist W. E. B. Du Bois was one of the few nonwhite students at Harvard in the late nineteenth century. Richard Theodore Greener, the first African American to graduate from Harvard, had only done so in 1870. Du Bois found the on-campus environment at Harvard difficult to manage. He did not even try to befriend white students, fearing he would be "disappointed and embittered by a discovery of social limitations." So he contented himself with being able to take classes and to use the Harvard library. Most of his friends were African Americans in the Boston area, not fellow students.

It was more typical for degree-seeking African Americans to go to the new independent black colleges. One of the most prominent of these schools was Tuskegee Institute in Alabama, the brainchild of former slave Booker T. Washington. By 1900, Tuskegee had 1,400 students learning a variety of practical trades and agricultural techniques. Du Bois's and Washington's relative fame in black educational circles set them up for one of the most important debates in American history with regard to education and social progress for people of color.

Washington stressed economic and social practicality as the key to advancement for African Americans in the post–Civil War South. "Cast down your bucket where you are," he urged poor blacks. It was in "agriculture, mechanics, in commerce, [and] in domestic service" that the vast majority of southern African Americans would find their place in the economy. There was little point for most blacks in seeking elite education and social transformation by "artificial forcing." "No race can prosper," Washington told the Atlanta Cotton States Exposition in a famous 1895 speech, "till it learns that there is as much dignity in tilling a field as in writing a poem. It is at the bottom of life we must begin, and not at the top." Washington conceded that social segregation of whites and blacks was unlikely to change soon, but that did not mean whites and blacks could not advance together. "In all things that are purely social we can be as separate as the fingers, yet one as the hand in all things essential to mutual progress." In time this approach would bring the South into material wealth and racial reconciliation. In time the South would seem like "a new heaven and a new earth," Washington predicted, referencing the book of Revelation.

Du Bois and other African Americans felt that Washington was conceding too much to dominant white power. In the late nineteenth century, the social and political conditions for blacks seemed to be getting worse, not better. Black voting rights were vanishing, and Jim Crow segregation was becoming more entrenched. Across the South white mobs were lynching African Americans with horrifying regularity. Booker T. Washington was not oblivious to these facts, but he preferred to emphasize black industriousness and responsibility as the best way to encourage racial harmony. Washington also excoriated the lynchings in a 1904 letter, noting the horrible incongruity of men and women being dismembered and burned in towns teeming with churches, YMCAs, and other Christian organizations. He demanded that pastors, newspaper writers, and other authorities denounce the mobs who were "bringing shame and ridicule upon our Christian civilization."

Small groups of African Americans took Washington's endorsement of segregated black communities as an impetus to set up independent black societies. Hundreds of blacks immigrated in the 1880s and 1890s to Liberia in West Africa. Liberia had begun in the antebellum era as a possible outlet for the "colonization" of freed American slaves. Other African Americans gathered into "black towns," which tried to operate as semiautonomous refuges for African Americans, free from white influence or control. Several branches of the extended Archer family established a black commune on hundreds of acres of Mississippi farmland they simply called the "Place." The family patriarch, a Baptist minister named John Perry Archer, sought to make the Place a self-sustaining agricultural community that kept debts and all other connections to the region's white community at a minimum. One of the group's members explained that while they agreed with much of Booker T. Washington's ideas, they regarded his famous mantra of "cast down your bucket where you are" as pessimistic and self-defeating.

Some blacks were more severe in their criticisms of Washington, who had become increasingly popular among whites because of his Cotton States Exposition speech and his 1901 autobiography, *Up from Slavery*. (One white admirer gushed that Washington was a "Christian statesman" and the "greatest man, save General Lee, born in the South in a hundred years.") Ida B. Wells thought black vocational education was just a "hobby" of Washington's. But Washington was "much too interested . . . in the decoration of Confederate graves to pay any attention to Negro rights," Wells said.

W. E. B. Du Bois had responded warmly to Washington's 1895 address, but he gradually became convinced that Washington was surrendering too much on the issues of legal and political rights for African Americans. In his 1903 *The Souls of Black Folk*, Du Bois took on Washington and his "Atlanta Compromise" directly. He argued that Washington's exclusive focus on economic and vocational matters made his program conspicuously appealing to whites in the age of big business. But Washington's focus overshadowed attention to the "higher aims of life" and virtually accepted many whites' belief in the "inferiority of the Negro races." Washington, Du Bois alleged, asked African Americans to give up any pretense to political power, civil rights, and higher education. Not surprisingly, the popularity of Washington's views was accompanied by the end of black voting rights, the rise of Jim Crow laws, and the constriction of blacks' opportunities for education. Du Bois asked whether African Americans could reasonably expect to make economic progress if they were "deprived of political rights, made a servile caste, and allowed only the most meager chance for developing their exceptional men." The answer, to Du Bois, was clearly no.

Du Bois conceded that the growing legal and social disadvantages for blacks were not a direct result of Washington's philosophy. But blacks across the ideological spectrum found few effective ways to counter the rising tide of discrimination. Jim Crow laws and policies became ever more pervasive nationally. Boston, once the country's hotbed of abolitionism, started segregating its schools after the Civil War and did not face serious legal challenge until the 1960s. Whites in the South sometimes went to incredible lengths to separate all aspects of white and black life: Atlanta courts, for example, used different Bibles to swear in white and black witnesses. Jim Crow did not always target blacks, however. San Francisco segregated its schools in 1906 due to concerns over the growing number of Japanese immigrant families in the city.

Jim Crow statutes found legal backing at the Supreme Court, which in the 1883 *Civil Rights Cases* had already ruled that the Fourteenth Amendment's guarantee of equal protection of the laws did not apply to actions by private

Figure 17.9. Dr. W. E. B. Du Bois.

businesses, such as hotels or restaurants. In 1890, however, Louisiana went a step further and passed a law *requiring* railway companies to provide separate accommodations for white and black passengers. Civil rights reformers in Louisiana decided to test the law in 1892. They sent Homer Plessy, a light-skinned man of mixed white and black ancestry, to ride in a white section of a Louisiana railroad car. Plessy told the conductor that he was partially black, and the conductor ordered him to leave the white section. Plessy would not leave, so he was arrested.

When the case of *Plessy v. Ferguson* came before the US Supreme Court in 1896, the justices ruled in a 7–1 decision that the Louisiana railroad segregation law was constitutional. The majority denied that "the enforced separation of the two races stamps the colored race with a badge of inferiority." Justice John Marshall Harlan was the lone dissenter in the case, and he predicted that one day *Plessy v. Ferguson* would be regarded as just as "pernicious" as the court's decision in *Dred Scott* in 1857. *Plessy* enshrined the principle that "separate but equal" public facilities were legal in America. In practice segregated facilities were often unequal or nonexistent for blacks. In *Cumming v. Richmond County Board of Education* (1899), the Supreme Court, with John Marshall Harlan this time writing the majority opinion, unanimously accepted a Georgia county's argument that it was shutting down its black high school because it was not financially feasible to keep it open.

Literature and Realism

As Americans wrestled with issues of racial justice in the aftermath of the Civil War, major changes were also afoot in fields including science, literature, art, and theology. One of the most significant changes was the turn toward "realism" and away from the sentimentalism and Romantic themes of the pre–Civil War era. Many writers and artists, inspired by the desire to expose and reform the conditions endured by everyday Americans, sought to portray life as it really was. Often this led to an emphasis on the mundane distinctives of regional cultures from mill workers to plantation workers to frontier farmers. One of the most celebrated early examples of such writing was Rebecca Harding's short story "Life in the Iron Mills," published in *Atlantic Monthly* in 1861. She offered an unflinching look at the lives of mill workers, with their "incessant labor, sleeping in kennel-like rooms, eating rank pork and molasses, drinking— God and the distillers only know what; with an occasional night in jail, to atone for some drunken excess. Is that all of their lives? . . . So many a political reformer will tell you . . . who has gone among them with a heart tender with Christ's charity, and come out outraged."

One of the best-remembered realist novels was Stephen Crane's *The Red Badge of Courage* (1895), which rejected idealistic views of the Civil War. The novel offered a gritty, morally ambiguous story of a young soldier who deserts his regiment, only to be given mistaken credit later for battlefield valor. A counterpart to Crane's realism in literature was Winslow Homer's in art. Homer's 1866 painting *Prisoners from the Front*, for example, portrayed Civil War soldiers in ragged garb, with little sense of the glory and heroism that marked much military-themed art up to that point.

The most celebrated realist author was Samuel L. Clemens, who went by the pen name Mark Twain. Twain based his most famous stories on his own experiences growing up in Missouri along the Mississippi River. He wrote in rough southern dialect, dealing humorously with issues of race, class, and religion. He skewered the pious pretensions of southern church culture, but usually he did so in such a good-natured way that it did not come off as anti-Christian. Twain recalled that his own Methodist Sunday school teacher kept giving him prizes for memorizing Bible verses even though he repeated the same five verses each Sunday. He was disappointed, however, in the "dreary" moralistic books he won as prizes. "There was not a bad boy in the entire bookcase. They were *all* good boys and good girls and drearily uninteresting, but they were better society than none."

Figure 17.10. *Prisoners from the Front*, Winslow Homer, 1866.

Twain has become such a fixture on the American literary landscape that his books can almost seem quaint at first glance. Their rough racial language, however, has led to the regular banning of *Tom Sawyer* and *Huckleberry Finn* in contemporary America. And when his books first appeared, they struck some observers as provocative and disgustingly lowbrow. A library in Concord, Massachusetts, home of the Transcendentalist movement, refused to circulate *Huckleberry Finn* when it was first published. One committee member for the library complained about the book's coarse humor, dealing with a "series of adventures of a very low grade of morality: it is couched in the language of a rough ignorant dialect, and all through its pages there is a systematic use of bad grammar. . . . The whole book is of a class that is more profitable for the slums than it is for respectable people." The Concord library concluded that *Huckleberry Finn* was "trash of the veriest sort."

Theological Conflict and the Rise of Fundamentalism

Twain's work seemed like just one small drop in the flood of attacks on traditional Christianity that began in the late nineteenth century. The turning point was the 1859 publication of English scientist Charles Darwin's *On the Origin of Species*, which spawned theological debates in Europe and America about the theory of evolution and its implications for the common Christian view of creation. Following the lead of Princeton theologian Charles Hodge, many Christians worried that the theory of evolution ruled out any divine purpose in the development of life. However, one of Hodge's successors at Princeton Theological Seminary, B. B. Warfield, argued that there was no necessary conflict between evolutionary processes and biblical views of creation. But Warfield knew that many evolutionists, including Darwin's more secular popularizers, had higher metaphysical aims: they implied that God was not behind the created order. For Warfield, when Darwinism served as a "complete account of the origin and state of the universe," it was "tantamount to atheism."

"Higher criticism" of the Bible, much of it emerging from the work of continental European scholars, also put the Bible under unprecedented scrutiny. What if the Bible was not "given by inspiration of God"? the critics asked. What if it was just another historical document, subject to the same kinds of limitations and imperfections as all other books? What if the great stories of Scripture were just myths, like the fanciful stories of gods and goddesses from other cultures of the ancient world, such as Greece and Rome? Books like the Frenchman Ernest Renan's *Life of Jesus* (1863) followed up on the furor caused by German writer David Strauss's book of the same name three decades earlier. Renan dismissed the miracles and the divine nature of Christ, trying instead to portray Jesus in his historic context as a great moral teacher and reformer of Judaism.

Most American denominations faced controversies about evolution and higher criticism. They also battled over the progressive trend toward the Social Gospel, which emphasized Christian service rather than calling on people to convert to faith in Christ. Many wondered whether the new perspectives on evolution, evangelism, and the Bible could be integrated into traditional Christian faith, or whether they essentially undermined historic Christian beliefs. Often these controversies came first to denominational seminaries, where some professors began teaching higher critical theories. For example, in the 1870s, Crawford Toy of the Southern Baptist Theological Seminary in Louisville, Kentucky, began instructing students about the views of the Dutch Old Testament scholar Abraham Kuenen, who believed the Pentateuch (the first five books of the Hebrew Bible) was written by a variety of authors, mostly at a much later date than the events those books described. In other words, significant parts of the Old Testament were not accurate as history. Toy also taught that three different writers had composed the book of Isaiah and that when the New Testament authors assigned messianic significance to Old Testament verses, they were not being faithful to the original meaning of the Hebrew Bible. Under pressure from seminary officials, Toy resigned in 1879 and eventually took a position teaching at Harvard.

Controversies over the new theology happened more often in northern Protestant denominations and seminaries than in the South, which remained more conservative theologically. Professor Charles Augustus Briggs of Union Theological Seminary, a Presbyterian school in New York City, was brought up on heresy charges for teaching that Moses had not authored the Pentateuch and that there was more than one author of Isaiah. Briggs also argued that Protestants had overemphasized the Bible alone as the source of religious truth and that the Bible was not inerrant. At first the New York presbytery in 1892 acquitted Briggs of heresy, but the Presbyterian General Assembly overturned the ruling and disciplined him. As a result, Union Theological Seminary withdrew from the Presbyterian denomination.

Another front for liberal criticism of the Bible came out of the women's rights movement. Some key figures in that movement, including Elizabeth Cady Stanton, became convinced that many churches propagated male domination of politics, society, and religion and that patriarchal teachings in Scripture were partly to blame. This concern resulted in Stanton's two-volume *The Woman's Bible* (1895, 1898), much of which Stanton wrote herself. In spite of the title, this was not a Bible translation or paraphrase but a series of commentaries on what the Bible taught about women and their roles in the church, family, and society. Stanton and her coauthors sometimes seemed to denounce the Bible for its anti-woman perspectives. At other times Stanton seemed to suggest that the true spiritual intent of the Bible was basically pro-woman. *The Woman's Bible* set off a widespread negative reaction not only from traditional Christians who rejected the book's critical approach but also from figures within the women's rights movement who saw the book as a distraction. Susan B. Anthony regarded the book as "flippant and superficial," writing that as proud as she was of many of Stanton's other writings and speeches, "of her Bible Commentaries, I am not proud—either of their spirit or letter."

In light of these theological threats, some church leaders developed a clearer sense of the "fundamentals" of Christianity. Of course, many denominations had creeds that dated back to the early centuries of the church, but the historic creeds were not crafted in response to the new challenges presented by higher criticism, evolution, and the Social Gospel. Conservative Protestants rallied around five doctrinal points of "fundamentalism" and expected seminary professors and pastors to teach these points without reservations. The five points were the inerrancy of Scripture, Jesus's virgin birth, Christ's atoning death for sinners, his physical resurrection from the dead, and (more generally) the validity of the Bible's miracles. Some conservatives also added particular views of the end times, including a belief in the imminent return of Christ to earth. These beliefs helped unify the emerging fundamentalist cohort, which opposed the higher critics' innovations.

Figure 17.11. Elizabeth Cady Stanton, seated, and Susan B. Anthony, standing, between 1880 and 1902.

Among the most important milestones in the development of fundamentalism, one that gave the movement its name, was the publication of the twelve-volume series *The Fundamentals* (1910–1915) by top conservative theologians and Christian apologists. Aside from defending the "five points," the volumes signaled the ambivalence of Christian traditionalists about evolution. While some writers denounced Darwinism as essentially anti-Christian, others argued that it could be compatible with the biblical view of creation. The main problem with Darwinism, the authors agreed, was when the theory claimed to explain away God's role in the created order or denied that men and women had any special role to play in that order.

Fundamentalists, the forerunners to many of today's evangelical Christians, showed other important signs of institutional and theological development. In 1909, Oxford University Press published the Scofield Reference Bible, which became arguably the most popular study Bible in twentieth-century America. Theologian C. I. Scofield was an advocate of "dispensationalist" theology, which emphasized how God had dealt with people in different dispensations through time, such as the dispensations of "law" and "grace." Dispensationalists also adopted a detailed biblical time line for end-time events, culminating in the return of Christ and the establishment of his "millennial" (thousand-year) kingdom on earth. Dispensational theology, and fundamentalist beliefs more generally, influenced the founding of new institutes and seminaries, such as Chicago's Moody Bible Institute (founded by evangelist Dwight Moody in 1886); the Bible Institute of Los Angeles, or Biola (1908); and Dallas Theological Seminary (1924), the most influential school for the promotion of dispensationalism in the twentieth century.

Gilded Age America was changing fast. Developments in immigration, entertainment, education, and theology made it appear that some of the most basic supports of American society were being undermined. People reacted in a range of ways, from indulging in nostalgia to accepting the new trends to seeking to counteract them. African Americans and other people of color faced challenges associated with white people's growing authority in the post–Civil War order. But as much as any other era of American history, the Gilded Age was simply a time of uncertainty and anxiety. Many Americans wondered which direction their nation, their cities, their schools, and their families would turn. As America became a more formidable commercial and imperial power, many Americans would work to make the nation as equitable as possible for those outside the circles of economic and political power.

■ SELECTED BIBLIOGRAPHY ■

Barrish, Phillip J. *The Cambridge Introduction to American Literary Realism.* New York: Cambridge University Press, 2011.

Beisel, Nicola. *Imperiled Innocents: Anthony Comstock and Family Reproduction in Victorian America.* Princeton, NJ: Princeton University Press, 1997.

Du Bois, W. E. B. *The Souls of Black Folk.* Chicago: A. C. McClurg, 1903.

Gorn, Elliott J., and Warren Goldstein. *A Brief History of American Sports.* New York: Hill and Wang, 1993.

Hale, Grace Elizabeth. *Making Whiteness: The Culture of Segregation in the South, 1890–1940.* New York: Vintage, 1999.

Hamburger, Philip. *Separation of Church and State.* Cambridge, MA: Harvard University Press, 2002.

Kennedy, David M. *Birth Control in America: The Career of Margaret Sanger.* New Haven, CT: Yale University Press, 1970.

Lebsock, Suzanne. *A Murder in Virginia: Southern Justice on Trial.* New York: W. W. Norton, 2003.

Marsden, George M. *Fundamentalism and American Culture.* 2nd ed. New York: Oxford University Press, 2006.

Moore, Jacqueline M. *Booker T. Washington, W. E. B. Du Bois, and the Struggle for Racial Uplift.* Lanham, MD: Rowman & Littlefield, 2003.

Washington, Booker T. *Up from Slavery.* New York: Doubleday, Page, 1907.

18

Populism and Empire

American politics after Reconstruction were closely divided between Republicans and Democrats. Republicans remained mostly a northern party, especially after the southern black Republican vote was snuffed out by white "Redeemers" in the 1870s. But the large and growing population of the North meant that if Republicans could control all of the North's electoral votes, they would win national elections. The Democrats retained considerable strength in parts of the North, however, strength that dated back to the antebellum era.

The most controversial political issues from 1876 to 1900 were financial ones, from trade policy to the best kind of currency. Only during the 1890s did foreign policy disputes associated with the Spanish-American War come to the fore in national debates. The financial controversies had roots in the Civil War, when the Union government had printed hundreds of millions of dollars' worth of "greenbacks." These notes were based on the government's assurances of their worth rather than a one-to-one backing in silver or gold. In the 1870s, wealthy businessmen favored putting America on the "gold standard" alone instead of backing the currency with both gold and silver. Populist farming interests in the South and on the frontier advocated for both silver and gold. A more expensive dollar made it more difficult for farmers and others of modest means to pay off their debts. The Coinage Act of 1873, however, resumed gold payments only, not silver, for American currency. Populists and agrarians called it the "Crime of '73," claiming that the legislation was born out of unholy collusion between financiers and corrupt congressmen.

The Gilded Age was marked by a series of one term presidents who won narrow elections often marked by disputes regarding financial policy. Rutherford Hayes won an extraordinarily close election in 1876 when a congressional commission awarded him the contested electoral votes of several southern states. Hayes came into office believing strongly in the gold standard, so he vetoed a congressional effort to allow for coinage of silver in 1878. Congress adopted the Bland–Allison Act—which required the Treasury to circulate silver dollars—over his veto, believing it would help alleviate the economic plight of many small-time farmers and debtors. Some went further and advocated that the national government continue its Civil War policy of not guaranteeing redemption of currency in either gold or silver. These "Greenbacks" argued that the government should make as much printed currency as was necessary to sustain economic growth. Doing so would make it possible for small businesses to challenge the supremacy of the great monopolies in oil, railroads, and steel. By 1878, the Greenback Labor Party was winning almost 15 percent of all votes nationally.

Hayes declined to run for reelection, and he was succeeded as president by Ohio Republican congressman and Union war hero James A. Garfield. Garfield won with an incredibly close margin over his Democratic opponent in the 1880 election. He won by just 10,000 votes, out of more than 9 million cast nationally. (The Greenback Party got no electoral votes, but it did receive 300,000 popular votes.) Garfield only got to serve for a few months as president, however. He was shot by an assassin, Charles Guiteau, at a Washington train station. Garfield lingered for two more months before dying from his wounds in September 1881. He was the second president to fall victim to an assassin, after Abraham Lincoln. Garfield was succeeded by his vice president, Chester A. Arthur, a New York Republican.

Failing health and an association with corrupt New York politics ensured that Chester Arthur would serve only one term as president. The 1884 election pitted a new Republican nominee, former Speaker of the House James Blaine, against New York's Democratic governor, Grover Cleveland. Worries about Catholic immigration tinged Blaine's campaign against the Democrats, which was typically the favored party for the new urban immigrants. Blaine was known for having sponsored a failed 1875 constitutional amendment that would have forbidden states from giving any tax funds to private religious schools. Supporters saw this measure as a way to bolster the "common school" movement but also to ensure that the growing Catholic parochial school system would not receive any state funding. Although the measure did not make it out of Congress, many states went ahead and passed their own versions of the Blaine Amendment. Though Blaine did not personally pander to anti-Catholic sentiment in the 1884 election, a pastor who supported him famously called the Democrats the party of "rum, Romanism, and rebellion." That comment helped to turn the 1884 election over to Grover Cleveland, who won by just 20,000 votes nationally. The Greenback and the Prohibition (anti-alcohol) parties polled hundreds of thousands of votes each.

Cleveland fought to reduce the size of government and to cut down on a burgeoning federal budget surplus. The government, Cleveland insisted, was taking far too much from Americans, especially in the form of the tariff on foreign imports. It was a "vicious, inequitable, and illogical source of unnecessary taxation," he told Congress. Cleveland vowed to reduce the tariff, over Republican protests that doing so would harm American business. Even a modest tariff reduction could not make it out of Congress, however. This illustrated the difficulty of passing major economic reforms in these years. The tariff became one of the defining issues of the 1888 election, as did a continuing scandal about Cleveland having fathered a child out of wedlock. Cleveland won the total popular vote nationally in 1888 by 90,000 votes, but he was routed in the Electoral College, doing poorly in the North and West. Republican Benjamin Harrison of Indiana became president.

In addition to passing the anti-monopoly Sherman Antitrust Act in 1890, the Republicans under Harrison raised the tariff. They also continued to crack down on the Catholic school system. In particular, Republican officials worked to end the contracts many Catholic schools had won to provide education on Indian reservations. Harrison's superintendent of Indian schools, Daniel Dorchester, was known as a veteran of the movement to stop public funding for Catholic schools, having authored a book titled *Romanism versus the Public School System*. Harrison's officials founded a new government school for Pueblo Indians in New Mexico. This public school sought to take students away from Santa Fe's Catholic boarding school. Officials explained that if the same Catholic education continued, then Pueblo students would remain in

Figure 18.1. *Another Voice for Cleveland.* Illustration shows a woman holding a baby, who is crying out, "I want my pa" as Grover Cleveland passes.

a "semilethargic condition, making little progress in civilization." A Bureau of Indian Affairs agent named Dolores Romero—atypical as a Hispanic woman with a federal government position—argued that Pueblo parents overwhelmingly preferred the old Catholic school system and that they regarded the government school as functionally Protestant. A Catholic backlash against the Harrison administration, plus worries about the effects of higher tariffs, helped return Grover Cleveland to the White House in 1892. Cleveland trounced Harrison in both the Electoral College and the popular vote.

Labor Movements in the Gilded Age

From the 1870s onward, America saw greater numbers of movements designed to defend the economic interests of the nation's laboring classes, from family farmers to industrial workers. National labor unions included the Knights of Labor and the American Federation of Labor (AFL). In 1905, total membership in labor unions had reached about 2 million workers, with the AFL dominating the national landscape. Collective action seemed necessary to workers who often labored under dangerous and grueling conditions and found little sympathy from courts, government officials, or business owners. One magnate spoke with typical patronizing sentiment when he expressed confidence that "the rights and interests of the laboring man will be protected and cared for, not by the labor agitators, but by the Christian men to whom God, in his infinite wisdom, has given control of the property interests of the country."

Each decade from the 1870s to the 1890s saw outbursts of labor unrest that sometimes spawned pitched battles and horrible violence such as that at Andrew Carnegie's Homestead factory in 1892. Chicago's factories were routinely racked by protests and strikes and severe government reactions to them. Workers went out on strike in 1886 at Chicago's McCormick Reaper Works (a farm machinery factory), and in a confrontation with police, several workers were shot and killed. This precipitated an even worse clash the next day at the city's Haymarket Square between police and anti-government anarchists. One of the anarchists threw a bomb at the police, killing seven of them. Although the courts could not prove the bomber's identity, four of the Haymarket protestors were executed for their involvement in the riot.

Another clash transpired at the Pullman Company of Chicago, which built railroad passenger cars. Amid a massive financial crisis, the Panic of 1893, the Pullman Company (like many businesses) cut workers' pay but did not cut costs of living in company housing or prices at the company's store. American Railway Union activists stepped in and gummed up railroad traffic throughout the region to force concessions by the company. When a federal court issued an injunction to stop the strike in 1894, President Cleveland sent in 2,000 federal troops to confront the protesting workers. Twelve workers perished in the resulting violence, and Eugene Debs, leader of the American Railway Union, went to jail for his role in the resistance. Debs went on to become one of the nation's most vocal advocates of socialism, arguing that the national government should put the railroads and other businesses under government ownership.

Violence erupted across the western states and territories in the late nineteenth century as well. Sometimes these riots had origins in both class and ethnic resentments. Dozens of "Chinatowns"—Chinese ethnic enclaves—in the West suffered attacks in cities from Seattle to Los Angeles. Railroad and mining companies traditionally used Chinese workers as cheap labor, and they sometimes brought them in as "scabs" or strikebreakers, raising the ire of white workers. The mid-1880s saw repeated anti-Chinese attacks and expulsions. In Rock Springs, Wyoming, twenty-five Chinese people were killed by a white mob, and attackers (some of them affiliated with the Knights of Labor) also drove hundreds of Chinese residents out of Tacoma and Seattle, Washington. These riots, combined with Congress's prohibition on Chinese immigration in the Chinese Exclusion Act (1882), caused the Chinese population of the West to drop sharply through the 1880s and 1890s. Other ethnic groups in the West, including Hispanics and Japanese people, faced periodic attacks from whites during this era. Sometimes the simplest altercation could explode into racial strife. An anti-Japanese riot in San Francisco was sparked in 1907 when an "intoxicated logger" fell through the window of a Japanese-run laundry. Before the ensuing brawl ended, dozens of whites and Japanese were injured. Hundreds of violent episodes like this one transpired across the Rocky Mountain region and along the West Coast during this period.

Small-time farmers, following on the legacy of the Grange societies of the 1870s, continued to organize and advocate for their economic interests. Global competition in crops from wheat to cotton squeezed the farmers' profit margins, and railroad companies often charged crippling prices to take crops and livestock to market. Two major regional alliances dominated the farmers' societies in the 1880s and 1890s: the Northwestern Alliance, based largely in the Great Plains, and the Southern Alliance. The Southern Alliance counted more than a million members. Because of racial tensions, the Southern Alliance was generally composed of whites, but the separate Colored Farmers' National Alliance also represented the interests of black farmers and farm workers.

Echoes of the debate regarding black advancement between W. E. B. Du Bois and Booker T. Washington appeared in the movement for African American farm laborers' interests. Some cotton pickers argued for a more aggressive stance, including strikes. Others cautioned against extreme tactics. "We banded together for the purpose of educating ourselves and cooperating with the white people, for the betterment of the colored people," one Colored Alliance leader explained. He thought that a strike could be "fatal" to those aims. Indeed, it was quite risky for any African American workers to organize formal protests or resistance. When some Colored Alliance cotton workers in Lee County, Arkansas, did try to strike for higher wages, it prompted a showdown between a white posse and the strikers. One white farm manager was killed, and fifteen black laborers died in the violence.

By the 1890s, farmers and farm workers were taking on more of a political posture as part of the Populist movement. This movement was led by a cast of dynamic leaders across the South and Midwest. One of the most formidable was South Carolina's "Pitchfork" Ben Tillman. Tillman, who as a teenager had lost an eye in the Civil War, struggled in the 1880s as a farmer, with indebtedness resulting from the purchase of expensive machinery. In 1884, he established the Agricultural Club in his native Edgefield district. As a representative to the South Carolina Grange meeting, he railed against the business elites and their political cronies who kept farmers in debt bondage. Tillman condemned the "drones and vagabonds" produced by South Carolina College, the favored institution of the state's elite families. He also reviled the elites of Charleston, which since the colonial era had been the center of high culture in the state. Charlestonians likewise scoffed at Tillman as representing the kinds of upstate bumpkins who "carry pistols in their hip pockets, who expectorate upon the floors, who have no tooth brushes, and comb their hair with their fingers."

Tillman wished to see the formation of an alternative agricultural college that could inculcate the best modern farming practices. He got his wish when in 1888 Thomas Green Clemson, a son-in-law of John C. Calhoun, gave hundreds of acres in his will for the creation of Clemson College in the northwest corner of the state. Tillman resisted attempts to create a Populist third party in South Carolina, and in 1890 he was elected governor as a Democrat. He made clear that he would serve the interests of the common white people. In his inaugural address Tillman repudiated the Jeffersonian belief in the equality of all people. "The whites have absolute control of the state government," he said, "and we intend at any and all hazards to retain it."

Midwestern Populists tended to be more open to cooperation with nonwhites (though of course the number of black farmers was highest in the South). They also produced some remarkable female leaders, such as Kansas schoolteacher Mary Elizabeth Lease, the child of Irish immigrants. Although Lease was born a Catholic, her speeches took on an evangelical tone. Her hundreds of orations across Kansas were like a "revival, a crusade, a Pentecost of politics," as one observer put it. "Wall Street owns this country," Lease thundered. "It is no longer a government of the people, by the people, and for the people, but a government of Wall Street, by Wall Street, and for Wall Street. The great common people of this country are slaves, and monopoly is the master."

In 1890, farmers' representatives from the Southern Alliance and the Colored Farmers' Alliance met in Ocala, Florida, and issued the "Ocala Demands," which would set the tone for the Populist political agenda in the coming years. It was an unusual instance of political cooperation across racial lines during the period. Some of the farmers' priorities carried on the desires of the Greenback Party, especially the expansion of the money supply and the use of silver coins. They also argued for a federal income tax that would put higher levies on the richest Americans and for direct election of US senators. (Constitutional amendments, the Sixteenth and Seventeenth, in favor of these two measures would pass in 1913.) The Ocala Demands' most innovative proposal for farmer relief was the creation of a federal "subtreasury" system in which farmers could store crops such as cotton, tobacco, and wheat in government warehouses until prices reached a profitable level and could secure low-interest government loans on the value of those crops.

The Populist Party

The Southern Alliance tended to promote candidates (like Ben Tillman) within the Democratic Party, but they often felt used by Democrats who did little to push forward Populist reforms. In the Midwest there was more momentum toward the establishment of a Populist third party to take on the Republicans and Democrats. In the 1890 election the Populist or "People's Party" candidates scored a number of local and state victories and dominated Kansas's congressional elections. One observer viewed the campaign as a combination of the "French Revolution and a western religious revival."

The height of the Populist movement as a national political force came in 1892 when farming interests from the mountain West, the Midwest, and even from much of the South joined together to create a national People's Party. Their platform reflected most of the priorities of the Ocala Demands. At the founding convention in Omaha, Nebraska, meeting on the Fourth of July, organizers painted a grim future of American economic inequality seen "in the midst of a nation brought to the verge of moral, political, and material ruin. Corruption dominates . . . [and] the people are demoralized. . . . The fruits of the toil of millions are boldly stolen to build up colossal fortunes for a few, unprecedented in the history of mankind; and the possessors of those, in turn, despise the republic and endanger liberty. From the same prolific womb of governmental injustice we breed the two great classes—tramps and millionaires." Citing 2 Thessalonians 3:10 ("If any would not work, neither should he eat"), they insisted that laborers should benefit from the fruit of their labor. But they also denounced an American immigration system that "opens our ports to the pauper and criminal classes of the world and crowds out our wage-earners," calling for "further restriction of undesirable emigration."

In the 1892 presidential election, the Populist Party hardly challenged the national power of the Republicans and Democrats, and Grover Cleveland reclaimed the presidency for the Democrats. Still the Populists won more than a million votes nationwide and got the electoral votes of five states in the Midwest and mountain West. They did even better in the 1894 elections, as the nation had plunged into the Panic of 1893, and the distress of farmers had only deepened. In the end, however, the Populist Party could not hope to successfully displace the Republicans or Democrats. In areas of substantial African American populations, white Populists could never balance their desire for black-white solidarity on issues of concern to farm labor and the problems created by conceding political power (or even the vote) to African Americans.

The Democratic Party also realized that if they did not satisfy Populist demands, they could risk cutting farmers out of their national coalition. By the 1896 election, the Democrats were catering to the priorities of Populism and the interests of industrial laborers. The frustrations of the working classes in the midst of a terrible economic depression came to focus on one issue—the expansion of silver coinage—as the best way to solve the nation's woes. As obscure as the issue of silver may seem today, the debate between those who would expand silver and those who wanted to restrict currency to the gold standard took on social and moral implications far beyond economic technicalities.

The 1896 Presidential Election

In the 1896 presidential election, Republicans nominated Ohio's William McKinley, a devout Methodist and congressman from Ohio. He campaigned on the gold standard, as Republicans insisted that "gold is the Universal Standard of the World." The Democrats nominated the equally devout Presbyterian William Jennings Bryan, a former congressman from Nebraska. In spite of opposition to silver coinage from Grover Cleveland's wing of the party, Bryan and his Populist-leaning Democrats made silver the center of their campaign. Bryan, one of the greatest orators in the history of presidential politics, delivered his "Cross of Gold" speech at the 1896 Democratic National Convention. Drawing on religious rhetoric and biblical images, Bryan assured the convention that the debate of 1896 was "not a contest among persons. The humblest citizen in all the land when clad in the armor of a righteous cause is stronger than all the whole hosts of error that they can bring. I come to speak to you in defense of a cause as holy as the cause of liberty—the cause of humanity." Bryan insisted that if they supported silver the Democrats would have the support of "all the toiling masses." Together they would answer the Republicans' "demands for a gold standard by saying to them, you shall not press down upon the brow of labor this crown of thorns. You shall not crucify mankind upon a cross of gold."

In the 1896 election McKinley and Bryan both experimented with new methods of campaigning that would come to mark modern American elections. McKinley and Mark Hanna, a prominent Republican businessman, raised unprecedented amounts of money for a national media blitz. Bryan had fewer businessmen as supporters so he just barnstormed across the nation, visiting twenty-seven states and speaking to approximately 3 million people during the campaign. The Populist Party decided to endorse Bryan, effectively ending their run as a national third party. When the election came, McKinley dominated Bryan, especially in cities, the Northeast, and the upper Midwest. McKinley won by almost 100 votes in the Electoral College. The Republicans had emerged as the dominant party nationally after decades of back-and-forth between one-term Democratic and Republican presidents.

Figure 18.2. *The Populist Paul Revere.* Illustration shows William Jennings Bryan riding through town on a horse fashioned out of the *Commoner* newspapers, announcing that representatives of the reorganized Democratic Party were coming, drawing out old men brandishing labeled weapons.

National Expansion

Aside from McKinley's defense of the gold standard, his administration would also mark a culmination of the United States' growing inclination toward expansion and empire after the Civil War. Of course, expansion was hardly a new theme, as it dated back to the competition between England, France, and Spain for American colonies. The first half of the nineteenth century had seen episodes such as the Louisiana Purchase, the Mexican War, and the spirit of "Manifest Destiny" spurring the procurement of lands all the way to the Pacific Ocean. In the late nineteenth century, the United States continued to compete with Britain, France, and Germany for influence and colonization around the world. Big business looked overseas for new markets. Tobacco magnate James Duke looked longingly at the Chinese market, for example. If its hundreds of millions of people could just be enticed to "average a cigarette a day," it would mean unfathomable new profits.

Evolutionary theory and Darwinism also gave ideological weight to the spirit of expansion. The subtitle of Darwin's *On the Origin of Species* was *The Preservation of Favoured Races in the Struggle for Life*. That struggle played out among and within species, Darwin contended. But that evolutionary competition was relevant to the global contest of civilizations and people of different races and religions too. "Civilized nations are everywhere supplanting barbarous nations," Darwin had observed. In his popular 1885 book, *Our Country*, Congregationalist minister Josiah Strong addressed the providential mandate for the expansion of Anglo-Saxon civilization. "God, with infinite wisdom and skill, is training the Anglo-Saxon race for an hour sure to come in the world's future." There were no new worlds to discover, Strong argued. The next stage in world history was "the final competition of races." Citing Darwin, Strong predicted that the Anglo-Saxons, "this race of unequaled energy, with all the majesty of numbers and the might of wealth behind it—the representative, let us hope, of the largest liberty, the purest Christianity, the highest civilization—having developed peculiarly aggressive traits calculated to impress its institutions upon mankind, will spread itself over the earth."

The first major US expansionist move after the Civil War was the 1867 acquisition of Alaska from Russia under the guidance of Secretary of State William Seward, who served under Lincoln and Andrew Johnson. While some observers scoffed at this massive tract of icy wilderness as "Seward's folly," the acquisition met a generally warm reception as a vast new source of natural resources and a possible step toward the annexation of parts of Canada. One newspaper reported that Alaska abounded with "furs, forest, and minerals, while its rivers and bays swarm with as fine fish as ever were caught. . . . As to the price, there can be but one opinion—it is dog cheap." At $7.2 million, or about two cents per acre, even critics had to admit that the Alaska Purchase was a bargain. Later discoveries of gold and oil in Alaska would make the deal look even better. Alaska would achieve statehood in 1959, becoming the nation's largest state by area.

Hawaii

Hawaii also presented an alluring target for US expansion. The Hawaiian Islands, in the middle of the Pacific Ocean, had long served as a stopover for ships during voyages between Asia and the Americas. Sailors had brought disease to the islands in the late 1700s, and by the beginning of the nineteenth century, the native Hawaiian population had dropped by half, to 150,000 people. Christian missionaries, many of them women, arrived in Hawaii in the 1820s. One of these missionaries was Betsey Stockton, a former slave in the household of Ashbel Green, an early president of the College of New Jersey (Princeton). Stockton had eventually gained her freedom, was baptized as a Christian, and gained a thorough Presbyterian education in the Princeton tradition. In 1823, Stockton went to Hawaii with missionaries of the American Board of Commissioners for Foreign Missions as a servant but also as a missionary in her own right. She was one of the first single American women, aside from widows, to serve as an overseas missionary. Stockton helped pioneer educational outreach to the families of commoner children in Hawaii, where only the children of the native nobility had previously received missionary education.

The missionaries also secured some prominent early converts among native Hawaiians, such as the chiefess Kapi'olani, who was converted to Christian beliefs by the first group of New England missionaries who arrived in the islands in 1820. In 1824, Kapi'olani engaged in a legendary act of defiance against Hawaii's fire goddess, Pele, entering an active volcanic crater and defiantly proclaiming her faith in Christ. Not all was easy for the missionaries, of course, as they struggled to convince some Hawaiians to accept the strictures of Christian sexual ethics. A number of American missionaries were accused of taking financial advantage of their proselytes by setting up coffee and sugar farms. Nevertheless, Hawaii's native population saw a major outbreak of Christian revival starting in 1837. Over the course of six years, tens of thousands of Hawaiians, a sizable portion of the islands' entire population, professed new faith in Christ. Mormon missionaries also arrived in the islands in 1850, however. They saw great successes, eventually making Hawaii one of Mormonism's greatest areas of strength outside of the mountain West.

In the post–Civil War era, Hawaii became more economically connected to the United States, particularly because of special trade arrangements that allowed Hawaiian sugar to enter the United States duty-free. In 1887, the United States gained the right to unchallenged use of Hawaii's Pearl Harbor as a naval station. Trade relations between the United States and Hawaii soured in the 1890s, and Hawaii's Queen Liliuokalani asserted the islands' economic and national independence from the continental behemoth to the east. Americans living in the islands rebelled against Liliuokalani's rule in 1893, and the US government sent hundreds of Marines into Hawaii to overthrow her government. After five years of halting efforts to do so, Congress finally annexed Hawaii in 1898. In 1959, Hawaii would become the fiftieth state in the union, and the only one thus far that is not part of continental North America.

The Spanish-American War

The island of Cuba was among the last of Spain's imperial possessions in the Americas, but in the 1890s, Cuba was shaken by economic and political instability. President Cleveland had advocated American neutrality on Cuba, as rebels there tried to free the island from Spanish control. President McKinley was more inclined to aid the Cuban rebels. American public sentiment turned more hostile toward Spain because of developments in 1898. First, a New York newspaper published a letter intercepted from a Spanish ambassador to the United States. It described McKinley as "weak and a bidder for the admiration of the crowd besides being a would-be politician." The letter also suggested that the Spanish were not sincere in their professed desire to seek a peaceful resolution of the Cuban unrest.

Far more provocative than the intercepted letter was the destruction of the US warship *Maine* in Havana harbor on February 15, 1898. Although the explosion was an unfortunate accident and not Spanish sabotage, more than 200 sailors died on the ship. Americans were incensed, assuming the Spanish were behind the incident. Many adopted the slogan "Remember the *Maine* and to hell with Spain!" As many clamored for an immediate declaration of war, McKinley hesitated, not wanting to rush into war if a peaceful resolution still looked possible. A furious Theodore Roosevelt, then working in the Department of the Navy, said that McKinley had "no more backbone than a chocolate éclair." The "yellow journalism" peddled by newspaper publishers such as William Randolph Hearst excoriated the Spanish and clamored for war. When Spain proved unwilling to bring an end to violence and to grant Cuba its independence, McKinley finally asked Congress in April 1898 to authorize an invasion of Cuba. Congress did so, but it also made clear that the United States did not intend to annex Cuba.

The Spanish-American War, though limited in its effects, took on global implications when word arrived in May 1898 that American navy ships trounced those of Spain in Manila harbor in the Philippines. The news boosted the US effort to recruit volunteers to go to Cuba. The standing US army remained small at about 28,000 men, many of whom were stationed in frontier outposts and only had experience, if any, in fighting Native Americans. McKinley sought to call up 125,000 new soldiers, but far more Americans than that responded to the summons.

The most famous recruits were Theodore Roosevelt's volunteer regiment called the "Rough Riders." Roosevelt resigned his position in the Department of the Navy in order to personally lead this motley crew into Cuba. The Rough Riders included a blend of top athletes from the Ivy League schools, western frontiersmen, sheriffs, and Texas Rangers. Roosevelt saw the Rough Riders as emblematic of America's manly independence and cultured civilization, which would crush the forces of the Spanish Empire. It was a priceless opportunity for them to demonstrate their valor, Roosevelt explained in his popular 1899 account of the regiment, with "many chances of death and hardship, of honor and renown."

Forgotten in many popular accounts of the war were more than 10,000 African American troops who served in the invasion of Cuba. As was often the case, the importance of African American servicemen put pressure on the racial discrimination they encountered during the war. Black troops traveling through and training in the South discovered that whites still expected them to cooperate with Jim Crow regulations of white-black segregation. Cavalry chaplain George Prioleau, accompanying African American troops training in Florida, found the inconsistency between American ideals and practice revolting. "You talk about freedom, liberty, etc.," Prioleau wrote. "Why sir, the Negro of this country is a freeman and yet a slave. Talk about fighting and freeing poor Cuba and of Spain's brutality. . . . Is America any better than Spain?" In spite of wearing the nation's uniform, these black troops could not even buy basic supplies at the same store counter as whites.

US forces invaded Cuba in June 1898, with Marines taking Guantánamo Bay in the southeast part of the island. From there tens of thousands of American troops moved overland toward the town of Santiago, assisted by Cuban revolutionaries. Outside of Santiago, African American regiments and Roosevelt's Rough Riders assaulted the Spanish position at San Juan Hill, with the Rough Riders taking heavy casualties. (Without the black soldiers' assistance, the Rough Riders might have been utterly decimated.) The Spanish regarded Santiago as a lost cause and tried to escape by sea, but American warships destroyed the Spanish fleet at Santiago Bay in early July.

The American victory at Santiago largely ended the fighting in Cuba. The deadliest foe American forces faced in Cuba was disease, which accounted for the vast majority of the 5,400 American deaths in the Spanish-American War. In August 1898, the Spanish also surrendered Manila, in the Philippines, to US forces. The United States

Figure 18.3. *Charge of the Colored Troops; San Juan.*

also occupied the Caribbean island of Puerto Rico and the Pacific island of Guam. The Spanish-American War was over, having lasted about four months.

In the initial peace agreement, Spain gave Guam and Puerto Rico over to US control. They finally conceded independence to Cuba. The United States retained the right to lease naval bases in Cuba, which in 1903 resulted in the creation of the American base at Guantánamo Bay. The Philippines' status remained uncertain, but the Spanish agreed to allow US naval forces to stay in Manila while the nations negotiated. President McKinley was hardly certain that he wanted the United States to keep the Philippines as part of a global empire, but he did not want to see Spain or another European power recolonize it either. McKinley reportedly told a group of Methodist church leaders that the best approach was for the United States "to educate the Filipinos, and uplift and civilize and Christianize them." (Many Filipinos were Catholics, but that did not dissuade many American Protestants from believing they needed evangelization.) From this perspective, uplift and civilization in the Philippines meant annexation. At the end of 1898, the United States and Spain signed the Treaty of Paris, in which Spain formally gave the Philippines to the Americans for a $20 million payment.

The prospect of annexing the Philippines unleashed a firestorm of criticism in the United States from figures as diverse as settlement house reformer Jane Addams, Democratic leader William Jennings Bryan, businessman Andrew Carnegie, and author Mark Twain. Although Bryan had enthusiastically supported US action in Cuba, he opposed any American seizure of territory overseas. "Is our national character so weak that we cannot withstand the temptation to appropriate the first piece of land that comes within our reach?" Bryan asked. Still the Senate narrowly approved the treaty between the United States and Spain in February 1899, giving the United States the Philippines and extending the nation's imperial reach into Southeast Asia.

The Philippine-American War

Many Filipinos were outraged with the US annexation of their country. Many had supported the US actions against Spain, assuming Spanish defeat would lead to independence for the Philippines. But when that hope was disappointed, a powerful insurgency arose, seeking independence for the Filipinos. The Filipinos' leader was Emilio Aguinaldo, who sustained a devastating guerrilla campaign against American forces. Aguinaldo's army launched incessant small surprise attacks and then disappeared back into the jungles or hid among civilian populations. Four thousand American troops died during the conflict from 1899 to 1902, which became increasingly frustrating for many American commanders. Filipinos and Americans alike committed outrages on the other side, but the US troops could make examples of Filipino civilians, including women and children, to vent their anger. Soldiers used racial epithets to describe Filipinos that were identical to derogatory names used for African Americans back home. One soldier wrote that "the boys say there is no cruelty too severe for these brainless monkeys." Another reported that after an American was discovered having been shot and mutilated by Filipino rebels, the commanding officer told his men to raze the town and kill every man, woman, and child in sight. The soldier worried that he was growing "hard-hearted, for I am in my glory when I can sight my gun on some dark skin and pull the trigger."

US forces sought to wear down the resistance of Filipino rebels by cutting off food supplies, executing their livestock, and rounding up residents of rebel areas into concentration camps. Hundreds of thousands of Filipinos died during the conflict, many of them from deprivation and duress that led to disease and starvation. In March 1901, Americans and some of their Filipino allies arrested Emilio Aguinaldo, who recommended that the rebels lay down their arms. Although some rebels continued to hold out, the back of the Filipino resistance was broken, and President Theodore Roosevelt announced an end to the conflict on July 4, 1902.

The Philippines remained under US control for four decades, but it never proved to be especially profitable from the American government's perspective. Missionaries and other Christian reformers seized the opportunity to evangelize Filipinos and to build schools and colleges. But many of the missionaries criticized the crass aspects of American imperialism and the exploitation of Filipinos and their resources. Nevertheless, evangelicals believed that centuries of Spanish Catholic rule had left much of the native Filipino population lost in ignorance and spiritual darkness. Evangelist George Pentecost, a prominent associate of Dwight Moody, spoke in Manila in 1902 and explained why American Protestant missionaries were in the Philippines: "We Protestant Christians are here because the door is set open before us. . . . We are here not to exploit the people but to do them good; to give them a simpler, a better and more spiritual form of Christianity."

Figure 18.4. "A welcome to Uncle Sam's protection—three Filipinos entering American lines, Pasay, P.I. Three Filipinos posed with American soldiers during Philippine War."

China and the Open Door Policy

Pentecost's language of an "open door," which alluded to words from the book of Revelation, also framed US policy in China, a near neighbor of the Philippines. In the late 1800s, China churned with political instability, and Western merchants and missionaries (both Catholic and Protestant) routinely fell under attack from local Chinese people called the "Boxers" (so named because some of their leaders were martial artists). McKinley administration officials did not want China to descend into violence and chaos, but they hesitated to attempt an aggressive colonization scheme there. So Secretary of State John Hay issued a series of policy directives known as the "Open Door Notes," asking the various colonial powers involved in China to maintain an open trade policy in their spheres of influence. All nations should "enjoy perfect equality of treatment for their commerce and navigation within such 'spheres,'" Hay argued in his first note in September 1899.

The key powers in China, including Japan and Britain, agreed to maintain this open policy. But then in 1900, the Boxer Rebellion exploded in China, and the Chinese empress embraced the anti-Western sentiment. Attacks began on missionaries, Chinese Christians, and non-Chinese businesses. Without securing approval from Congress, President McKinley ordered thousands of American troops into China to aid a multinational force gathering there to counteract the Boxer uprising. (Some experts have argued that this was a critical turning point in the war powers of the president and the president's ability to act quickly to meet military crises around the world.) The Americans and their allies broke the Boxers' siege of Peking (Beijing), saving many diplomats, missionaries, businessmen, and Chinese Christians who had sought refuge there. The foreign armies and anti-Boxer Chinese governors brutally suppressed the Boxers. Secretary of State Hay reemphasized the Open Door policy and committed the United States to preserving China's independence while maintaining American access to Chinese markets. The principle behind the Open Door policy—using American power to maintain free trade and access to international markets—has remained a fixture of US foreign policy through the present day.

The Rise of Theodore Roosevelt

The election of 1900 was a rematch between McKinley and William Jennings Bryan. In spite of lingering trouble in the Philippines, the Spanish-American War was widely viewed as a successful conflict for the United States. McKinley's original vice president had died, and as his replacement McKinley chose New York governor and celebrated Rough Rider Theodore Roosevelt. In spite of a history of disagreements over the Spanish-American War, Roosevelt became McKinley's most effective champion. Roosevelt loved the barnstorming campaign style that Bryan had mastered in 1896. The popularity of the war and the attractive figure of Roosevelt as vice president helped McKinley defeat Bryan easily. McKinley won by almost a million popular votes and dominated Bryan in most areas of the country except for the solidly Democratic South.

Seven months into his second term, however, McKinley fell victim to an assassin's bullet. Leon Czolgosz was a Polish American steelworker who had lost his job in the Panic of 1893 and had come under the influence of radical anti-government anarchist philosophy. He traveled to Buffalo, New York, where McKinley was scheduled to appear at the city's Pan-American exhibition, confronted the president in a receiving line, and shot McKinley in the stomach. McKinley lingered for a week before succumbing to his wounds, and Roosevelt ascended to the presidency. At age forty-two Roosevelt was the youngest man yet to become president.

As a domestic reformer and advocate of US power on the world stage, Roosevelt exemplified two of the most important political trends of the era. He exhibited enormous energy as president, wanting to make the presidency the center of American political initiative instead of Congress. Roosevelt spoke of the office of president as the "bully pulpit," the preeminent platform in America from which to shape national and international policy.

On the international front Roosevelt crystallized McKinley's desire to strike a balance between muscular imperialism and cringing isolationism. Roosevelt generally dismissed the idea of new American colonies but wanted to enhance US influence around the world, not least in the Western Hemisphere. The United States, he said, could not help but be concerned about "chronic wrongdoing, or an impotence which results in a general loosening of the ties of civilized society" in countries near to the American mainland. Citing the Monroe Doctrine and its connection between the United States and the nations of the Western Hemisphere, Roosevelt proposed that instability in or threatening behavior by neighboring nations sometimes required American intervention with "international police power." This idea came to be called the "Roosevelt Corollary" to the Monroe Doctrine. Shortly after articulating this principle of foreign policy, America intervened and took over parts of the trading and banking system in the Dominican Republic. In 1916, the United States took even more aggressive action by sending marines into the Dominican Republic to protect US financial interests there. American officials since have often used the Roosevelt Corollary to justify US intervention in "trouble spots" in the Caribbean and Central America.

Concern for trade with neighbors both near and far precipitated one of Roosevelt's most ambitious initiatives, the Panama Canal, a ship channel across the isthmus of

Panama. This would enable far shorter shipping routes between America's eastern, western, and southern ports, cutting out the long and dangerous passage around the southern tip of South America. It would also mean that all the nation's ports would have much quicker access to Asia, including the Philippines and China. The United States helped Panama achieve independence from Colombia, but in exchange America secured virtually sovereign control over the territory of the channel.

In one of the greatest engineering feats in modern world history, US engineers and workers from many nations built the canal between 1904 and 1914. Huge numbers of workers came from the Caribbean islands—perhaps as many as 60,000 came from the British colony of Barbados alone, out of a total Barbadian population of 180,000. About 5,600 workers died during the canal's construction, both from work-related accidents and from diseases such as malaria. Although the United States would invade Panama in 1989 to secure the canal and to depose dictator Manuel Noriega, by treaty the canal transferred to Panamanian control at the end of 1999.

Empire and Prosperity

Advocates of annexation of places from Cuba to the Philippines predicted that American expansion would lead to greater prosperity for all, both for the places annexed and for the American worker back home. One writer in 1906 said that American imperial

Figure 18.5. President Roosevelt running an American steam shovel at Culebra Cut, Panama Canal. Stereograph.

influence would revitalize the "insular possessions" of the United States. By the mid-1920s, he predicted, a visitor to the Philippines would everywhere "perceive the evidences of a people awakening to their opportunities and happy in the beginnings of a vast prosperity. American capital and American enterprise will ere then have made their vivifying effects felt in the land." Those benefits would accrue to the American farmers and factory workers who helped fuel the economic renaissance in far-distant lands. While one could certainly point to many instances where free trade and global interconnectedness have improved standards of living, the linkage between empire and prosperity has never been that simple. Nevertheless, American leaders moved into the twentieth century with enormous confidence that, with wise plans and energetic effort, they could alleviate America's own ills and extend its influence for good around the world.

■ SELECTED BIBLIOGRAPHY ■

Ayers, Edward L. *The Promise of a New South: Life after Reconstruction*. New York: Oxford University Press, 1992.

Gould, Lewis L. *Theodore Roosevelt*. New York: Oxford University Press, 2012.

Greene, Julie. *The Canal Builders: Making America's Empire at the Panama Canal*. New York: Penguin, 2009.

Harris, Susan K. *God's Arbiters: Americans and the Philippines, 1898–1902*. New York: Oxford University Press, 2011.

Hutchison, William R. *Errand to the World: American Protestant Thought and Foreign Missions*. Chicago: University of Chicago Press, 1987.

Kazin, Michael. *A Godly Hero: The Life of William Jennings Bryan*. New York: Knopf, 2006.

Postel, Charles. *The Populist Vision*. New York: Oxford University Press, 2007.

Roosevelt, Theodore. *The Rough Riders*. New York: P. F. Collier, 1899.

Smith, Carl. *Urban Disorder and the Shape of Belief: The Great Chicago Fire, the Haymarket Bomb, and the Model Town of Pullman*. 2nd ed. Chicago: University of Chicago Press, 2007.

Strong, Josiah. *Our Country*. New York: American Home Missionary Society, 1885.

19

The Progressive Era

The Progressive Era, which lasted from the 1890s to the 1920s, was inspired by the conviction that America's ills could be solved by hard work, creative planning, and moral zeal. One of the reformers' most basic tasks was to bring the darker aspects of American life to light in order to touch the consciences of average middle-class Americans. The "muckrakers," those journalists and writers who sought to expose the abuse of American workers and the plight of America's poor, specialized in stories that stirred Americans' hearts with compassion for America's downtrodden classes.

One of the most effective exposés was novelist Upton Sinclair's *The Jungle* (1906), which revealed horrid conditions in Chicago's meatpacking plants. Sinclair painted revolting scenes of butchers with swollen joints and missing fingers and "men who worked in the cooking-rooms, in the midst of steam and sickening odors, by artificial light; in these rooms the germs of tuberculosis might live for two years, but the supply was renewed every hour."

The conditions were worst of all for the men who worked at the enormous cooking vats. "Their peculiar trouble was that they fell into the vats; and when they were fished out, there was never enough of them left to be worth exhibiting. Sometimes they would be overlooked for days, till all but the bones of them had gone out to the world as 'Durham's Pure Leaf Lard!'" Sinclair's account was so sickening that he worried that he had failed in his muckraking aims. He wanted to draw the nation's attention to the "wage-slaves" in the food industry, but instead all the focus went to the horrific corruption of the food supply. "I aimed at the public's heart," Sinclair confessed, "and by accident I hit it in the stomach!" From the factories to impoverished farms, and from immigrant ghettos to the cotton plantations, Progressives saw outrages that demanded action.

Changes in American Industry

The American economy had begun to recover from the depression caused by the Panic of 1893. The continued growth of American industry in the early 1900s created difficult and dangerous conditions for many workers, especially recent immigrants, the poor, and the uneducated. The scale of American business continued to escalate and consolidate in the early decades of the twentieth century, creating behemoths such as J. P. Morgan's U.S. Steel Corporation.

New technologies kept revolutionizing the marketplace too. Perhaps the most distinctive technological change in the early years of the 1900s was the coming of the automobile. The key figure in the automobile industry was Henry Ford, the child of Irish immigrant farmers who grew up in Dearborn, Michigan, outside Detroit. In Detroit, Ford went to work for the Edison Illuminating Company, where he learned from Thomas Edison's vision of pairing invention and the production of consumer products. Ford was a talented engineer and machinist, and in 1896 he unveiled his prototype car, called the Quadricycle. In 1903, he founded the Ford Motor Company, believing he could design cars that would be affordable for middle-class American families. "I will build a car for the great multitude," he said. "It will be so low in price that no man making a good salary will be unable to own one—and enjoy with his family the blessings of hours of pleasure in God's great open spaces." Until that point automobiles were exotic luxuries. In 1895, only four cars total were operating on the nation's roads.

Although Ford's Model N car was a commercial success, in 1908 he introduced the Model T, a product that would permanently transform American life. His company produced 6,000 Model Ts in 1908, each selling for $850. As Ford streamlined the production process, he ratcheted up the number of cars he was making and slowly dropped the price. By 1916, Ford Motor Company was making almost 600,000 cars a year and selling them for $360 each. Along with competitors like General Motors and Chrysler, Ford not only revolutionized American transportation but also transformed many other sectors of the economy. Demand shot up for gasoline, oil, rubber, and other car-related products. The landscape of American towns and highways changed, with shops lining newly paved roads. Traffic signals coordinated the unprecedented flow of automobile traffic passing through cities.

Ford realized that the traditional way of making machinery like a car, with a small number of craftsmen working on each stage of assembly, was inefficient. His factory standardized each stage of the car production process to make it quick and reliable. Individual workers each performed a simple task, like turning bolts or putting on a single part of the automobile. Ford also installed conveyer belts so the cars moved automatically down the assembly line to the next task station. Workers no longer moved from their stations. The car came to them. By 1920, Ford factory workers could construct a Model T in one minute.

Like many industrialists, Ford feared worker unrest and union movements. So he decided in 1914 to raise his factory laborers' pay to five dollars per eight-hour workday. At the time this was triple the average amount an industrial worker was making in America, and Ford figured that it would help him attract and keep the best workers. All his innovations made Ford the pioneer of mass production. In 1923, 2 million Model Ts rolled off Ford assembly lines.

Corporations, trusts, and other large businesses were the only ones that could invest in the kinds of infrastructure, equipment, and laborers required to perform mass production of affordable products. Local craftsmen and small-shop industries became less and less common. On the eve of the Great Depression of the 1930s, incorporated businesses were responsible for making 92 percent of the manufactured goods in America. The 200 largest corporations held a fifth of America's combined wealth.

Mass Production and the Workers

Some workers, like the higher-paid ones at the Ford factory, benefited from the expansion of mass production. Others found the transition challenging at best. The simple nature of mass-production factories meant that an individual worker ideally learned to do just one task as expertly and quickly as possible. If that meant turning one bolt on one car part countless times a day, that meant more efficiency. But many workers found that kind of work mind-numbing. (Part of the reason Ford raised wages in 1914 was because they were already seeing massive rates of turnover among the workers.) Increased efficiency could also make old-fashioned jobs superfluous, leading to layoffs. Other factory employees, like Upton Sinclair's meatpackers, found themselves working in extraordinarily dangerous conditions.

The dangers for factory workers were illustrated by the horrors of the Triangle Shirtwaist Factory fire in 1911 in New York City. The fire began on the eighth floor of a ten-story building. There a labor force made up mostly of immigrant Jewish women sewed "shirtwaists," a popular kind of women's blouse. The fire was of uncertain origin, but it swept through the factory and its abundant supply of flammable materials. Lacking any kind of modern alarm or fire-extinguishing equipment, the panicked workers found many of the factory doors locked, as owners were trying to cut down on unscheduled breaks, thievery, and unwelcome guests. An elevator and a fire escape were both inoperable at the time of the fire. The New York City fire department was ill-equipped to counteract a blaze so high up in a building. Desperate women leapt to their deaths out of factory windows. Some of those left inside were burned beyond recognition. One hundred forty-six shop workers died in the conflagration. Many of the dead were teenagers. Factory owners were charged with manslaughter, but they were acquitted. They settled charges in a civil lawsuit by paying seventy-five dollars for each dead worker.

Eighty thousand people marched in the New York City funeral procession for the Triangle factory workers. A twenty-nine-year-old labor organizer named Rose Schneiderman said that the good wishes of civic and religious leaders in the city did nothing to help. Though the Triangle fire was one of the worst industrial accidents in American history, Schneiderman argued that it was hardly exceptional. "Every week I must learn of the untimely death of one of my sister workers," she said. "Every year thousands of us are maimed. The life of men and women is so cheap and property is so sacred. There are so many of us for one job it matters little if 146 of us are burned to death. . . . It is up to the working people to save themselves. The only way they can save themselves is by a strong working-class movement."

Although episodes like the Triangle fire did inspire some reforms in workplace safety, the early 1900s were not an era of growth for the labor union movement. Corporations such as Ford Motors were successful at adopting strategies to keep unions at bay. The prosperity of the 1910s and 1920s also meant that joining a union seemed less urgent to many workers. Key Supreme Court decisions weakened legislative and constitutional protections for workers too. One of the most significant decisions was *Lochner v. New York* (1905), which struck down a New York law that had tried to cap the maximum allowable working hours for employees at bakeries. The court's majority argued that this kind of law violated

Figure 19.1. Rose Schneiderman, between 1909 and 1920.

the Fourteenth Amendment's guarantee of "due process" and an individual worker's right to make contracts of his or her choosing.

Legal historians often call the next three decades of Supreme Court jurisprudence the "Lochner era" because of a series of decisions that tended to favor business owners over workers and that limited the effectiveness of unions. In decisions such as *Loewe v. Lawlor* (1908), known as the "Danbury Hatters' Case," the court sometimes applied antitrust legislation to the efforts of unions and workers to boycott companies that prohibited union organizing. Antitrust legislation, including the Sherman Antitrust Act (1890), was originally designed to break up monopolies that suppressed competition. In cases such as *Loewe*, however, the court applied antitrust principles to forbid groups such as the United Hatters union and the American Federation of Labor (AFL) from organizing national boycotts against nonunionized companies. Doing so, the court contended, violated such companies' ability to participate freely in interstate commerce. The court also made clear that individual workers, not just their unions, could be held financially accountable for violating antitrust provisions. This had a chilling effect on workers' willingness to get involved in strikes and boycotts.

The labor union movement was also hampered by internal divisions. Some groups—for instance, the Industrial Workers of the World (the "Wobblies")—were openly radical and socialist. Socialists sought to recruit unskilled workers, nonwhites, and women, segments of the working population that organizations such as the AFL tended to ignore. Early efforts at organizing more marginalized workers resulted in unions for women, such as the Women's Trade Union League, or for African Americans, such as the Brotherhood of Sleeping Car Porters, organized in 1925 by A. Philip Randolph. Randolph was influenced by the writings of nineteenth-century German philosopher Karl Marx, who had addressed the perpetual struggle between capital and labor. But the horrors of the Bolshevik

Figure 19.2. J. W. Mays, Pullman car porter.

Revolution in Russia in the 1910s sobered Randolph, who became an outspoken anti-communist even as he sought to organize African American railway workers.

In a 1926 speech on the sesquicentennial of the Declaration of Independence, Randolph cited the Declaration's principle that "all men are created equal" and insisted that blacks should share fully in that ideal. To those who would exclude African Americans, Randolph declared that the "Negro is, doubtless, the most typically American. He is the incarnation of America. His every pore breathing its vital spirit, without absorbing its crass materialism." But blacks were also the most exploited workers in American history. So Randolph predicted that "the Negro's next gift to America will be in economic democracy. . . . Experience and necessity are teaching him of the value of labor organization. . . . This will rescue him from the stigma of being regarded by organized white labor as the classic scab of America." In 1929, Randolph would affiliate the Sleeping Car Porters union with the AFL, tapping into the broader national power of the white-led labor movement. In 1937, the Sleeping Car Porters union also won a labor contract with the Pullman Company, the key employer of the brotherhood's members.

Immigration

Waves of new immigrants kept supplying much of the unskilled, and least unionized, segments of the American workforce. Since 1900, much of that immigration was coming from southern and eastern Europe and from Mexico. In the first two decades of the twentieth century, a record-setting 14.5 million immigrants arrived in the United States. Some of these came as entire families, with no plan to return to their place of birth. Some immigrants came by themselves, hoping to earn money to help their families back home or to earn money in America that would help them get established once they returned to their land of origin. Companies like Ford offered English-language instruction and courses on American culture to help immigrant employees get acclimated. But some union activists believed these courses were mainly intended to produce compliant workers. On the West Coast, Japanese immigration outpaced Chinese because of laws specifically prohibiting Chinese settlement. By 1920, more than 100,000 Japanese people lived in the United States, mostly in California.

Mexican immigration had begun to pick up after 1900, especially as southwestern ranches, farms, and businesses needed more labor to replace the excluded Chinese. Then in 1910, the Mexican Revolution began with the ouster of Mexico's longtime ruler Porfirio Díaz. The Mexican Revolution would continue to convulse the nation for ten years as Mexico went through multiple revolutionary regimes. The violence and instability sent tens of thousands of Mexican immigrants across the US border. There was no effort to tally up US border crossings until 1907, and there was no border patrol until 1924. Thus, the numbers of immigrants and of Hispanics living in the United States were difficult to track. Nevertheless, the total number of Mexican-born people in the United States probably went from fewer than 5 million in 1900 to about 15 million on the eve of the Great Depression in the late 1920s. They spread out across the country from Alaska to the East Coast, but the preponderance of Mexican immigrants lived in the Southwest, from California to Texas.

In the southwestern states, the number of Mexicans was often doubling every decade between 1900 and 1930. In some places the growth was even faster. Mexicans often settled in barrios, or Mexican-majority sections of southwestern towns. The barrio in El Paso, Texas, was called Chihuahuita, a name derived from the Mexican state that lay directly south across the Rio Grande. Chihuahuita grew quickly from the 1890s forward, with most adult men in the neighborhood working in the railroad industry. Others used barrios such as Chihuahuita as a transit point: once having crossed the border into the United States, Mexican workers might fan out to wherever they could find seasonal work and then return to the border town in the off-season. A visitor to Chihuahuita in 1900 noted that most of the Mexicans there lived in dirt-floor adobe huts with outhouses and little sanitation.

Christian churches and missionary organizations worked to alleviate some of the problems in the barrios, offering spiritual help and social assistance of various kinds. St. Ignatius Catholic Church was one of the key parishes serving the Chihuahuita neighborhood, whose residents were overwhelmingly from a Catholic background. Tens of thousands of Catholic Mexicans would participate in Corpus Christi parades each June in the 1910s in El Paso. Protestants also sought to make inroads, and by the early 1900s virtually every major Protestant denomination had founded a church designed to reach out to El Paso's Mexicans. Probably more successful than the churches were the efforts of the YMCA to attract young Mexicans in Chihuahuita. The YMCA offered Bible and English-language classes as well as various sports leagues and other forms of entertainment. Although much of this activity was designed to foster "Americanization," the YMCA did put Mexican Americans in leadership positions. It also accommodated Mexican culture by sponsoring events such as a Cinco de Mayo celebration each May. By 1920, tens of thousands of Mexicans were participating in YMCA functions in El Paso.

White-owned businesses were eager to use Mexican labor, but many whites expressed concern about the cultural and racial influences Mexicans brought to America. In particular, white men worried about Mexican men and their potential desire to marry white girls. One Los Angeles agricultural official during the era assured constituents that

Mexicans "don't try to marry white women" (though he thought that Filipino men did try to do so). A San Diego school superintendent was not so sure, saying that "American parents don't want their lily-white daughters rubbing shoulders with the Mexicans with their filthy habits." Such sentiments encouraged the segregation of Mexicans into their own schools and neighborhoods in the Southwest.

Progressives

The Progressive movement responded to a host of issues raised by rapid urbanization, industrialization, and immigration. Progressivism was a large and not always consistent movement. It ran the gamut from admirable causes, such as alleviating the worst abuses of factory workers, to troubling ones, such as restricting the birth rates of "undesirable" races. Progressives worked in political offices, journalism, academia, churches, and social relief agencies.

Progressives focused on at least three major areas of social reform. One was regulating big industry and business. The successes of companies like Ford Motor and Standard Oil depended on the freedom of businesses to grow and compete as they saw fit. But Progressives argued that there came a point where business success undermined human dignity and the public good. Theodore Roosevelt declared that the government must resist those businessmen who believe that "every human right is secondary to his profit." Progressives argued for reforms of child labor practices, workplace safety, and the maximum working hours and minimum pay laborers could expect. Some Progressives believed the government must take an active role in breaking up monopolies for the good of the economy and the individual consumer.

A second major focus of Progressives was ensuring responsive, democratic government. In this priority they drew on parts of the legacy of Populism from the late 1800s. Progressives lamented corruption in politics and the power of Democratic and Republican party operatives over the people at large. They sought to put more political power in the hands of more people, advocating for causes such as the direct election of US senators and the right of women to vote.

Finally, Progressives sought to address the problems created by immigration, urban crowding, and poverty. Some initiatives took a positive approach, offering basic services to the urban poor and to immigrant newcomers. The settlement house movement encouraged education, job training, health, and safe living conditions. Some reforms took a more negative approach, seeking to restrict immigration, especially of Jews, Catholics, and Asians. Others sought moral reforms that seemed especially pressing among the urban population, such as prohibiting the sale and consumption of alcohol.

Progressives were often split among themselves on issues such as racial integration and voting rights for nonwhites. Many of the Progressives' concerns were not new in American history, but the Progressive movement became the first nationwide effort at systematic reform since crusades such as the temperance cause of the pre–Civil War era.

The Progressives produced a remarkable cadre of female leaders, pioneered by Frances Willard, the leader of the Women's Christian Temperance Union, which had already become the nation's largest women's organization by the 1890s. Jane Addams's Hull House in Chicago also cultivated key female leaders in the Progressive movement. One of them, Florence Kelley, lived at Hull House for much of the 1890s before becoming the head of the National Consumers League from 1899 to 1932. Kelley's organization campaigned for labor and educational reform but was especially known for restricting the use of young children as laborers in factories.

Kelley, who was influenced by European socialist thought, explained the tumultuous changes coming to America if the nation did not give due attention to suffering workers:

> We are nearing the point at which the blind movement of industrial development must involve us in utter social chaos, the means of production all concentrated in a few irresponsible hands . . . the army of the unemployed swollen to such proportions as to burden and cripple all industry. . . . The old order of society is passing away, the new has yet to be evolved. The transition may excel the horrors of the French Revolution, or be ushered in as calmly as the dawning of the day. That will depend upon the insight of the workers and the women of the nation.

To ease the transition, Kelley insisted, the children of even the poorest Americans must have access to public schooling. Americans should not allow children, forced by economic need, to go into the factories at an early age, which was common in the late 1800s. In a successful national campaign, Kelley's league also put labels of approval on consumer products from companies that did not exploit workers or children.

New experts like Kelley (who earned a law degree from Northwestern) touted scientific analysis as key to alleviating social ills. They performed unprecedented surveys of cities such as Chicago and New York, documenting patterns of poverty and unsanitary conditions. Although some Progressives still emphasized that no one could hope to escape poverty without making good individual choices, many of the new reformers pointed to structural and generational causes of the impoverished classes' struggles.

The studies of poverty reflected a broader trend toward creating academic, scientific, and professional societies of all kinds across America. Hundreds of such societies were founded between the end of Reconstruction and the US entry into World War I. Among the most influential was the American Bar Association (1878), which has set many standard practices for the law profession. The American Medical Association (AMA) had been founded in 1847, but a 1901 reorganization of it helped turn the AMA into a major advocate for standardized protocols of doctors' care and use of medication. Because of its focus on "professional" medicine, the AMA has also historically been resistant to the recognition of "alternative" medical practices, such as naturopathy and chiropractic treatments.

The Muckrakers

One of the most powerful tools of the Progressive movement was publishing. The men and women who wrote exposés of the abuses in industry and politics were labeled "muckrakers" in 1906 by Theodore Roosevelt. This was initially a negative term that referenced the character of the "Muck-raker" in John Bunyan's spiritual classic *The Pilgrim's Progress*. Although Roosevelt had his own Progressive inclinations, he thought that some muckraking authors were too negative about the corruption and exploitation in America. But muckrakers such as Upton Sinclair and Ida Tarbell (the nemesis of John D. Rockefeller and Standard Oil) found a ready audience for their work in popular newspapers, magazines, and books. The muckrakers spun lurid and sensational but usually fact-based stories about the appalling suffering in the nation's cities and leading industries.

Writers such as Samuel Hopkins Adams lambasted the producers of patent medicines that were laced with alcohol and cocaine, which might bring temporary relief but also bred false hopes and addiction. Writing in *Collier's Weekly*, Adams exposed the "Great American Fraud" of the popular remedies, including

> the alcohol stimulators, as represented by Peruna, Paine's Celery Compound, and Duffy's Pure Malt Whiskey (advertised as an exclusively medical preparation); the catarrh powders, which breed cocaine slaves, and the opium-containing soothing syrups, which stunt or kill helpless infants; the consumption cures, perhaps the most devilish of all, in that they destroy the hope where hope is struggling against bitter odds for existence; the headache powders, which enslave so insidiously that the victim is ignorant of his own fate; the comparatively harmless fake as typified by that marvelous product of advertising and effrontery, Liquizone; and finally, the system of exploitation and testimonials upon which the whole vast system of bunco rests, as upon a flimsy but cunningly constructed foundation.

Adams's work prompted the passage of the Pure Food and Drug Act of 1906, which required that commercially sold medicines list their ingredients on the label. Another law in 1914 greatly reduced the use of cocaine and opium in common medicines.

The Social Gospel

As we have seen, by the late 1800s some American Christians were adopting the "Social Gospel," or the belief that Christianity was best lived out in loving service. The Social Gospel blended with the spirit of Progressivism in the early 1900s. Social Gospelers believed that all Christians should seek the good of the most troubled communities and people in the nation. Some Christians went so far as to espouse socialism. Some of the same kinds of people attracted to the Populist movement of the late 1800s gravitated toward socialist principles. For example, in Oklahoma and other parts of the Great Plains, socialist candidates received the most support from Pentecostals and Primitive Baptists. These denominations tended to appeal to working-class Christians anyway, and some who felt left out of the burgeoning capitalist system combined the messages of Christianity and socialism. They scoffed at the more affluent denominations' religion as the "church of greed." One socialist appealed to ministers by saying that the time for choosing your allies was at hand: "If you are with the crowd that Jesus drove from the temple, you will have to show it, and if you want to come out from among the thieves and money changers and join the battle for humanity it's time to show your hands."

The most famous Social Gospel advocates were not Great Plains farmers, however, but eastern Protestant theologians and pastors. Walter Rauschenbusch, a Baptist professor at

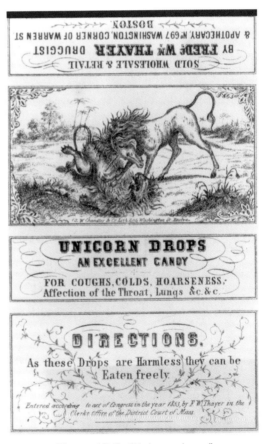

Figure 19.3. "Unicorn drops" medicine, ca. 1853.

Rochester Theological Seminary, produced some of the key works on the Social Gospel, including *Christianity and the Social Crisis* (1907). Instead of viewing Jesus's teachings as focused on individual salvation or the afterlife, Rauschenbusch insisted that Jesus's ethics were meant for the here and now. Christians should be known for working on behalf of the "least of these" (see Matt 25:31–46) and for economic equality and fairness. "Christianizing the social order," Rauschenbusch explained in 1912, meant "bringing it into harmony with the ethical convictions which we identify with Christ. . . . These moral principles find their highest expression in the teachings, the life, and the spirit of Jesus Christ." Of broader impact was the phenomenally popular novel *In His Steps: What Would Jesus Do?* (1896) by Congregationalist pastor Charles Sheldon. The book told the story of how a town was revolutionized when its citizens took up the challenge of asking, "What would Jesus do?" before taking any action. Sheldon's novel went on to sell tens of millions of copies.

Although many of the Social Gospel advocates came out of traditional Christian backgrounds, the movement also became associated with some pastors who de-emphasized or even denied essential Christian beliefs. Some of the Social Gospel's leaders, such as Congregationalist pastor Washington Gladden, positioned themselves as foes of the emerging "fundamentalist" Christian movement. For example, Gladden denied the infallibility of the Bible. He acknowledged that as of the late 1800s, the "great majority of Christians" believed in the Bible's perfection and infallibility. But "intelligent pastors do not hold it," Gladden said. This sort of critical view of the Bible led many fundamentalists to view the Social Gospelers with skepticism. As an essay in *The Fundamentals* put it, the church should indeed proclaim the "social principles of Christ." But that did not "mean the adoption of a so-called 'social gospel' which discards the fundamental doctrines of Christianity and substitutes a religion of good works."

African American Social Gospel advocates were often influenced by the debates between W. E. B. Du Bois and Booker T. Washington and disagreed among themselves about the best approach to black "uplift" in the era of Jim Crow. Leaders of the Women's Convention of the National Baptist Convention (NBC), for example, called not only for equal treatment of women and African Americans but also for alleviating the struggles of the urban poor and factory workers. The Women's Convention, the largest organization for black women at the time, was also evangelistic, sending missionaries to Africa and elsewhere. In her 1900 speech "How the Sisters Are Hindered from Helping" at an NBC meeting, the Woman's Convention founder and leader, Nannie Helen Burroughs, declared, "For a number of years there has been a righteous discontent, a burning zeal to go forward in [Christ's] name among the Baptist women of our churches and it will be the dynamic force in the religious campaign at the opening of

the 20th century. It will be the spark that shall light the altar fire in the heathen lands."
Burroughs recruited Booker T. Washington as a regular keynote speaker for National
Baptist women's meetings.

Progressives and Race

In addition to concerns for the unfair treatment of the poor and other groups, black
Progressives and muckrakers carried the additional burden of protesting the treatment of
African Americans. Although many black workers were poor too, blacks also dealt with
the additional burdens of segregation, disenfranchisement, and lynchings. Thousands of
African Americans were murdered by lynching in the last two decades of the 1800s, with
many of the victims subjected to torture in public spectacles. Ida B. Wells, a teacher and
journalist in Memphis, gained notoriety in 1892 when she published the anti-lynching
exposé *Southern Horrors: Lynch Law in All Its Phases*. Wells not only documented many
instances of lynching but insisted that the strategy of hoping to appeal to white people's
consciences was an insufficient plan of resistance. Under the category of "Self-Help,"
Wells noted that the only way blacks
had averted lynchings was when
they took up arms in self-defense. A
"Winchester rifle should have a place
of honor in every black home," Wells
concluded. "It should be used for
that protection which the law refuses
to give. When the white man who is
always the aggressor knows he runs
as great risk of biting the dust every
time his Afro-American victim does,
he will have greater respect for Afro-
American life." Wells suggested that
the common accusation of black men
raping white women was a myth.

Many whites were outraged by
Wells's provocative publication. One
newspaper declared that "the fact that
a black scoundrel is allowed to live
and utter such loathsome and repulsive calumnies is a volume of evidence

Figure 19.4. Nannie Helen Burroughs,
between 1900 and 1920.

as to the wonderful patience of Southern whites. But we have had enough of it." A Memphis newspaper openly called for the editors of Wells's newspaper, the *Free Speech and Headlight*, to be lynched themselves. Whites wrecked the office and equipment of the newspaper in 1892. Fortunately for Wells, she was attending a conference of the African Methodist Episcopal Church in Philadelphia when the attack happened, or she might have also become a victim. Realizing the risks of staying in Memphis, Wells permanently relocated to Chicago.

African Americans wanting a more aggressive approach to civil rights organized the Niagara Movement in 1905. Led by W. E. B. Du Bois, the group adopted a platform committed to "full manhood suffrage" (keeping distance from women's suffrage), the "abolition of all caste distinctions based simply on race and color," and the "recognition of the highest and best human training as the monopoly of no class or race." That last point was a swipe at the views of Booker T. Washington. Washington opposed the Niagara Movement as a threat to his dominant role in the African American community.

The Niagara Movement struggled to gain traction and ceased to exist after several years. Of more enduring significance was the National Association for the Advancement of Colored People (NAACP), founded in 1909 by black and white leaders, including Ida B. Wells and Jane Addams. Du Bois was the only African American on the executive board of the NAACP at the outset. But the NAACP and Du Bois's magazine, the *Crisis*, became the vehicle by which Du Bois's brand of civil rights activism overtook that of Booker T. Washington, who died in 1915. The NAACP engaged in legal efforts to enfranchise blacks and to expose and punish lynching. They struggled to get anti-lynching legislation passed in Congress, however.

The NAACP scored its first Supreme Court victory in 1915 in the case of *Guinn v. United States.* In this ruling the court struck down an Oklahoma grandfather clause that exempted voters from literacy tests if their grandfather was eligible to vote. This functionally meant that many illiterate whites could still vote while illiterate blacks (or those deemed insufficiently literate) could not. The court ruled that the Oklahoma law violated the Fifteenth Amendment, which banned racial discrimination in voting rights. The ruling invalidated similar grandfather clauses that many southern states had adopted since the Civil War, but it left many legal and extralegal options in place for states to keep nonwhites from voting.

Political Reform in the States

Most political activity in the late 1800s and early 1900s still took place in states and towns, not at the national level. Some of the most fundamental changes of the Progressive Era came from outside of Washington, DC. Beginning in 1902, the state of Oregon passed a series of Populist-style reforms that became known nationwide as the "Oregon system." These included the ballot initiative, which gave regular citizens the power to propose laws; the referendum, which gave voters the opportunity to vote on some new laws at the ballot box; and a recall provision, which made it possible for voters to remove politicians from office for corruption, incompetence, or other reasons. Oregon also instituted a system of direct primary elections, which allowed voters instead of political bosses to choose a party's nominee for various offices. Oregon followed the example of several other western states when it gave women the right to vote in 1912, before the passage of national women's suffrage, the Nineteenth Amendment, in 1920.

Oregon also led the way in changing the method by which Americans choose US senators. The Constitution had stipulated that state legislatures would choose a state's US senators. That meant senators, unlike US representatives, were not directly accountable to the people's votes. There were routine accusations about the problems this caused, including the introduction of corruption, favoritism, and bribery into the process of choosing senators. Oregon modified the system by requiring members of the state legislature to promise to support the winner of a party primary for US Senate, making the legislature's role a mere formality. The House of Representatives began adopting constitutional amendments for the direct election of senators in the 1890s, but the Senate would not agree to it until 1912. The requisite number of states agreed, and direct election of senators was ratified as the Seventeenth Amendment in 1913. Whereas the framers of the Constitution had imagined the Senate would be somewhat detached from the people by the senators' indirect election and six-year terms, the Seventeenth Amendment made the character of the Senate more like that of the House.

The Presidency of Theodore Roosevelt

As the youngest president in American history, Theodore Roosevelt made a major impact on international and domestic policy. With his vision of the presidency as the "bully pulpit," Roosevelt broke out of the mold of a string of relatively inactive or ineffective presidents since Reconstruction. He believed government should be a force for moral good, although it could never substitute for thriving families and other units of society that stood between the government and the individual. Roosevelt explained in a 1910 book that

> the object of government is the welfare of the people. The material progress and
> prosperity of a nation are desirable chiefly so far as they lead to the moral and

material welfare of all good citizens. Just in proportion as the average man and woman are honest, capable of sound judgment and high ideals, active in public affairs,—but, first of all, sound in their home life, and the father and mother of healthy children whom they bring up well,—just so far, and no farther, we may count our civilization a success. We must have—I believe we have already—a genuine and permanent moral awakening, without which no wisdom of legislation or administration really means anything; and, on the other hand, we must try to secure the social and economic legislation without which any improvement due to purely moral agitation is necessarily evanescent.

On race relations Roosevelt embraced Booker T. Washington as an advisor and even hosted him for dinner at the White House. Such a move was repulsive to much of the white southern press. A Memphis newspaper howled that Roosevelt had "committed a blunder that is worse than a crime, and no atonement or future act of his can remove the self-imprinted stigma. This is a white man's country. . . . Race supremacy precludes social equality." Likewise, a New Orleans newspaper took the dinner as a "studied insult to the South . . . forcing upon the country social customs which are utterly repugnant." But Roosevelt's overall record on race relations was complex, as he struggled to negotiate an alliance with white southern Republicans, many of whom (the "lily-white" Republicans) wanted to purge the party of black voters. Roosevelt, wishing to be seen as tough on black crime, dishonorably discharged hundreds of black soldiers because of an episode of racial violence in Brownsville, Texas, in 1906. Though there was little evidence and no trial, Roosevelt still concluded that the "Buffalo Soldiers" from Fort Brown were to blame. He discharged them without honor from the army. Booker T. Washington told the president it was a mistake, and W. E. B. Du Bois called the action a "sin."

Still, Roosevelt was eager to use the power of the executive branch to bring about reform in areas that captured his attention. Prominent journalist Walter Lippmann wrote that Roosevelt was the "first president who realized clearly that national stability and social justice had to be sought deliberately. . . . He was the first president to grasp the fact that justice, opportunity, and prosperity were not assigned to Americans in perpetuity as the free gift of Providence." Convinced that the federal government and its agencies could serve as forces for social good, Roosevelt and his immediate successors presided over a doubling of the number of federal employees.

Some of Roosevelt's most celebrated actions came against the power of the trusts and big corporations. Courts had been reluctant to rigorously enforce measures such as the Sherman Antitrust Act (1890). Even though Roosevelt recognized that big business was the source of much innovation and employment, he also believed with his fellow Progressives that unchecked corporate power could threaten workers, small businesses, and the general welfare. He pressured Congress into creating a Department of Commerce and Labor, which used its investigative powers to expose some of the worst abuses of large corporations.

Roosevelt also prompted the Justice Department to challenge J. P. Morgan's gargantuan railroad trust, the Northern Securities Company. Roosevelt contended that Morgan was failing to abide by the Sherman Antitrust Act and its prohibition on monopolies. In the case of *Northern Securities Co. v. U.S.* (1904), the Supreme Court narrowly ruled against Morgan's corporation, mandating that it be broken up into several smaller companies. The Roosevelt administration initiated similar actions against monopolistic trusts in tobacco, chemicals, and meat production. His suit against John D. Rockefeller's Standard Oil eventually led to its breakup as well in 1911. Roosevelt was not always as consistent as his "trust-busting" reputation might suggest, however. For example, in 1907 he permitted Morgan's U.S. Steel to acquire a key steel competitor in the South, explaining that the move was critical to avert an economy-shaking collapse in that sector. Morgan also donated more than $100,000 to Roosevelt's 1904 campaign.

At times Roosevelt also acted aggressively on behalf of workers, especially when he regarded big business as acting against the nation's interests. The most celebrated instance came in Roosevelt's extraordinary intervention in the United Mine Workers' (UMW) 1902 coal strike in Pennsylvania. Coal-rich northeastern Pennsylvania supplied much of the fuel for heating in America, so this product had a direct bearing on life in many American homes. Irish-born socialist and UMW organizer "Mother" Mary Harris Jones described the plight of many of the mine workers, noting that many of the miners were recent arrivals from Europe. "Hours of work down under ground were cruelly long. Fourteen hours a day was not uncommon. . . . Families lived in company owned shacks that were not fit for their pigs. Children died by the hundreds due to the ignorance and poverty of their parents."

The UMW represented many of the coal miners in Pennsylvania. When the union called for a wage increase and an eight-hour workday, the mine owners would not make concessions, believing that doing so would damage the industry and perhaps send the American economy into a tailspin. One hundred fifty thousand miners went on strike. The head of the mining companies, George Baer, saw the strikers as criminals and called for prayer that "right may triumph, always remembering that the Lord God Omnipotent still reigns, and that His reign is one of law and order." As the strike dragged into late summer of 1902 and winter loomed, the price of heating coal quadrupled in some areas of the country.

Roosevelt summoned the head of the UMW and the mine owners to the White House, but the owners still refused to negotiate. The president was incensed, and he directed the secretary of war to begin preparations to go into northeastern Pennsylvania with federal troops and take over the mines. Even as he prepared for such drastic measures, however, he asked J. P. Morgan to intervene on the administration's behalf. The threat of military intervention and the nationalization of the mines broke the mine owners' resistance, and they agreed to federal arbitration of the dispute with the UMW. The miners also agreed, and they went back to the mines in October 1902. Lawyers for the UMW, including Clarence Darrow (who would become famous two decades later for his role in the Scopes Trial over teaching evolution) pointed to the monopolistic collusion between the mine owners, the railroads that controlled them, and financiers such as Morgan who lorded over the whole system. Those were the forces keeping wages artificially low, Darrow argued.

The federal commission eventually awarded some concessions to the workers, including wage increases and fewer hours. It declined to give the UMW official recognition as the miners' representative, however. Although this did not give the UMW everything it had asked for, the outcome of the strike was a victory for organized labor and represented one of the first times the federal government had intervened on behalf of striking workers. As Roosevelt explained later, he expected that "big business give the people a square deal; in return we must insist that when any one engaged in big business honestly endeavors to do right he shall himself be given a square deal." The concept of Roosevelt's "square deal" meant the federal government should take an activist role in curtailing the worst abuses of major corporations, especially when those actions threatened to impact the daily lives of many Americans. Roosevelt's philosophy was not hostile to business in general, but it positioned the federal government as police and arbiters in business and labor disputes.

Roosevelt's desire to curb the excesses of big business also explains his interest in the conservation of natural areas and sustainable land development. Roosevelt did not agree with the philosophy of preservationists, who touted the value of leaving land pristine and untouched. He wanted land used for the benefit of the people but in a manner that was sustainable. Dating back to his brief, ill-fated time as a rancher in the Dakota Territory in the 1880s, Roosevelt also believed in the restorative value of being in nature. The frontier was a staple theme in his prolific writing career, including his popular four-volume *The Winning of the West* (1889–1896). He also felt that the government should restrain the uncontrolled development of lands by big business, which, left unchecked, could harm the long-term economic prospects of the nation because of the depletion of forests, mines, and other resources.

Roosevelt's primary contribution to conservation as president was the creation of government preserves of land. The total amount of land in government-controlled preserves when Roosevelt became president was 45 million acres; by 1908, that number had swelled to 195 million acres. Much of that acreage protected forests, mining regions, and areas of special beauty or geological significance, such as the Grand Canyon in Arizona or Devil's Tower in Wyoming. Roosevelt made Devil's Tower the country's first national monument in 1906. Much of the preserved land was in the West, where timber and mining companies and ranchers took a keen interest in the fate of acreage not yet used in their businesses. In 1907, Congress presented a bill that would prevent the president from adding any new national forests in the Northwest from Colorado to Washington State. Roosevelt signed the bill but not before creating or expanding thirty-two national forests, one of his most controversial moves. Western politicians were outraged, calling Roosevelt's forests the "Midnight Reserves."

The Taft Presidency

In the 1904 election Roosevelt trounced his Democratic opponent by two and a half million votes and more than doubling his rival's total in the Electoral College. (The Socialist candidate Eugene Debs got no electoral votes but did receive 400,000 popular

Figure 19.5. Devil's Tower. Devil's Tower or Bear Lodge (Mato [i.e., Mateo] Tepee of the Indians), as seen from the east side. Located near the Belle Fourche River in Wyoming.

votes.) Having filled out most of President McKinley's second term already, Roosevelt vowed not to seek reelection in 1908. His handpicked successor was his secretary of war, Ohio Republican William Howard Taft. In 1908, Taft easily defeated William Jennings Bryan, who was the Democratic nominee for the third time. But Taft's comparatively laid-back approach offered an opportunity for latent factions among the Republicans to come to the surface. Most of his time in office, he struggled to contend with Republican infighting over tariff policy and the control of Congress.

Nevertheless, Taft's administration continued Roosevelt's approach to extending American influence in the Caribbean, Central America, and East Asia. With a philosophy of "dollar diplomacy," Taft argued that economic intervention was much preferable to using the military to get America's way overseas. Thus, Taft got involved in debt crises in Honduras, Nicaragua, and Haiti. He also persuaded a group of bankers to help finance a major railway project in China, hoping to keep the Open Door policy alive in trade with the Chinese.

On the domestic front, among the signature achievements under Taft's watch were the congressional passage of the Sixteenth and Seventeenth Amendments to the Constitution, which authorized a federal income tax, and the direct election of US senators. Article I of the Constitution had prohibited Congress from passing "direct" taxes. An 1895 Supreme Court decision had ruled that an earlier income tax had violated that prohibition. In the nineteenth century the small federal government had largely relied on revenue sources such as trade duties and the sale of public lands. Tariffs continued to be a much-debated source of government funds, with opponents arguing that high tariffs impacted poorer people the most, partly because higher prices hurt those with the least money.

Progressives argued that it was only fair for those with the highest incomes to shoulder more of the tax burden. Opponents of the income tax and the Sixteenth Amendment worried that the government might eventually raise income tax rates to crippling levels. Some also contended that wealthier people should not have to pay higher percentages of their incomes in taxes—doing so was penalizing them just because of their wealth. Nevertheless, Congress passed the Sixteenth Amendment as a way to bolster government income in the face of lower tariff duties. The requisite number of states ratified the amendment by 1913, and Congress adopted a progressive system of tax rates, with gradually higher rates based on the amount of income people or companies earned. The issue of income tax rates has remained a perennial point of debate in American politics through the present day. Wartime rates have often gone particularly high, with the highest "marginal" tax rate on the top-earning Americans reaching an astounding 94 percent of income during World War II.

Disagreements with other Republicans kept dogging Taft's administration, which inadvertently gave signals that it was trying to roll back parts of Roosevelt's legacy. Most notably, Taft's secretary of the interior, Richard Ballinger, engaged in an ugly feud with Gifford Pinchot, who had served as head of the forestry department under both Roosevelt and Taft. Ballinger sought to open up previously protected federal lands to miners and other businesses. Some Progressives suggested that Ballinger had a personal financial stake in opening these lands. Pinchot went public with his criticisms of Taft and Ballinger's policies, and Taft subsequently fired him. Although Taft actually put a great deal of western land under federal protection and subsequent investigations exonerated Ballinger of the corruption charges, a public impression developed that Taft and Ballinger stood on the side of big business and against Roosevelt and Pinchot's conservationist efforts.

The Return of Theodore Roosevelt and the Election of Woodrow Wilson

Progressive-leaning Republicans urged Roosevelt to consider another run for the White House. His frustration with Taft had pushed Roosevelt in an ever more Progressive direction, more so than when he was president. In 1910, he laid out a program of federal initiatives that Roosevelt labeled the "New Nationalism," a philosophy that "regards the executive power as the steward of the public welfare," Roosevelt explained. He advocated the kind of democratic reforms associated with the "Oregon system," including the popular referendum and the option to recall elected officials. He also pushed for a progressive income tax, more aggressive regulation of large corporations, and protecting public lands from use by anyone but small-time settlers.

Roosevelt's dissatisfaction with Taft and his continuing popularity in the nation made him a formidable challenger for the Republican nomination in 1912. Taft had secured the allegiance of many key Republican leaders in the states, however. Many states had not yet adopted the direct primary system, which tended to favor Roosevelt. So in mid-1912, the Republican Convention nominated Taft for reelection. The disgusted Roosevelt left the convention and decided to run a third-party campaign.

In August 1912, Roosevelt received the nomination of the Progressive Party, sometimes also called the "Bull Moose" Party (so named because during the campaign Roosevelt said that he felt as strong as a bull moose). As with the Progressive movement generally, the Progressive Party drew people from many sectors of American life, such as leaders from both the business world and labor unions. The Progressive Party was committed to women's voting rights. Settlement house reformer Jane Addams seconded Roosevelt's nomination for president, an unusually public political role for any woman yet in American history. Roosevelt's campaign took on a revivalist tone as the candidate cast his platform as a matter of good versus evil by citing the apocalyptic battle of Revelation 16:

> Here in this great republic it shall be proved from ocean to ocean that the people can rule themselves, and thus ruling can gain liberty for and do justice both to themselves and to others. We who stand for the cause of the uplift of humanity and the betterment of mankind are pledged to eternal war against wrong by the few or the many . . . fearless of the future; unheeding of our individual fates; with unflinching hearts and undimmed eyes; we stand at Armageddon, and we battle for the Lord.[*]

Realizing that the divisions among the Republicans signaled their best chance for victory since Grover Cleveland in 1892, the Democrats nominated Woodrow Wilson, the governor of New Jersey. Wilson grew up in the Southern Presbyterian Church, and his father was a key church leader. Wilson's deep sense of morality and the obligation to serve animated his work as the president of Princeton University and as the reform-minded New Jersey governor. In many ways the Democrats' priorities in 1912 resembled those of the Progressives': balancing the need for business growth with the need to protect workers and consumers. Although Wilson had lived and worked in New Jersey in the 1890s, he was steeped in the states-rights tradition of southern politics. Therefore, he was warier of top-down schemes led by the federal government than was Roosevelt.

In the general election of 1912, Wilson only won 42 percent of the popular vote, but he dominated Roosevelt and Taft with 82 percent of the electoral votes. Roosevelt and Taft had so divided the Republican Party that they gave a resounding victory to Wilson. The sitting president finished third and managed to gain only eight electoral votes. The Socialist Eugene Debs made his best showing yet, with almost a million votes, but this also cut into the support for the Progressive Party. The Democrats also won control of both houses of Congress, and Wilson understandably believed he had a broad mandate to govern.

In his inaugural address Wilson offered an explanation for the Democratic triumphs of 1912. "The Nation has been deeply stirred, stirred by a solemn passion, stirred by the knowledge of wrong, of ideals lost, of government too often debauched and made an instrument of evil," he said. "The feelings with which we face this new age of right

---

[*] "Progressive Covenant with the People," audio recording, 3:21, https://www.loc.gov /item/99391565.

Figure 19.6. President Woodrow Wilson throwing out the first ball, opening day, 1916.

and opportunity sweep across our heartstrings like some air out of God's own presence, where justice and mercy are reconciled." Wilson laid out a political program he called the "New Freedom," centered on lower tariffs, limitations on monopolistic trusts in business, and Progressive reforms in the nation's financial systems. Wilson and the Democrats backed up the "New Freedom" with laws such as the 1913 Underwood-Simmons Tariff, which dramatically lowered the duties charged on imported goods. Wilson promised that this measure would lower consumer costs for everyone, but he also forecast that lowering the tariff would induce other countries to do likewise, opening global markets to more American products.

Reformers had called for change in the American banking system since a devastating financial panic in 1907 had nearly swamped tens of thousands of local banks. Although the idea of a national bank operated by the federal government had been controversial since Alexander Hamilton had first proposed one in the 1790s, advocates insisted that a central banking system could help stabilize the economy and avert crippling mass withdrawals from the banks in times of turmoil. They also argued that the central bank would reinforce the American currency, as it could boost or reduce the money supply according to current economic conditions.

William Jennings Bryan and other populist-leaning Democrats argued that consolidating the banking system would put even more power in the hands of elite financiers in New York City. These critics worried that the proposed Federal Reserve would really serve to protect the interests of big bankers rather than common people. Wilson encouraged lawmakers to establish a dozen regional branches of the central bank in an attempt to allay the concerns of the populists. With this adjustment made, Congress passed the Federal Reserve Act of 1913 to establish the Federal Reserve System. The Federal Reserve sets the "prime" interest rate for loans charged to banks, which influences the interest rates for consumers who wish to borrow money to make purchases. The Federal Reserve Act was the most important domestic legislation of Wilson's presidency, especially in terms of its enduring significance in American history. The Federal Reserve remains the chief governing unit of the banking system in the United States. The power and biases of the "Fed," and its performance during periodic financial panics since 1913, has remained a topic of heated political debate.

Wilson was also inspired to take on the power of the trusts and financial elites by his advisor Louis Brandeis, who in 1916 would become the first Jewish member of the Supreme Court. In a series of muckraking articles that became the book *Other People's Money and How the Bankers Use It* (1914), Brandeis warned of the unchecked power of America's "financial oligarchy" who by "gradual encroachments" of power had taken over vast sectors of the economy and who exercised undue influence in the workings of government. "It was by processes such as these that Caesar Augustus became master of Rome," he wrote. "The makers of our own Constitution had in mind like dangers to our political liberty when they provided so carefully for the separation of governmental powers."

At Brandeis's urging, Wilson and the Congress created the Federal Trade Commission, which possessed broad investigative power over "unfair methods of competition," and the ability to give cease-and-desist orders to businesses violating antitrust laws. Brandeis was disappointed in the relative lack of enforcement power given to the Federal Trade Commission, however. The Clayton Antitrust Act of 1914 extended the anti-monopoly policies of the federal government too. Most important, from the unions' perspective, it limited the courts' ability to stop labor activists from striking.

Wilson was reluctant to embrace more radical aspects of the Progressive agenda. Many African Americans were discouraged by his administration's record on race relations. The Democrats remained a heavily southern-oriented party, and the Republicans had traditionally counted on African American voters. But higher numbers of African Americans and civil rights activists had supported Wilson, who had courted them during the election of 1912. When Wilson became president, however, many of his cabinet appointees were white southerners who objected to integration in federal departments. Postmaster general Albert Burleson of Texas suggested that the departments begin the process of racial segregation of offices, bathrooms, and other facilities, and Wilson did not object. When leaders such as Booker T. Washington and Oswald Garrison Villard (the head of the NAACP) objected, Wilson informed them that segregation was "distinctly to the advantage of the colored people themselves" and that he believed many African Americans supported the policy. Wilson further explained that he did not believe there was any "discrimination along race lines but that there was a social line of cleavage which, unfortunately, corresponds with the racial line." More aggressive protests against federal segregation did move the administration to curtail some of the most egregious examples of discrimination, but Wilson's reputation among African Americans was damaged.

During his 1916 reelection campaign, Wilson instituted more labor reforms, such as a law providing compensation for injured federal workers, restrictions on child labor, and an eight-hour workday for railroad employees. These measures helped secure Progressives' support for him, and he narrowly defeated the nominee of the reunified Republican Party in the 1916 election. But since the outbreak of World War I in Europe in 1914, the domestic priorities of the Progressives had started to fade in political importance. Campaigning on the slogans "America First" and "He Kept Us out of War," the issues of the 1916 campaign increasingly centered on foreign affairs and the question of US intervention in World War I. In that sense the 1916 election marked the beginning of the end for the Progressive movement. Muckrakers and social reformers remained attentive to the excesses of American industry, but the eyes of most Americans focused on events in Europe.

■ SELECTED BIBLIOGRAPHY ■

Bissett, Jim. *Agrarian Socialism in America: Marx, Jefferson, and Jesus in the Oklahoma Countryside, 1904–1920*. Norman: University of Oklahoma Press, 1999.

Chambers, John Whiteclay, II. *The Tyranny of Change: America in the Progressive Era, 1900–1917*. New York: St. Martin's Press, 1980.

Curcio, Vincent. *Henry Ford*. New York: Oxford University Press, 2013.

García, Mario T. *Desert Immigrants: The Mexicans of El Paso, 1880–1920*. Repr. ed. New Haven, CT: Yale University Press, 1981.

Gerin-Gonzales, Camille. *Mexican Workers and American Dreams: Immigration, Repatriation, and California Farm Labor, 1900–1939*. New Brunswick, NJ: Rutgers University Press, 1994.

Greenwald, Richard A. *The Triangle Fire, The Protocols of Peace, and Industrial Democracy in Progressive Era New York*. Philadelphia: Temple University Press, 2005.

Hankins, Barry. *Woodrow Wilson: Ruling Elder, Spiritual President*. New York: Oxford University Press, 2016.

Higginbotham, Evelyn Brooks. *Righteous Discontent: The Women's Movement in the Black Baptist Church, 1880–1920*. Cambridge, MA: Harvard University Press, 1993.

Leonard, Thomas C. *Illiberal Reformers: Race, Eugenics, and American Economics in the Progressive Era*. Repr. ed. Princeton, NJ: Princeton University Press, 2016.

McGerr, Michael E. *A Fierce Discontent: The Rise and Fall of the Progressive Movement in America, 1870–1920*. New York: Free Press, 2003.

Painter, Nell Irvin. *Standing at Armageddon: The United States, 1877–1919*. New York: W. W. Norton, 1987.

20

World War I

When World War I began, President Wilson vowed to keep America out of it. But as time wore on, it became more difficult for Wilson to maintain neutrality. Not only was Germany taking hostile actions against American ships, but it seemed that great world events were passing America by. Some Progressives demanded that Wilson keep his promise of neutrality. Reformers such as Jane Addams and Florence Kelley formed the American Union Against Militarism. Getting involved in a massive war overseas would inevitably undermine social reform at home, they argued. The pacifists vowed to throw a "monkey wrench into the machinery" of war preparations.

Others, including journalist Walter Lippmann of the *New Republic*, thought Wilson had dithered in the face of a war that could become the greatest engine of social reform America had ever known. "We Americans have been witnessing supreme drama, clenching our fists, talking, yet unable to fasten any reaction to realities," Lippmann wrote. Out of the "horror" of war would come fresh opportunities for change in America. "We shall call that man un-American and no patriot who prates of liberty in Europe and resists it at home. A force is loose in America as well." Lippmann and other Progressives were naïve about the effectiveness of using war to bring about positive domestic change. But as has always been the case in American history, this new war did bring about unpredictable transformations of American society and government.

Mexican Revolution

World War I was not the only foreign policy crisis facing the Wilson administration. Although the United States had major financial interests in Mexico, it was not too concerned with the initial phase of the Mexican Revolution, which began in 1911 when the reformer Francisco Madero overthrew longtime Mexican ruler Porfirio Díaz. Just as Wilson was about to be sworn in as president in 1913, however, a Mexican military coup led by General Victoriano Huerta overthrew Madero's government and killed Madero. With that Mexico descended into bloody chaos, and Wilson insisted that he would not recognize the new military regime. The Wilson administration supported Huerta's enemies, and Huerta ultimately resigned in 1914. Wilson was reluctantly supportive of a new government headed by Venustiano Carranza, but Carranza met fierce opposition from an army headed by Francisco "Pancho" Villa. Villa, operating in northern Mexico, decided to resupply his army and provoke the Wilson administration by engaging in a 1916 cross-border attack at Columbus, New Mexico. Eighteen Americans were killed in Villa's assault on the town.

Wilson found this attack intolerable, so he sent General John J. Pershing with a 10,000-man army on an expedition into Mexico to capture Pancho Villa. Chasing after Villa gave Pershing, who would play a key role in World War I, experience in using new war technologies, including trucks, airplanes, and machine guns. Pershing's army suffered few casualties, but in the end Pershing failed to capture Villa. Wanting to avoid a larger war between the United States and Mexico, Wilson instructed Pershing to withdraw from northern Mexico. Pershing was disappointed, writing that "having dashed into Mexico with the intention of eating the Mexicans raw . . . we are now sneaking back home under cover like a whipped cur." Pancho Villa's forces would periodically reappear to threaten Mexican authorities and American border towns. When a 1919 battle in Juárez, Mexico, endangered El Paso, Texas, American commanders sent 3,600 soldiers across the Rio Grande to help defeat Villa's army, the final loss of Villa's career. Villa developed a daring image that turned him into a Mexican folk hero, an image that has endured among many Mexicans and Mexican Americans.

The Lusitania Incident

World War I, or the Great War, was sparked by the assassination of Archduke Franz Ferdinand of Austria-Hungary in 1914. A complex tangle of international alliances accounted for the alignments in the war, as the Allied Powers of Britain, France, and Russia faced off against the Central Powers of Austria-Hungary, Germany, and Turkey. The United States, a major player in the European economy, stood to make enormous profits from the war. Even before it formally entered the war, US economic interests were firmly aligned with the Allied Powers. US businesses exported billions of dollars' worth of munitions, food, and steel to them. Much of the trade was facilitated by J. P.

Morgan's banking firm, which also made hundreds of millions of dollars of loans to the Allied Powers.

America's deep business connections to the warring European powers fed directly into the crisis that led the United States into the war. The United States and Britain had ongoing disagreements about America's freedom to trade with the Central Powers, even though the amount of goods the United States was shipping to them (mostly to Germany) was shrinking rapidly. But the most acute issue came when German submarines, or U-boats, began menacing American ships in the Atlantic. Germany printed advertisements in the United States warning Americans of the danger of ship travel in the war zone (which included the waters in and around Britain), but Americans considered such threats belligerent and unreasonable.

Figure 20.1. Portrait of Pancho Villa, general of the Mexican Revolution.

In May 1915, a German U-boat torpedoed the British passenger steamship *Lusitania* off the coast of Ireland. More than half of the boat's 2,000 passengers, including 124 Americans, perished when the ship sank. It was the worst Atlantic disaster since the *Titanic* sank after colliding with an iceberg in 1912. But this was different from the *Titanic* tragedy: the *Lusitania* was sunk by an enemy ship. The American public was outraged, and even many who had favored neutrality now called for war. Others, including Wilson, thought diplomacy could still avert US entrance into the war. Wilson demanded the Germans honor the "freedom of the seas" for neutral powers and warned that any more sinkings of passenger ships with Americans on board would be viewed as "deliberately unfriendly." Although the language sounds tepid in retrospect, Wilson was effectively guaranteeing that another incident would mean war with the United States. The Germans backed down and promised they would stop attacks on passenger vessels, but the *Lusitania* incident had done much to push America toward entering the war.

Although some isolationists and pacifists kept insisting that America stay out of the European conflict, Wilson's critics saw the *Lusitania* as the definitive confirmation of why the United States must get involved. Theodore Roosevelt lamented that "President Wilson has lacked the courage and the vision to lead this nation in the path of high duty. . . . The cause of preparedness [for war] is inseparably connected with the cause of Americanism, of patriotism, of whole-hearted loyalty to this nation." Even Walter Lippmann, who did not want to see the United States enter the war as a full participant, admitted that as the sinking of the *Lusitania* had "united Englishmen and Americans in a common grief and a common indignation," it might also "unite them in a common war and conceivably a common destiny."

The United States and the War

Protestants were all over the map regarding the United States' role in the war. The pacifist William Jennings Bryan, Wilson's secretary of state, resigned his position rather than continue on a path to war. Conversely, evangelist Billy Sunday competed with Theodore Roosevelt's stridency about getting into the war. Sunday even seemed to make support for the war a condition of one's standing as a Christian. "Christianity and Patriotism are synonymous terms," he said, "and hell and traitors are synonymous." Conservative pastors and theologians associated with the early Christian fundamentalist movement tended to be skeptical of politics and were cautious about supporting entry into World War I. This drew the ire of more liberal theologians who thought the fundamentalists' belief in Jesus's imminent return was a dangerous distraction from the pressing need to support the Allies. Once the United States entered the war, however, fundamentalists became much more supportive, seeing Germany in particular as a great threat to both traditional Christian beliefs (because it was the home of "higher criticism" of the Bible) and to Christian civilization.

After Wilson's reelection victory, he addressed Congress early in 1917 and argued that the only sustainable peace in the war would be a "peace without victory." He warned that victory imposed by military force would leave a crippling legacy of bitterness and make the resumption of war more likely. "Only a peace between equals can last," Wilson insisted. (The hostile European powers were, of course, not interested in such a negotiated outcome.) He proposed the formation of a League of Nations, which would seek to avert war in the future.

Still the direction of the war steered America closer to the brink of intervention. Germany had been inconsistent in its promises to respect the neutrality of American shipping in European waters, but it announced that as of February 1, 1917, its U-boats would attack any and all ships encountered in the seas around Britain or France. The Germans believed this was the only way to strangle the Allied Powers and bring an end to the war. In March, the Germans followed through on their warnings, as U-boats attacked and sank four American ships.

The final provocation came in February when British intelligence agents intercepted a telegram from German foreign secretary Arthur Zimmerman, telling the German ambassador in Mexico that if the United States entered the war against Germany, Germany should seek an anti-US alliance with Mexico. Zimmerman floated the possibility that Germany could help Mexico reclaim territories it had once lost to the United States, including Arizona, New Mexico, and Texas. When pacifists in Congress resisted Wilson's appeals to equip American merchant ships with guns, Wilson released the Zimmerman telegram to the media.

America Enters the War

The combined effects of U-boat aggression and the Zimmerman telegram made US entry into World War I inevitable. Wilson asked Congress for a declaration of war. He regretted that the nation must "accept the status of belligerent which has been . . . thrust upon it." The United States had been called to fight because the "world must be made safe for democracy," Wilson asserted. Congress responded overwhelmingly with the Senate approving war by an 82 to 6 vote.

The optimism many felt about the war was reflected in the conflict's most popular tune in America, "Over There," written by New York composer George Cohan.[*]

> Over there, over there,
> Send the word, send the word, over there
> That the Yanks are coming, the Yanks are coming,
> The drums rum-tumming everywhere.
> So prepare, say a prayer
> Send the word, send the word to beware,
> We'll be over, we're coming over,
> And we won't be back till it's over over there.

Cohan gave the song to a popular vaudeville singer, and soon it was widely available as sheet music and on disc records, which had been introduced for use with the phonograph in the early 1900s.

---

[*] Copyright Canada 1917 by Whaley, Royce and Co. for William Jerome Pub. Corp.

In spite of such cheery views of the United States' role in the European war, the nation was hardly ready to mobilize. The US armed forces remained fairly small as of early 1917, with a combined army and national guard membership of 208,000 when the United States entered the war in April. But Wilson planned on sending millions of Americans to Europe as soldiers. The buildup's strain on the nation would be massive, and it made supporters of the war angry toward anyone perceived as reluctant or hostile to the war effort. Conservative Protestants found themselves countering charges that the "premillennial" theology many of them embraced made them passive about the war. (Premillennial theology took a dim view of the direction of world history before Christ's return to earth.) Liberal church historian Shirley Jackson Case of the University of Chicago Divinity School warned of the "Premillennial Menace," observing that as the nation was "engaged in a gigantic effort to make the world safe for democracy, it would be almost traitorous negligence to ignore the detrimental character of premillennial propaganda."

Many immigrants, especially German-language speakers, fell under much harsher scrutiny, as pro-war Americans worried about disloyal elements in their midst. German pacifist Christians may have suffered the most harassment because of their ethnicity and their religious views. Hundreds of conscientious objectors were brought up on court-martial charges during the war for refusing to cooperate with military conscription. Many ended up in jails, from the one at Alcatraz Island in San Francisco Bay to Fort Leavenworth in Kansas. Four young Hutterite men (members of a German Anabaptist sect) from South Dakota arrived at Alcatraz in mid-1918, having refused to participate in training exercises to which they were forcibly sent in Washington State. Hutterites in South Dakota had already seen some of their livestock seized and sold to pay for war bonds, which they refused to buy. When the four Hutterite dissenters had been drafted and sent to Washington, other soldiers had set upon them on board the train and cut off their hair and beards (a distinctive marker of their faith). When they would not even fill out information cards at the military camp, the Hutterites were court-martialed, convicted, and sentenced to captivity in the dungeons of Alcatraz. Two of the men, brothers Joseph and Michael Hofer, died in detention after they were transferred to a prison at Fort Leavenworth. Most of the remaining Hutterites of South Dakota immigrated to Canada to escape further persecution.

Congress supported both the war effort and the suppression of dissent via measures including the Selective Draft Act (1917), the Espionage Act (1917), and the Sedition Act (1918). Under the draft tens of millions of fighting-age men had to register for possible military service, and nearly 3 million of them were actually drafted and conscripted into such service. The Espionage Act gave the postmaster general, Albert Burleson, the power to enforce the measure by preventing the mail from carrying literature deemed to be in violation of the act. Burleson took an expansive view of what counted as "espionage," so he went after publications of socialist groups, labor unions, foreign-language newspapers, and any others who might "impugn the motives of the government and thus encourage insubordination." Critics of the war were appalled. Muckraking writer Upton Sinclair regarded it as a travesty that Burleson was given the power "to decide what may or may not be uttered by our radical press."

The Sedition Act went further, broadening the Espionage Act's definition of seditious speech to include "any disloyal, profane, scurrilous, or abusive language about the form of government of the United States," its Constitution, its flag, or its military, or language that might bring "contempt, scorn, contumely, or disrepute" to any of those national institutions. Even the Sedition Act fell short of some aggressive anti-dissent proposals, such as one that considered handing matters of espionage and sedition over to domestic military enforcement rather than keeping it in the hands of the Justice Department. The Wilson administration also encouraged private citizens to join in the surveillance of dissenters. Hundreds of thousands of Americans joined the American Protective League, which investigated and reported on neighbors and coworkers that the Protective League members suspected of disloyalty.

Figure 20.2. "Draft World War. Drafted Men; Camp Meade."

Obviously the Espionage and Sedition Acts raised constitutional problems, especially about the right to free speech during time of war. (The treatment of pacifist Christians also raised questions of religious liberty.) Several cases along these lines came before the Supreme Court after the war was over. In each instance the high court upheld convictions under the Espionage Act. In *Schenk v. United States* (1919), Justice Oliver Wendell Holmes Jr. wrote for a unanimous court and argued that speech that might be acceptable in peacetime might not be acceptable during a war, especially if that speech directly hindered the war effort. Thus, the First Amendment's protection of free speech did not represent an unlimited right. Schenk was a socialist who had mailed flyers urging people to resist the draft. Holmes established a legal standard that if the speech in question created a "clear and present danger" of lawbreaking, it was not protected by the First Amendment.

Likewise, in *Debs v. United States* (1919), the court upheld the conviction of Socialist Party leader Eugene Debs for seditious speech. Although Debs had not directly advocated illegal behavior, he still praised the courage of those Americans who would not comply with the draft. Debs was sentenced to ten years in a federal penitentiary for his crimes, although President Warren G. Harding commuted his sentence to time served in 1921. Debs still received almost a million votes as the Socialist candidate for president in 1920. Congress repealed the Sedition Act after the war was over, but it left the Espionage Act on the books.

The War in Europe

The war between the Allied and Central Powers was grinding and gruesome. Entrenchment spread across the heart of the European continent, with enemy soldiers often separated by just hundreds of yards. Attacks across "no man's land" in between the trench lines were suicide missions. Weapons such as poison gas and the new machine gun kept the armies in place indefinitely. The lack of movement and the horrid conditions in the trenches took a terrible toll on the soldiers. When the armies did launch offensives, the costs were heavy. The 1916 German campaign at Verdun, France, took the lives of 600,000 soldiers.

As American Navy destroyers curtailed the attacks of the U-boats, American troops led by General John Pershing began arriving in France in June 1917. As the number of American soldiers was reaching 300,000, in March 1918 the Germans tried to break the stalemate in western Europe. In a vast offensive the Germans broke through British and French lines and pushed toward Paris. The fresh American troops were essential to halting the German advance. As the other Allied powers before them had, the US

NO·MANS LAND
ONCE A FOREST "IN FLANDERS FIELDS" X217

Figure 20.3. No Man's Land in World War I, ca. 1919, by F. J. Lamphere.

forces took terrible losses. After experiencing his first battle, African American soldier John F. Dixon of New York wrote home to his family and tried to encourage them by saying, "We are real soldiers now and not afraid of Germans. . . . War is more than a notion. Our boys went on the battlefield last night singing, you can't beat them, they are surely game and a happy bunch. . . . We'll get that [German] Kaiser yet."

Among the most critical contributions of the American forces came in June 1918, at the battles of Château-Thierry and Belleau Wood. At Château-Thierry, American soldiers and Marines helped the French defend bridges over the Marne River, successfully stalling the German advance on Paris. Near Château-Thierry, Marines also fought for several weeks to expel the Germans from Belleau Wood. Marines dug trenches with their bayonets and fought in vicious combat with the Germans, often grappling in hand-to-hand fights to the death. It required a terrible price for the Marines' commanders to learn the foolishness of sending assaults against machine gun nests. The American forces took some 9,777 casualties at Belleau Wood, but much heavier losses were ahead.

By mid-July 1918, momentum had begun to turn against the Germans. Pershing's army scored another major victory against them at St. Mihiel in September, setting the stage for the decisive battles of the Meuse-Argonne, which began in late September.

Pershing brought more than a million men against the heavily fortified German defenses in the Argonne forest in eastern France. Again the Americans confronted lines of barbed wire and concrete huts with German gunners. Among the most heroic acts of the battle were those performed by Corporal Alvin York of Tennessee. York was a devout Christian, having experienced conversion through a Church of Christ in 1914. He considered declaring himself a conscientious objector, recalling, "I didn't want to go and kill. I believed in my bible. . . . And yet Uncle Sam wanted me." When York went to training camp, an officer convinced him that the Bible sanctioned a Christian's participation in a just war.

At Meuse-Argonne, York and his fellow soldiers were tasked with flanking a German machine gun position. York's best friend was killed in the assault, but York, an expert sharpshooter, picked the Germans off one after another with his rifle and pistol, he said, the "way we shoot wild turkeys at home." York convinced the Germans to surrender with the assistance of a captured German officer and brought back 132 prisoners of war. But York still struggled with the morality of the killings, not entirely sure God approved of his actions.

The massive American phalanx moved slowly forward through the German defenses at Meuse-Argonne, and after two weeks of fighting, more than 26,000 Americans had died. The Meuse-Argonne battles lasted longer than some of America's more famous battles, and they were the deadliest in American history in terms of total men who perished. By the second week of November, however, it had become clear to the Germans that there was no point in fighting on. They accepted the Allies' peace terms and signed the armistice ending the fighting. In six months of fighting, the United States had lost almost 49,000 dead, with 230,000 injured. Another 63,000 Americans died of disease during the war. These losses paled compared to those endured by the British, the French, or the Germans, but it still made World War I the third-deadliest war in American history, behind the Civil War and World War II, both of which lasted far longer than the America's fighting role in the First World War. It was a lesson in just how devastating a modern mechanized war could become.

The Great Migration

It would be hard to overstate the level of change World War I brought to the American home front. The great flood of immigration from Europe stopped abruptly because of the threat of the U-boats. Millions of American men went into the armed forces just as factory production was ratcheting up for the war effort. For the men not drafted, and many women who had previously been out of the industrial workforce, new job opportunities became abundant, especially in the cities of the Midwest and Northeast. This resulted in the beginning of the "Great Migration" of black farmers and share-croppers out of the South to the North. African American men were subject to the draft, and almost 400,000 of them enlisted in the armed forces. But even more African Americans moved north from 1916 to 1918. It was the largest geographic shift for African Americans since the Civil War, and for the first time it gave northern cities a sizable black population.

African Americans were often drawn by higher income, even though they often took the lowest-paying entry jobs in the factories, such as janitors. Continuing racial tension and violence in the South also pushed blacks to leave. There were some 3,000 lynchings in America between 1889 and 1918, most of them in the South. The year 1916 had seen the horrific murder, dismemberment, and burning of a teenager named Jesse Washington in a public square in Waco, Texas. Washington had been accused of killing a white woman and was hastily convicted by an all-white jury. A photographer captured the scene of a crowd of whites milling around Washington's smoldering corpse.

Even the presence of black enlisted men in the South sparked racial tensions. In 1917, African American soldiers stationed at Camp Logan near Houston grew weary of the daily indignities they and African American civilians endured under Jim Crow segregation rules. A violent confrontation between black soldiers and Houston police erupted into a spasm of racial violence by hundreds of black soldiers against whites. They had vowed to take revenge on white police officers, but some of the soldiers ran-domly shot white civilians too. By the time the riot had ended, sixteen whites and four black soldiers were dead. Unfortunately, the violence, committed entirely by the rogue soldiers, led to a crackdown on Houston's black community in general. Thousands of African Americans left Houston after the incident, even though the city had banned northern employers from openly recruiting them, fearing a labor shortage in Houston.

Black activists implored poor African Americans to seek safety and opportunity in the North. But the urban centers of the Northeast and Midwest were often not wel-coming to blacks either. In East St. Louis, Illinois, metalworking factories had begun to recruit African Americans to counteract the power of labor unions, which were run and dominated by white workers. Whites' anger at the black workers spilled over in July 1917, when mobs attacked the African American section of East St. Louis, leaving forty-seven people dead and thousands of blacks without homes. Cities from Omaha, Nebraska, to Washington, DC, saw additional racial violence.

Still many blacks felt as if World War I was a time of unfolding possibilities for what they called the "New Negroes." Freed not only from the shackles of slavery but from burdens of the post–Civil War South, many migrating African Americans felt a new sense of independence, led by the veterans who had served in World War I. If blacks had fought for freedom in the war, then surely they could do so on the home front too. W. E. B. Du Bois wrote in 1919, "By the God of Heaven, we are cowards and jackasses if now that that war is over, we do not marshal every ounce of our brain and brawn to fight a sterner, longer, more unbending battle against the forces of hell in our own land. We *return*. We *return from fighting*. We *return fighting*. Make way for Democracy! We saved it in France, and by the Great Jehovah, we will save it in the United States of America."

The popular song "Lift Ev'ry Voice and Sing," composed in 1900, spoke to the sense of growing black independence. Its first verse said:

> Lift every voice and sing
> Till earth and heaven ring,
> Ring with the harmonies of Liberty;
> Let our rejoicing rise,
> High as the list'ning skies,
> Let it resound loud as the rolling sea.
> Sing a song full of the faith that the dark past has taught us,
> Sing a song full of the hope that the present has brought us,
> Facing the rising sun of our new day begun,
> Let us march on till victory is won.

In 1919, the NAACP adopted this song as the "Negro National Anthem."

Wartime Reform

African Americans were not alone in seeing the potential for political and moral reform in the Great War. Momentum had been building before the war for a constitutional amendment guaranteeing women the right to vote. Women contributed to the war effort in innumerable ways: they replaced men in industrial and office jobs; they worked in charitable and Christian organizations such as the Red Cross, the YMCA/YWCA, and the Salvation Army to provide care and supplies to soldiers; and they served in the tens of thousands as military nurses. President Wilson came to endorse the voting rights amendment for women in 1918 partly because of the invaluable wartime service women had provided. The Nineteenth Amendment became part of the Constitution in 1920. Jane Addams calculated that votes for women came so soon after the war that "it must be accounted as the direct result of war psychology."

The long-standing American campaign against alcohol also reached its apex during World War I. Led by organizations such as the Anti-Saloon League and Frances

Willard's Women's Christian Temperance Union, many argued that alcohol had a uniquely destructive influence in American society and should be banned. The crusade for prohibition took on added urgency during the war. Temperance advocates painted Germans and German Americans as beer guzzling and disloyal. Alcoholic beverages seemed a terrible extravagance at best, given Americans' need to conserve for the war effort. The military also sought to keep soldiers away from alcohol's stupefying effects.

The rate of alcohol consumption remained quite high in America on the eve of Prohibition. The rate increased rapidly from Reconstruction to World War I, when adults drank an average of more than thirty gallons of beer, wine, and hard liquor a year (mostly beer). An Alabama congressman spoke for many when he declared in 1914 that alcohol

> undermines and blights the home and the family, checks education, attacks the young when they are entitled to protection, undermines the public health, slaughtering, killing, and wounding our citizens many fold times more than war, pestilence, and famine combined; that it blights the progeny of the Nation, flooding the land with a horde of degenerates; that it strikes deadly blows at the life of the Nation itself and at the very life of the race, reversing the great evolutionary principles of nature and the purposes of the Almighty. There can be but one verdict, and that is this great destroyer must be destroyed.

White Protestant Christians heavily backed the prohibition cause, but African American Christians were more mixed in their response. The fact that groups such as a resurgent Ku Klux Klan supported prohibition made many blacks wary of a racial agenda behind the anti-alcohol movement. Catholics and Jews in America generally did not support prohibition either. In the end the Eighteenth Amendment was ratified in 1919. It banned the manufacture, sale, and transportation of alcoholic beverages in America. Historians generally agree that Prohibition was a failure because it created an enormous black market for alcohol and was a boon to organized crime and "bootleggers," who illegally trafficked in alcohol. Nevertheless, Prohibition did lead to an apparent decline in overall alcohol consumption, which would not rise to pre-Prohibition levels for many decades even after the Eighteenth Amendment was repealed in 1933.

The Fourteen Points

In 1917, President Wilson became troubled by reports coming from Europe, made public by communist revolutionaries in Russia, that the Allied Powers planned to divvy up Germany's and Turkey's colonies once the war was over. The idealistic Wilson did not want the war to result in mere switching of colonial powers and retribution against the losing side. With the help of journalist Walter Lippmann, Wilson drew up a fourteen-point plan for a just peace settlement, which he presented to Congress in January 1918. "The day of conquest and aggrandizement is gone by," Wilson declared. "What we demand in this war, therefore, is nothing peculiar to ourselves. It is that the world be made fit and safe to live in; and particularly that it be made safe for every peace-loving nation which, like our own, wishes to live its own life, determine its own institutions, be assured of justice and fair dealing by the other peoples of the world as against force and selfish aggression."

The Fourteen Points focused especially on national self-determination (as opposed to control by empires), free navigation of the oceans, transparent diplomacy, and the formation of a "general association of nations," which would help guarantee "political independence and territorial integrity to great and small states alike." In a break from the tradition of previous wars, Wilson professed no desire to destroy Germany, nor even a desire to lessen Germany's "legitimate influence or power." The Allies should simply expect Germany to live in peace and equity with other nations, Wilson declared.

Not only did Wilson wish to avoid a peace based on crushing Germany and its allies, but he also needed to counteract the new communist threat emerging from Russia. In late 1917, Bolshevik revolutionaries led by Vladimir Lenin had overthrown the Russian government. The Bolsheviks sought the destruction of the capitalist system and called for workers everywhere to rise up against business and political authorities. "We summon you to this struggle, workers of all countries! There is no other way. The crimes of the ruling, exploiting classes in this war have been countless. These crimes cry out for revolutionary revenge." Inspired by the philosophy of German philosopher Karl Marx, they prohibited private property and set up a radical workers' democracy. Lenin believed Russia needed to seek peace with Germany at virtually any cost to secure the communist revolution within Russia itself. So in March 1918, Russia and Germany signed the Treaty of Brest-Litovsk, under which Russia surrendered its claims to territories including Poland, Ukraine, and Finland, which accounted for a quarter of the Russian empire's population. Worried about communism and about German influence in Russia, Wilson sent thousands of American troops into Russia to aid anti-Bolshevik fighters there. In doing so, Wilson himself seemed to contradict one of his Fourteen Points, the right to national self-determination in Russia.

Wilson staked his reputation on the peace conference in Paris in early 1919. He personally attended the talks at the palace of Versailles, to much fanfare. The Fourteen Points would not fare well in Paris, as a scramble for colonies and the desire to punish Germany animated the leaders of Britain, France, and other nations. The Allied Powers understandably blamed Germany for the awful suffering of the war. They forced the Germans to sign a devastating (and unrealistic) program of reparations, which would amount to $33 billion. Most of Wilson's Fourteen Points were either ignored or compromised at Versailles. But Wilson insisted on the creation of the League of Nations, which would feature a nine-nation council including Britain, France, Italy, Japan, and the United States. Members would promise to consult with one another when war loomed and would commit to protect one another's sovereignty.

Wilson saw the League of Nations as a modern, internationalist means to prevent more war. But his Republican opponents at home disagreed. They thought the League of Nations would make war more likely, as it bound the United States to get involved in the conflicts and concerns of foreign nations. Many Americans were weary of war and feared that the League of Nations would compromise America's independence on the world stage. Opponents such as Republican senator Henry Cabot Lodge of Massachusetts saw in the League of Nations a zeal for "internationalism" that smacked of Bolshevism. "We must not lose by an improvident attempt to reach eternal peace all that we have won by war and sacrifice," Lodge told the Senate in February 1919. "We must build no bridges across the chasm which now separates American freedom and order from Russian anarchy and destruction. . . . America and the American people are first in my heart now and always."

Before the Treaty of Versailles was finished, Lodge and almost forty senators had already pledged to oppose it if the treaty included US membership in the League of Nations. Because the Senate must ratify treaties by a two-thirds majority, this was a serious threat to the League. Wilson secured adjustments to the League in order to emphasize members' independence. In June 1919, delegates signed the Treaty of Versailles, and Wilson came back to America to campaign for the treaty's ratification. Wilson appealed directly to the American people, declaring that the United States had a moral obligation to support the League. "We have come to redeem the world by giving it liberty and justice. Now we are called up before the tribunal of mankind to redeem that immortal pledge." Conflating the Christian language of salvation with America's place on the global stage, Wilson thundered, "At last the world knows America as savior of the world."

After a speech in Pueblo, Colorado, the exhausted Wilson became ill and returned to Washington. On October 2, 1919, Wilson suffered a stroke that caused partial paralysis. His wife, Edith, closely guarded information about the president's health, and some critics speculated that she was really in control of the presidency. As Woodrow Wilson convalesced, he spent all of his limited energy trying to salvage the League. Lodge and some Republicans offered compromise versions of the treaty, but Wilson thought they undermined the original purpose of the League. The Senate voted repeatedly on the treaty and amendments to it but never could muster the two-thirds majority required.

In 1921, Congress adopted a resolution technically ending US involvement in the war since they had rejected the terms of the Treaty of Versailles.

Wilson had lost on the initiative he had hoped would define his presidency. European powers went ahead and created the League of Nations. But the alliance was badly hampered by the absence of the United States and communist Russia, now called the Soviet Union. The League would continue to exist until 1946, when in the aftermath of World War II, it was superseded by the United Nations.

The Red Scare

For decades the socialist and labor movements in America had commanded widespread support. Even communist groups claimed tens of thousands of American members. But with the heightened patriotism of World War I and the calls for workers' revolution coming out of Russia, America became far less hospitable to any movements that critics could associate with Bolshevism. Labor strikes that had once garnered some popular favor with their calls for humane working conditions and decent pay now became associated with the terror of the communist insurgency.

A string of mail and house bombings in the spring and summer of 1919 spawned a wave of fear about the possible work of communist operatives in the United States. One bomb destroyed part of the Washington, DC, home of attorney general Mitchell Palmer and frightened his neighbors, including future presidential couple Franklin and Eleanor Roosevelt. There did not seem to be any conspiracy behind the bombings, but they remained terrifying nevertheless. Attorney General Palmer warned that the wildfire of communism was "eating its way into the homes of the American workman . . . licking the altars of the churches, leaping into the belfry of the school bell, crawling into the sacred corners of American homes, [and] burning up the foundations of society." The Justice Department conducted raids on communist party offices, confiscating Marxist literature and rounding up and deporting thousands of noncitizens suspected of having Bolshevik sympathies.

Perhaps the most controversial case associated with the "Red Scare" was the trial and execution of Italian immigrants Nicola Sacco and Bartolomeo Vanzetti, who were accused of robbery and murder in South Braintree, Massachusetts. Although their role in the crime was unclear, Sacco and Vanzetti were anarchists and atheists who spoke limited English. They seemed to embody the murderous threat posed by European radical philosophy. Sacco and Vanzetti were arrested and tried in 1920, and liberal critics from around the world insisted that they did not receive an adequate defense or a fair hearing. Appeals dragged on until 1927, when the two were executed by electrocution.

There were important philosophical differences between communists, socialists, anarchists, and other left-wing radicals, but to worried observers they all seemed attached to the internationalist Marxist menace.

The 1920 Election and the Rise of Calvin Coolidge

War-weariness and controversy over the League of Nations dominated the 1920 presidential election. Republican nominee Senator Warren Harding of Ohio insisted that the nation needed no more Wilsonian adventures. Americans wanted a return to "normalcy," Harding said. He believed Americans were ready for "not the dramatic but the dispassionate, not experiment but equipoise, not submergence in internationality but sustainment in triumphant nationality." The Democrats were hamstrung by uncertainty over Wilson's health and future. Some imagined that Wilson, who played such a dominant role in Democratic politics, might run for a third term, but those close to him knew his physical condition would not allow it. So the Democrats nominated Ohio governor James Cox to run against Harding. Cox's vice-presidential running mate was Franklin D. Roosevelt of New York. Although Progressives were generally unhappy with the choice presented between Cox and Harding, they could not coalesce around a third-party candidate. In spite of his imprisonment, Socialist Eugene Debs still got more than 900,000 votes in the 1920 election.

An economic recession in 1920 sealed the fate of the Democrats. Harding won a smashing 60 percent of the popular vote and more than 400 electoral votes. Republicans now controlled the House and Senate by large margins. But scandals in the Harding administration would squander much of the Republicans' advantage. Harding was surrounded by old political allies that critics called the "Ohio Gang," who made a series of shady deals, exchanging political favors for cash. Most notoriously, Harding's interior secretary, Albert Fall, was exposed for taking bribes in exchange for granting oil leases on federal land, including at Teapot Dome, Wyoming. The Teapot Dome Scandal landed Fall in jail. Harding was deeply distressed by his unraveling presidency. In 1923, he suffered a fatal heart attack, and the presidency passed to Calvin Coolidge of Massachusetts, Harding's vice president.

Coolidge was able to redeem the presidency for the Republicans, removing some of the key players in Harding's scandals. He easily defeated the Democratic nominee John W. Davis of West Virginia in the 1924 election, in spite of the third-party Progressive candidacy of Robert La Follette of Wisconsin. Coolidge won almost the entire Northeast, Midwest, and West, while the Democrats only managed to win the South. Coolidge was the champion of small, business-friendly government. He was the antithesis of the interventionist bent of Theodore Roosevelt or Wilson, on the domestic and the international front. Boosted by the federal income tax, higher tariffs, and lower government spending, the federal government under Coolidge cut debt and actually took in more revenue than it spent. Older Progressive leaders felt as though they were living in a different America than the one that had preceded World War I and Wilson's presidency. "What has become of this movement that promised so much twenty years ago?" asked reformer Frederic Howe in 1925. "What has become of the prewar radicals?" Disillusionment over the war, a healthy economy under Coolidge, and Progressive gains in areas like women's suffrage had changed the political environment dramatically. The era of internationalism and aggressive reform seemed, for the moment, to be over. Americans entered an era of exuberant prosperity in the 1920s, but the nation's carefree days were not to last.

■ SELECTED BIBLIOGRAPHY ■

Browne, George. *An American Soldier in World War I*. Edited by David L. Snead. Lincoln: University of Nebraska Press, 2006.

Capozzola, Christopher. *Uncle Sam Wants You: World War I and the Making of the Modern American Citizen*. New York: Oxford University Press, 2010.

Dumenil, Lynn. *The Second Line of Defense: American Women and World War I*. Chapel Hill: University of North Carolina Press, 2017.

Goldberg, David J. *Discontented America: The United States in the 1920s*. Baltimore: Johns Hopkins University Press, 1999.

Jenkins, Philip. *The Great and Holy War: How World War I Became a Religious Crusade*. New York: HarperOne, 2014.

Keegan, John. *The First World War*. New York: Knopf, 1999.

Kennedy, David M. *Over Here: The First World War and American Society.* New York: Oxford University Press, 1980.

Murphy, Paul L. *World War I and the Origin of Civil Liberties in the United States*. New York: W. W. Norton, 1979.

Sánchez, George J. *Becoming Mexican American: Ethnicity, Culture, and Identity in Chicano Los Angeles, 1900–1945*. New York: Oxford University Press, 1993.

Smith, Tony. *Why Wilson Matters: The Origin of American Liberal Internationalism and Its Crisis Today*. Princeton, NJ: Princeton University Press, 2017.

Stoltzfus, Duance C. S. *Pacifists in Chains: The Persecution of Hutterites During the Great War*. Baltimore: Johns Hopkins University Press, 2013.

Williams, Chad L. *Torchbearers of Democracy: African American Soldiers in the World War I Era*. Chapel Hill: University of North Carolina Press, 2010.

21

The Roaring Twenties

For Americans in the 1920s, it seemed that good times had come to stay. The horrors of World War I were behind them, as were the interminable squabbles over the League of Nations. Calvin Coolidge's presidency inaugurated six years of unprecedented prosperity, and even the embarrassing scandals of the Harding administration were fading into the past. Of course, the good times of the 1920s could not obscure ongoing tensions related to race and economic classes in America. And no one could have foreseen just how hard America would fall after its decade of excess.

The 1920s were marked by soaring industrial output and household incomes. This meant that more Americans could purchase the new appliances and industrial goods of the era, such as vacuum cleaners, washing machines, and automobiles. More Americans also had disposable income to spend on entertainment, including radios for the home or going to the movies. The 1920s were perhaps the key decade when American culture became consumed with popular entertainment, a trend that still endures today.

One of the greatest stars of the "silent era" of moviemaking was Mary Pickford. Pickford emerged in the 1910s, usually portraying independent-minded and even rebellious women. By the end of World War I, Pickford was making sometimes millions of dollars a year and conspicuously displayed her wealth with fancy cars and clothes. In 1919, she cofounded United Artists with other movie titans, including the actors Charlie Chaplin and Douglas Fairbanks. By then she had become arguably the most powerful woman in the history of the movie business. She would divorce her first husband and marry Fairbanks in 1920. In the past a divorce might have severely damaged a woman's reputation, but for Pickford and other media celebrities, such scandals seemed only to add to the fascination they generated.

Figure 21.1. Mary Pickford, ca. 1916.

Women and Family

Although Mary Pickford's life was highly unusual, her independence and power in business signaled a new openness in American society to public roles for women. Her divorce also signaled new instability in traditional family structures. World War I made it more common than ever for women to seek employment outside the home or farm. Still, women most commonly worked in clerical positions, domestic service, teaching, and nursing, while professions such as doctors, lawyers, or professors were still largely the domain of men. Liberal reforms made divorces easier to obtain, and the frequency of divorce doubled between 1900 and 1928.

Young people in the cities became increasingly drawn to fashions set by the new celebrities. Young urban women sometimes tried to emulate the style of Mary Pickford, but by the 1920s the image of the "flapper" was all the rage. The term *flapper* was once derogatory, referring to an immoral young woman. But in the 1920s, it came to refer to a woman who followed the popular styles of the time, most notably short, "bobbed" hair that looked similar to the traditional hairstyles of men. Movies and Broadway shows featured flapper characters, and songwriter and composer Hoagy Carmichael said the "postwar world came in with a bang of bad booze, flappers with bare legs, jangled morals and wild weekends." Critics believed the glorification of the flapper image encouraged reckless behavior and promiscuity.

Poorer women, including African Americans and immigrants from Europe, Asia, or Mexico, usually did not have the kind of resources or leisure time to embrace the flapper lifestyle. Black women who came north during the Great Migration found some work in industries but usually in less desirable, entry-level positions. As one New York publication noted, they typically were "doing work which white women will not do." Many other African American women found work as domestic servants, maids, and cooks. Mexican migrant women in the Southwest were commonly employed in farm

Figure 21.2. *Where There's Smoke There's Fire*. Full-length illustration of a fashionably dressed flapper. 1920s.

businesses, often working in the fields alongside other family members. Some Hispanic women did find office work in cities. Sometimes businesses found it advantageous to have bilingual employees on staff in cities such as Los Angeles. Japanese women typically found employment in agriculture or as household servants too.

Of course, large numbers of women of every class and ethnicity worked in their own homes, taking care of their children and other domestic responsibilities and did not draw pay from an employer. Popular movies and plays often highlighted the risks of unchecked youthful independence among women. These movies featured women who paid a heavy price for their wild living or were redeemed from it by getting married. Christian activists such as the National Baptist Convention's Nannie Helen Burroughs warned about the dangers of flapper culture. A brochure for her National Training School for Women and Girls declared, "There are no flappers in Nannie Burroughs's school."

Even some women's rights activists thought the radical style of flapper culture was potentially harmful to women. If the freewheeling sociability of the 1920s led to increased use of contraception (and even abortion), some worried, it would turn sex into a recreational pursuit and damage the stability of the family. Feminist writer

Charlotte Perkins Gilman believed unfettered use of contraception was a "free ticket for selfish and fruitless indulgence, and an aid in the lamentable behavior of our times." She later came to accept birth control as useful in the cause of eugenics, or controlling the population of less-desirable peoples.

Advertising

Whatever their social or economic status, American women in the 1920s were buffeted with advertisements and media images promoting the importance of female physical attractiveness. Beauty became big business. The number of "beauty shops" skyrocketed in America between 1920 and 1930, from about 5,000 to 40,000. The flapper image typically came with makeup, and cosmetics became vastly more common and lucrative. Cosmetic sales went from about $17 million in 1914 to $141 million just eleven years later. An advertisement for a corset company echoed many manufacturers of goods designed for women when it said that within a "woman's soul burns still the flame of her desire for charm and beauty." Although the emphasis on women's physical attractiveness had much deeper cultural roots, companies had never so aggressively marketed products associated with style and beauty to American women. Men similarly had clothes and other fashions marketed to them that would ostensibly make them attractive to women.

Stylish clothes and cosmetics were hardly the only products hawked by advertisers. Although advertising also had deeper precedents, the mass media of radio and magazines made advertisements more alluring and effective than ever before. In 1914, American businesses spent about $680 million on advertising; by 1929, advertising expenditures had shot up to almost $3 billion. Countless ads promised that if buyers consumed their products, they would be healthier, more stylish, and well-adjusted. Products such as mouthwash, deodorant, and perfume, little known in the nineteenth century, became common by the 1920s. Advertisements promised these products would make consumers more socially desirable and save them from social humiliation due to bad breath or body odor. As one advertisement for Cosmo Buttermilk Soap put it, "Pretty women appreciate a pure toilet soap, a healthy, soft, and white skin. All women and men desire beautiful faces and pretty hands—suggestion: use a good, pure toilet soap."

Some sought to sanctify the new culture of consumption and advertising by tying it to Christianity or to Jesus himself. The most notable instance of this effort was Bruce Barton's wildly popular book *The Man Nobody Knows* (1925). Barton, an advertising executive and the son of a Baptist minister, said the church's popular image of a "sissified," suffering Jesus was nothing like what he saw in the Gospels. Jesus, the "most popular dinner guest in Jerusalem. . . . picked up twelve humble men and created an organization that won the world," Barton wrote. "Jesus would be a national advertiser today . . . as he was the great advertiser of his own day." The parables of Jesus were perfect examples of effective advertising, Barton insisted.

Sports

As in the movies, the sports industry focused on small numbers of celebrities and their rivals who seemed to define an entire sport. Baseball produced perhaps the greatest sports celebrity of the age, George Herman "Babe" Ruth. Ruth had a preternatural talent for baseball, and especially

Figure 21.3. "The Best article in the world, Laird's bloom of youth, or liquid pearl for preserving & beautifying the complexion & skin." Ca. 1863.

for hitting home runs. After the Boston Red Sox sold Ruth's services to the New York Yankees, Ruth helped turn the Yankees into a dynasty. Ruth seemed to embody the commercial excesses of the 1920s, as his talent allowed him to pursue hard drinking, eating, and night life with little effect on his on-field performance. Ruth was the first sports celebrity to employ a press agent, who helped the "Sultan of Swat" make more money through off-season touring and product endorsements than Ruth did from baseball itself.

In college football national power shifted away from the Ivy League schools, who had dominated the sport in the late 1800s, to new powers such as midwestern universities Michigan, Ohio State, and Notre Dame. Colleges erected cavernous stadiums to accommodate the crowds that attended big games. In 1927, Michigan played Ohio State at Michigan's new stadium before a reported crowd of more than 84,000 people. Notre Dame football became the pride of countless American Catholics. Notre Dame's famous player and coach Knute Rockne turned Notre Dame into a major national contender in the 1920s, capped by its undefeated 1924 season and Rose Bowl victory in

Pasadena, California. In the 1940 film *Knute Rockne, All American*, future American president Ronald Reagan portrayed the dying Notre Dame player George Gipp, a role that accounted for Reagan's nickname "the Gipper."

Probably the greatest celebrity in football in the 1920s was Harold "Red" Grange, a running back for the University of Illinois and the professional Chicago Bears team. Sports celebrities typically garnered nicknames, and a sportswriter dubbed Grange the "Galloping Ghost." A three-time All-American at Illinois, Grange became the first sports figure to grace the cover of *Time* magazine in 1925. The same year, he signed with the Bears for a contract promising $100,000 a year in salary. Grange's presence helped invigorate the National Football League, which had begun competition in 1920. Grange also used his fame in sports to appear in films about his career.

Boxing remained enormously popular, and of all sports boxing may have been the most dominated by promoters. Jack Dempsey was the most celebrated fighter of the era, but his promoter, "Tex" Rickard, was key to Dempsey's lucrative career. Dempsey,

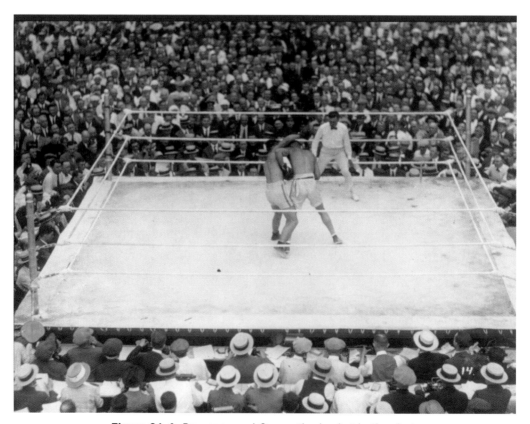

Figure 21.4. Dempsey and Carpentier boxing in the ring.

known as the "Manassa Mauler" in homage to his small Colorado hometown, reigned as heavyweight champion from 1919 to 1927. Like Babe Ruth, Dempsey's personal life was as much of interest to the sports media as his boxing career. Dempsey's first wife had once worked as a prostitute, and she accused him of dodging the draft for World War I after they divorced. The issue of wartime service hung over the 1921 "Fight of the Century" when Dempsey brawled with French champion and war veteran Georges Carpentier before 80,000 spectators in Jersey City, New Jersey. Ticket sales for the fight netted $1.7 million, and Dempsey knocked Carpentier out in the fourth round.

Figure 21.5. "'Strangler' Lewis defeats Cossack giant. Ed 'Strangler' Lewis is seen applying the deadly headlock to Ivan Linow at the International Championship Wrestling Tournament."

Like Ruth and Grange, Dempsey enhanced his popularity and income by commercial endorsements, exhibition tours, and movie appearances. His boxing career ended when he lost two fights to his great rival, the "Fighting Marine" Gene Tunney, in 1926 and 1927.

Professional wrestling's blend of sport and theater made it enduringly popular, and in the 1920s it produced stars that competed with the likes of Dempsey and Ruth for national prominence. Wrestling had transitioned from the non-choreographed marathon grappling sessions of the nineteenth century into scripted, time-limited matches featuring acrobatic moves and dreaded submission holds. The matches often pitted crowd favorites against a "heel," who earned a crowd's ire through rude talk and dirty tactics. Ed "Strangler" Lewis was the dominant wrestler of the 1920s, a 220-pound hulk whose signature move was the devastating headlock. Like Dempsey, Lewis's success depended a great deal on the work of a business team, including a manager and a promoter. Lewis's key rival was Jim Londos, the "Man with the Million-Dollar Body." Londos's attractiveness supposedly accounted for the new popularity of wrestling among women, according to some observers. Ladies had lifted "wrestling from a dubious barroom-brawl status to a position where it threatens soon to take its place with boxing in the million-dollar gate class," one newspaper writer said. In 1934, Lewis and

Londos clashed for the world wrestling title before an audience of more than 35,000 at Chicago's Wrigley Field.

The Jazz Age

The 1920s are often called the "Jazz Age," a name derived from a book of short stories published by the writer F. Scott Fitzgerald. The 1920s brimmed with new forms of popular music and dance, including jazz. Jazz was first created by African American musicians in cities such as New Orleans and New York. Music promoters could easily distribute songs by new means, including sheet music, phonograph records, radio programs, movies, and Broadway musicals. African American pianist James P. Johnson introduced the song and accompanying dance "The Charleston" in a 1923 Broadway show, and by the late 1920s the dance had become wildly popular across the nation.

Figure 21.6. "Frank Farnum coaching Pauline Starke. And now the Charleston is moving into the movies! Pauline Starke will introduce it to the movie public at large when in the role of a chorus girl in Metro-Goldwyn-Mayer's 'A Little bit of Broadway,' she performs it on the screen. Frank Farnum, originator of the step, gave her first-hand (or foot) instructions." 1925.

Probably the most popular male singer of the 1920s was Al Jolson, who was born in the 1880s to a Jewish family in Lithuania. Jolson's family moved to the United States in the 1890s, and Jolson became a popular vaudeville star, often performing in blackface as stereotyped African American characters. Jolson recorded a number of hit songs before starring in the movie *The Jazz Singer* (1927). This Warner Brothers film was the first major "talkie," or film that synchronized the sounds of actors' words with the motions of their mouths. Sophie Tucker was arguably the most popular female singer of the 1920s. She had a similar biographical background to Jolson's, as she was born to a Jewish family in Poland who had fled Russia for the United States in the late 1880s. Tucker, who made her way on the vaudeville circuit and sometimes performed in blackface, was known for brash, racy songs, including her signature hit "Some of These Days" (1926). She also introduced ethnic distinctives into her performances with songs such as "My Yiddish Momme" (1925).[*]

"Jazz" is a broad musical category, and music historians debate how much the popular music of the best-known white performers was really jazz at all. Among the undisputed pioneers of 1920s jazz, however, were African American performers on the New Orleans circuit, including the trumpet (cornet) virtuoso Louis Armstrong. Some have viewed Ferdinand Joseph La Menthe, better known as Jelly Roll Morton, as the key inventor of jazz music. Morton was born in the 1880s into a Creole (mixed African and French heritage) family in New Orleans. Morton got his start playing in the bars and brothels of "Storyville," the red-light district of New Orleans. As a pianist Morton drew on influences from the blues, ragtime, and a Hispanic style he called the "Spanish tinge." One of Morton's signature songs was "The Jelly Roll Blues," published as sheet music in 1915 and recorded with his band, the Red Hot Peppers, in 1926. Morton and other major African American artists such as W. C. Handy (the "father of the blues") eventually relocated to New York City, drawn in part by the vibrant music and literature scene of the "Harlem Renaissance" of the 1920s.

If jazz and the blues drew from African American folk traditions, "hillbilly music" originated in rural white culture in Appalachia and other parts of the South. The most significant distributor of hillbilly music (the forerunner of country music) was *The Grand Ole Opry*, which began broadcasts on station WSM out of Nashville in 1925. The first major country star of the 1920s was Jimmie Rodgers, who parlayed his background as a railroad worker into a fabulously successful singing career. The "Singing Brakeman" appeared in a 1929 film by the same name and recorded hits including "In

---

[*] "1927—The Jazz Singer," YouTube video, 2:39, https://www.youtube.com/watch?v=UYOY8dkhTpU.

the Jailhouse Now" (1928). With his distinctive yodeling style, Rodgers' songs spun tales about the kinds of drifters and gamblers one might meet on the railroads.

The Limits of the Roaring Twenties

The popular images of the 1920s were all about individual expression and breaking traditional restraints. This cultural mood was perhaps best captured by the most celebrated individual achievement of the decade, Charles Lindbergh's pioneering transatlantic flight in his airplane the *Spirit of St. Louis* in 1927. (Not surprisingly, Lindbergh's flight precipitated a host of popular songs, movies, and books about him.) But many American critics saw serious problems lying beneath the carnival of excess during the decade.

Many immigrants, African Americans, and poor people did not share in the economic boom of the 1920s, of course. In their groundbreaking study *Middletown* (1929), sociologists Robert and Helen Lynd analyzed Muncie, Indiana, and concluded that the difference between the "working" and the "business" classes represented the "outstanding cleavage" in Muncie society. "The mere fact of being born upon one or the other side of the watershed roughly formed by these two groups is the most significant single cultural factor tending to influence what one does all day long throughout one's life." (If they had considered a more ethnically diverse town, the Lynds might have also noted the role of race in such divides.) The Lynds surmised that the working classes did not enjoy the same prosperity and opportunities as the business-class families did. The working-class families still lived in the more traditional world of the pre–World War I era.

Some of the greatest writers of the era were a group Gertrude Stein called the "Lost Generation." These writers, including Ernest Hemingway, Sinclair Lewis, and F. Scott Fitzgerald, raised questions about the emptiness of American life and the lingering cultural damage done by World War I. Hemingway's novel *The Sun Also Rises* (1926), which took its title from the book of Ecclesiastes, focused on the personal struggles of British and American expatriates living in continental Europe in the 1920s. The book echoed some of Hemingway's own experiences, as he was wounded during the war while working for the American Red Cross in Italy, and he also lived as a correspondent in Paris during the postwar years.

Sinclair Lewis's 1922 *Babbitt* used the character of the fictional midwestern businessman George Babbitt to eviscerate the era's culture of consumerism and conformity. The "kernel" of Babbitt's vacuous Christianity "was that it was respectable, and beneficial to one's business, to be seen going to services." F. Scott Fitzgerald's novel *The Great Gatsby* (1925) likewise showed that Jay Gatsby's indulgent lifestyle could not ultimately hide the emptiness of his life and that of his wealthy New York friends. The

Lost Generation in America often focused on the themes of loss, disillusionment, and the seeming purposelessness of life. In Britain some key literary figures who came of age during World War I, such as J. R. R. Tolkien, C. S. Lewis, and the American-born T. S. Eliot, offered more explicitly Christian answers to the era's unease. If the modern world was vacuous, they argued, then the depths of the Christian tradition in the West could fill the emptiness.

A group of white southern authors, most of them associated with Vanderbilt University in Nashville, also sought to counter the rising culture of industrialism in their collected volume *I'll Take My Stand: The South and the Agrarian Tradition* (1930). Although some dismissed this book as a nostalgic defense of the Confederate "Lost Cause," it raised serious questions about the corrosive effects of consumerism and industrial society, trends that had already swept the urban North. Contributor John Crowe Ransom explained that all the authors "tend to support a Southern way of life against what may be called the American or prevailing way; and all as much as agree that the best terms in which to represent the distinction are contained in the phrase, Agrarian versus Industrial." Because the South had been relatively exempt from the rampant spread of industrialization, it offered the best hope for an alternative, more traditional way of life in America. The Southern Agrarians believed the South could still preserve Thomas Jefferson's vision of humble farmers as the best guardians of liberty. One of the contributors to *I'll Take My Stand*, Robert Penn Warren, went on to win the Pulitzer Prize in 1947 for *All the King's Men*, a fictional account of a populist politician based on the actual career of Louisiana governor Huey P. Long.

Fundamentalism and the Scopes Trial

The most enduring reaction to the cultural changes of the 1920s came from traditional Christians. As we have seen, some, including Baptist leader Nannie Helen Burroughs, saw flapper culture as frivolous and indulgent at best. Many American Catholics shared Protestants' concerns about the apparent rise in promiscuous behavior in the era and vigorously opposed the liberalization of the use of birth control. But the most famous Christian opposition to cultural and intellectual trends came from Protestant "fundamentalists." By the end of World War I, many conservative Protestants viewed American culture and churches as beset by a myriad of threats, both foreign and domestic. These included sexual permissiveness, communism, Darwinian evolution, and higher criticism of the Bible.

In 1918, the World's Christian Fundamentals Association was founded to combat these threats inside and outside the church. "Thousands of false teachers, many of them occupying high ecclesiastical positions, are bringing in damnable heresies, even denying the Lord that bought them," Association leaders proclaimed. A leading fundamentalist Presbyterian writer insisted that luxurious consumption and moral laxity had brought America to a point of spiritual crisis. He called for Bible-believing churches to counteract the "German destructive criticism . . . and the conception and propaganda of the Reds [communists]." He proclaimed that "the Bible and the God of the Bible is our only hope" against these menaces. Although conservative Protestants like these were certainly concerned about wider cultural changes, their primary concern was the weakening of biblical doctrine within the churches themselves. More Christians began to describe themselves as defending the "fundamentals" of biblical doctrine, especially in large denominations such as the Northern Baptist Convention and the Presbyterian Church in the United States of America, where those doctrines seemed tenuous.

Theological modernists pushed back against fundamentalist critics. In his 1922 sermon "Shall the Fundamentalists Win?," liberal New York City pastor Harry Emerson Fosdick defended the concept of theological progress and railed against the conservatives' insistence on "fundamental" doctrines:

> They insist that we must all believe in the historicity of certain special miracles, preeminently the virgin birth of our Lord; that we must believe in a special theory of inspiration—that the original documents of the Scripture, which of course we no longer possess, were inerrantly dictated to men a good deal as a man might dictate to a stenographer; [and] that we must believe in a special theory of the Atonement—that the blood of our Lord, shed in a substitutionary death, placates an alienated Deity and makes possible welcome for the returning sinner.

Fosdick said that he did not object to Christians holding such beliefs, but he did object to Christians making them a test for whether someone was truly a Christian.

Conservatives argued that Christianity utterly depended on correct doctrines about God, the Bible, and humankind. Princeton Seminary theologian J. Gresham Machen insisted that advocates of modernism such as Fosdick were not simply Christians with whom he disagreed; they were representatives of a non-Christian religion that masqueraded as Christianity. "The great redemptive religion which has always been known as Christianity is battling against a totally diverse type of religious belief, which is only the more destructive of the Christian faith because it makes use of traditional Christian terminology. This modern non-redemptive religion is called 'modernism' or 'liberalism,'" he wrote. Many Presbyterians rejected Machen's views, leading him eventually to help found a new Presbyterian denomination, the Orthodox Presbyterian Church. Machen also left Princeton Theological Seminary to create Westminster Theological Seminary in Philadelphia in 1929.

The immediate postwar years also saw increasing fundamentalist scrutiny of cultural trends. Some fundamentalist reformers worried as much about keeping American morals pure as they did about keeping the churches' doctrine pure. John Roach Straton, who had responded to Fosdick with a rejoinder titled "Shall the Funnymonkeyists Win?," pastored a Baptist church in New York City. In sermons such as "Will New York Be Destroyed if It Does Not Repent?," Straton deplored the city's theaters, dance halls, and other haunts of vice. In spite of the nation's rampant immorality, Straton also believed God had given American Christians a special role in the war against "irreligion and political radicalism." Undermining the authority of the Bible, Straton and other conservative Protestants argued, would undermine American Christians' ability to play that redemptive role. To the fundamentalists, the conflicts over the Bible were intimately connected to a broader struggle for the fate of Western civilization.

With the legal prohibition of alcohol secured in the Eighteenth Amendment (1919), the fundamentalists' energy focused on two primary causes: winning the major denominations for conservative theology and prohibiting the teaching of evolution in public schools. Northern denominations such as the Northern Baptist Convention and the Presbyterian Church in the United States of America saw the most heated battles because there were numerous advocates of both fundamentalism and modernism within those churches. But "exclusivist" conservatives, meaning those who wished to remove liberal pastors and theologians, could never reach solid majorities in those denominations. The modernists also enjoyed significant support at major divinity schools such as New York's Union Theological Seminary and in influential Christian publications. The Chicago-based *Christian Century* became one of the key advocates of modernist theology, encouraging submissions that detailed the "embarrassment and evils of denominationalism, revivalism, traditional theology, etc." African American denominations tended to side with more traditionalist theology but were not usually eager to identify themselves as "fundamentalists." White-dominated southern denominations, such as the Southern Baptist Convention, endured some struggles over modernist theology, but liberal beliefs gained little traction among rank-and-file Protestant pastors in the South. Lutheran churches, which by 1900 counted more than 1.6 million members, also largely avoided quarrels over modernism because of American Lutherans' prevailing traditionalism at that time.

Since the advent of debates over Darwinian evolution, conservative Protestants were never totally unified about just how damaging evolutionary theory was to traditional

Christian beliefs. From the beginning, many had seen evolution as a fatal compromise of the plain teaching of Scripture about the process of creation and God's means of creating humankind through Adam and Eve. Other Christians believed the churches could fold evolution into traditional theology but Christians must reject secular evolutionists' contention that evolution was not directed by God's providential hand. Until 1920, evolution had been just one among many fundamentalist concerns. That year William Jennings Bryan, the three-time Democratic nominee for president, embraced the anti-evolution cause and took it to new levels of prominence. The effort to ban the teaching of evolution in public schools, championed by Bryan, gave the fundamentalist movement a new political focus.

The most controversial moment in the history of American fundamentalism came in 1925, with the Scopes "Monkey Trial" in Dayton, Tennessee. There Bryan took on liberal lawyer Clarence Darrow in a great showdown over the teaching of evolution in America's schools. Many figures in the trial, from Bryan to the American Civil Liberties Union to the leaders of the city of Dayton, had vested interests in turning the trial into a media spectacle. Dayton's boosters had even encouraged John Scopes, a local teacher and hardly a militant evolutionist, to violate Tennessee's 1925 state law against teaching evolution. Dayton leaders hoped a great national show trial would happen there as a result and bring publicity to the sleepy town. National and international journalists depicted the trial as a clash between rural southern religion and cosmopolitan northern progress.

There was no question about Scopes's guilt—he readily admitted he had violated the law and was convicted, though the decision was later reversed for technical reasons. But Scopes was not really the focus of the trial. The focus was the battle between Darrow and Bryan over evolution. Bryan was one of America's greatest orators, but he was no match for Darrow in a courtroom debate. Nevertheless, Bryan himself took the stand in defense of the Bible against evolution. Bryan's health was failing anyway, and he came off as addled. It became clear that he did not have much expertise in refuting higher criticism of the Bible. Darrow unleashed a fusillade of questions about Jonah being swallowed by the great fish, the sun standing still in the book of Joshua, and the date of Noah's flood. Bryan actually believed in a very old earth, unlike many conservative Christians, who held that the earth was no more than 10,000 years old. Still their exchange on Noah's flood was devastating for Bryan:

DARROW. You believe the story of the flood to be a literal interpretation?
BRYAN. Yes, sir.
DARROW. When was that Flood?

BRYAN. I would not attempt to fix the date. The date is fixed, as suggested this morning.

DARROW. About 4004 B.C.?

BRYAN. That has been the estimate of a man that is accepted today. I would not say it is accurate . . .

DARROW. But what do you think that the Bible, itself, says? Don't you know how it was arrived at?

BRYAN. I never made a calculation.

DARROW. A calculation from what?

BRYAN. I could not say.

DARROW. From the generations of man?

BRYAN. I would not want to say that.

DARROW. What do you think?

BRYAN. I do not think about things I don't think about.

DARROW. Do you think about things you do think about?

BRYAN. Well, sometimes.

The audience exploded in laughter at Bryan's puzzled statement, and "fundamentalist" became associated with the image of rural ignorance and buffoonery. In a conclusion that no one could have scripted, Bryan died just days after the trial, utterly worn out from the experience. His death marked the supposed national destruction of fundamentalism.

Of course, the fundamentalist movement was hardly finished, though its political and denominational power was diminished by the embarrassment at Dayton. In the 1955 play and 1960 movie *Inherit the Wind*, the Scopes Trial became concretized for millions of Americans as the stereotypical American clash between the forces of secular rationality and religious irrationality. Matthew Harrison Brady, the movie character patterned after Bryan, is phenomenally popular and seems formidable at first. But in the closing scenes of Brady/Bryan's interrogation and collapse, the movie exposes him as closed-minded and pathetic.

Other popular evangelists and pastors also brought controversy to the conservative Protestant movement in America. The evangelist Billy Sunday preached before packed audiences from New England to California before World War I, but his extravagant theatrical style and big-business supporters drew numerous critics. One of the most popular evangelists of the 1920s was Aimee Semple McPherson, whose Pentecostal preaching and healing ministry were based in Los Angeles. In 1923, she opened the Angelus Temple in Los Angeles, which could seat 5,000 worshippers and was the largest church building on the West Coast at the time. She became a key leader in the International Church of the Foursquare Gospel, with an associated Bible college and radio ministry. She too came under scrutiny in 1926, however, when she mysteriously disappeared while swimming. She was gone for more than a month and most assumed she was dead, but then she reappeared in Mexico and claimed she had been kidnapped. Critics charged that she had run away with her radio station manager, but what exactly happened during that month was never proven.

In spite of the efforts to retain the northern Baptist and Presbyterian denominations, fundamentalists (as well as Pentecostals, with their distinctive focus on holiness and the gifts of the Spirit) often established their own denominations and colleges instead of trying to hold on to the large church organizations. Dallas Theological Seminary, founded in 1924, became the flagship American seminary for the teaching of dispensational theology, a key component of many fundamentalists' beliefs. Dispensationalism focused on God's various "dispensations" through history and the anticipated events before Jesus's return to earth. Evangelist Bob Jones, a leader in the World's Christian Fundamentals Association, founded Bob Jones University in Florida in 1926. The school went through financial struggles and relocations until finding a permanent home in Greenville, South Carolina, in 1947. Bob Jones University has maintained the position that fundamentalism requires separation from theological modernists and liberals. Over time, the "exclusivist" wing of fundamentalism was the only segment that remained comfortable with the label "fundamentalist." More irenic conservative Protestants who still affirmed the full authority of the Bible increasingly became known as "neo-evangelicals," or just "evangelicals."

Pentecostals founded the Assemblies of God in 1914, which remains one of America's fastest-growing denominations. Today its numbers globally far outnumber its American adherents, however. Both the Assemblies of God and the Church of God in Christ grew in part out of the Azusa Street revival in Los Angeles in the early 1900s. This Pentecostal revivalist movement was multiethnic at its outset, but the founding of the Assemblies of God signaled a parting of ways between white and black Pentecostal leaders, as the Church of God in Christ remained predominantly African American. Although the membership of the Church of God in Christ is still rooted in the United States, it is an international fellowship with millions of adherents in countries from Mexico to India.

As we have seen, one of the most distinctive conservative institution-builders was J. Gresham Machen, originally of Princeton Theological Seminary. Machen and many conservatives like him belied the stereotype that "fundamentalists" were ignorant bumpkins. But the liberal trends at Princeton Seminary and in the Presbyterian Church left Machen feeling that he had no option but to separate, leading him and other conservative Presbyterians to found Westminster Theological Seminary and the Orthodox Presbyterian Church. Even those outside of the fundamentalist movement, such as the journalist Walter Lippmann, admired Machen. Lippmann, who was slowly trending away from the secularism of his youth, praised Machen's *Christianity and Liberalism* as a "cool and stringent defense of orthodox Protestantism" and "the best popular argument produced by either side" in the fundamentalist-modernist controversy. Lippmann was even sympathetic to the World's Christian Fundamentalist Association when they stated that liberals resorted to a "weasel method of sucking the meaning out of words" in order to pose as authentic Christians. But Lippmann feared the fundamentalist movement generally was intellectually and ethically damaged because of some fundamentalists' entanglement with "bizarre and barbarous agitations, with the Ku Klux Klan, with fanatical prohibition, with the 'anti-evolution laws,' and with much persecution and intolerance."

The Ku Klux Klan Reborn

As Lippmann's comments suggested, the 1920s had seen a resurgence of the Ku Klux Klan, which often packaged its animosity toward blacks and immigrants in Christian-sounding language. Fascination with the Klan boomed with the release of the movie *Birth of a Nation* in 1915. This film, with its favorable portrayal of Klansmen, was extraordinarily innovative in its use of moviemaking technology, but it brazenly portrayed Reconstruction-era African Americans as horrid brutes. The NAACP denounced the film, but the controversy seems only to have made the film more popular. *Birth of a Nation* went on to become the highest-grossing silent film of all time, in spite of its epic three-hour length.

A Methodist minister named William Simmons was inspired partly by *Birth of a Nation* to relaunch the Ku Klux Klan. He and a small group of followers burned a cross on top of Stone Mountain near Atlanta and proclaimed themselves as the successors to the Klansmen of the Reconstruction decades. Through effective marketing and recruiting techniques, the second Klan grew by leaps and bounds in the early 1920s. Although this Klan remained hostile to African Americans, its targets were ethnically, culturally, and religiously broader than just blacks. The Klan of the 1920s was fundamentally a nativist movement trying to preserve the so-called purity of Protestant American culture against the threat of Catholics, Jews, immigrants, and those who embraced the licentious style of the flappers. Even in the South the new Klan often targeted whites they perceived as immoral such as known adulterers.

The Klan was hamstrung by repeated accusations that some of its own leaders were adulterers or that they violated Prohibition's ban on alcohol. Nevertheless the Ku Klux Klan grew steadily in the early 1920s across the nation. The second Klan had a strong presence outside the South in states from New Jersey to Oregon. It also thrived in cities, not just rural areas. Part of the appeal of the Klan in the urban North was its opposition to Catholic and Jewish immigration. Chicago, for example, had twenty "klaverns" (chapters) of the Klan in the 1920s, with possibly as many as 50,000 members in the city. One Ku Klux Klan march in Chicago in 1921 drew 10,000 participants. One of the largest Klan meetings ever took place in Kokomo, Indiana, where in 1923 as many as 100,000 people attended a Fourth of July rally. Nationally, the Ku Klux Klan probably had about 2 million members during the 1920s.

Klan leaders such as Hiram Evans of Dallas echoed the eugenic concerns of anti-immigration leaders, contending that white Protestants needed to protect their racial stock from lesser peoples. Even though immigration was significantly restricted by the 1920s, Evans called for an entire halt to it in his popular 1924 speech and pamphlet, *The Menace of Modern Immigration*. Evans, who expelled William Simmons as Klan leader and declared himself "imperial wizard" of the Klan in 1922, originally delivered *The Menace* before a gargantuan audience of 75,000 people during "Klan Day" at the Texas State Fair in 1923. Evans explained that Anglo-Saxon Protestant America could never assimilate with people of certain races and religions. These unassimilable groups began with "the negro," who could never "attain the Anglo-Saxon level" because of the "low mentality of [their] savage ancestors, of jungle environment." Jews, although physically wholesome and law-abiding, were unassimilable because they were always destined to be outsiders. They could never embrace true American patriotism, Evans claimed. Finally, he believed Catholics could never assimilate because they owed ultimate allegiance to a foreign power, the pope in Rome. He argued that if the tide of immigration must be allowed to continue, then the United States should establish a quota restricting "inferior foreign elements." He warned Klansmen and their sympathizers that "ten percent of all the aliens coming to us were from Mexico" and that the United States needed to work on fortifying its borders to stem the flow.

Most Ku Klux Klan activism took the form of rallies and threats of vigilante violence. The Klan did make notable legislative efforts to shut down Catholic and other religious schools and to keep Catholics from serving as public school teachers. Most of these laws did not enjoy enough support to overcome concerns about religious liberty protections. Oregon voters did pass a law in 1922 that required all students between the ages of eight and sixteen to go to a public school. This was a direct assault on

Catholic parochial schools in the state, but it would have also prohibited children from attending denominational schools run by Lutherans, Seventh-day Adventists, and others. Before the law went into effect, however, the US Supreme Court unanimously ruled that it was unconstitutional in the landmark case *Pierce v. Society of Sisters* (1925). In that decision the justices affirmed that the Constitution "excludes any general power of the state to standardize its children by forcing them to accept instruction from public teachers only." This precedent had enduring significance, as it enshrined the principle that parents should have the final decision about what kind of education their children would receive, whether public or religious (or, as has become more common since the 1980s in America, whether parents would teach their children at home).

Figure 21.7. Dr. H. W. Evans, Imperial Wizard of the Ku Klux Klan, leading his Knights of the Klan in the parade held in Washington, DC, September 13, 1926.

By 1925, this second wave of the Klan had begun to collapse. Its enemies did push back against the Klan. For example, Catholics routinely confronted Klan rallies in the North, such as when a group of students from the University of Notre Dame rumbled with Klansmen in the streets of South Bend, Indiana, in 1924. African Americans publicized a continuing wave of lynchings, especially in the South, such as the killing of three members of the Lowman family before a crowd of thousands in Aiken, South Carolina, in 1926. Subsequent investigations showed that many of the white officials who were involved in the Lowman family killings were part of the Klan.

The resistance to the Klan added to the group's own internal problems. The organization had almost no effective national leadership. Some of those who did seek to give the Klan that kind of leadership were exposed in sex and financial scandals. By the late 1920s, the Klan had dwindled to a shadow of what it had been earlier in the decade.

But its brief flowering had illustrated the extreme counterreaction the cultural changes of the 1920s created in some segments of American society.

African American Activism

The NAACP continued to work hard to expose racial violence and to seek political reforms. In the 1920s, however, it was eclipsed by the Universal Negro Improvement Association (UNIA), led by Marcus Garvey, as the nation's biggest black advocacy organization. Garvey's philosophy was reminiscent of Booker T. Washington's older ideas about African American uplift and of Washington's lack of emphasis on integration. Garvey was even more pessimistic about white America than Washington had been, however, believing that racial justice in the US would always be illusory. The Jamaican-born Garvey had lived and worked in the Caribbean, Costa Rica, and England before moving to Harlem in New York City in 1916. Through speaking tours and his newspaper, *Negro World*, Garvey had become arguably the most famous person of African ancestry in the world by the early 1920s.

Garvey's philosophy was rooted in pan-African nationalism, or the idea that African peoples around the world had common interests and struggles. Africans must take it upon themselves to work for the betterment of their own race, Garvey taught. "The Negro of yesterday has disappeared," Garvey said, "and his place taken by a new Negro who stands erect, conscious of his manhood rights and fully determined to preserve them at all costs." Garvey helped set up black-run businesses and built a shipping company that would allow African Americans to move out of the United States, going to Africa if they so wished. He also sought to establish an African Orthodox Church, which would use

Figure 21.8. Marcus Garvey, 1887–1940.

Christian terminology but employed black representations of Jesus and the Virgin Mary in worship.

The UNIA became a fully transnational organization, with branches in countries from Panama to South Africa to Australia, in addition to the more than 700 UNIA chapters in the United States. Although the UNIA developed a huge following among working-class blacks, Garvey alienated NAACP leaders such as W. E. B. Du Bois because of his lack of support for integration. Garvey went so far as to meet with Ku Klux Klan leaders, affirming the Klan's views on the need for black-white separation. Financial problems with Garvey's shipping company led to charges of deception and mail fraud, which eventually landed Garvey in jail in 1925. In 1927, President Calvin Coolidge pardoned Garvey but deported him from the United States. Garvey returned to Jamaica, and the UNIA in America and elsewhere floundered.

Herbert Hoover and the 1928 Election

Although groups like the UNIA illustrated the widespread discontent in some sectors of American society, the Republican president Coolidge seemed to govern placidly over America, content to let business run its own affairs. Coolidge decided not to run for reelection in 1928, and Herbert Hoover was the obvious new standard-bearer for the Republicans. Hoover was a classic American rags-to-riches story, having been orphaned when he was a boy. Through family connections and sheer effort of will, Hoover became part of the inaugural class of students at Stanford University in 1891. He became wealthy as he worked as a mining engineer and consultant in places such as China and Australia. Hoover helped coordinate American relief programs during World War I and then served in government positions, including as secretary of commerce under presidents Harding and Coolidge.

During the 1928 presidential campaign, Hoover explained his belief in the American ideal of "rugged individualism." With the end of World War I and the rise of communism in Europe, America faced a "choice between the American system of rugged individualism and a European philosophy of diametrically opposed doctrines—doctrines of paternalism and state socialism." The Republican Party, Hoover insisted, had become the nation's great defender of individualism and free enterprise. He believed the economic results of Republican presidential governance under Harding and Coolidge were obvious. Under the "principles of decentralized self-government, ordered liberty, equal opportunity, and freedom to the individual, our American experiment in human welfare has yielded a degree of well-being unparalleled in the world. It has come nearer to

Figure 21.9. Woman mounting a "This Home is for Hoover" sign.

the abolition of poverty, to the abolition of fear of want, than humanity has ever reached before." As a candidate for president, Hoover was asking for a chance to further that legacy.

Hoover's opponent in the 1928 election was Al Smith, an Irish German Catholic and a product of the Democrats' Tammany Hall political machine in New York City. Smith was the first major Catholic candidate for the presidency in American history. This signaled that European immigrants—many of them Catholic—were becoming a more central part of the Democratic Party base. But the animosity toward Catholics in broad swaths of the country still meant that a Catholic candidate such as Smith would struggle outside of the urban North and the lower South, a region that remained solidly Democratic because of the legacy of Reconstruction. Smith did dominate America's largest cities, but Hoover and the Republicans wiped him out almost everywhere else. He lost his home state of New York. Smith even lost southern Democratic strongholds, including Texas and Florida, partly due to charges that Smith favored "negro equality" and that, as a Catholic, Smith "worships the Pope" (as one Arkansas Baptist minister put it). Nationally, Hoover won almost 84 percent of the electoral vote. Smith's only regional pocket of strength was in the southern states from South Carolina to Louisiana.

It remained to be seen how a new Democratic candidate could fuse rural southern voters with those of the urban North into a winning coalition. Few would have forecast that 1928 would be the last presidential victory for the Republicans until 1952. Moreover, few understood just how fragile the American economy was after the decade of excess that had followed World War I.

■ SELECTED BIBLIOGRAPHY ■

Dumenil, Lynn. *The Modern Temper: American Culture and Society in the 1920s.* New York: Hill and Wang, 1995.

Finan, Christopher M. *Alfred E. Smith: The Happy Warrior.* New York: Hill and Wang, 2002.

Gioia, Ted. *The History of Jazz.* 2nd ed. New York: Oxford University Press, 2011.

Giordano, Ralph G. *Satan in the Dance Hall: Rev. John Roach Straton, Social Dancing, and Morality in 1920s New York City.* Lanham, MD: Scarecrow Press, 2008.

Goldberg, David J. *Discontented America: The United States in the 1920s.* Baltimore: Johns Hopkins University Press, 1999.

Hankins, Barry. *Jesus and Gin: Evangelicalism, the Roaring Twenties and Today's Culture Wars.* New York: St. Martin's Press, 2010.

Larson, Edward J. *Summer for the Gods: The Scopes Trial and America's Continuing Debate over Science and Religion.* New York: Basic Books, 1997.

Marsden, George M. *Fundamentalism and American Culture.* 2nd ed. New York: Oxford University Press, 2006.

Roberts, Randy. *Jack Dempsey, the Manassa Mauler.* Urbana: University of Illinois Press, 2003.

Stein, Judith. *The World of Marcus Garvey: Race and Class in Modern Society.* Baton Rouge: Louisiana State University Press, 1991.

22

The Great Depression and the New Deal

The Great Depression was arguably the most crushing economic downturn in American history. Its devastating impact did more than ruin many family's finances. It tore apart families themselves. Pauline Kael was a student at the University of California–Berkeley in the 1930s. She noticed how the Depression had left many students fatherless, both functionally and literally. Some fathers had left their families to seek work elsewhere. Some had permanently abandoned their wives and children, in part because of their distress and embarrassment over being unable to provide for them. Men who were once comfortably middle-class could not cope with the stress of abject poverty. Some even committed suicide, she recalled, with the despairing thought that at least their families could collect their life insurance.

At Berkeley, some of the students had nowhere to stay, so they slept under bridges on the campus. Even Kael, who had a scholarship to Berkeley, had to skip some meals due to her lack of money. She worked as a teacher's assistant for seven courses per semester, which earned her fifty dollars a month. Stewing with economic and political resentment, Berkeley was becoming a "cauldron" for socialist and communist thought in that era. "You no sooner enrolled than you got an invitation from the Trotskyites and the Stalinists," Kael remembered.

The Crash of 1929

It is easier to describe *what* happened in the financial disaster of late 1929 than to explain *why* it happened. Scholars ever since have disagreed about whether the government could have done more to avert, or at least to alleviate, the meltdown. Some of the problems at the root of the Depression were caused by the immense changes in the American economy since World War I. It is doubtful whether any Republican or Democratic administration could have designed policies that would have addressed all the economy's structural weaknesses. The 1920s had seen enormous increases in consumer spending on goods such as automobiles and household appliances, but the huge increases masked deep fractures undermining the economy.

Many people, especially in the middle and upper classes, had put a great deal of money into the stock market. Although the market for consumer products had slowed down in the years before the crash, stock values continued to crest. Total share values on the New York Stock Exchange went from $27 billion in 1925 to $67 billion at the beginning of 1929. The number of active traders in the market (about 500,000 people) remained a small fraction of the American population, but the sales volume still surged from about 236 million trades in 1923 to more than 1.1 billion in 1928. Much of the stock was being sold on speculation. You only had to put a fraction of the dollar value down to buy stocks on the assumption that the value would continue to soar and you could make a killing without needing much money up front. Banks similarly engaged in dangerous lending practices. The economy was becoming a house of cards, precariously built on risky credit and rising stock prices. But few realized the risks. The *Wall Street Journal* issued an infamous forecast in August 1929 that "the outlook for the fall months seems brighter than at any time in recent years."

Instability shook the stock market in September, and then in late October the house of cards collapsed. Top stocks such as the Radio Corporation of America and Westinghouse dropped by half almost instantly. By mid-November the market's industrial sector overall had shed half of its stock value compared to September. Some expected speculators to return and boost the market once again, but the stomach-churning decline continued for years. The department store and mail-order company Montgomery Ward, for example, eventually saw its stock price drop from a high of $138 to just $4.

The Great Depression

The market crash began a crippling spiral of economic contraction that lasted for years. Banks that survived had to cut back on their lending. Reducing the amount of lending meant less spending by consumers on everything from homes to entertainment. Reduced spending meant that factories and service providers had to cut back on their operations, and they laid off many workers and cut the wages and hours of others. That led to further reductions in consumer spending, and the vicious cycle continued. America's gross national product (the value of the total amount of goods and services produced) fell by two-thirds. Steel and auto plants were often operating at 20 percent of capacity, or even less.

Unemployment shot up to 25 percent by 1932. In some towns, especially in the industrial Midwest, unemployment was much higher. Half of the working-age population of Cleveland, Ohio, was unemployed. In Toledo unemployment hit 80 percent. African American unemployment in the cities was twice the rate of whites, as factories tended to lay them off first. Desperate unemployed whites became more willing to take what had traditionally been seen as "Negro jobs," such as being household servants or garbage collectors. Conditions were even worse for poor black and white laborers in the rural South. The flow of African Americans to the urban North continued during the Depression in spite of the lack of ready work there.

In the Southwest the Depression reversed the flow of Mexican immigration into the United States. By 1930, some 1.5 million Mexican immigrants lived in the United States, mostly in states from California to Texas. Mexico (like many other nations) was also hit hard by the Depression, so returning there offered no particular economic advantage for these immigrants. Frustration over the economic suffering encouraged another wave of anti-immigrant backlash, however. Like blacks, Mexicans were often the first to lose their jobs. Even before the stock market crash, Congress passed the Deportation Act (1929), which gave local authorities enhanced powers to expel Mexicans and other immigrants. As the hardships of the Great Depression deepened, many argued that the country could not afford to provide immigrants with social services and welfare benefits. Between 1929 and 1939, some 1 million Mexicans and Mexican Americans were deported from the United States. Perhaps another million left because of duress caused by unemployment and the denial of social services. Many of those who left or were forced out were US citizens or could have claimed US citizenship. Immigration officials routinely engaged in Hispanic roundups. If those suspected of being Mexican could not produce proof of residency, they were sent to Mexico. Four hundred worshippers at Los Angeles's La Placita Church were detained and deported as they left Catholic mass one Sunday in 1931.

Many Jews, Catholics, and Protestants sought to expand their traditional efforts to minister to the poor during the Great Depression. Abyssinian Baptist Church, the largest church in Harlem and one of the largest Protestant churches in the country, had for years provided services to the poor and the elderly in its largely African American community. But when the Great Depression struck, Pastor Adam Clayton Powell Sr. insisted that the church needed to do more. Citing a phrase from Jesus in the Gospels, Powell warned, "The axe is laid at the root of the tree and this unemployed mass of black men, led by a hungry God, will come to the Negro churches looking for fruit and finding none, will say cut it down and cast it into the fire." Powell said he was committing a third of his annual salary to help those suffering. Emotional congregants responded with generosity, and the church increased its programs to give home heating fuel, food, and clothing to the poor. During 1930–1931 alone, Abyssinian Baptist assisted more than 40,000 people. Even heroic efforts like these, however, could not keep pace with the crushing burdens of the Depression.

Farmers and the Dust Bowl

Urban dwellers were not the only ones to endure the ravages of the Depression. Poverty and want were perhaps most pervasive among the farming and sharecropping people of rural America. Farmers' income in America dropped by two-thirds between 1929 and 1932. Reporter Lorena Hickok toured rural areas during the mid-1930s and was stunned by what she saw. In the South she observed starving blacks and whites who would "struggle in competition for less to eat than my dog gets at home, for the privilege of living in huts that are infinitely less comfortable than his kennel." The Depression took its toll on such sharecroppers and farmers, of course, but the economic collapse was also just perpetuating problems that dated back to the era of slavery.

The statistics of the era reveal deep patterns of poverty and a lack of education and sanitary facilities for many Americans. In 1934, the average annual income per person in farming families across America was a mere $167. Only a tenth of farmhouses had an indoor toilet; "outhouses" remained the standard. Only a fifth of farmhouses had electricity. Many rural Americans suffered from ailments related to malnutrition that doctors could have easily cured if doctors were available. In more than 1,300 counties in rural regions, there was not a single hospital. In rural America almost a million children between the ages of seven and thirteen were not attending school. Older children attended school even less frequently.

The climate and overworked soils across much of the Southwest and Great Plains only exacerbated the economic trials of the 1930s. For the first half of the decade, those regions endured the "Dust Bowl," a prolonged drought that wrecked the fields and livelihoods of countless farming families. The 1920s had seen more and more intensive farming, which left topsoil more vulnerable to drought and erosion. When the rains stopped, the soil became bone-dry and powdery, and winds swept it away in massive dust storms. John Steinbeck's novel *The Grapes of Wrath* (1939) immortalized the experience of the Joad family of Oklahoma and the "Okies'" great out-migration to California. But farmers from Colorado, Kansas, Texas, and Arkansas also had to leave, often with virtually no possessions, to find work elsewhere—usually in California.

The Dust Bowl migration gave California's culture a new dose of southern character. The parents of the great country singer Merle Haggard, for example, left Oklahoma during the Dust Bowl and moved to Bakersfield, California. In 1937, Haggard was born

Figure 22.1. *Migrant Mother*. Iconic Dorothea Lange photo of a thirty-year-old California pea picker and mother of seven. February 1936.

in a train boxcar the Haggards had converted into a home. The Dust Bowl and the migration west remained a staple theme of Haggard's music. He was probably best known for his 1969 hit "Okie from Muskogee," which extolled the simple values of small-town America.

The Political Response to the Depression

President Herbert Hoover has gained a somewhat unfair reputation as having done nothing to avert the economic collapse of the Depression. That criticism presumes that the national government could have enacted a better plan than Hoover's to stave off or at least alleviate the worst of the Depression. That it could have done so is highly doubtful since the nation really did not emerge from the Depression until World War II, well into Franklin Roosevelt's long presidency. Hoover did act against the Depression, although he preferred to leave jobs and relief in the hands of businesses and private agencies rather than the government. Even so, Hoover ramped up federal construction programs

Figure 22.2. Dust is too much for this farmer's son in Cimarron County, Oklahoma.

to create more jobs and signed major legislation establishing farmers' cooperatives to help stabilize agricultural markets. He also encouraged the creation of the National Credit Corporation, which was designed to keep small banks afloat. He pleaded with businesses not to lay off more workers and to maintain a basic minimum wage for employees. Drawing on his experience in coordinating relief efforts in post–World War I Europe, Hoover helped coordinate private agencies' assistance to the poor and unemployed. He also implored local governments to take care of their own people. But Hoover was reluctant to get the national government involved in direct handouts of assistance, believing that would only worsen the economic malaise, escalate the national debt, and create a culture of dependence on government assistance that would prove hard to break.

Hoover's modest federal initiatives, combined with private charity and local government assistance, did not do much to curtail the terrible crisis. States and cities found themselves swamped with new requests for public assistance, even as declining tax revenues made sustaining relief at their current levels difficult. By 1932, many cities had completely run out of funds to help the newly unemployed or destitute. Some cities, such as Dallas and Houston, cut corners by giving assistance only to white families, not to Mexicans or African Americans. Whether it was fair or not, Hoover took the blame for the Depression—he was the nation's political figurehead, and he was president when the crash happened. His name became a term of derision for many Americans. Across the nation shantytowns called "Hoovervilles" sprang up. Migrants and the homeless living in Hoovervilles "squatted" on public lands, erecting tiny shacks with scrap and discarded materials.

The Depression and Radical Unrest

Given the grotesque deprivations of the Depression, it is no surprise that signs of unrest and radicalism appeared across the nation such as at Pauline Kael's University of California. People across the socioeconomic spectrum began to consider socialism,

Figure 22.3. Home of Mexican squatters in San Antonio, Texas, made of scrap and discarded materials. Photograph by Russell Lee, March 1939.

Marxism, and even Soviet-style communism. After reading Karl Marx's work, novelist F. Scott Fitzgerald wrote that "to bring on the revolution, it may be necessary to work inside the communist party." Communist operatives gained a hearing in seemingly improbable areas, such as in parts of the Deep South. The Bethel Baptist Church, in a predominantly African American neighborhood in Birmingham, Alabama, was riven by terrible controversies over communism. Several members in the early 1930s were communist activists, but the pastor, Milton Sears, was vehemently anti-communist. When the pastor helped police find an accused black suspect in a criminal investigation in 1933, Sears drew the ire of many of the city's African Americans as well as Communist Party activists. Communists passed out a brochure calling Sears a "preacher for the Lord, spy for the police, and framer-up of workers." When a communist-led crowd confronted Sears during a service, the pastor pulled out a shotgun and drove his antagonists from the sanctuary. (Two decades later Bethel Baptist was the church of pastor and renowned civil rights activist Fred Shuttlesworth.)

In San Francisco frustrated longshoremen and dock workers shut down the city's port for two months in 1934. When business leaders finally sent in substitute workers to try to break the strike in July, longshoremen attacked them with rocks and iron pipes. Police accompanying the strikebreakers struck back, opening fire on the dock workers and flooding the streets with tear gas. The police dispersed the workers, but two of the strikers were killed in the clash. Harry Bridges, the openly communist head of the International Longshoremen's Association, called for a general strike in the city in response to the killings; 130,000 workers responded, representing a wide range of trades. Virtually all business in the whole city of San Francisco came to a halt until feuding between rival unions resulted in a resumption of work and negotiations for better working conditions also resumed.

The incident that best illustrated the breakdown of the relationship between many of the American people and the Hoover administration was the federal crackdown on the "Bonus Army" of veterans in Washington, DC, in 1932. Tens of thousands of out-of-work World War I veterans had descended on Washington in the spring of 1932 to demand early payment of a cash "bonus" that Congress had authorized to be paid to them. The bonus was not due until 1945, but the veterans argued that given the dire conditions, Congress should issue the payments early. Congress declined. Many of the Bonus Army's members left the capital city, but a few thousand stayed

Figure 22.4. Bonus Army marching to the US Capitol; the Washington Monument is in the background, July 5, 1932.

in Washington. District police tried to remove them from their encampment in July, but some of the veterans refused to budge. In the ensuing violence two of the protestors were shot and killed.

President Hoover summoned federal soldiers to assist the police confronting the Bonus Army. Tanks and infantrymen went in, led by Army Chief of Staff Douglas MacArthur, who would later become famous for his roles in World War II and the Korean War. (MacArthur's assistants in 1932 included future World War II generals George S. Patton and Dwight D. Eisenhower, who would also become US president in 1953.) MacArthur's forces used tear gas to evict the marchers from their camp, and then they burned down the protestors' ramshackle tent village. MacArthur's tactics had clearly exceeded Hoover's intentions, yet Hoover did not discipline him. MacArthur regarded the marchers as a "mob . . . animated by the essence of revolution" who threatened the stability of the federal government. The image of the administration turning the force of government against impoverished veterans was one of the last, and worst, public relations disasters for President Hoover.

The Election of 1932

Republicans reluctantly renominated Hoover to run for president in 1932. It is hard to imagine a candidate having less of a chance of winning. Unless the Democrats had committed some stupendous mistake, they were virtually guaranteed to recapture the White House for the first time since Woodrow Wilson. The Democrats committed no such mistake, wisely nominating the experienced and savvy New York governor Franklin D. Roosevelt (FDR) to run against Hoover. Roosevelt was from a wealthy New York family and was a distant cousin of former president Theodore Roosevelt, who had died in 1919. FDR had lost the ability to walk without assistance because of a bout with polio in 1921. His own struggles may have helped him identify with those of regular American people in spite of his elite background. Roosevelt had a clear, confident style of communication that worked superbly in the new radio era, and he was eager to employ new communication methods as a candidate and as president.

When he accepted the Democratic nomination in Chicago, Roosevelt immediately began speaking of how he would make a "new deal" with the American people. After several years of the Depression, it was a message the majority of American voters were eager to hear. In 1928, the New Yorker Al Smith had been unable to unify the Democrats' traditional constituencies in the urban North and rural white South. Roosevelt put those constituencies back together again. Outside of winning a few northeastern states, Hoover lost badly in the Electoral College. Roosevelt won by a margin of 472 votes to Hoover's 59, and Roosevelt won a clean sweep in the states of the Midwest, West, and South.

Roosevelt Confronts the Depression

The crisis of the Depression showed little sign of improving when FDR took office. A quarter of the American workforce remained unemployed, and states were routinely declaring "bank holidays" to keep their financial institutions from collapsing. Roosevelt himself had narrowly avoided being assassinated even before he took office (the assassin's bullet did take the life of the mayor of Chicago). In his first inaugural address, which was filled with biblical allusions, Roosevelt set a decisive but reassuring tone for his presidency. "This great Nation will endure as it has endured, will revive and will prosper," Roosevelt declared. "So, first of all, let me assert my firm belief that the only thing we have to fear is fear itself." Insisting that the time had come for aggressive national action against the ravages of the Depression, FDR indicated that he would ask Congress for "broad Executive power to wage a war against the emergency, as great as the power that would be given to me if we were in fact invaded by a foreign foe."

One of FDR's biblical allusions in the first inaugural was to the "unscrupulous money changers" in the financial sector who sacrificed the public good for personal gain. His first move as president was to secure the passage of the Emergency Banking Act, which sought to keep the banks solvent after a short national banking holiday. Congress hastily passed the law before some of its newest members had even settled in. FDR used the first of his "fireside chats," delivered in national radio addresses, to assure Americans that they could safely leave their money deposited in banks. His assurances worked: the flood of withdrawals slowed when the banks reopened. Congress and the president followed up with other regulations that prohibited risky speculation by financial institutions, and they created the Federal Deposit Insurance Corporation, which protected people's bank deposits from catastrophic losses.

Although FDR would soon authorize huge increases in federal spending under the "New Deal," his early inclination was to cut spending and to generate new sources of revenue for the government. Remarkably, FDR was able to get a coalition of Republicans and Democrats to agree to cut payments to veterans, exactly the issue that had prompted the crisis of the Bonus Army late in Hoover's presidency. But FDR was riding a wave of popularity that allowed him to do it, and Congress cleverly paired the budget cuts with the beginning of the end of Prohibition. Congress had passed an amendment repealing Prohibition before Roosevelt took office, based on the belief that the banning of alcohol had been a failure and that taxing the sale of alcohol represented an appealing source of government income. The required number of states had ratified the Prohibition repeal by the end of 1933, and it became the twenty-first amendment to the Constitution. In anticipation of that amendment, Roosevelt signed the Beer-Wine Revenue Act within two weeks of taking office, legalizing the sale and taxation of beer and wine in America.

The Hundred Days

With these early measures out of the way, FDR's administration and Congress entered upon the "Hundred Days." Whatever critics thought of their propriety and success, the legislation passed during the Hundred Days was the quickest and most transformative set of laws ever at the outset of an American presidency. During these months FDR put fifteen major requests before Congress, and Congress returned fifteen laws to him for signature. Some of them created institutional legacies that have persisted through the present day in America. These programs reflected the opposite of Hoover's hope that relief could be handled privately or by the states. Although states were given increased recovery funds under the Federal Emergency Relief Administration, Congress and the president created a dizzying array of agencies and federal employers that gave the New Deal a distinctly top-down, centralized tone. There were so many new abbreviated agencies such as FERA, TVA, CCC, and WPA that critics like former presidential candidate Al Smith said the national government was "submerged in a bowl of alphabet soup."

The concept behind work programs like the Tennessee Valley Authority (TVA) and the Civilian Conservation Corps (CCC) was to put people to work doing public jobs that would have lasting benefits but that employees of private businesses were unlikely to perform. The TVA took on the gargantuan challenge of bringing electrification and flood control to a large swath of Appalachia. It transformed the landscape of this region, centered on East Tennessee but extending to parts of seven states, by building hydroelectric dams and creating new lakes. The CCC, Roosevelt's favorite, sent workers across the nation to engage in conservation projects in America's national parks and national forests. It would eventually give work to almost 3 million people. CCC workers built countless trails, small dams, bridges, and miles of fencing and terracing. The CCC was eliminated in 1942 in the midst of the demands of World War II. But in the intervening years, they had left traces and structures that remain visible today in parks from coast to coast.

A man named Blackie Gold, who went on to become a car dealer with a comfortable middle-class life, experienced the depths of the Depression personally before enlisting in the CCC. His father died when Gold was an infant, and he and his siblings had to beg for heating coal. His mother could not afford to take care of Gold any longer, so she placed him in an orphanage where he stayed until he was seventeen. He joined the CCC in 1937. Gold traveled the country with the CCC, planting trees in Michigan and fighting forest fires in Idaho. The CCC provided for his basic needs, including three meals a day. "They sure made a man out of ya," he said, "because you learned that everybody here was equal." Gold thought this belief extended even to race relations. (The CCC usually operated in segregated units, but it did employ African Americans and Mexican Americans and paid them the same as whites.) "We never had any race riots," Gold recalled. There were a "couple of colored guys there, they minded their business; we minded ours." Black CCC workers did encounter overt hostility at some camps, however. Local white residents near Tennessee's Shiloh National Military Park, which was hosting a team of African American laborers, asked that the workers be removed because "ours is not a negro community and we do not know how to handle them."

New Deal Bureaucracy

Agencies like the CCC remained helpful and popular, but some units of the New Deal struggled to fulfill their intended functions. The National Recovery Administration (NRA), for instance, represented a vast national effort to coordinate industry and labor leaders into a system of pricing, hours, and production limits. NRA leaders hoped they could stabilize American businesses and ensure both profitability for industry and fair treatment for workers. In reality the NRA turned into an enormous bureaucratic mess. Compliance was voluntary, and many business leaders became convinced that America's most powerful companies were dictating the NRA's codes and regulations to their benefit. Workers also felt that the regulations were tipped in favor of business

Figure 22.5. CCC (Civilian Conservation Corps) workers putting up a fence. Greene County, Georgia, 1941.

over labor. The NRA drowned in a sea of regulatory complexity, with thousands of NRA desk workers creating intricate codes for American businesses. Even obscure industries faced mountains of regulations: corkmakers alone operated under thirty-four sets of codes, each with its own lists of regulations. Within two years the NRA had produced codes that filled 13,000 pages with their rules. Critics said the NRA really stood for "No Recovery Allowed." Journalist Walter Lippmann observed that because of top-down efforts like the NRA, the "excessive centralization and the dictatorial spirit are producing a revulsion of feeling against bureaucratic control of American economic life."

In the 1935 case *Schechter Poultry Corporation v. United States*, the Supreme Court unanimously ruled that many of the NRA's activities were unconstitutional. The Schechter company was a kosher poultry seller in Brooklyn that had been charged with a number of violations of NRA regulations, including selling "unfit chickens." The Supreme Court agreed that the rules, and the law enabling them, exceeded both the president's and Congress's powers to regulate local commerce. According to the Tenth Amendment, the court contended, such regulatory powers should be left to the states. *Schechter* was one of the first judicial roadblocks President Roosevelt faced in the implementation of his New Deal programs.

Roosevelt made similar centralizing efforts in farming with the creation of the Agricultural Adjustment Administration (AAA). In farming a classic problem was that farmers always brought as much produce and meat to market as they could, though doing so reduced prices and profits for all farmers. By using subsidies, the AAA encouraged farmers to cut production, taking acreage out of use and in some cases even plowing under crops such as cotton and killing piglets so they would not become the bacon and pork of tomorrow. (Critics worried about the morality of such "pig infanticide" when millions of Americans did not have enough to eat anyway.) In the short term such tactics did help raise farm prices and revenue overall. The Dust Bowl ironically was one of the biggest aids to the AAA because the forces of drought and wind took so much land out of production involuntarily.

Like the NRA's programs the AAA often benefited big agricultural companies and independent farmers and left poor farm workers and sharecroppers out. Owners were theoretically supposed to share the proceeds of their subsidies with workers, but in practice that often did not happen. Mexican workers were some of the most vulnerable, especially if they were recent arrivals to the United States or spoke little English. On Colorado's sugar beet farms, which were the largest beneficiaries of the state's AAA payments, farmers took so much acreage out of use that many Mexican workers were left without work. Unemployed Mexicans in Colorado and elsewhere were often specifically prohibited from receiving state or local relief funds, and they found it difficult to get approved for federal relief as well. In one Colorado county individual beet farm workers earned an average of seventy-eight dollars per year.

Perhaps the most important legacy of the AAA is that it put major farming sectors under the authority of the federal government. The government has continued to provide subsidies to keep crops and meats affordable, but the subsidies affect only certain kinds of grains and grain-fed meats. Historically, farmers who grow cotton, sugar, wheat, and soybeans have received the bulk of US agricultural subsidies, while fruit and vegetable farmers have been left out. Regardless of the relative nutritional merit of sugar and grains, they have remained cheap and have become ever more central to the American diet. Sugar and grains are especially common in processed and packaged foods.

Disparities in the recipients of farm subsidies have also persisted. Again big farming companies have been more likely to receive government payments than small family farmers. Large farming operations in the Midwest and Great Plains regions receive the bulk of the payments. Other farmers, whether large or small, in fruit- and vegetable-producing states such as Michigan, California, and Florida receive few subsidies. Since the creation of the AAA, Congress has been responsible for passing major farm bills every five years or so, but reform of the subsidies system has proven elusive.

Critics of the New Deal

The New Deal was massive and ambitious. By the end of FDR's first term in office, the federal budget deficit had grown to $4.5 billion, 55 percent larger than when he became president. The total federal debt had also more than doubled since the time of Hoover. Yet many of the Depression's problems had hardly budged. FDR's policies inevitably drew out critics from across the political spectrum. Some socialists and communists welcomed the New Deal, while others thought it did not go far enough to rein in businesses. Many conservative Protestants echoed concerns like those voiced by Walter Lippmann about the consequences of government central control. Some even speculated that the New Deal was a precursor or a "rehearsal" for the evil one-world government headed by the Antichrist in the last days. Some fundamentalists suggested that the ubiquitous Blue Eagle symbol of the National Recovery Administration was a forerunner to the Antichrist's "mark of the beast." One fundamentalist writer conceded that the Roosevelt administration was well-intentioned in its desire to alleviate Americans' suffering during the Depression but said that the New Deal was "preparing people for what is coming later . . . the big dictator, the superman, the lawless one."

Detroit-based Catholic priest Charles Coughlin was one of America's pioneers in using radio to spread a religious-political message. Originally an FDR supporter, Coughlin eventually used his vast radio platform of perhaps 40 million listeners to criticize the New Deal for not going far enough. Coughlin blamed "predatory capitalists" for much of America's financial woes. FDR should have broken the power of the bankers and redistributed income in a just manner, Coughlin insisted. Calling FDR "Franklin Double-Crossing Roosevelt," Coughlin accused him of being a faithless politician who had "promised to drive the money changers from the temple, [but] had succeeded in driving the farmers from their homesteads and the citizens from their homes in the cities." By the late 1930s, Coughlin's views had become progressively exotic, conspiratorial, and anti-Semitic (anti-Jewish). He spoke positively about the rise of Nazism in Germany and suggested that Jews and communists controlled the American government and economy. Once America entered World War II, the threat of arrest for sedition by the Roosevelt administration finally silenced Coughlin.

Another key Catholic figure of the era, Dorothy Day of the Catholic Worker Movement, was more reserved in her criticisms of FDR, focusing more on ministering to the poor themselves. Day had become a socialist in the 1910s, but in the late 1920s she converted to Catholicism. Day and French priest Peter Maurin founded the journal the *Catholic Worker* in 1933. The *Catholic Worker* advocated for pacifism and Catholic socialism and reached a circulation of 150,000 by 1936. Day renewed the older tradition of settlement houses in impoverished districts of New York and other American cities. She certainly preferred FDR to the Republican presidents of the 1920s, but she also thought FDR delivered too little on his promises to the workers and farmers. They saw him as a "savior," she said. "The problem was . . . he wasn't their savior. His policies were an emergency response to a situation that threatened the country's stability. By the end of the 1930s the same problems were there, as serious as ever." Day went on later to protest America's roles in foreign wars and its nuclear armament buildup in the 1950s. In the 1960s, she became a vocal supporter of César Chávez's United Farm Workers of America movement in solidarity with Mexican migrant laborers.

The most flamboyant critic of the New Deal was undoubtedly Huey P. Long, governor and senator from Louisiana. Long helped resurrect the populist tradition as the answer to his state's woes during the Depression. Long was elected governor in 1928, running on a platform of opposition to elite financial interests before the Depression even began. (Like many southern states Louisiana still struggled with disproportionate poverty levels that dated back to Reconstruction.) Like his ally Father Coughlin, Long originally supported FDR but came to believe the New Deal was unduly favorable to big business. FDR, for his part, scoffed at Long's "crackpot" ideas. In 1934, Long began to eye his own presidential run as he launched his "Share Our Wealth" program, which was based on high taxes for the rich and for business sectors such as the oil industry. Long envisioned massive redistribution of wealth and huge investments in public projects from roads to the facilities of Louisiana State University. He also called for a guaranteed minimum income for all people to maintain a basic standard of living for everyone. Long also built a ruthless and corrupt political machine, requiring payoffs from any person or business who wished to remain in good standing in the state. Long generated an enormous debt for the Louisiana state government. Even so, Long remained enormously popular in Louisiana when he was killed by an assassin in 1935.

The Second Hundred Days and Social Security

Mindful of critics like Long and Coughlin, and realizing that the effects of the Depression remained debilitating, FDR launched a new legislative program in 1935 that some call the "Second Hundred Days." Congress raised taxes on businesses and the wealthy, with the top income tax rate reaching 79 percent. Much of the new spending was reflected in the Emergency Relief Appropriation Bill, or what FDR called the "Big Bill." This spending measure cost $5 billion, which by itself was greater than the entire federal budget in the last year of the Hoover administration. The Big Bill gave new funding to agencies such as the Civilian Conservation Corps, but it also created the Works Progress Administration (WPA), which would eventually employ more than 8 million Americans.

Figure 22.6. Huey P. Long.

Critics noted that WPA funds became tools of local Democratic machines and party bosses. Nonwhites often suffered discrimination from local WPA agents. But for millions who had few employment prospects, the WPA supplied work for people building roads and bridges. Workers from the CCC and the WPA helped construct the iconic Blue Ridge Parkway in North Carolina and Virginia. At the behest of First Lady Eleanor Roosevelt, the WPA also employed many out-of-work artists, musicians, and writers. One of the most valuable results of the Federal Writers' Project of the WPA was an incomparable collection of thousands of interviews with former slaves. Although the interviews reflect biases of the WPA employees, the project produced 10,000 pages of recollections of life in the South that otherwise would surely have vanished from history's written records.

The New Deal program with the broadest lasting significance was the Social Security Act of 1935. FDR entrusted the design of this program to Frances Perkins, who as the secretary of labor was the first woman ever appointed to head a presidential cabinet office. Perkins was a disciple of the settlement house reformer Jane Addams. In 1911, she had led an official New York state investigation into the horrific Triangle Factory fire, which had resulted in the deaths of 146 women workers. This had secured her commitment to Progressive principles and labor reform.

Until the Social Security Act, the nation had little in the way of old-age pensions or of unemployment or disability insurance. Although the Constitution spoke of serving the "general welfare," what contemporary Americans think of as "welfare" programs

Figure 22.7. Mrs. Mary Crane, 82-year-old ex-slave, Mitchell, Indiana, between 1937 and 1938.

were limited as of the early 1930s outside of pensions given to military veterans and their dependents. "Retirement" was not really an option for most workers. If Americans got too sick or feeble to work, the best option for many was depending on the help of adult children or other family members. The influential physician and reformer Francis Townshend had proposed that the government should start providing guaranteed old-age pensions of $200 per month. FDR thought the administration should consider a "cradle to grave" system of insurance and benefits so no one would become destitute because of a job loss, an injury, or old age. But any old-age program this comprehensive would be phenomenally expensive, and there was much pressure to leave pension and insurance plans in the hands of the states. So Perkins and other presidential advisors sought to craft an economically and politically feasible plan.

In the end the Social Security Act left the planning and distribution of unemployment and disability insurance mostly to the states. The administration originally imagined that the act might take on the enormous burden of health insurance too, but the final version effectively abandoned that issue. Government health insurance for the poor and elderly would wait another three decades until the advent of Medicaid and Medicare. The major part of the act that fell under direct federal supervision was the old-age pension system (a system that has become synonymous with the name "Social Security"). Americans would be required to make "contributions" to the old-age pension system. In fact, these were taxes on individuals, forcing them to contribute to the system. Social Security would theoretically provide a minimum income for them when they reached old age.

Critics noted that the burden of Social Security taxes fell hardest on poor Americans. But many of the poorest Americans, including farm workers and domestic servants, were explicitly excluded from coverage under the old-age pension plan. Disproportionate numbers of these workers were African Americans, leading the NAACP to comment that Social Security was like a "sieve with the holes just big enough for the majority of Negroes to fall through." Amendments including the unrepresented workers were not adopted until the 1950s. Some of those workers who were not included did not object, however, because it meant they did not have to make compulsory contributions to Social Security. FDR realized that making the Social Security fund partly dependent on individual contributions would likely secure Social Security's existence indefinitely. Once having paid into the system, workers became insistent (whatever their political preferences) that they get their fair share back when they retired. In 1940, a seventy-six-year-old Vermont woman received the first Social Security old-age support check. It was for $41.30. With annual payments today totaling in the hundreds of billions of dollars, Social Security (with its related health insurance programs added in the 1960s) went on to become the biggest expenditure in the federal budget.

Organized Labor and the New Deal

The Depression saw a revitalization of the labor movement in America. Depression-era workers (those who were able to maintain employment) felt the pinch of declining wages. They often saw themselves as having collective interests that were at odds with business owners. But unions had declined in importance during the 1920s, and in certain sectors, including automobiles and steel, union organizing was largely absent. The 1935 Wagner Act, or National Labor Relations Act, gave new life to the unions. It gave workers stronger access to collective bargaining with their employers and created the National Labor Relations Board, which was tasked with enforcing the law and policing anti-union tactics by businesses.

Leaders of the American Federation of Labor (AFL) were not interested in trying to organize assembly-line factory workers, prompting the creation of the Congress of Industrial Organizations (CIO) in 1935. CIO founder John L. Lewis was so angry at the AFL's unwillingness to act that he got into a fistfight with another union leader at the 1935 AFL convention. Lewis, who served as the president of the United Mine Workers of America, led a cohort of eight unions out of the AFL to start the CIO. In 1937, the CIO sponsored a series of successful "sit-down" strikes in automobile factories in Flint and Detroit, Michigan, to get the car manufacturers to recognize the United Auto Workers union. The Roosevelt administration signaled an unwillingness to break up these strikes and others launched by the CIO. Its successes made the CIO more attractive to factory workers, and by the end of 1937, the conglomerate of unions had 3 million members. The CIO and other unions became closely aligned with the Democratic Party and helped many workers gain a number of basic benefits such as pensions, paid days off, and health insurance. The CIO entered a season of decline in the post–World War II era. It was torn by internal dissension over the presence of communists in its ranks, and the CIO launched a massive but failed attempt to extend union organizing to the South. The weakened CIO merged with the AFL in 1955.

The New Democratic Coalition

The New Deal helped forge an enduring coalition in the Democratic Party, uniting many who might have seemed to have contradictory priorities. Southern whites had been the base of the Democratic Party since the Civil War era. Now union members and many others in the urban North became solidly Democratic too. The most dramatic shift in allegiance came from African American voters, however. African Americans, when allowed to vote, had historically tended to vote Republican because it was the party of Lincoln and the abolition of slavery. By FDR's reelection campaign in 1936, however, three-quarters of African American voters supported him.

The New Deal brought benefits to many African Americans, even though many parts of it discriminated against nonwhites in official and unofficial ways. Blacks and other nonwhite workers were often paid less than white workers in the same federal jobs. FDR's agricultural programs were disastrous for many farm workers who did not own the farms. Again these workers were disproportionately nonwhite, though many poor whites also fell victim to the farming programs' effects. Tenant farmers, sharecroppers, and migrant workers often found themselves without work as the government paid farmers subsidies to curtail production of crops and meat. And Social Security's old-age program excluded many African Americans because they were farmworkers or domestic servants. Still, as many as four in ten African Americans did receive support or employment through New Deal programs. The WPA, in particular, gave jobs to more than a million blacks by the end of the 1930s.

The Roosevelt administration also gave unprecedented positions of power to small but influential numbers of African American leaders. One of the most prominent was Mary McLeod Bethune, who headed the National Youth Administration's Office of Negro Affairs, which supplied jobs and training to hundreds of thousands of young blacks. Bethune was born to a cotton farming family in rural South Carolina. A devout Methodist, Bethune attended the Moody Bible Institute and once aspired to become a missionary to Africa, but she found doors closed to her because of her race. She returned to the South and became a leading advocate for Christian education for African Americans. In the early 1900s, she founded what became Bethune-Cookman College in Florida.

Taking on a variety of leadership positions in national education and civil rights organizations, Bethune befriended Eleanor Roosevelt. Bethune accepted her administration position with the National Youth Administration in 1936. With access to the president, by the late 1930s Bethune became arguably the most influential African American leader in the United States. She saw the church as having enormous potential for generating social change in the nation, but she insisted the church must live out its beliefs in order to be effective. "The church has been and must continue to be the great gateway to these spiritual influences which lead us to the realization of the Fatherhood of God and the brotherhood of Man. But this influence can be willed only by a living, breathing church that puts this concept into practice."

Perhaps the most important symbolic moment for race relations during the Roosevelt administration came when Eleanor Roosevelt and Secretary of the Interior Harold Ickes arranged for a performance on the steps of the Lincoln Memorial in Washington, DC, by the great contralto singer Marian Anderson in 1939. Anderson had been refused the opportunity to perform at the city's largest concert venue, the Constitution Hall of the Daughters of the American Revolution. Eleanor Roosevelt resigned from the

Figure 22.8. Mary Bethune, in charge of the "Colored Section" of the NYA. Ca. 1938.

Daughters of the American Revolution over the episode. When Anderson performed on the national mall on April 9, a vast integrated throng of 75,000 spectators came to hear her sing. It was broadcast live on radio networks.[*]

Challenging the New Deal

Regardless of the New Deal's limitations, a majority of voting Americans believed Roosevelt had handled the Depression well. His new Democratic coalition led him to a landslide victory in 1936 over Republican presidential nominee Alf Landon. Winning all the states except Maine and Vermont, FDR trounced Landon in the Electoral College by 523 to 8 votes.

Feeling that the election had given him a renewed mandate, FDR set his sights on the primary obstacle to New Deal legislation: the Supreme Court. The court had struck down certain parts of the New Deal program. Roosevelt was frustrated by his inability to replace the aging justices, some of whom seemed determined to stay on the court as long as necessary to restrict FDR's legislative agenda. Because the Constitution does not stipulate how many members the Supreme Court has, FDR asked Congress to institute a measure to expand the number of justices by up to six new members. This would have given FDR a solid majority of supporters on the court. But the scheme ended up damaging FDR politically.

Critics saw the "court-packing" plan as a crass politicization of the Supreme Court, which ideally was supposed to stand above the nation's political turmoil. Even some Democrats resisted FDR's proposal. The court, perhaps chastened by the threat of expanding its membership, approved the constitutionality of key measures such as the Wagner Act and the Social Security Act in the meantime, indicating that they were not going to stand in the way of every New Deal measure. FDR's Supreme Court expansion proposal eventually died in Congress. By the end of the 1930s, FDR had been able to replace a number of retiring justices anyway, so the issue became moot. But Roosevelt had spent a lot of political capital on the battle, and it set the stage for the emergence of more effective political opposition to his agenda.

FDR's electoral triumph in 1936 was clouded by the court-packing controversy. Then the United States spiraled into a renewed economic downturn in 1937. The recession brought into question whether all of FDR's huge spending programs had been for naught. A group led by Democratic senators such as Josiah Bailey of North Carolina

---

[*] "Marian Anderson Sings at the Lincoln Memorial," YouTube video, 1:50, https://www.youtube.com/watch?v=XF9Quk0QhSE.

drew up a "Conservative Manifesto," questioning the New Deal's dependence on spending the public's money as an answer to the nation's economic woes. They encouraged policies that would lower taxes and encourage private investments in businesses and the stock market as well as balance the federal budget and restore confidence in the government's stability. They urged the administration to steer away from the temptations of socialist state ownership of business and mass government employment programs. American private enterprises were not foolproof, they acknowledged, but "they are far superior to and infinitely to be preferred to any other so far devised. They carry the priceless content of liberty and the dignity of man. They carry spiritual values of infinite import, which constitute the source of the American spirit." Increasing numbers of southern Democrats, along with the national Republican Party, wanted to keep the New Deal from undermining the American ideal of free market capitalism.

The "Conservative Manifesto" represented the beginnings of the modern conservative movement in America. From the 1930s forward, political battle lines in America were often drawn around the question of whether more government or less government was needed for citizens to flourish. The New Deal had undoubtedly alleviated some of the worst effects of the Depression, but it also represented a phenomenal increase in the size and intrusiveness of national government agencies. Of course, some Americans of a more radical persuasion wanted the New Deal to go further into state ownership and collectivism represented by socialism or communism. The Cold War, beginning in the late 1940s, would help many Americans understand the murderous extremes to which communism could run. In the meantime the specter of fascism and Nazism began to darken America's international horizons.

■ SELECTED BIBLIOGRAPHY ■

Biles, Roger. *The South and the New Deal*. Lexington: University Press of Kentucky, 2006.

Brinkley, Alan. *Voices of Protest: Huey Long, Father Coughlin, and the Great Depression*. New York: Vintage, 1982.

Carpenter, Joel A. *Revive Us Again: The Reawakening of American Fundamentalism*. New York: Oxford University Press, 1997.

Greenberg, Cheryl Lynn. *"Or Does It Explode?" Black Harlem in the Great Depression*. New York: Oxford University Press, 1991.

Kelley, Robin D. G. *Hammer and Hoe: Alabama Communists during the Great Depression*. 2nd ed. Chapel Hill: University of North Carolina Press, 2015.

Kennedy, David M. *Freedom from Fear: The American People in Depression and War, 1929–1945*. New York: Oxford University Press, 1999.

Leuchtenberg, William E. *The Perils of Prosperity, 1914–1932*. Chicago: Rand McNally, 1958.

McElvaine, Robert S., ed. *Down and Out in the Great Depression: Letters from the Forgotten Man*. Rev. ed. Chapel Hill: University of North Carolina Press, 2008.

Sitkoff, Harvard. *A New Deal for Blacks: The Emergence of Civil Rights as a National Issue: The Depression Decade*. Classic ed. New York: Oxford University Press, 2008.

Terkel, Studs. *Hard Times: An Oral History of the Great Depression*. New York: Pantheon Books, 1970.

Walker, Melissa, ed. *Country Women Cope with Hard Times: A Collection of Oral Histories*. Columbia: University of South Carolina Press, 2012.

Worster, Donald. *Dust Bowl: The Southern Plains in the 1930s*. 25th anniv. ed. New York: Oxford University Press, 2004.

23

World War II

Since the end of World War I, isolationism had been the dominant approach in American foreign policy. When the Senate refused to approve the Treaty of Versailles, it kept the United States from joining the League of Nations. Many hoped Americans' role overseas would be restricted to trade and diplomacy. That hope was reflected in the 1928 Kellogg-Briand Pact, an effort by American and French politicians to ban war altogether. Most countries in the world signed on to the Kellogg-Briand Pact, but in retrospect the agreement looked idealistic and naïve. The Great Depression only intensified Americans' reluctance to get involved with international affairs. As so many Americans struggled for daily sustenance, who had time for meddling in the affairs of other nations?

Circumstances would not allow Americans to stay out of international conflict forever. Indeed, the Japanese attack on Hawaii's Pearl Harbor naval station in 1941 ultimately forced war upon the United States. Japan, Italy, and Germany had turned to militarism in the midst of the global travails of the Great Depression. Japan fell under the leadership of nationalist military officers who expanded the nation's armed forces and sought to expand Japan's imperial influence into China and the rest of southeast Asia. Many Japanese people regarded themselves as the "Yamato race," the superior ethnic family in Asia and perhaps the world. Japan invaded the Chinese territory of Manchuria in 1931 and then embarked on an invasion of China as a whole in 1937. The United States increasingly sided with China in these conflicts, and Japanese leaders saw America as their number-one enemy on the global stage.

In 1922, Italy had come under the rule of strongman Benito Mussolini. As a young man Mussolini had worked as an agitator for the Italian Socialist Party. During World

War I, he paired his socialist inclinations with Italian nationalism. Breaking with the Italian Socialist Party, Mussolini's Blackshirts battled in the early 1920s for control of Italy's radical political movements. His faction represented themselves with the ancient symbol of the *fascio*, a bundle of sticks not easily broken. From this symbol came the movement's "fascist" name. Under Mussolini, Italy invaded Ethiopia in 1935. League of Nations sanctions were unable to stop Italy from conquering the East African nation.

Germany turned out to be the gravest threat of all, as Adolf Hitler assumed power there in 1933 as the head of the National Socialist, or Nazi, Party. In violation of the Versailles Treaty, Hitler's Germany began an aggressive program of rearmament. Nazi police rooted out critics of the regime, and Hitler blamed Germany's woes on a host of shadowy enemies, especially Jews. Anti-Semitic laws revoked Jews' citizenship. Then, on November 9, 1938, the Nazis initiated a direct campaign of violence and arrests against Jews. A hundred Jews died, and tens of thousands were arrested on *Kristallnacht*, the "night of broken glass." Congressional efforts to increase quotas for fleeing Germans to come to America proved futile. Large majorities of Americans, and even a sizable minority of American Jews, opposed making more room for refugees. Smaller efforts did extend visas for certain Europeans already staying in the United States, such as the Jewish scientist Albert Einstein, who was working at Princeton's Institute for Advanced Study.

War in Europe Begins

Many in the United States, observing the developments in Asia and Europe, renewed their insistence that America should not get dragged into foreign conflicts. In Europe in the late 1930s, Germany and Italy backed fascist forces during the Spanish Civil War, while Communist Russia and thousands of individual Americans supported Spain's liberal revolutionaries. Worrying that the conflict in Spain might become the trigger for American intervention, Congress repeatedly passed measures in the 1930s mandating American neutrality. The acts, labeled the Neutrality Acts, prohibited loans, arms sales, and other assistance to nations at war.

The American neutrality policy may have emboldened Hitler, who was plotting the conquest of Germany's neighbors. In 1936, he occupied the Rhineland of western Germany, which by treaty was supposed to remain a demilitarized zone between France and Germany. Then in 1938, the Nazis took over Austria. Months later Hitler announced his intention to annex the Sudetenland, a German-dominated province of Czechoslovakia. European powers led by British prime minister Neville Chamberlain

Figure 23.1. America gains a famous citizen. Albert Einstein receiving from Judge Phillip Forman his certificate of American citizenship.

agreed to give up the Sudetenland at the Munich Conference in hopes that it would satisfy Hitler and avert war. Even though he privately condemned Chamberlain's weakness, President Roosevelt publicly approved of the agreement and informed Hitler that the United States had "no political involvements in Europe, and will assume no obligations in the conduct of the present negotiations."

In retrospect it is easy to see that there would be no appeasing Hitler. In British Parliament, future prime minister Winston Churchill struck a prophetic note when he called Chamberlain's agreement with Hitler a "total and unmitigated defeat." Citing the book of Daniel, Churchill said that "terrible words have been pronounced against the Western democracies: 'Thou art weighed in the balance and found wanting.'" Churchill insisted that there could never be peace with Nazi power, "that power which spurns Christian ethics, which cheers its onward course by a barbarous paganism. . . . This is only the beginning of the reckoning. This is only the first sip, the first foretaste of a bitter cup which will be proffered to us year by year unless . . . we rise again and take our stand for freedom."

Hitler broke the Munich agreement just six months later when Germany took over the rest of Czechoslovakia. Alarmed, FDR pleaded with Congress to modify the Neutrality Acts. Isolationist congressmen, failing to realize the seriousness of the Nazi threat, stonewalled the attempt to allow trade on a "cash and carry" basis. Cash and carry meant the United States would trade only if the purchasing nation paid up front and provided its own ships for transport. Hitler mocked the United States for its fecklessness, and in August the Nazis announced a nonaggression pact with the Soviet Union. This agreement freed Germany to invade Poland, which began on September 1, 1939. Hitler and Soviet dictator Joseph Stalin agreed to split Poland in two. The invasion of Poland marked the beginning of World War II. FDR, awakened in the middle of the night to the news of German forces rampaging across Poland, said, "It has come at last. God help us all!"

Maintaining Neutrality

By 1937, Germany, Italy, and Japan had already indicated their common interests against threats from the Soviet Union. In 1940, the three nations would sign the Tripartite Pact, solidifying their alliance as the Axis Powers. American opinion was overwhelmingly hostile toward Germany and Japan. But the question of intervention, or how to aid the Allied Powers of France and Britain, remained controversial even after the invasion of Poland. FDR's renewed calls for a "cash and carry" policy finally broke through the isolationist logjam in Congress in late 1939. But isolationist congressmen and popular leaders, including Father Charles Coughlin and the celebrated aviator Charles Lindbergh, warned that revising the neutrality provisions would become the first step toward war. Lindbergh went on radio to assert that the "destiny of this country does not call for our involvement in European wars." As he knew well from his flying experiences, the ocean was a formidable barrier, and he contended that Germany posed no real threat to the United States.

Lindbergh and others helped form the America First Committee in 1940 to urge the nation to stay out of war. Their antiwar stance reflected a deep, enduring commitment among many Americans, at least until the bombing of Pearl Harbor. Lindbergh tarnished the reputation of America First agitation when he expressed anti-Semitic suspicions about the small number of Jews who were supposedly driving America to war. (FDR privately regarded Lindbergh as a Nazi sympathizer.) President Donald Trump would resurrect the phrase "America First" in his 2016 inaugural address, reflecting his belief that America had spent too much on foreign aid and tolerating illegal immigration while neglecting its own citizens and workers.

Momentum for more American action grew when the Nazis struck against Denmark, Norway, the Netherlands, Belgium, and finally France. All of them fell before the Nazis' blitzkrieg tactics between April and June 1940. Many Americans had assumed World War II would bog down in Europe, just as World War I had. The Nazis demonstrated just how wrong that assumption was. Britain was the last holdout against the Nazi domination of Europe. If Britain fell to the Nazis, the Germans might secure the use of the surviving British navy. This could mean the Atlantic would not present a barrier to Nazi power after all and could put the East Coast of the United States in jeopardy.

The America First advocates scoffed at such scenarios as paranoid scare tactics. But the conquest of France convinced more Americans that they must prepare for war and do whatever they could to keep Britain from succumbing to German power. By June 1940, 80 percent of Americans favored giving the British more material support to help fight the Nazis. In an address that month at the University of Virginia, FDR acknowledged that

> some indeed still hold to the now somewhat obvious delusion that we of the United States can safely permit the United States to become a lone island, a lone island in a world dominated by the philosophy of force. Such an island may be the dream of those who still talk and vote as isolationists. Such an island represents to me and to the overwhelming majority of Americans today a helpless nightmare of a people without freedom. . . . Overwhelmingly we, as a nation—and this applies to all the other American nations—are convinced that military and naval victory for the gods of force and hate would endanger the institutions of democracy in the western world.

That same month, Roosevelt submitted a plan to Congress for a military draft. Later that year FDR agreed to give Britain fifty older American destroyer ships, and Britain leased America the right to establish air and naval stations in British territories in the Caribbean and in Canada. Churchill, who had become British prime minister earlier in 1940, was delighted. The airborne German attacks in the Battle of Britain had started to reach their most critical phase. Churchill took the exchange of destroyers for bases as a sign that America was beginning to stir. He thought the American-British alliance against Nazism was inevitable. The "English-speaking democracies, the British Empire and the United States, will have to be somewhat mixed up together in some of their affairs for mutual and general advantage," he told Parliament.

The 1940 Election and Lend-Lease

George Washington had set a previously unbroken precedent of retiring after two terms as president. But there was as yet no constitutional requirement that limited presidents' service to two terms. The 1940 election proceeded in a time of anxiety over the outcome of the Battle of Britain and fear that the Nazis or Japanese could eventually threaten the United States. These concerns were foremost in FDR's mind when he decided to run for a third term as president. The Republicans might have considered nominating an isolationist stalwart, which would have offered a serious ideological alternative to FDR. But instead they nominated Indiana's Wendell Wilkie, a business executive and a former Democrat who was critical of the New Deal but who supported FDR's aid to Britain. As the 1940 election approached, international issues had eclipsed domestic ones for the moment, so the differences between the two candidates did not seem significant. Roosevelt won another Electoral College landslide, with 449 votes to Wilkie's 82.

The electoral victory emboldened FDR to ramp up assistance to Britain. Churchill pleaded with the president for direct aid, as Britain was out of money to continue paying for "cash and carry" military supplies. So Roosevelt proposed the "Lend-Lease" Act, which offered the (somewhat dubious) arrangement that the United States could "lend" military equipment to foreign nations or (more realistically) lease it in exchange for other economic concessions or future payments. Isolationists scoffed, noting that the United States would hardly be interested in receiving back used military supplies at the end of the war. Nevertheless, the bill passed easily in Congress in March 1941, representing a major turn away from the policy of isolation. Although Churchill wished the aid had come sooner, he nevertheless expressed public thanks on behalf of Britain "for this very present help in time of trouble." Britain would ultimately receive $40 billion in assistance under Lend-Lease. One immediate benefit the United States secured under Lend-Lease was forcing Britain to open its global empire to trade with America by lowering Britain's high tariffs.

The Soviet Union also became a major beneficiary of Lend-Lease after Hitler invaded it in June 1941. Instead of focusing on securing its domination of central and western Europe, the Nazis decided to extend Germany's armed forces into the vast reaches of Russia. This strategic error would be a key element of Germany's demise in World War II. The invasion of the Soviet Union took some pressure off Britain, but German submarines (U-boats) continued patrolling the waters of the North Atlantic.

In response to Churchill's pleas for naval assistance, FDR agreed to use American warships to help escort British shipping in the western parts of the Atlantic, closer to the US mainland. Although FDR and Hitler both remained reluctant to provoke open naval war between the United States and Germany, incidents between the U-boats and American ships were inevitable. Several altercations between German and American ships culminated in the October 1941 sinking of the American destroyer *Reuben James*, resulting in the deaths of 115 sailors. In November an indignant majority in Congress voted to remove all remaining limitations on American ships' movements through the war zones around Britain and the Soviet Union. Although large segments of the American population still professed reluctance about war, the United States had functionally entered the conflict in the Atlantic by the beginning of December 1941.

Pearl Harbor and the Pacific

Japanese aggression in China and in other nations of southeast Asia led the United States to gradually cut off all trade with Japan. Most critically, the United States stopped sending oil exports, on which the Japanese economy and military heavily depended. The Japanese premier, General Hideki Tojo, made pretenses of continuing negotiations while Japan actually prepared for war against the United States, its Pacific bases, and its territory in the Philippines. The Japanese preparations included practice attacks on a mock-up of Hawaii's Pearl Harbor naval base, which they had erected in Japan's Saeki Bay.

In the early morning (Hawaii time) of December 7, 1941, the Japanese launched a massive surprise assault on Pearl Harbor. The United States had established the naval station at Pearl Harbor in 1908, following the US annexation of Hawaii. Pearl Harbor was the foremost base for the American Pacific fleet, and the airborne attack decimated it. Japanese fighter pilots sank or crippled eighteen warships, destroyed 180 military airplanes, and killed more than 2,000 American sailors and servicemen, with more than 1,000 others wounded. Close to half of the dead had been on board the battleship *Arizona*—the attack had ignited a bomb in the ship's hold, sinking the *Arizona* almost immediately. Dorie Miller of Waco, Texas, served on the USS *West Virginia* as a mess attendant, one of the only positions open to African Americans in the navy. When the attack began, Miller helped move wounded sailors to safety and then took command of an antiaircraft machine gun and shot at Japanese planes until ordered to abandon ship. Miller was awarded the Navy Cross for his bravery. A chaplain at Pearl Harbor recalled the difficulty they had in identifying the dead, using "every means possible to determine the identity of bodies: clothes, letters, contents of pockets, billfolds, laundry marks, organization insignia, [and] fingerprints."

"above and beyond the call of duty"

DORIE MILLER
Received the Navy Cross
at Pearl Harbor, May 27, 1942

Figure 23.2. Above and beyond the call of duty—Dorie Miller received the Navy Cross at Pearl Harbor, May 27, 1942. By David Stone Martin.

The tragedy at Pearl Harbor represents one of the greatest turning points in American history. It is not entirely clear why, other than retribution for America shutting down oil shipments, the Japanese decided to attack Pearl Harbor. Some Japanese leaders may have believed that war with the United States was inevitable. If they could preemptively devastate the American fleet from the outset of that war, perhaps it could give Japan freer rein in Asia and force the United States into negotiating peace. But if that was Japan's intent, the attack backfired. It would be hard to imagine anything that could have inflamed American public sentiment more than Pearl Harbor. And as devastating as Pearl Harbor was, it left key elements of American Pacific naval strength intact, including the enormous stores of fuel oil at the base. The Japanese also failed to strike at American aircraft carriers, which were all absent from Pearl Harbor for various reasons on the day of the assault.

Since 1939, FDR had been torn between his concern over Axis aggression and the strength of isolationist sentiment at home. Pearl Harbor totally changed the equation. Calling December 7, 1941, "a date which will live in infamy," FDR asked for a declaration of war against Japan, and Congress overwhelmingly approved it.* (The lone dissenting vote was from Jeanette Rankin, Republican representative of Montana, who also happened to be the first woman elected to Congress.) Chinese leader Chiang Kai-shek, who was battling Japan for control of China, hoped the attack would finally shift America's attention to the Asian-Pacific theater. Winston Churchill recalled being relieved that America would finally enter the war with full force, but he wanted to

---

* "'A Date Which Will Live in Infamy': FDR Asks for a Declaration of War," audio, 4:14, http://historymatters.gmu.edu/d/5166.

make sure the new American focus on Asia would not drain resources from Britain. Adolf Hitler believed it would be "impossible" for the Axis powers to lose, now that Japan had brutally taken the war to the United States. Germany and Italy formally declared war against the United States four days after Pearl Harbor.

The months following Pearl Harbor were a grim time for the Allies in the Pacific. Japan followed up Pearl Harbor by taking American bases at Wake Island and Guam and by overwhelming Allied forces in the Dutch East Indies. Japan seized the valuable

Figure 23.3. Pearl Harbor naval base and USS *Shaw* ablaze after the Japanese attack, 1941.

oil fields of the East Indies, which the Japanese needed to replace the oil supply from America. They dominated British shipping in the Indian Ocean. Japan had decimated General Douglas MacArthur's aircraft fleet in the Philippines the day after Pearl Harbor. Tens of thousands of American and Filipino soldiers retreated to the Bataan Peninsula, on the Philippine island of Luzon. MacArthur was eventually evacuated to Australia, vowing, "I shall return." The Japanese continually bombed the remaining American forces in the Philippines. One army nurse in the Philippines, Juanita Redmond, recalled the "endless, harrowing hours" of caring for the injured and dying after a bomb struck their camp. The nurses and doctors worked unceasingly, with "hours of giving injections, anesthetizing, ripping off clothes, stitching gaping wounds, of amputations, sterilizing instruments . . . [and] covering the wounded we could not save."

The remaining American and Filipino forces in the area around Bataan were forced to surrender in the spring of 1942. The Japanese took 70,000 prisoners, including 10,000 American soldiers. Japanese commanders subjected many of these prisoners to the infamous Bataan Death March, an eighty-mile hike to prisoner-of-war camps. The captives were humiliated, tortured, and denied food and water, and stragglers were summarily executed. About 600 Americans died during the march, along with far greater numbers of Filipinos.

By the summer of 1942, the Japanese controlled much of the western Pacific Ocean and southeast Asia. But American forces soon pushed against the edges of Japanese control. Japanese and American pilots and aircraft carriers fought a vicious but inconclusive battle at the Coral Sea, northeast of Australia, in May 1942. American code-breakers then informed Admiral Chester Nimitz, the US commander in the Pacific, that the Japanese intended to attack Midway, a small island at the far northwestern end of the Hawaiian Island chain. At Pearl Harbor naval mechanics were hastily repairing the aircraft carrier *Yorktown*, which had been damaged at the Coral Sea. Unknown to the Japanese, Nimitz fortified Midway's defenses with ships like the *Yorktown*.

American forces repulsed the initial Japanese assault on Midway on June 4, 1942, and Japanese planes returned to their carriers to resupply. American dive-bombing planes suddenly attacked the Japanese carriers, sinking four of them, along with many of their pilots and aircraft. Of its carriers the Americans lost only the *Yorktown*. Since aircraft carriers were becoming the key to the Pacific War, the victory at Midway virtually

Figure 23.4. USS *Yorktown* (CV-5) was hit on the port side, amidships, by a Japanese Type 91 aerial torpedo during the midafternoon attack by planes from the carrier *Hiryu*, in the Battle of Midway, on June 4, 1942. *Yorktown* is heeling to port and is seen at a different aspect than in other views taken by USS *Pensacola*, indicating that this is the second of the two torpedo hits she received. Note the heavy antiaircraft fire. Photographed from the USS *Pensacola* (CA-24).

flipped the balance of power in that theater from the Japanese to the Americans. Midway was arguably the most significant battle in the Pacific theater of World War II.

War and the Home Front

As devastating as the Great Depression had been, World War II was even more transformative for the American economy and society. The vast industrial demands of the war and the departure of so many men for the war front created unprecedented job opportunities for people who traditionally had been excluded from many industrial sectors, including women, African Americans, and Hispanics. All these changes led to movement: people enlisting in the armed services moved to their bases or with their deploying units, people left their homes to take new jobs in other parts of the country, and rural areas lost population to regions with military bases and large industries, especially those related to wartime production.

Countless enlistees and factory workers found themselves swept up by the course of the war into places and experiences they could have never imagined. (Some of those experiences, of course, they would have preferred to have missed.) Robert Lekachman, who would go on to become a distinguished economics professor at the City University of New York, got the first steady job of his life in the army when he was drafted right after Pearl Harbor. He was by his own admission a "helplessly awkward intellectual sort of kid" with bad vision and no mechanical or shooting skills. The army sent him to Fort Jackson in South Carolina as part of the "Statue of Liberty" Division, a mix of New Yorkers and southerners. He regarded himself lucky to avoid becoming an officer; junior officers "got slaughtered in heaps in Japan and in the Pacific, where my unit ultimately went," he recalled. He became a clerk and wrote letters for officers from his regimental headquarters. His first overseas assignment was in Guam. "That was the first time I saw a dead Japanese," he said. "He looked pitiful . . . like an awkward kid who'd been taken right out of his home to this miserable place."

The movement and transitions put new strains on the lives of American families. The rate of both marriages and divorces went up during World War II. There were millions of absent fathers and husbands, some of whom never returned. Women entered the workforce in unprecedented numbers, with the total number of women employed outside the home in the United States increasing from 14 million in 1940 to 19 million in 1945. Many of the new female entrants to the workforce were married and had children. The lines between men's and women's professions also became more blurred. Women found jobs in physically demanding occupations such as in steel mills or shipyards. Augusta Clawson remembered working under grueling conditions as a welder at a shipyard in Oregon. In her diary she described her increasing confidence and hardening muscles as she wielded her blowtorch in the factory's sweltering heat. She became convinced that women welders got exhausted not because of the "work, nor the heat, nor the demands upon physical strength. It is the apprehension that arises from inadequate skill and consequent lack of confidence." But as she mastered the tools and methods of welding, she came to enjoy the job. Some of the growing trends in women's employment reversed after the war, of course, but the war marked a distinct change in the professional status of women.

As in World War I, African Americans found new opportunities in World War II to improve their economic and social standing. Fighting a war against fascism made the inequalities on the home front more conspicuous. The majority of African Americans still lived in the South, but World War II hastened the movement of blacks into other parts of the nation. Some 700,000 African Americans moved out of the South during the war. They found new jobs in war-related industries and the military, but they also found that discrimination lingered in hiring practices and pay. As illustrated by sailor Dorie Miller's work as a mess attendant, the navy explicitly barred blacks from combat and leadership roles at the beginning of the war. The secretary of the Navy during the war excused this policy by arguing that blacks could never exercise authority over whites in the military and that "teamwork, harmony and ship efficiency" would be jeopardized if African Americans became officers. In 1940, as part of the plans for instituting the military draft, the War Department explained that segregation of troops remained its official policy.

Still, people of color found opportunities to serve in critical capacities in the armed services. Mexican Americans were not as subject to rigorous segregation as were blacks. The Eighty-Eighth Division, which served with distinction in Italy, was made up largely of Hispanics, both officers and soldiers. The Second Division had many Mexican Americans from south Texas, and they participated in the invasion of France in 1944. During a German counteroffensive in Belgium in December 1944, Mexican-born Sergeant José López realized his company was about to be overrun by German tanks and troops. He saved the company almost single-handedly by grabbing a machine gun and shooting incessantly at the advancing forces until he ran out of ammunition. He recalled praying to the Virgin of Guadalupe, the patroness of Mexico, to save his life and protect his brother soldiers. When American observers surveyed the field after the battle, they calculated that López had killed at least 100 Germans. López was awarded the Medal of Honor in 1945.

Native American men also joined the US armed forces in disproportionately large numbers. Drawing on precedents from World War I, American commanders employed a number of Native Americans as "code talkers," people who used little-known native languages to prevent the enemy from capturing and deciphering transmissions. Code talkers served from Indian groups including the Choctaws and Comanches, among others. The most famous of the World War II code talkers were Navajos. A son of missionaries serving among the Navajos convinced a Marine major general to use them as code talkers, and the Navajo code talkers devised a secret method of communication for the Pacific theater that the Japanese could never break. The code was so complex that even Navajo prisoners of war, subject to torture by the Japanese to force them to divulge the meaning of the transmissions, could not understand it. By the end of the war, the Marines had trained about 400 Navajos as code talkers.

African Americans also found official fighting roles in the armed services. The army created an African American infantry division as well as a tank battalion. There were several airborne African American units, the most celebrated of which was the Ninety-Ninth Pursuit Squadron, or the "Tuskegee Airmen." They trained at the Tuskegee Institute in Alabama, the educational brainchild of Booker T. Washington. Pilots from the Ninety-Ninth served in North Africa and Italy. Eventually, the US Army Air Corps consolidated several squadrons of Tuskegee Airmen into the 332nd Fighter Group, which posted an active and successful combat record. They became best known for escorting bomber runs over enemy territory, and Tuskegee-trained pilots were responsible for the destruction of approximately 112 German airplanes in the air and 150 more on the ground.

In spite of the celebrated efforts of individual soldiers, sailors, and airmen, military and civilian discrimination against blacks remained common. In 1941, the black labor leader A. Philip Randolph, seizing upon the incongruities of how blacks were often treated in America, proposed that tens of thousands of African Americans should march on Washington in protest of employment discrimination. FDR pleaded with Randolph to call off the march, but he would not do so until he received assurances that the administration would announce

Figure 23.5. Photograph of several Tuskegee Airmen attending a briefing in Ramitelli, Italy, March 1945, by Toni Frissell.

a formal change in employment policy. Randolph got such an announcement with Executive Order 8802 in June 1941. It prohibited employment discrimination "in defense industries or government because of race, creed, color, or national origin." This did not directly address segregation and discrimination in the armed forces. (A directive by President Truman in 1948 would formally desegregate the military.) But Executive Order 8802 was a turning point in federal employment policy.

From World War II forward, the government has often used such policies to prohibit workplace discrimination against women, ethnic minorities, or people with disabilities. The Civil Rights Act of 1964 would ban employment discrimination against people on the basis of race, color, religion, sex, or national origin. The scope and ambition of antidiscrimination orders has continued to expand, more recently moving into areas related not just to race or gender but to sexuality. An executive order signed in 1995 by President Bill Clinton was the first instance of the federal government including "sexual orientation"—a legal term promoted by gay and lesbian activists—as a category protected from discrimination.

The desperate need for workers in war-related industries during World War II as well as those industries' new openness to African Americans fueled the surge of black out-migration from the South. During 1943, about 10,000 African Americans were arriving in Los Angeles per month. Sybil Lewis had been earning $3.50 a week in small-town Oklahoma. But she went to Los Angeles and found work as a riveter at Lockheed Aircraft, where she made $48 a week. She said that when she got her first paycheck, she had never seen so much money before. Lewis was able to go to college and eventually secured a government job. The influx of blacks and Mexicans in many American cities bred racial resentments and unrest, however. Detroit saw some of the worst violence between whites and blacks. The city had seen tens of thousands of blacks arrive in the city during the war years. But even more whites came to Detroit, many of them from Appalachia. In June 1943, the ethnic tension in Detroit erupted into open rioting. Before federal troops quelled the fighting, nine whites and twenty-five blacks had died.

Japanese Internment

National bitterness over the surprise attack on Pearl Harbor precipitated the relocation and detention of more than 110,000 Japanese Americans during the war. The majority of the interned Japanese were American citizens. Smaller numbers of German and Italian Americans were interned during the war as well. Roosevelt gave military commanders the power to carry out the relocation program in Executive Order 9066, justifying it by the need to take "every possible protection against espionage and against sabotage." Although evidence for planned Japanese attacks on the West Coast was negligible, the roundups of Japanese Americans began in February 1942. Strangely, US officials left the Japanese population of Hawaii largely untouched, even though the territory had the largest American concentration of Japanese population at the time.

Japanese evacuees were sent to rural detention camps across the West and South. The centers were "concentration" camps in the sense that they sought to isolate and detain a suspect population behind barbed wire, overseen by armed guards. (America saw nothing like the mass extermination programs of the Nazi death camps, however.) One of the largest camps was the Manzanar Relocation Center in a desert area of east-central California. Detainees lived in sparse barracks and were largely responsible for feeding themselves by gardening. Tensions could run high at the camps. In December 1942, protesters at Manzanar demanded that authorities release one of their leaders who was arrested after fighting with a suspected Japanese informant. Military police tried to disperse the protestors with tear gas and then opened fire into the crowd. Two detainees died.

The forced relocation of so many Japanese American citizens raised obvious questions about their due process rights and the government's powers in wartime. One Japanese American man, Fred Korematsu of San Leandro, California, was arrested for refusing to leave his home, and Korematsu challenged his conviction in court. In 1944, the Supreme Court affirmed his conviction in a 6–3 ruling in the case of *Korematsu v. United States*. The court argued that singling out Japanese Americans for detention was warranted in a time of urgent military need.

US officials began to allow many detainees to leave if they convincingly professed their loyalty to the American government and the Allied cause in World War II. Remarkably, thousands of fighting-age Japanese Americans left the camps to enlist in the American military. In all more than 25,000 Japanese Americans would serve in the US armed forces during the war. The segregated Japanese 442nd Regimental Combat Team served with great distinction in the European theater, with members earning more than 1,000 commendations for brave actions in combat.

The War in Europe

US assistance and British determination saved the United Kingdom from Nazi conquest, and the Nazi invasion of the Soviet Union bogged down outside Leningrad (St. Petersburg) in 1941–42. The Nazis then failed to conquer Stalingrad (Volgograd) in the titanic battle there in 1942–43, which resulted in some 2 million total soldiers dead,

Figure 23.6. "Evacuees of Japanese ancestry attending Memorial Day services at Manzanar, California, a War Relocation Authority center. Boy Scouts and American Legion members participating in the services appear in the foreground. 1942."

wounded, or captured. But the Allies struggled to find a way to open up a new offensive front within Europe. FDR agreed to Churchill's suggestion that the Allies first strike at the "soft underbelly" of the Axis Powers in the Mediterranean Sea, first in North Africa and then in Italy. Forces under American general Dwight Eisenhower entered Algeria and Morocco in late 1942 and then moved into Tunisia. There German general Erwin Rommel humiliated the American forces in the Battle of Kasserine Pass in early 1943. Eisenhower charged General George Patton with renewing the morale of the army and with better implementing America's industrial advantages in aircraft, artillery, and tanks. A combined British-American offensive in the spring of 1943 resulted in the Allied capture of some 250,000 Axis troops.

Patton, a former Olympic athlete in the pentathlon, proved to be one of the more feared and flamboyant of America's commanders when he led American forces onto the Italian island of Sicily in summer 1943. Patton was supposed to play a supporting role to British forces in the invasion, but instead he sped across the island to the key seaport of Messina. Along the way critics charged that his men had massacred German and

Figure 23.7. *People Leaving Buddhist Church, Winter II, Manzanar Relocation Center, California*, by Ansel Adams, photographer, 1943.

Italian prisoners of war in an incident at Biscari. Then Patton himself fell under criticism for berating and slapping soldiers recovering from "battle fatigue" in Allied field hospitals. He questioned the men's toughness and shouted that one of them should be "lined up against a wall and shot." An embarrassed Eisenhower had to temporarily relieve Patton of command. (The actor George C. Scott would portray the general in the 1970 war epic *Patton*, which won the Academy Award for Best Picture.) Italians deposed Mussolini when the Allies invaded Sicily. The subsequent Allied invasion of the Italian mainland effectively took Italy out of the war. In 1945, as the final vestiges of Axis power crumbled, Mussolini was executed by Italian communists, who publicly desecrated his corpse in Milan.

The American Army

By 1944, as the Allied invasion of France loomed, the US Army had more than 7 million men and women serving in it. That number had ballooned from the paltry 200,000 American troops in the army in 1940. All told, some 16 million Americans would work for the armed forces during World War II. Most of the men who served were draftees. The typical World War II "GI" was twenty-six in the year 1944, which meant he had been born the year World War I ended. This average soldier weighed 144 pounds and stood five feet eight inches tall. Less than half of white soldiers, and even fewer black soldiers, had finished a high school education.

The army established vast training camps, most of them in the South, which offered abundant undeveloped land and warm weather. Among the largest of the camps was Fort Benning, a site outside of Columbus, Georgia, that could accommodate as many as 100,000 soldiers in training. Soldiers in basic training typically awoke at 6:05 a.m., participated in the day's exercises from 8 a.m. to 5:30 p.m., and turned out the lights at 9:45 p.m. They learned basic military tactics, engaged in physical exercise, and learned about the reasons for the war from the film series Why We Fight, created by the celebrated Hollywood director Frank Capra. For many of the soldiers who grew up during the Depression, military service meant a steady job and three meals a day. The soldiers even got a life insurance policy with $10,000 of coverage.

The infantry divisions had no regional separations. Aside from some racial segregation, people from all over the United States served together, from rural and urban areas, from different economic classes, and from different religious backgrounds. World War II unintentionally was one of the most powerful forces in the twentieth century for reinforcing a sense of common American culture as millions of young men and hundreds of thousands of young women interacted with Americans quite different from the people back home. One midwesterner ironically noted, "The first time I ever heard a New England accent was at Fort Benning [Georgia]. The southerner was an exotic creature to me. People from the farms. The New York street-smarts. You had an incredible mixture of every stratum of society." The bonds the servicemen formed when they went overseas became even stronger. The same midwestern soldier said, "The reason you storm the beaches is not patriotism or bravery. It's that sense of not wanting to fail your buddies."

D-Day

The soldier's reference to "storming the beaches" suggested the turning point (from the American point of view) of the European theater of the war: the Allies' D-Day invasion of France in 1944. General Eisenhower and his British colleagues knew they would have to invade western Europe to break the Nazi stranglehold on the continent. How and where to invade was the greatest strategic challenge of the war. They ultimately focused on striking at the Normandy peninsula, west of Paris and across the English Channel from Portsmouth, the site of Eisenhower's headquarters. By summer 1944, Eisenhower and the Allies had assembled a force of 3 million troops and vast amounts of war-related materiel, positioned in the south of England and ready to cross the English Channel.

Eisenhower, who had served in numerous army positions before becoming the American commander in the European theater in June 1942, had to make the excruciating decision of when to launch the D-Day invasion. Factors from the light of the moon to the timing of tides came into play for the date of the complex operation. They originally settled on June 5, but a stormy forecast forced the Allies to delay D-Day until June 6.

American and British paratroopers began dropping into France in the predawn darkness of June 6, 1944. The Nazis were confused about whether this line of parachutists represented a small probing action or the full invasion they knew the Allies had long planned. (As the invasion began, Hitler was in a drug-induced deep sleep and would not hear about the assault until noon on the sixth.) More than 6,000 Allied ships moved across the Channel, and Allied aircraft would run 15,000 individual missions on that single day. Troops on the Allied transport ships carried sixty-eight pounds of gear as they prepared to face German guns in Normandy. The US Fourth Division at the beach code-named Utah took only light casualties. The First Division at Omaha Beach met fierce resistance from German machine guns and artillery, and many American soldiers died there without even making it out of the surf. One of the first groups to make it through the beach and up the cliff overlooking it was a Ranger Assault Group that scaled and captured the 100-foot Pointe du Hoc. These Rangers lost more than half their men during the first two days of the invasion. Total American casualties during the Normandy landings on June 6 have been estimated at about 6,600.

In his D-Day message to the troops, Eisenhower called the invasion a "Great Crusade" and assured the soldiers, "The eyes of the world are upon you. The hope and prayers of liberty-loving people everywhere march with you. In company with our brave Allies and brothers-in-arms on other Fronts, you will bring about the destruction of the German war machine, the elimination of Nazi tyranny over the oppressed peoples of Europe, and security for ourselves in a free world."

As FDR announced the D-Day invasion to Americans, he asked that they join him in prayer.

Almighty God: Our sons, pride of our Nation, this day have set upon a mighty endeavor, a struggle to preserve our Republic, our religion, and our civilization, and to set free a suffering humanity. . . . With Thy blessing, we shall prevail over the unholy forces of our enemy. Help us to conquer the apostles of greed and racial arrogancies. Lead us to the saving of our country, and with our sister Nations into a world unity that will spell a sure peace, a peace invulnerable to the schemings of unworthy men. And a peace that will let all of men live in freedom, reaping the just rewards of their honest toil.

Once the Allies broke through the German lines in France, there was little to stop them as they raced across the French countryside. They liberated Paris and approached the French-German border faster than the commanders had anticipated, creating major supply problems and leaving the Allies vulnerable to counterattack. In December 1944, the Germans launched a surprise offensive through the Ardennes Forest, resulting in a struggle that became known as the "Battle of the Bulge." Nazi forces cut through a lightly guarded section of the Allied front, creating a German "bulge" in the line that ran sixty miles into territory the Allies had once held. In one of the most celebrated exchanges of the war, the Germans offered an "honorable surrender" to Anthony McAuliffe, acting commander of the US 101st Airborne Division, which was stationed at the key French junction of Bastogne. McAuliffe coldly rejected the offer, writing, "To the German commander: Nuts! The American commander." The encircled 101st staged a heroic defense of Bastogne until the (reinstated) General George Patton swiftly sent three American divisions into the flank of the German bulge and relieved the besieged troops at Bastogne.

The Battle of the Bulge lasted for a month until the Allied forces—led mostly by American fighters—drove the Germans back to their previous position, sealing off the bulge. Although the episode was really more a series of separate engagements than a single event, 600,000 US troops participated in the Battle of the Bulge, arguably the largest battle in the history of the American army. The Americans took heavy casualties, with 19,000 soldiers dying during the offensive. But the Germans also suffered terrible losses, ones they could not afford since they were fighting in the west and in the east against the Soviets. The Battle of the Bulge undoubtedly hastened the Nazis' demise.

The War Ends in Europe

In the late stages of the war, Allied commanders debated how to bring the conflict to the speediest end possible, with the fewest Allied deaths. In both the Pacific and in Europe, this quandary led some to argue for taking the war directly against Japanese and German civilian populations. Although some American pilots worried that indiscriminate bombing of cities would tar them as "baby killers," both British and

American commanders expressed some interest in doing whatever it took to devastate the "morale" of the Axis nations. In Europe this desire led to Allied bombing of Berlin and Dresden in February 1945 that killed tens of thousands of German civilians.

Dresden became an especially notorious episode because the bombing unleashed a literal firestorm in the city, killing some 35,000 people, many by burning or asphyxiation. In 1969, the American writer Kurt Vonnegut published a satirical novel, *Slaughterhouse-Five*, which included a semiautobiographical account of the Dresden bombing. Vonnegut himself had been a prisoner in Dresden when it happened. American critics in 1945 contended that the American commanders ordered the "terror bombing of the great German population centers as a ruthless expedient to hasten Hitler's doom."

Allied forces closed in on Berlin from the east and the west. As they proceeded, some of the American troops got a firsthand look at the aftermath of the Holocaust, or the Nazis' systematic murder of 6 million Jews and other peoples regarded as dangerous or undesirable. In April 1945, George Patton's army liberated prisoners who were left at Buchenwald, one of the largest of the death camps in Germany. (Some of the largest camps, such as Treblinka and Auschwitz, were constructed in Nazi-occupied Poland.) Edward R. Murrow described the horrific scenes at Buchenwald for millions of American listeners to the CBS radio network. He told of the cadaverous prisoners, smelling of death and packed into impossibly close quarters. At the crematorium the Nazis had run out of fuel to burn the bodies of those they executed, so they had just started stacking the naked corpses in piles. Elsewhere Murrow saw piles of gold teeth, human hair, and children's shoes in the thousands. He pleaded with the American audience: "I pray you to believe what I have said about Buchenwald. I have reported what I saw and heard, but only part of it."

CBS, the *New York Times*, and other media outlets had been warning Americans since 1942 that the Nazis were planning the "greatest mass slaughter in history." But aside from small numbers of special cases, such as Albert Einstein, the US government was reluctant to receive many European Jewish refugees. The State Department issued a number of new regulations designed to keep most Jews out, as many Americans worried that some of the prospective Jewish migrants might actually be Axis collaborators. On the heels of the Depression, much of the nation remained fearful about impoverished foreigners taking American jobs. Jewish leaders insisted that the Allies should at least launch air strikes on Auschwitz and other camps to disrupt the killing factories of the Holocaust. But doing so never became a priority for the Americans and British, so they were left to liberate the small numbers of prisoners who remained alive. For the Nazi orchestrators of the Holocaust, the end had also come. When Soviet troops entered

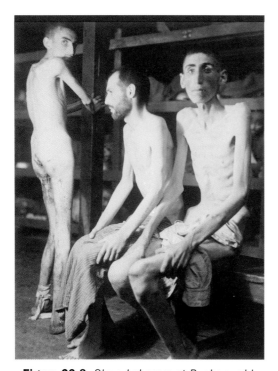

Figure 23.8. *Slave Laborers at Buchenwald.*
(Original title: *These Russian, Polish,
and Dutch slave laborers interned at the
Buchenwald concentration camp averaged
160 pounds each prior to entering camp
11 months ago. Their average weight is now
70 pounds. Germany, April 16, 1945.*)

Berlin in late April 1945, Adolf Hitler chose to commit suicide rather than face capture and trial. The remaining German forces unconditionally surrendered to General Eisenhower on May 7, 1945.

FDR did not live to see the Germans surrender, either. He had handily defeated the Republican challenger Thomas Dewey in the 1944 presidential election, winning an unprecedented fourth term in the White House. In spite of his declining health, in February 1945 Roosevelt attended a summit of Allied leaders in the Black Sea town of Yalta, in the Soviet Union. There the Russian premier Joseph Stalin began to set the stage for Soviet domination of Eastern Europe, even though Stalin, Churchill, and FDR affirmed the need for free elections in postwar Europe. When FDR returned to the United States, he sought rest at his retreat in Warm Springs, Georgia, where he suffered a stroke and died on April 12, 1945. Harry S. Truman, a Missouri senator who had joined FDR's ticket as vice president for the 1944 campaign, became president.

Victory in the Pacific

Following the turning point at the Battle of Midway in 1942, Allied forces pushed back Japanese control of the Pacific theater in fighting that often moved from island to island. The first American offensive came against the Solomon Islands in the south Pacific, including the key Japanese base at Guadalcanal. Marines captured the Japanese airfield at Guadalcanal in August 1942, but the Japanese repeatedly attacked the American foothold there. In November, American and Japanese naval forces engaged in an incredibly destructive battle in and around Guadalcanal. The Americans won, though at the price of a number of naval vessels sunk by the Japanese. The Japanese soon determined it was futile to try to hold Guadalcanal and prepared to evacuate the island, vacating it in early 1943. After Guadalcanal the Japanese were forced into a defensive stance in the Pacific. American forces under Douglas MacArthur and Chester Nimitz inched closer and closer to the Japanese home islands.

By summer 1944, the Allies had taken islands such as Guam, Saipan, and Tinian, which put them within the range of bombers to conduct runs over Japan itself. As in Germany this allowed Allied commanders to consider a campaign that would decimate and demoralize the Japanese population. Air Force commander Curtis LeMay engaged in a new campaign in early 1945, using bombs and incendiary weapons to wreak destruction on Japanese towns and homes. Enough bombing and conflagrations could, as in Dresden, create firestorms engulfing entire cities. LeMay's forces targeted sixty-six Japanese cities, but the most controversial attack came against Tokyo in March 1945. Hundreds of bombers precipitated a firestorm in the city, enveloping hundreds of thousands of the city's mostly wooden homes and killing an estimated 90,000 Japanese people. The Tokyo firestorm may have initially killed more Japanese than even the atomic bombs America soon dropped on Hiroshima and Nagasaki.

American strategists were divided about the best way to end the war with Japan. Even with the horrific results of the firebombings, it was not clear whether Japan would ever agree to an unconditional surrender. If they did not, the Allies feared an invasion of Japan would mean hundreds of thousands more Allied casualties. The Battle of Okinawa, beginning on Easter Sunday 1945, was the largest amphibious assault of the war's Pacific theater. It claimed approximately 82,000 American casualties. (Okinawa is a large island 340 miles from mainland Japan.) So the Truman administration turned to the atomic bomb as the means to end the Pacific war. Albert Einstein and other physicists had warned FDR before World War II began that such a weapon was feasible and the American government should start developing one before the Germans beat them to it. That knowledge prompted the creation of the secret Manhattan Project. A team of scientists and engineers led by physicist Robert Oppenheimer developed the enriched uranium and plutonium required for the bomb, which they tested for the first time in an isolated area of New Mexico on July 16, 1945. The weapon sparked a chain reaction of nuclear fission, setting off an explosion of unfathomable power and destructive energy. The scientists at the Los Alamos, New Mexico, laboratory produced two nuclear bombs, the uranium-based "Little Boy" and the plutonium weapon "Fat Man."

A number of the nuclear scientists had qualms about using the bomb against a city, but President Truman and Secretary of War Henry Stimson decided to drop the bomb on Hiroshima with little prior notice to the Japanese. "When you have to deal with a beast you have to treat him as a beast," Truman explained shortly after the bombings. Hiroshima was struck on August 6, 1945. A B-29 bomber dropped the 8,000-ton Little Boy over Hiroshima, and it detonated at just under 2,000 feet of altitude to maximize the damage. The bomb incinerated four square miles of the city, killing some 60,000 people. Estimates suggest that another 60,000 people died in Hiroshima within a year of the explosion due to injuries and radioactive fallout.

Two days after Hiroshima the Soviet Union declared war on Japan and invaded the Japanese-controlled Chinese region of Manchuria. Then, on August 9, the United States dropped the second atomic bomb, Fat Man, on Nagasaki. (Cloud cover spared the people of the Americans' initial target, the city of Kokura.) The devastation at Nagasaki was contained somewhat by the city's mountainous terrain, but still the death tolls were appalling: perhaps 80,000 fatalities were attributed to the bomb by the end of 1945. Fat Man exploded almost directly over a hospital, which was obliterated along with a square mile of Nagasaki. The emperor of Japan realized the nation could not afford to continue its struggle against the Allied powers, and he agreed to an unconditional surrender on August 14, 1945.

In America some Christian critics said that such indiscriminate killing of civilians and noncombatants did not live up to the standards of the Christian tradition of just-war theory. Others argued that the bombs, horrific as they were, ended up sparing the lives of Allied forces who fought against Japanese tyranny. Still others believed nuclear weapons made clearer how the Bible's grim descriptions of the last days could come true, such as 2 Peter 3:10's forecast that the world's elements would "melt with fervent heat, the earth also and the works that are therein shall be burned." The American people generally supported the use of the atomic bomb at the time. Support for atomic weapons waned after the war, especially as details of the terrible consequences in Hiroshima and Nagasaki became better known.

The Dawn of American Global Dominance

With much of Europe in ruins, the United States emerged from World War II as the world's new superpower. Its military, especially the navy and air force, was the most powerful in the world. America alone had successfully used the atomic bomb. Spurred by the ravenous demands of the war, America's gross national product had more than doubled during the conflict. The United States now possessed half of the entire world's

Figure 23.9. V-J Day celebrations in Jackson Square,
Oak Ridge, Tennessee, August 14, 1945.

capacity for manufacturing, created more than half of the world's supply of electricity, and produced more than twice the oil of all other nations combined. The statistics could go on, but the point was that the United States was ascendant in a unique way. The Soviet Union would go on to challenge the United States militarily. Multinational organizations, such as the Organization of the Petroleum Exporting Countries (OPEC), would contest American dominance in certain economic sectors. But in terms of sheer military and economic might, there was no doubt about the preeminent stature of the United States in the post–World War II era. America and its allies had vanquished the threat of the totalitarian powers together, but the United States stood alone after the war as the world's preeminent nation, militarily and economically.

■ SELECTED BIBLIOGRAPHY ■

Breitman, Richard, and Allan J. Lichtman. *FDR and the Jews*. Cambridge, MA: Harvard University Press, 2013.

Hartmann, Susan M. *The Home Front and Beyond: American Women in the 1940s*. Boston: G. K. Hall, 1982.

Iriye, Akira. *Pearl Harbor and the Coming of the Pacific War: A Brief History with Documents and Essays*. Boston: Bedford/St. Martin's, 1999.

Keegan, John. *The Second World War*. New York: Viking Penguin, 1989.

Kennedy, David M. *Freedom from Fear: The American People in Depression and War, 1929–1945*. New York: Oxford University Press, 1999.

Moye, J. Todd. *Freedom Flyers: The Tuskegee Airmen of World War II*. New York: Oxford University Press, 2012.

Murray, Williamson, and Allan R. Millett. *A War to Be Won: Fighting the Second World War*. Cambridge, MA: Harvard University Press, 2001.

Piehler, G. Kurt, ed. *The United States in World War II: A Documentary Reader*. Malden, MA: Wiley-Blackwell, 2013.

Robinson, Greg. *By Order of the President: FDR and the Internment of Japanese Americans*. Cambridge, MA: Harvard University Press, 2001.

Symonds, Craig L. *The Battle of Midway*. New York: Oxford University Press, 2011.

Tomblin, Barbara Brooks. *G.I. Nightingales: The Army Nurse Corps in World War II*. Lexington: University Press of Kentucky, 1996.

Winkler, Allan M. *Home Front U.S.A.: America during World War II*. 3rd ed. Wheeling, IL: Wiley-Blackwell, 2012.

24

The Cold War

Winston Churchill resigned as British prime minister in July 1945 after his party suffered a crushing defeat in a general election. He remained a key opposition leader in Parliament and warned Britain and America that the next great threat to their interests—and to freedom around the world—would be Soviet communism. In a 1946 address at Missouri's Westminster College, with President Harry Truman sharing the platform, Churchill described the sphere of Soviet influence in Europe as an "iron curtain":[*]

> A shadow has fallen upon the scenes so lately lighted by the Allied victory. We welcome constant, frequent and growing contacts between the Russian people and our own people on both sides of the Atlantic. It is my duty however, for I am sure you would wish me to state the facts as I see them to you, to place before you certain facts about the present position in Europe. From Stettin in the Baltic to Trieste in the Adriatic, an iron curtain has descended across the Continent. Behind that line lie all the capitals of the ancient states of Central and Eastern Europe. Warsaw, Berlin, Prague, Vienna, Budapest, Belgrade, Bucharest and Sofia, all these famous cities and the populations around them lie in what I must call the Soviet sphere.

He reminded the audience that he had recognized the Nazi threat for what it was earlier than most observers in the 1930s. "Last time I saw it all coming and cried aloud to my

---

[*] "Winston Churchill's 'Iron Curtain speech' regarding USSR and Eastern Bloc," YouTube video, 7:07, July 2, 2014, https://www.youtube.com/watch?v=lMt7zCaVOWU.

own fellow-countrymen and to the world, but no one paid any attention." He did not want the Western powers to make the same tragic mistake again.

Soviet leader Joseph Stalin scoffed at Churchill's speech and accused Britain and America of trying to provoke a new war with Russia. The Truman administration would come to promote a doctrine of "containment" against the extension of Soviet power in Europe and Asia. Journalist Walter Lippmann, skeptical of the globalist ambitions of the Truman administration, published a 1947 book titled *The Cold War*, in which he warned against pursuing a worldwide clash with Russia. Lippmann's term "Cold War" stuck. This conflict between America and its allies and the Soviets and their allies lasted four and a half decades and represented the central concern of American foreign policy. The Americans and Soviets furiously sought to extend and protect their global spheres of influence, as well as to prepare their militaries for eventual war. Both sides understood, however, that the next world war could precipitate the use of the next generation of nuclear bombs, far more powerful than the ones America had used against Japan in 1945. That prospect was so frightening that many wished to keep the Cold War as "cold," or as noncombative, as possible. "Hot" war between the West and the Soviets could result in nation-killing destruction on both sides.

The Coming of the Cold War

Whether the Cold War was inevitable, the ideological differences between the United States and Soviet Russia were stark. The United States largely embraced capitalism and the private ownership of businesses while the Soviets touted socialism and state ownership of businesses. Although America had its own outbreaks of persecution against dissenters, the United States professed a constitutional commitment to freedom of speech and religion. The Soviet Union ruthlessly suppressed critical political speech and persecuted people of devout beliefs. John Foster Dulles, secretary of state under President Eisenhower, argued that atheism was the foundation of all other Soviet beliefs: "Soviet communism starts with an atheistic, Godless premise. Everything else flows from that premise. If there is no God, there is no moral or natural law." Dulles and other critics of Soviet power argued that because of their Marxist philosophy, the Soviets expected continual war against the capitalist powers.

During World War II common enemies in Germany and Japan had made allies of the United States and the Soviet Union. But theirs was always an alliance of convenience. The end of the war left Russia and the United States scrambling in Europe and Asia to maintain as much influence as possible as nations entered the new postwar order. The Soviets were deeply concerned about the American use of the atomic bomb and vowed to develop and test a bomb of their own. This, the Soviets believed, would provide some balance against the enormous military advantages the Americans enjoyed. The Soviets resented the fact that the US government had advised Britain about the Manhattan Project but did not inform Russia. At the Yalta Conference in February 1945, Stalin, Churchill, and FDR agreed on the need for the establishment of what would become the United Nations. They also professed a desire to afford all nations the right of political self-determination, free from outside interference. However, they also divvied the world up into zones of special influence for each of their countries, including Eastern Europe for the Soviets. FDR and then Truman would disagree with Stalin about just how much influence the Soviets should exercise in countries such as Poland and in the Soviet zone of control in Germany. By the late 1940s, the Soviets had helped install communist governments in Poland, Hungary, Romania, Czechoslovakia, and East Germany.

Containment

In February 1946, American diplomat George Kennan sent the "long telegram" from Moscow that helped many American leaders interpret Soviet actions. Americans should expect the Soviets to be paranoid and aggressive, Kennan said. "At bottom of Kremlin's neurotic view of world affairs is traditional and instinctive Russian sense of insecurity. . . . They have always feared foreign penetration, feared direct contact between Western world and their own, feared what would happen if Russians learned truth about world without or if foreigners learned truth about world within. And they have learned to seek security only in patient but deadly struggle for total destruction of rival power." Kennan warned Truman administration officials that the Soviets could never accept "peaceful coexistence."

The Truman administration watched with concern as the nations of Eastern Europe turned communist and fell under the sway of the Soviets. The president knew the Soviets were also working to extend their influence into Turkey and Greece, and in 1947 he asked Congress to send assistance to help these nations counteract that influence. The president articulated what became known as the Truman Doctrine, or America's obligation to "support free peoples who are resisting attempted subjugation by armed minorities or by outside pressures."

An important corollary to the Truman Doctrine was the policy of "containment," which George Kennan first articulated in a 1947 article. Kennan contended that

> the main element of any United States policy toward the Soviet Union must be that of long-term, patient but firm and vigilant containment of Russian expansive tendencies. . . . Soviet pressure against the free institutions of the western

world is something that can be contained by the adroit and vigilant application of counter-force at a series of constantly shifting geographical and political points, corresponding to the shifts and maneuvers of Soviet policy, but which cannot be charmed or talked out of existence.

He believed God's Providence had specially positioned Americans to take responsibility for containment, the moral and political challenge of their generation.

Kennan was a foreign policy realist who felt it was best to assume the Soviets were always plotting against the free nations of the world. Some of his convictions about Russia surely derived from his Presbyterian faith and dim view of human nature. "I have a great horror of people who have no fear of God," Kennan explained. After having worked for the State Department in the Soviet Union, Kennan regarded Russia as the "most impressive example of hell on earth that our time has known."

Aside from aid to threatened nations such as Greece and Turkey, Truman knew his administration had to help the free nations of postwar Europe become stable again. If they did, then those nations presumably could stave off any possible Soviet-backed insurgencies. So, in 1947, Truman's secretary of state, George Marshall (a general and former army chief of staff during World War II), announced what became known as the Marshall Plan for European recovery. The plan's aims, Marshall explained, were to alleviate "hunger, poverty, desperation, and chaos. . . . In this trying period, between a war that is over and a peace that is not yet secure, the destitute and oppressed of the earth look chiefly to us for sustenance and support until they can again face life with self-confidence and self-reliance."

The winter of 1946–47 had been unusually harsh in western Europe, compounding people's suffering in the aftermath of World War II. As spring 1947 came around, Winston Churchill said that Europe was a "rubble-heap, a charnel house, a breeding ground of pestilence and hate." Although congressional critics worried about the enormous expense of the Marshall Plan, Congress eventually sent more than $13 billion in recovery aid to European countries between 1948 and 1952. The Marshall Plan helped rebuild the wrecked infrastructure of western Europe and restore industry and farming to prewar levels of production. Most observers agree that the Marshall Plan stabilized postwar Europe and protected the western European countries from communist rule. The program of aid also set a pattern of US government spending in foreign countries as a tool of diplomacy. In many other cases (through the present day), the benefits of foreign aid have been less clear than they were with the Marshall Plan.

National Security

The fear of communist power also spurred the Truman administration to create a stronger "national security" establishment. In 1947, Congress passed the National Security Act, which would become one of the most consequential measures of the postwar years. It replaced the Department of War with the Department of Defense, which consolidated American military operations under the secretary of defense. It also expanded the president's resources for defense planning and intelligence gathering by creating both the National Security Council and the Central Intelligence Agency. In 1952, Truman would also create the National Security Agency, a top-secret military spy department. The work of these intelligence agencies caused enduring controversy, not least because of unauthorized leaks in 2013 that suggested the NSA was gathering information on the telephone records and electronic communications of millions of US citizens. In the short term, however, Truman's CIA and NSA remained relatively small and noncontroversial.

The United States also assured its democratic allies in Western Europe that it would come to their aid in the event of Soviet attack. This intention was confirmed by the creation of the North Atlantic Treaty Organization (NATO) in 1949. The United States and Canada joined ten European countries, including Britain, France, and Italy, in a mutual defense pact affirming that an attack on one member of NATO represented an attack on all members. This unprecedented peacetime alliance reflected US policymakers' intense concern that Western Europe had to be saved from the Soviets, even if joining NATO risked dragging America into another European war. Many in America believed isolationism had allowed the Nazis to become a much direr threat, and they vowed not to let the Soviets run roughshod over the rest of Europe. The Soviets saw the NATO alliance as a significant escalation of tensions in the Cold War. In 1950, Truman appointed Dwight Eisenhower, who had coordinated the D-Day invasion in 1944, as supreme commander of NATO forces in Europe.

The tensions between the democratic powers and the Soviets came to a head over the division of Berlin, Germany, in 1948–49. After World War II, Berlin was divided into French, British, American, and Soviet zones of occupation, but the whole city lay within the eastern part of Germany, which was controlled by the Soviets. In June 1948, Joseph Stalin cut off democratic West Berlin from all incoming road and rail traffic. Slowly the city ran out of food and supplies. Truman decided to break the blockade by airlifting thousands of tons of aid to the city every day. The president feared that the United States and Russia would go to war over the confrontation in Berlin. But Stalin did not wish to provoke a military conflict by shooting down the cargo planes flying into Berlin. The Soviets remained mindful that the Americans could employ nuclear weapons should a war begin. The airlift succeeded, and by the middle of 1949, the Soviets had backed down and allowed traffic into Berlin to resume. But later in 1949, communists backed by the Soviet Union proclaimed the creation of communist East Germany, or the so-called German Democratic Republic. Its capital was East Berlin. (In 1961, East Germany constructed the Berlin Wall to divide the city permanently and to prevent unauthorized departures from the East into Western-aligned West Berlin.)

Truman and the 1948 Election

In spite of his successful fight against the blockade of Berlin, Truman's prospects for election in 1948 looked grim until the eve of voting. He faced a host of critics within the Democratic Party, many of whom wished to replace him as the 1948 nominee. African Americans and progressive whites in the party demanded civil rights reforms. For Truman, taking a strong stance against segregation would surely provoke anger among southern whites, one of the pillars of FDR's Democratic coalition. When Truman ordered the gradual desegregation of the armed forces and indicated his support for a progressive civil rights plank in the Democratic Party platform, it created a backlash among Deep South Democrats. Some southern delegates staged a noisy walkout at the Democratic convention and nominated South Carolina's Strom Thurmond for president as a States' Rights Democrat, or "Dixiecrat."

A staunch defender of racial segregation, Strom Thurmond had been elected governor of South Carolina in 1946. He had served in World War II, participating in the D-Day invasion by using a glider to land in Normandy as part of the Eighty-Second Airborne Division. Thurmond couched his opposition to civil rights reform in ideological appeals to states' rights and to anti-communism. Progressive aggression on racial and employment issues would foment "race and class hatred," Thurmond warned, and "create the chaos and confusion which leads to communism." As a presidential candidate, Thurmond temporarily broke the Democrats' hold on the "solid South," winning the electoral votes of four Deep South states. The Dixiecrats also hinted at the Democrats' fundamental problem in trying to maintain their hold on both northern black and southern white voters. Thurmond himself would switch to the Republican Party in the 1960s, heralding the transformation of the Democrats' solid South into a Republican one by the 1980s. He would go on to become the longest-serving US senator in American history, representing South Carolina from 1956 to 2003. He died shortly after retiring from the Senate, at the age of 100.

In 1948, liberal Democrats also wanted more decisive action from Truman on civil rights, and they recoiled against his interventionist stance on Soviet power in Europe. With the Democrats so badly divided, the Republicans saw their best chance at winning the presidency since 1928. But their nominee, New York governor Thomas Dewey, proved to be a lackluster candidate. Truman primarily campaigned on the social reforms he favored, including a higher minimum wage, increased Social Security coverage, inflation and price controls, and a more progressive tax code. Returning to common Democratic themes of the Depression era, Truman succeeded in painting Dewey as a tone-deaf Republican who favored business interests over common people.

The political media, focused on the disarray within Democratic ranks, failed to realize that Truman's enthusiastic campaign was building a populist insurgency in his favor. As Truman railed against Republican "bloodsuckers" and Wall Street elites, large crowds shouted encouragement, saying, "Give 'em hell, Harry!" That phrase became a nickname for Truman. Almost all political analysts picked Dewey to win, and the *Chicago Tribune*'s Election Day evening edition proclaimed, "Dewey Defeats Truman." But Truman had the last laugh, winning almost half of the popular vote, in spite of third-party runs by Thurmond and by Henry Wallace on the Progressive Party ticket. Truman won 303 electoral votes to Dewey's 189.

Truman and the Hydrogen Bomb

Truman had originally proposed that the United States begin to scale back its defense spending in 1949. But Soviet aggression turned the administration toward escalating military spending and prompted the development of the hydrogen bomb as the next-generation nuclear weapon. In 1948, a Soviet-backed communist coup overthrew the government of Czechoslovakia. Then, in 1949, the Soviets successfully tested their own atomic bomb. That same year communists took control of China. The fear of communist power prodded the Truman administration into an "arms race" to develop the hydrogen bomb before the Soviets did. Key scientists, including Albert Einstein, called on the United States to restrain the arms race and the quest for the hydrogen bomb. Einstein said the contest between the Soviets and the United States was taking on a "hysterical character"; he worried that "annihilation of any life on earth" was becoming a real technological possibility. Diplomat George Kennan also opposed the development of the "Super," as the hydrogen bomb was known, preferring a minimalist approach to deterrence. As illustrated by the destruction of Hiroshima and Nagasaki, the United States already possessed more than enough power to wreak mass devastation. Kennan contended that the Soviets and the United States should negotiate an end to the contest for ever-greater numbers of phenomenally powerful weapons. They should accept the reality that both sides possessed the power to unleash crippling damage on the other and make a firm agreement never to be the first to use that power.

Other American leaders argued that refusal to develop the hydrogen bomb smacked of appeasement. The Soviets would presumably build their own hydrogen bomb, regardless of what they promised. Truman agreed, and in early 1950 he authorized the project to build the Super. Of course, Truman hardly wished for the nation to use such a weapon, knowing that doing so would unleash massive retaliation by the Soviets. But he believed the new weapon was needed as an ever-present threat that could contain Soviet aggression.

Scientists at the Los Alamos National Laboratory, led by the anti-communist Hungarian physicist Edward Teller, worked feverishly to solve the technical and mathematical dilemmas involved with setting off a thermonuclear explosion. Such an explosion required achieving the kind of extreme heat only found naturally in stars. The Los Alamos scientists employed computers, one of the first major American projects to use this new technology. The first hydrogen bomb, code-named "Mike," weighed more than a million pounds and stood three stories high. The United States tested it at a small atoll in the Marshall Islands in the North Pacific on November 1, 1952. The resulting explosion was unlike any man-made event seen before in world history. The telltale mushroom cloud the bomb created was 1,200 miles wide and 25 miles high. Observers estimated that a similar explosion set off in the United States would have annihilated any midsize city, such as Washington, DC.

The Soviets conducted their own successful test of a hydrogen bomb in 1953. Although both nations had to keep working on a version of the bomb that was deliverable by missile, the Cold War had entered the era of nuclear "proliferation." Other nations, including Britain and China, would go on to develop their own nuclear bombs. Many in the international community have expressed grave concern about the spread of the technology and its possible use by terrorists or rogue states such as North Korea, which began to develop thermonuclear weapons in the early twenty-first century.

The policy behind the arms race was framed by National Security Council Document 68 (NSC-68), drawn up by Paul Nitze, Kennan's replacement at the State Department. This secret document was issued in April 1950 and painted a grim view of the clash between Soviet and American power. NSC-68 explained that "the Soviet Union, unlike previous aspirants to hegemony, is animated by a new fanatic faith, antithetical to our own, and seeks to impose its absolute authority over the rest of the world. . . . With the development of increasingly terrifying weapons of mass destruction, every individual faces the ever-present possibility of annihilation should the conflict enter the phase of total war." Massive increases in defense spending were required so that America and its NATO allies would always possess more military force than the Soviets and their allies. One historian has called NSC-68 the blueprint for waging the Cold War.

The Communist Threat and Korea

American observers watched Asia with keen interest, waiting to see if communism would spread there as it had in Eastern Europe. American authorities led by General Douglas MacArthur tightly controlled the postwar rebuilding of Japan, keeping Soviet influence out. But the ideal of containment suffered a terrible blow in 1949 when the nationalist government of China fell to Chinese communist insurgents led by Mao Zedong. Soon thereafter, Mao and Stalin struck an agreement that confirmed Americans' worst fears: China was now part of the Soviet sphere of influence. The Chinese-Soviet relationship would sour a decade later, but at the outset of the Cold War, many American observers expected much of the world to fall into Soviet and American spheres of influence, leaving little room for "third world" nations. The United States could not afford, they believed, to lose more nations in southeast Asia.

This concern set the stage for conflict between the US-backed government of South Korea and the Soviet-backed communists of North Korea. The Korean peninsula, which bordered both China and the Soviet Union, had been freed from Japanese control at the end of World War II. Allied forces split the country at the thirty-eighth parallel. The Soviets helped the communist North Koreans, under the rule of Kim Il Sung, to develop a powerful army. Then, with both Stalin's and Mao's blessings, the North Koreans invaded South Korea in June 1950, seeking to unify the nation under communist control.

Truman saw the invasion of South Korea as a repeat of Nazi-style aggression from the 1930s, and he was determined not to repeat the mistake of appeasement. His administration went to the United Nations (created in 1945) and secured a Security Council resolution condemning the North Koreans' actions and authorizing a military response. The Soviets boycotted the vote, even though they were permanent members of the Security Council. Small numbers of troops from fifteen member nations of the UN participated in this "police action," but the United States supplied about 90 percent of the UN fighting force against the North Koreans. Because the authorization came from the United Nations, Truman decided not to call the Korean conflict a "war." Thus, he did not believe he needed to approach Congress for a formal declaration of war. This set an important precedent: from Korea forward the United States engaged in a number of small- and large-scale conflicts overseas for which the president did not get a formal declaration of war from Congress. This change has significantly increased the president's powers as "commander in chief" and reduced congressional oversight over making war.

At first the formidable North Korean army ran roughshod over the South. But in September 1950, Douglas MacArthur launched a successful counteroffensive, landing his forces on the west coast of Korea near Seoul and trapping much of the North Korean army in the south. MacArthur's campaign was so successful it convinced President Truman to take the war into the north, trying to unify Korea under pro-American control. The administration and MacArthur assumed China would not intervene to save North Korea for communism. They were wrong. As UN forces approached the China–North Korea border in November 1950, the Chinese sent hundreds of thousands of troops into North Korea in a counterattack.

The shocked American and UN army was forced to retreat under dire winter conditions in nighttime temperatures that reached as low as −35 degrees Fahrenheit. The US First Marine Division, trapped at the Chosin Reservoir, fought through waves of Chinese soldiers and ice and snow to get to their escape at the port of Hungnam on the northeast coast of the peninsula. The cold temperatures rendered supplies useless, including everything from rifles to jeep batteries and medical equipment. Andy Anderson, a Marine from Fond du Lac, Wisconsin, recalled that the "worst was the guys who froze to death, mostly the enemy. They were even worse off than us. Some of them didn't have boots. You'd see them all stiff and frozen, their legs sticking up, their feet wrapped in rags. And you'd move on." Even for the Marines who were fully equipped, the insides of their boots often froze onto their legs during the retreat from Chosin.

UN forces retreated to the thirty-eighth parallel. As the war became increasingly unpopular in America, growing political pressure and frustration over the Chinese invasion led Truman to seek a negotiated peace with China. His peace terms included leaving North Korea under communist control. Douglas MacArthur was indignant, believing American-led forces should regroup, destroy the communist army, and unify Korea under the pro-American government. MacArthur became brazen in his criticism of the Truman administration, telling a Republican congressman in a public letter in 1951 that Korea was the focus of the great global struggle between communism and freedom. Losing in Korea would have cascading effects around the world, including in Europe. "We must win. There is no substitute for victory," MacArthur wrote. Truman felt this public insubordination left him no other option, so he fired MacArthur in April. Even after MacArthur's termination, the war and peace negotiations dragged on. The Korean War did not officially conclude until July 1953, by which time 37,000

Figure 24.1. A column of troops and armor of the First Marine Division move through communist Chinese lines during their successful breakout from the Chosin Reservoir in North Korea. The Marines were besieged when the Chinese entered the Korean War on November 27, 1950, by sending 200,000 shock troops against Allied forces.

Americans had died in the war, Soviet leader Joseph Stalin had died, and America had elected a new president: Dwight D. Eisenhower. The peace agreement left the boundaries of North and South Korea nearly the same as before the war began. It also left intractable hostility between the two Koreas. North Korea remained a grim, isolated, and unpredictable communist holdout, even after the collapse of communism in the Soviet-bloc nations in the 1980s and 1990s.

The Postwar Economy

The end of World War II brought a temporary reduction in military and government spending, but it spiked again during the Korean War. The two world wars and the New Deal, following on the establishment of the income tax and the Federal Reserve System in the 1910s, radically transformed the size and scope of the national government and military. Federal expenditures went up from $3 billion in 1929 to $9 billion in 1939 to a stunning $95 billion in 1945. The Cold War kept spending high: even in the nonwar year of 1960, the government spent $90 billion, half of which went to the military or military-related industries.

The government made major investments in installations related to the arms race. In 1950, the DuPont Company, operating under a contract from the Atomic Energy Commission, broke ground on a massive nuclear facility, the Savannah River Site in western South Carolina. At a $2 billion cost of construction, the task of building the plant was compared to that of building the Panama Canal. Its five nuclear reactors and many other facilities focused primarily on the production of tritium and plutonium-239, essential elements in the new generation of nuclear weapons. The plant lay on 310 square miles where small towns such as Ellenton and Dunbarton, South Carolina, had once stood, but authorities relocated the towns, or they vanished altogether. (Ellenton was reincarnated as "New Ellenton," standing just outside the northern gates of the site.) By the mid-1950s, the plant was fully operational and began shipping tritium and plutonium-239. Plants, factories, and bases related to the cold war routinely ended up in the South, coordinated by powerful southern congressmen. These ventures gave the historically agrarian South a new dose of industrialism and federal spending.

Reconverting the American economy to a peacetime basis after World War II came with a number of strains. Wages and prices shot up quickly, but workers found themselves falling behind since they could no longer depend on factories running around the clock and paying overtime as they had during the war. Women had replaced many men in traditionally male professions in sectors such as heavy industry, but the number of women in the workforce dropped temporarily once the war ended. World War II represented a permanent turning point for women's employment, however, and by 1953 the number of women working outside the home had returned to 1945 levels.

Labor unions remained powerful, but they had tried to avoid strikes during the war to escape charges of disloyalty. That changed with the end of the war, and in 1946 millions of workers participated in nearly 5,000 strikes. Walkouts by mine and railroad workers threatened to cripple the economy. The strikes caused a backlash against the unions in Congress, which passed the Taft-Hartley Act in 1947. This act sought to weaken the unions by softening the rules established under the pro-union Wagner Act in 1935. The Taft-Hartley Act made it easier for states to ensure that employees had the option not to join the union as a condition of working at a factory. (Unions depended on having "closed" shops and a totally unionized workforce to negotiate most effectively with owners.) Taft-Hartley also required union leaders to swear that they were not communists before they could interact with officials of the National Labor Relations Board. Truman was ambivalent about the power of the unions, but he thought Taft-Hartley went too far. He vetoed the law, but bipartisan majorities over-rode his veto in Congress.

African Americans found expanded employment opportunities in civilian and military sectors during World War II, and they sought to consolidate those gains in the postwar era. They also contended that if African Americans were capable of con-tributing to the nation's fight against totalitarianism, then they deserved political rights equal to whites. The National Association for the Advancement of Colored People slowly chipped away at the myriad ways blacks suffered political discrimination. In the 1944 Supreme Court case of *Smith v. Allwright*, justices declared the all-white primary system of many southern states a violation of the Fourteenth and Fifteenth Amendments. Because the Democratic Party dominated the politics of many southern states, their primary elections were more significant in many cases than the general elec-tions. Democrats often ran unopposed in southern general elections. White Democrats argued that since they were a political party and not an arm of the government, they could restrict voting however they liked. A number of southern states banned blacks, as well as Mexican Americans and other minorities, from voting in Democratic prima-ries. In *Smith v. Allwright* the court ruled that Texas's all-white primary was uncon-stitutional because the state had entrusted a critical part of the electoral system to the party. Thus, the Democratic primary was answerable to constitutional mandates regarding voter discrimination and equal protection of the laws.

Spurred by this decision and emboldened by their experiences in World War II, a number of returning African American soldiers attempted to vote in southern Democratic primaries. Medgar Evers, who would later be murdered for his civil rights activism, was one of those who sought to cast a ballot. He and his brother Charles were students at Alcorn A&M College (later Alcorn State), and in July 1946 they went to the courthouse in Decatur, Mississippi, to cast their votes. A crowd of white men—many of whom Evers knew—blocked their entry to the polls. The whites, carrying baseball bats and guns, told them to go home. Evers quietly opened a jackknife in his pocket, but he decided to leave before a fight broke out. Voter registration was on the rise among southern African Americans, however, growing from 2 percent in 1940 to 12 percent in 1947.

Thurgood Marshall, a lawyer who directed the NAACP's Legal Defense and Educational Fund, and who would later become a Supreme Court justice, argued *Smith v. Allwright* in addition to a series of other high-profile civil rights cases. In 1946, Marshall was also a cocounsel in the case of *Morgan v. Virginia*. This case involved Irene Morgan, an African American woman traveling on a bus from Maryland to Virginia, who was arrested when she refused to give up her seat for white passengers. The NAACP successfully contended that the Supreme Court should invalidate the Virginia statute on segregated buses because the federal government had the right to regulate interstate commerce (under Article I, Section 8, of the Constitution). Justices agreed that contradictory state laws about segregation on buses represented an undue burden on this form of commerce. The question of blacks' access to buses and bus terminals would continue to fester, prompting the Freedom Ride protests in 1961, in which African American passengers challenged southern states' unwillingness to desegregate interstate transportation.

Perhaps the most powerful symbol of desegregation on a national level was Jackie Robinson, the first black man to play in Major League Baseball since the league's early years in the late 1800s. Robinson, a phenomenal multisport athlete, army veteran, and devout Christian, was a perfect candidate to break the color barrier in baseball. Robinson received ruthless harassment from fans and other players. Branch Rickey, the president of the Brooklyn Dodgers and also a committed Christian, called Robinson up to the majors in 1947. Rickey believed Robinson could help the Dodgers win, but he was also convinced that desegregating baseball was the right thing to do morally. Rickey's bet paid off more than he could have hoped, as Robinson went on to win the Rookie of the Year award in 1947 and was eventually inducted into the Baseball Hall of Fame. Robinson made it possible for many more African Americans to join the major leagues: Larry Doby started playing for the Cleveland Indians just months after Robinson joined the Dodgers. Soon other African American players, including Hank Aaron, Ernie Banks, and Willie Mays, had become among the greatest stars in baseball. Integration also signaled the beginning of the end of baseball's Negro Leagues, just as integration would weaken other distinctive black institutions such as all-black colleges.

Anti-Communism

The combined effects of the Cold War, the communist takeover of Eastern Europe and China, and the Korean conflict fueled a resurgence of anti-communist fears in America. Open sympathy for communism in America was rare, and the American Communist Party was miniscule. Nevertheless, its leaders were subjected to prosecution for plotting to overthrow the government, and many states banned Communist Party activities.

The greatest fear in America was not about outspoken communists, however, but secret communist operatives and sympathizers. In Congress, the House of Representatives' Un-American Activities Committee (HUAC) took the lead in 1947 in investigating communist activities in the Hollywood movie industry. Some in Hollywood approved of the effort to root out communists while others saw the hearings as a witch hunt. Frank Sinatra, the popular singer and actor who had released his debut album in 1946, said that if the government got "the movies throttled, how long will it be before we're told what we can say and cannot say into a radio microphone?" Sinatra and many others feared that anyone expressing liberal political views could be labeled a "commie" and blacklisted, making it impossible for them to get work. Ten film industry figures, citing their First Amendment right to free speech, refused to answer the HUAC's questions and were found in contempt of Congress. Each of the "Hollywood Ten" spent up to a year in prison.

The Truman administration also issued an executive order in 1947 that established "loyalty boards" to oversee federal government agencies. The order stipulated that federal employees could be fired if there were "reasonable grounds" to suspect they were disloyal to the government. If a

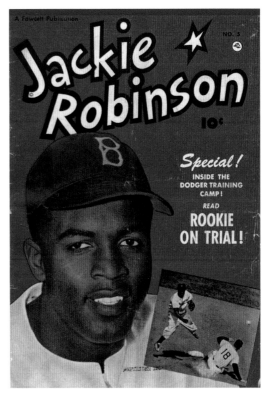

Figure 24.2. Front cover of *Jackie Robinson* comic book, ca. 1951. The inset image shows Jackie Robinson covering a slide at second base.

person belonged to a group the attorney general designated as "totalitarian, fascistic, communistic, or subversive," that was sufficient grounds for dismissal. Although the accused were afforded some procedural protections, the standard of "disloyalty" was vague and difficult to refute. The military established similar programs to evaluate civilian contractors. By 1952, authorities had dismissed more than 1,000 people under the federal disloyalty investigations. Many more resigned instead of undergoing questioning from the loyalty boards.

The anti-communist purges were frightening and reckless, and many people were tarred as "disloyal" simply for liberal political associations. But the Soviets did, in fact, have spies working in the United States, so the communist "witch hunt" was not based entirely on paranoia. One of the most spectacular communist spy accusations came from Whittaker Chambers, a *Time* magazine editor who confessed to having worked as a

Soviet agent in the 1930s. He subsequently embraced Christian beliefs and became an anti-communist activist. Chambers accused Alger Hiss, a high-ranking State Department official, of having worked as a communist operative. Hiss denied the charges but struggled to explain suspicious documents Chambers said Hiss had given him. Republican congressman and future president Richard Nixon championed the investigation of Hiss, who was eventually convicted of lying to Congress and sentenced to five years in prison.

British officials also arrested physicist Klaus Fuchs, who had worked at America's Los Alamos nuclear facility and served as a Soviet spy. The investigation of Fuchs's activities led American authorities to Jewish communists Julius and Ethel Rosenberg. Julius had access to sensitive information as part of his work for the army during World War II, and American officials charged the couple with conspiracy to commit espionage by passing on secrets to the Soviets. They were convicted in 1951 and sentenced to death. (Hiss had gotten off with a much lighter sentence because the statute of limitations on espionage had expired for him.) Many observers have argued that anti-Semitic hatred fueled the animosity toward the Rosenbergs, but many prominent American Jewish groups supported their convictions. Although there were charges of procedural irregularities in the Rosenbergs' trial, and even though the couple had two young children, federal authorities had them executed by electrocution in 1953.

The most controversial figure in the anti-communist investigations was Republican senator Joseph McCarthy of Wisconsin. In 1950, McCarthy declared that the free people of the West were "engaged in a final, all-out battle between communistic atheism and Christianity." He said he knew of hundreds of Communist Party members and sympathizers working in the State Department alone. Even though McCarthy was a heavy drinker and not known as a paragon of virtue, he couched the war on communism as a Christian crusade, calling Alger Hiss "the man who sold out the Christian world to the atheistic world." For a time McCarthy became phenomenally popular in America. His supporters included Catholics and Protestants who liked his straight talk about the menace of atheistic communism. Prominent fundamentalist pastor Carl McIntire pushed Congress to investigate communist influences among modernist Protestant pastors. One of McCarthy's investigators declared that Protestant pastors represented the "largest single group supporting the communist apparatus in the United States."

President Eisenhower, a Republican who took office in 1953, disliked McCarthy but was reluctant to take on the popular senator directly. In the end McCarthy did himself in by overreaching. Trying to settle a score for one of his associates, McCarthy attacked the army in 1954 for sheltering communists. The armed forces were not nearly as easy a target as the elites of Hollywood, liberal pastors, or prominent universities. Congress initiated hearings into McCarthy's charges, and they were aired on national television to audiences as large as 20 million people. McCarthy's bullying tactics did not come off well. In a key exchange with army special counsel Joseph Welch, McCarthy impugned a liberal lawyer who worked with Welch. Welch upbraided McCarthy for his incessant attempts to ruin people's reputations. "Have you no sense of decency, sir?" Welch asked.* The confrontation crystallized the public's growing disgust with McCarthy. By the end of the year, senators voted 67 to 22 to condemn McCarthy's actions as having damaged the honor of the Senate. McCarthy remained in office, but he died three years later of a liver condition exacerbated by his heavy drinking.

Eisenhower and the 1952 Election

The 1952 presidential election was marked by fears over the Cold War and communism, as well as frustration over the conflict in Korea, which had bogged down after the Chinese invasion of North Korea in 1950. Because of his nonpartisan demeanor and sparkling military record, Dwight Eisenhower had emerged as a formidable candidate for the Republicans. Eisenhower believed the best thing for the United States to do was get out of Korea, promising that as president he would bring the war to an "early and honorable end." Eisenhower chose the much younger senator Richard Nixon as his running mate. Nixon not only offered Eisenhower the likelihood of winning his home state of California but also contributed a hard-edged anti-communist bent that he had cultivated in his attacks on Alger Hiss.

Eisenhower's rival, Democratic Illinois governor Adlai Stevenson, was not that different politically from Eisenhower. Stevenson did not connect with ordinary Democratic voters as much as Truman had. Eisenhower pioneered the use of the television "spot," or advertisement, in the 1952 campaign. The general was not adept at public speaking, but producers filmed him giving short answers to questions posed by "everyday" voters. Stevenson and many observers were contemptuous of this tactic. Stevenson scoffed that the election wasn't "Ivory Soap versus Palmolive." The Democrats failed to realize that television was transforming media and the political landscape. By 1952, about a third of American households already owned a television. Paid advertising could carefully manage the public impression a candidate gave while also putting the candidates' image and views in a new format for tens of millions of potential voters.

When the November election came, Eisenhower trounced Stevenson, winning 442 electoral votes to 89. Stevenson only managed to carry nine states, mostly in the South.

---

* "Army McCarthy Hearings," YouTube video, 0:17, May 25, 2009, https://www.youtube.com/watch?v=fqQD4dzVkwk.

(Stevenson's running mate, Senator John Sparkman of Alabama, helped the Democrats avoid a repeat of the Dixiecrat secession in 1948.) Virtually the first thing Eisenhower did was visit Korea and secure the cease-fire, which went into effect on July 27, 1953. Given the anti-communist furor of the early 1950s, the former general was one of the only people in America who could have pulled off ending the Korean War without falling victim to charges of being weak on communism. The Cold War's first great clash over the policy of containment ended in disappointment for many Americans, with a split Korea returning to its prewar status quo. It would not be the last time the goal of containing communism would run into difficult realities in Asia.

■ SELECTED BIBLIOGRAPHY ■

Boyer, Paul. *By the Bomb's Early Light: American Thought and Culture at the Dawn of the Atomic Age.* Rev. ed. Chapel Hill: University of North Carolina Press, 1994.

Clune, Lori. *Executing the Rosenbergs: Death and Diplomacy in a Cold War World.* New York: Oxford University Press, 2016.

Frederickson, Kari A. *Cold War Dixie: Militarization and Modernization in the American South.* Athens: University of Georgia Press, 2013.

Gaddis, John Lewis. *George F. Kennan: An American Life.* New York: Penguin, 2011.

Gilpatrick, Kristin. *The Hero Next Door: The Korean War.* Middleton, WI: Badger Books, 2010.

Inboden, William. *Religion and American Foreign Policy, 1945–1960: The Soul of Containment.* New York: Cambridge University Press, 2008.

Patterson, James T. *Grand Expectations: The United States, 1945–1974.* New York: Oxford University Press, 1996.

Powaski, Ronald E. *The Cold War: The United States and the Soviet Union, 1917–1991.* New York: Oxford University Press, 1997.

Ruotsila, Markku. *Fighting Fundamentalist: Carl McIntire and the Politicization of American Fundamentalism.* New York: Oxford University Press, 2015.

Sandler, Stanley. *The Korean War: No Victors, No Vanquished.* Lexington: University Press of Kentucky, 1999.

Swan, Patrick, ed. *Alger Hiss, Whittaker Chambers, and the Schism in the American Soul.* Wilmington, DE: ISI Books, 2003.

Tushnet, Mark V. *Making Civil Rights Law: Thurgood Marshall and the Supreme Court, 1936–1961.* New York: Oxford University Press, 1994.

25

The 1950s

The 1950s were boom times for America in everything from consumer spending to the average number of children per family. Manufacturers met Americans' new influx of disposable income with a bounty of updated and innovative products. Television was perhaps the defining product of the decade, making entertainment ever more central to American culture. Radio had dominated the electronic media culture of the Great Depression and World War II. But starting in the late 1940s, television went from being an oddity to a common feature of American living rooms. In 1948, 172,000 American homes owned a TV; by 1952, 15.3 million did. As TVs became more affordable, even relatively poor American households came to own one. By 1960, about 90 percent of American homes had a TV set. TVs originally showed black-and-white moving images, but in the 1970s color television became increasingly common.

Television shows such as Lucille Ball's *I Love Lucy* captivated many Americans. Because of the relatively small number of shows available at first, the most popular shows and stars generated enormous audiences and advertising revenue. Even though many Americans still did not have access to a television, one *I Love Lucy* episode in early 1953 drew an audience of some 44 million people, out of a total of 160 million Americans. *I Love Lucy* also broke with popular conventions in depicting the relationship of "Ricky and Lucy," the real-life married couple Lucille Ball and Desi Arnaz, a white woman and a Cuban man. The show also joked frankly about Lucy's pregnancy, which producers regarded as a sensitive topic, particularly for an interethnic couple.[*]

---

[*] "I Love Lucy—Pregnancy Cravings," YouTube video, 3:43, August 20, 2013, https://www.youtube.com/watch?v=oOfuoA146Y0.

Sports slowly became a staple of television programming, but live-action ball games were often difficult to capture well with early television camera technology. Relatively stationary sports, including boxing and professional wrestling, worked much better. Boxing still routinely produced ethnic champions, such as African American champion Sugar Ray Robinson, Italian brawler Rocky Marciano, and native Mexican Gaspar "Indio" Ortega. All of them regularly appeared on popular programs such as NBC's *Cavalcade of Sports*, sponsored by Gillette razors.

Professional wrestling, with its dramatic preplanned scripts and results, was arguably the perfect form of early television sports entertainment. Because personality drove professional wrestling as much as athleticism did, television turned some 1950s wrestlers into national cultural icons. These included "Nature Boy" Buddy Rogers, whose bleached hair, impressive physique, and arrogant style made him a much-loathed but compelling wrestler. (Rogers, whose real name was Herman Gustav Rohde, was the son of German immigrants.) Rogers became the model for a number of future wrestlers, most notably Ric Flair (who also used the name "Nature Boy"), one of the most popular and successful wrestlers of the 1970s and 1980s. In the 1950s, however, there was no more controversial wrestler on television than "Gorgeous George" Wagner. Gorgeous George cultivated a preening, effeminate style, with outrageously coiffed platinum blond hair. He would come to the ring to the booming sounds of "Pomp and Circumstance," and his "valet" would spray perfume in the ring, ostensibly to make it a tolerable setting for the "Gorgeous One." Male audiences loved to hate Gorgeous George. But at the height of his fame, he may have been the highest-paid athlete in the world.[*]

Some Christian leaders in America worried about the cultural and spiritual effects of television and mass entertainment. That concern was largely overshadowed, however, by the willingness of Catholic, mainline Protestant, and evangelical leaders to use television as a means to distribute the Christian message. Evangelists such as Billy Graham and Oral Roberts became nationally known in the 1950s partly because of their innovative use of television. Still, some observers wondered if television was making Americans more isolated, unreflective, and susceptible to marketing and advertising. The great Christian poet T. S. Eliot marveled that TV was a "medium of entertainment which permits millions of people to listen to the same joke at the same time, and yet remain lonesome."

---

[*] "Gorgeous George vs. Hans Schnabel (11/03/1950)," YouTube video, 27:02, September 11, 2014, https://www.youtube.com/watch?v=fVpTpuWSU48.

The Postwar Boom

Everywhere you looked were signs of prosperity in the late 1940s and 1950s America. Some people still lagged behind, of course, but overall the economic circumstances in the postwar world positioned America for a lengthy period of growth. Unemployment remained under 5 percent, price inflation stayed under 2 percent, and the widespread poverty of the Depression era was much diminished. Workers' hours dropped and their wages grew. Leisure time and disposable income increased for many average workers. This led typical American families to buy and to watch televisions and to enjoy many other kinds of entertainment. Families felt more confident about having larger numbers of children, so the 1950s saw the peak of the "baby boom" that had started even before the end of World War II. Birth rates had been lower during the Depression era, but now it was not unusual for Americans to have four or five children per married couple.

Builders and marketers were ready to sell Americans on their dream home in the "suburbs," or new planned communities on the outskirts of cities. The suburbs came with associated ideas about what the good life entailed: a single-family home with a yard, automobiles for workers (usually fathers) to go into the city, enough bedrooms to house growing numbers of children, and space for new consumer products such as the TV. For urban dwellers who had only known the confines of apartment or tenement living, the suburbs seemed to offer the promise of an older American dream: individual land ownership.

The pioneer suburban developer was William Levitt, who in 1947 began work on a community in suburban New York that he called "Levittown." Levitt sold thousands of homes, many to the families of returning World War II veterans, with little money down and low monthly payments to pay off the home loan over time. By 1951, the original Levittown had more than 17,000 houses, and Levitt built two more of these communities in New Jersey and Pennsylvania. The homes were virtually identical, except for some variations on the exteriors, to give some visual character to the rows of houses. The houses were simple and small (720 square feet) by today's standards. A refrigerator, washing machine, and stove came standard with each house. By 1960, communities like Levittown had revolutionized the residential patterns of American life, as one-third of Americans already lived in suburbs. By the 1990s, nearly half of all Americans lived in suburbs.

America was increasingly becoming a nation of consumers. The growth of the suburbs undergirded much of the new spending on electronics, cars, and other new commercial products. Detroit automakers struggled to keep up with burgeoning demand for cars. In the boom year of 1955, American companies sold 8 million automobiles. The Eisenhower administration backed the adoption of the $50 billion Interstate Highway Act in 1956, which would revolutionize the nation's system of roads. The United States had built an older road system in the 1920s, with the advent of mass ownership of cars. But the Interstate Highway System modernized and often bypassed those older roads, prioritizing quick transportation across the country. One of the most famous of the old roads was Route 66, known in popular lore as America's "Mother Road." Route 66 ran from Chicago, Illinois, to Santa Monica, California. But the interstates made many roads like Route 66 obsolete. Whereas Route 66 had passed through countless towns, spawning innumerable gas stations, motor inns, and diners along the way, the interstates bypassed the center of towns to keep traffic from stopping. The interstates became a fixture of life for traveling Americans, including those taking personal trips and truck drivers hauling goods across the country. At interstate stops chain restaurants and hotels replaced the old local businesses. Holiday Inn opened its first hotel in 1952, heralding the beginning of the end for many independent hotels and lodges. In 1955, Ray Kroc opened his first McDonald's restaurant in Des Plaines, Illinois. By 1960, America had 228 McDonald's franchises. It would go on to become one of the largest companies in the world.

New shopping venues made it easier and more convenient for customers to buy goods. The first enclosed mall in America opened in Minnesota in 1956. Now customers could shop in a number of different stores in a climate-controlled environment, which was crucial for stores to boost sales during the winter months in the North and the summer months in the South. Big Town Mall, one of the first air-conditioned malls in the South, opened in 1959 outside of Dallas, Texas. A half century later, many of the earliest malls had fallen on hard times. (Big Town Mall was demolished in 2006.) Malls have come to suffer from competition by "big box" retail centers, such as Wal-Mart, and from growing online competition from shopping websites, including Amazon.com.

Banks also made it easier for consumers to spend money on credit, especially through the use of credit cards. Henry Ford had pioneered the system of paying for cars on an "installment" plan so buyers did not have to pay the whole cost up front. Home sellers likewise made it possible for consumers to occupy a house with a down payment and a promise to make monthly payments until the loan and interest were paid off. But a major turn came in 1950 when Diner's Club introduced a credit card with which diners could pay on credit at dozens of New York City restaurants. Banks decided to try this payment model for many different retailers and purchase types. In 1958, Bank of America introduced the BankAmericard program, which would later be named Visa. By the mid-1960s, Americans were using some 5 million credit cards. Buying on credit (and being charged interest for outstanding balances) was standard practice by the end of the twentieth century, when credit card purchases in the United States approached $1 trillion annually.

Searching for Meaning and Salvation amid Consumption

Critics worried about the dulling effects of mass consumption. Some wondered if America had become enmeshed in a culture of "conformity," in which people all bought the same products, watched the same shows, and tried to meet the same social expectations. Of course, beneath the images portrayed in TV shows and advertisements, America remained diverse regionally, ethnically, and religiously. But books such as sociologist David Riesman's *The Lonely Crowd* (1950) expressed concern that much of the American population was focused on living up to others' social expectations of them. This fostered a "close behavioral conformity," Riesman said, and an "exceptional sensitivity to the actions and wishes of others." No "ideal of independence or of reliance on God alone" could modify such a person's desire to share in the lifestyle and experiences of others, Riesman explained. William H. Whyte Jr.'s 1956 *The Organization Man* similarly registered fear that the lockstep, soulless quality of large businesses was making America into as much of a collective state as the Soviet Union.

Much of American religion in the 1950s was shaped by the growing consumer culture as congregations moved into the suburbs and religious leaders adapted to new forms of electronic communication. But Americans' religion also reflected a desire to find meaning that transcended the mundane cycles of working and buying more things. Easily the most well-known Protestant leader in America in the 1950s was the evangelist Billy Graham. Graham's long and enormously influential ministry was reminiscent of the popularity of the evangelist George Whitefield during the eighteenth-century Great Awakening. Both men developed a level of fame that far transcended any church or denomination. They were media sensations, ready to use their celebrity to reach many more people with their gospel preaching. Born in North Carolina at the end of World War I, Graham graduated from Wheaton College in Illinois in 1943. He soon began working as an evangelist for the interdenominational ministry Youth for Christ. With a boost from newspaper mogul William Randolph Hearst, Graham launched a series of major revival meetings beginning in Los Angeles in 1949. Lasting two months, the Los Angeles revival assemblies drew some 350,000 total attendees.

Graham drew criticism from many quarters. Some secular critics saw him as just another ranting Bible-thumper. Some fundamentalist Christians believed Graham was too willing to cooperate with a broad range of Christian churches, including liberal ones.

Figure 25.1. Billy Graham, April 11, 1966.

Graham represented the "neo-evangelical" movement, which would become more commonly known as evangelical Christianity. He denounced the modern trends in Western cultures that had turned people's hearts against God. But he also favored cooperation with all kinds of Christians who supported his message rather than demanding doctrinal purity before he would work with them. Graham began live television broadcasts of his revival meetings during his 1957 crusade in New York City. Polls that year showed that some 85 percent of Americans knew who Graham was and that the majority of respondents had a positive view of him.

Graham's early sermons commonly warned about the modern alternatives to the Christian gospel, including communism, rationalism, and the idolatry of science. "We have an age of skepticism, unbelief, atheism and agnosticism," he told a Houston audience in 1952. He also registered concern about the massive expansion of government since the New Deal. Millions had become convinced, he said, "that the problems of sin can be cured by government; they have renounced faith in Christ as the Savior of the human race from the curse of sin and have put their faith in government." Graham touted the time-honored message of faith in Christ and the "new birth" of conversion as the solution to humankind's ills. Graham maintained personal relationships with presidents from Eisenhower to George W. Bush (the latter crediting Graham with helping him accept Christ as his Savior). By the end of his career, Graham, who died in 2018, had preached around the world to estimated live audiences totaling 210 million people. Many more saw Graham speak on TV or read his books.

The new evangelicals often bridged the worlds of church and "parachurch" ministries, such as the Billy Graham Evangelistic Association, which Graham started in 1950. Dynamic local churches often spun out niche ministries seeking to reach high school or college students, for example. One of the most influential church-based ministries of the post–World War II era was led by Henrietta Mears at First Presbyterian Church, Hollywood, California. Mears's dynamic teaching in the church's college ministry impacted Graham at a critical moment when, as the story goes, Graham had begun to doubt the Bible's reliability. Mears assured him that he could trust the Bible, setting the stage for the enormous successes of the 1949 Los Angeles crusade.

Mears also made an indelible impact in her mentoring relationship with Bill and Vonette Bright. The Brights both experienced Christian conversion in the 1940s, and in 1951 they founded Campus Crusade for Christ (now called Cru) at the University of California–Los Angeles. In the early 1950s, Bill Bright developed the "Four Spiritual Laws," Campus Crusade's signature method of sharing the gospel with college students. The Four Spiritual Laws, along with the Bright-produced *Jesus* film (1979), have become among the most widely distributed religious media in world history. By the beginning of the twenty-first century, Campus Crusade was operating in 191 countries around the world. Campus Crusade and other parachurch organizations such as the Fellowship of Christian Athletes, the Navigators, InterVarsity Christian Fellowship, and Young Life helped reach Americans (and people around the world) in the military, in colleges and high schools, and in other places where traditional churches were having limited influence.

Catholics also adjusted their methods of outreach to the post–World War II culture. Bishop Fulton Sheen had already developed a major radio ministry in the 1930s, which he parlayed into a popular TV show called *Life Is Worth Living* in the 1950s. Sheen was not overtly evangelistic in the way Graham was, but he covered a wide range of political and human-interest topics from a Catholic perspective. Like Graham, Sheen was fiercely anti-communist, calling on his viewers to "join him in a 'Holy War' against the godless forces of communism." Sheen's messages resonated far beyond a Catholic audience, making him the best-known national Catholic figure of the era in America.

Although religious adherence can be difficult to track with accuracy, the 1950s seem to have represented one of the greatest peaks of religious commitment in all of American history. By 1960, more than 60 percent of Americans claimed membership in a religious organization or denomination, and almost half of Americans claimed to attend religious services every weekend. Jewish sociologist and theologian Will Herberg's 1955 book *Protestant, Catholic, Jew* argued that even if ethnic identifications went away in the face of homogenizing American culture, religious identity would remain crucial to the way Americans viewed themselves. Herberg wrote that "to be an American today means to be either a Protestant, a Catholic, or a Jew. . . . Not to be a Catholic, a Protestant, or a Jew today is . . . not to be anything, not to have a *name*." This analysis was undoubtedly accurate for a strong majority of Americans in 1955, though social changes in the post-1965 era would erode that tripartite religious uniformity.

Critics of Big Government and Consumer Society

From the political left and right came criticisms of American institutions and culture in the 1950s. On the left many believed the culture of conformity and consumption was soulless and inauthentic. Writers such as Jack Kerouac and Allen Ginsberg became identified with a literary and social movement known as the "Beat Generation," or the Beatniks. Kerouac's *On the Road* (1957) detailed the semiautobiographical journeys of Kerouac and his Beat friends as they rambled across the country. *On the Road* helped set the tone for the Beat Generation with the novel's iconic proclamation: "The only people for me are the mad ones, the ones who are mad to live, mad to talk, mad to be saved . . . the ones who never yawn or say a commonplace thing, but burn, burn, burn like fabulous yellow roman candles exploding like spiders across the stars." The number of Americans fully embracing the carefree (and often drug-addled) Beat life-style was probably never more than 1,000, mostly among people in New York and San Francisco. But the Beats had great cultural influence on future writers and musicians such as the folk singer Bob Dylan. And they set the stage for the larger "hippie" movement of the 1960s.

Conservatives criticized consumerism too. But they worried that the rage for buying the newest products and the ever-increasing scale of the national government would drain all that was noble and distinctive from the storehouses of American traditions and local cultures. Russell Kirk published one of the seminal books of the modern conservative movement in his 1953 *The Conservative Mind*. Kirk touted the American founding as fundamentally conservative and argued that radical secular philosophy had threatened the conservative tradition's survival ever since. "If the conservative order is indeed to return," Kirk wrote, "we ought to know the tradition which is attached to it, so that we may rebuild society; if it is not to be restored, still we ought to understand conservative ideas so that we may rake from the ashes what scorched fragments of civilization escape the conflagration of unchecked will and appetite."

While Kirk familiarized Americans with the intellectual tradition undergirding conservatism, William F. Buckley became arguably the best-known public figure representing conservatism before the 1980s. Buckley published *God and Man at Yale* (1951) to criticize his alma mater's entrenched opposition to religion and to free-market capitalism. In 1955, Buckley founded *National Review* magazine as a counterweight to the liberal dominance of national periodicals such as the *Nation* and the *New Republic*. In his founding editorial, Buckley famously explained that *National Review* "stands athwart history, yelling Stop." With liberal philosophy in command of so many leading cultural institutions, Buckley argued, being conservative was about the most radical thing an American could do. *National Review* offered a "position that has not grown old under the weight of a gigantic, parasitic bureaucracy, a position untampered by the doctoral dissertations of a generation of Ph.D.'s . . . [and] uncorroded by a cynical contempt for human freedom. And that, ladies and gentlemen, leaves us just about the hottest thing in town." Buckley went on to found the long-running TV show *Firing Line* in the 1960s, bringing his distinctive brand of conservatism to an even wider audience.

Youth Culture and Rock and Roll

A concern about wild teenagers is as old as American history itself. But in the 1950s, worries about young people were focused on popular literature, music, and movies that idealized rebelliousness and an independent teenage culture. J. D. Salinger's 1951 novel *The Catcher in the Rye* centered around the fictional experiences of the alienated New York teenager Holden Caulfield. Movies such as Marlon Brando's biker film *The Wild One* (1953) and James Dean's *Rebel without a Cause* (1955) glorified characters (especially young men) who refused to live up to social norms.

Nothing represented the burgeoning youth culture of the 1950s as much as rock-and-roll music. Through the early 1950s, American pop music tended to be somewhat quaint and innocuous. Growing out of older forms of jazz, rhythm and blues, and country, rock and roll burst onto the music scene in the mid-1950s. Its songs featured radio-ready tunes driven by heavy drums, electric guitars, and barroom-sounding pianos. Bill Haley and the Comets scored what some see as the first full-blown rock-and-roll hit with the 1954 "Rock around the Clock," which reached number one on the music charts in both the United States and Britain. African American artists enjoyed unusual popularity in the rock-and-roll era too, with early hits coming from Little Richard, Chuck Berry, and Chubby Checker.

The single most important figure of 1950s rock and roll, however, was Elvis Presley. Elvis grew up in poverty in Mississippi and learned a great deal about music by performing with friends from his Assemblies of God church. Elvis moved to Memphis, Tennessee, as a teenager and began recording music for the local producer Sam Phillips. Elvis admired movie stars such as James Dean and Marlon Brando, mimicking their style and look. Phillips believed Elvis was unique because he could make music with a "Negro sound," but he did not face the traditional white prejudices against black artists. Soon Elvis was cranking out smash hits, including "Heartbreak Hotel" and

"Hound Dog." Elvis cultivated an overt sexuality in his performances, particularly with his signature gyrating hips. Variety show host Ed Sullivan once vowed not to have such a lewd performer on his show but changed his mind when he realized what an unprecedented star Elvis was becoming. Elvis appeared on *The Ed Sullivan Show* three times, breaking previous records for the largest TV audience up to that time.* (The Beatles would break Elvis's record in 1964, also on *The Ed Sullivan Show*.)

Listening to rock and roll became a key habit of teen culture of the 1950s. Many Christian leaders responded negatively to the genre, suggesting that the music endorsed sin. Billy Graham advised Christian teens not to listen to rock and roll. "If I were 17 today I'd stay as far away from it as I could," he said in 1960. Even though rock and roll became associated with sexual license and teenage rebellion, it was as much a part of consumer culture as cars and washing machines. Radio and TV catapulted musicians like Elvis to fame, raking in advertising dollars to do so. Middle-class American teenagers had more disposable income (or allowance money) to spend on vinyl records. At least they had coins to drop in a local diner's jukebox, which would play the hit songs of the day. Record players became more and more affordable in the 1950s and were just one more electronic appliance that many Americans wanted to have in their homes.

Race and Civil Rights

However "conformist" the culture of 1950s America was, there were still deep divides in American society. Some of the most obvious divides ran along racial and ethnic lines. The flight to the suburbs was an almost exclusively middle- and upper-class white phenomenon. African Americans, and increasingly Latinos, flowed into urban centers in the 1950s. Hundreds of thousands of Puerto Ricans left their home island (a US territory since 1898) in the 1940s and 1950s, attracted by better economic prospects on the American mainland. New York City, especially East Harlem, took the majority of these immigrants.

Mexicans also came to the United States in greater numbers. A new influx began during World War II as part of the "bracero" program, which funneled Mexicans into low-paying manual labor in the railroad or farming sectors. Mexican authorities worried about abuse of the workers, however, even suspending the bracero program in Texas in 1943 because of reports of "extreme, intolerable racial discrimination." Many

---

* "Elvis Presley 'Hound Dog' on The Ed Sullivan Show," YouTube video, 1:04, June 17, 2013, https://www.youtube.com/watch?v=sGZm7EOamWk.

white Americans in the Southwest, conversely, worried that the growing numbers of Mexican laborers would drive down wages and take jobs from whites.

One bracero, Manuel Padilla, recalled the troubles he encountered in the 1940s when he tried to secure fair treatment. While working in a lemon orchard, he got fired for going to the bathroom without permission. At an orange grove he got into an altercation with the field boss because the boss gave Padilla worthless, blunt scissors for harvesting. When Padilla left the bracero program, he kept trying to work illegally, but he eventually got deported to Juárez, Mexico. But undocumented Mexicans kept coming to the United States because the opportunities for making money seemed better than in Mexico.

Braceros and undocumented immigrants lived in constant fear of deportation as resentment against Mexicans and fear of criminal elements rose along with the number of Hispanics coming to America for work. Whites often called Mexicans the derogatory term "wetbacks" because they had supposedly swum the Rio Grande to get into the country. (Never mind that the Rio Grande is only the southern border of Texas, not of New Mexico, Arizona, or California.) In 1954, the Eisenhower administration authorized what became known as Operation Wetback, a mission led by a general from the 101st Airborne Division, to deport hundreds of thousands of Mexicans. Under Operation Wetback the U.S. Immigration Service claimed that 1.3 million Mexicans were forcibly deported or convinced to leave by threat of deportation.

Before the late 1940s, civil rights litigation had focused on issues such as segregating interstate transportation and all-white southern primaries. Segregated schools became a major focus after the war. A key early decision undermining racial segregation in schools was *Mendez v. Westminster School District* (1947), a federal court verdict that ruled it was unconstitutional for a California district to create separate schools for Hispanics. Then in 1951, the National Association for the Advancement of Colored People, led by lawyer Thurgood Marshall, initiated a series of suits against school segregation laws. These actions coalesced into the Supreme Court case of *Brown v. Board of Education* (1954), named for a black family in Topeka, Kansas. The Brown family's daughter was bused to an all-black school in spite of an all-white school being a few blocks away from their home.

Brown challenged the precedent in *Plessy v. Ferguson*, the 1896 Supreme Court ruling that had affirmed that "separate but equal" public facilities were constitutionally permissible. Marshall argued that segregated schools were inherently unequal, regardless of the quality of the facilities, and that attending an inferior school "branded" African American children psychologically as inferior. The Supreme Court, led by Eisenhower appointee Chief Justice Earl Warren, unanimously agreed with Marshall. They ruled that state-mandated school segregation violated the Fourteenth Amendment's guarantee of "equal protection of the laws." But the court was hesitant about making desegregation move too quickly. A follow-up ruling in 1955 suggested that the process should go forward "with all deliberate speed."

In some parts of the country, desegregation did proceed, but a number of white politicians in the Deep South states called for what Senator Harry Byrd of Virginia called "massive resistance" to integration of the public schools. One hundred one congressmen and senators, including Byrd, signed the "Southern Manifesto" (formally, Declaration of Constitutional Principles) in 1956, calling *Brown* a "clear abuse of judicial power." The manifesto warned that "outside agitators are threatening immediate and revolutionary changes in our public school systems." President Eisenhower was also cautious about forcing desegregation on the white South, believing it was foolish for the government to try to change deep-seated cultural habits overnight. Eisenhower did push forward with the desegregation of federal facilities, however, and of the school system in Washington, DC.

The question of desegregating southern schools was forced on Eisenhower in 1957. The school district of Little Rock, Arkansas, had agreed to comply with a federal order to desegregate Little Rock Central High School. Claiming this order jeopardized the public order, Arkansas governor Orval Faubus called up troops from the Arkansas National Guard to stop black students from enrolling. Eisenhower finally sent in soldiers from the 101st Airborne to protect the black students, called the "Little Rock Nine," as they went to their classes. The students were able to attend Central High School under guard for a year, but then Little Rock officials decided to close the school temporarily rather than allow desegregation to become entrenched.

As some in the white South promised to keep resisting desegregation, some African Americans faced the continuing threat of lynching and racial murder. Emmett Till was a black teenager from Chicago who was visiting family in Mississippi in the summer of 1955. Till supposedly whistled at a white woman in the town of Money, Mississippi. Vengeful whites kidnapped, mutilated, and murdered Till, throwing his body into a river. Two white defendants accused of perpetrating the murder were acquitted by an all-white, all-male jury. The defendants later freely admitted to killing Till but with no legal consequences. Till's almost unidentifiable body was sent back to Chicago for a funeral where his mother insisted upon having an open-casket ceremony, which was attended by thousands.

Standing up for civil rights on the local level, especially in the South, could be fearful. But key African American leaders still vowed to bring about desegregation throughout America. Individual African Americans had for decades occasionally refused to

Figure 25.2. *Operation Arkansas: A Different Kind of Deployment.* "Soldiers from the 101st Airborne Division escort the Little Rock Nine students into the all-white Central High School in Little Rock, Arkansas," 1957. Photograph by the US Army.

comply with segregation policies on public transportation, such as on buses. In 1953, African American Baptist minister T. J. Jemison led protests against fare increases and the segregated bus system of Baton Rouge, Louisiana. Church leaders arranged a system of rides so black workers could avoid using the buses. Jemison's protestors and the city of Baton Rouge quickly came to a settlement, but it left some segregated seating in place on city buses. Nevertheless, Jemison's tactics became a model for other bus protests in the South, most notably in Montgomery, Alabama, in 1955.

Montgomery's bus boycott was sparked by the refusal of Rosa Parks to give up her seat to white passengers. Parks was a seamstress at a department store and a member of the city's NAACP and of a local African Methodist Episcopal Church. Parks herself had been removed from a bus ten years earlier for refusing a similar request from a bus driver. She was such a dignified, devout person that the NAACP realized Parks would make an ideal candidate to test the city's bus segregation ordinance. Recruiting Parks was a stroke of genius, as it mobilized legions of African Americans to begin organizing a boycott. Although these local people do not often get the recognition they deserve, a boycott required widespread participation in order to succeed.

The boycotters created the Montgomery Improvement Association to coordinate the protests. They chose the young Baptist minister Martin Luther King Jr., a recent arrival in the city as the pastor of the Dexter Avenue Baptist Church, to head the boycott. King was a bracing preacher with sterling credentials, as he was finishing a PhD from Boston University. King was first and foremost a product of the black church. His father was a prominent minister in Atlanta. But King also drew on a variety of intellectual influences, including theologian and ethicist Reinhold Niebuhr. Niebuhr, who taught at Union Theological Seminary in New York, was known for advocating Christian realism. This philosophy touted the priority of Christian love but also recognized that even the best-intended actions were often tainted with sin and short-sightedness. King also valued the writings of figures such as the Indian independence leader Mohandas Gandhi and Gandhi's promotion of nonviolent resistance to oppressive powers.

Parks was convicted of refusing to give up her seat on the bus, and when she would not pay the fine, she was put in prison. She also lost her department store job. King and dozens of other boycotters were also jailed in Montgomery, charged with participation in illegal tactics against the city's transportation system. The burgeoning controversy drew out white supremacist rivals, including a rejuvenated Ku Klux Klan. White supremacists bombed some leaders' homes, including King's. Yet King and the boycotters still insisted on nonviolent tactics. King testified that shortly before the bombing of his home he had reached a point of spiritual crisis, not knowing if he could stand the stress and pressure. (He had just received another of a number of death threats.) As he prayed at the kitchen table, he said, "I experienced the presence of the Divine as I had never experienced Him before. It seemed as though I could hear the quiet assurance of an inner voice saying, 'Stand up for righteousness, stand up for truth; and God will be at your side forever.'" Some believe this was the most important moment of King's life, steeling him for what lay ahead.

The boycott garnered widespread participation from Montgomery's African American community, and protestors initiated a lawsuit to challenge the bus segregation policy. A US district court ruled in *Browder v. Gayle* (1956) that Montgomery's segregation ordinance violated the equal protection clause of the Fourteenth Amendment. The Supreme Court upheld the district court ruling, and the city was forced to desegregate its buses. It was a major victory, but it left the growing civil rights movement with a lot of work to do. Segregation remained legal in countless places across America, from all-white restaurants to city parks and drinking fountains. It was difficult to see how boycotts would work to effect change in those situations. Nevertheless, in 1957 King founded the Southern Christian Leadership Conference (SCLC) to lead the charge against segregation. King and his allies believed that a majority of Americans accepted, in principle, the Judeo-Christian obligation to love one's neighbor and that nonviolent resistance had a real chance to generate broad-based sympathy, even among southern whites. The SCLC meant to appeal to the "conscience of the great decent majority who through blindness, fear, pride or irrationality have allowed their consciences to sleep," King said.

In February 1960, a new phase of the civil rights movement began, sparked by a "sit-in" at a department store lunch counter in Greensboro, North Carolina. Four freshman students from the black college North Carolina A&T employed nonviolent resistance tactics by sitting down at the counter, which was reserved for white customers, and refusing to leave. No one would serve them, but their example sparked similar sit-ins in other segregated places across the nation. Ella Baker, the executive director of the SCLC, summoned hundreds of protestors from black colleges to meet for a strategy session at North Carolina's Shaw College in April 1960. Methodist leader James Lawson, who was expelled from Vanderbilt Divinity School for his role in Nashville sit-ins, gave a keynote address at the Shaw College conference. He emphasized that racial prejudice and segregation were sinful and that the "matter is not legal, sociological or racial, it is moral and spiritual." Some at the Shaw assembly felt college students needed a new organization focused on their role in civil rights and to complement or challenge SCLC, which they perceived as moving too slowly. So the students organized the Student Nonviolent Coordinating Committee (SNCC).

The sit-ins generated a backlash among some whites. Thousands of sit-in protestors went to jail in 1960, usually accused of disturbing the peace or trespassing. In April 1960, a "wade in" protest at a public beach in Biloxi, Mississippi, precipitated a race riot. A mob of whites attacked the black swimmers using bats, metal pipes, and chains. As the fighting spilled into the town of Biloxi, eight blacks and two whites were shot. Some African American leaders felt the sit-ins were overly provocative and fruitless. Thurgood Marshall urged students to support legal measures to end segregation instead. The president of Louisiana's Southern University, a black college, suspended eighteen students who had participated in sit-ins and vowed to root out all troublemakers from the student body.

Political Anxiety and the Cold War

Dwight Eisenhower was reelected president in 1956. In a rematch with Adlai Stevenson, Eisenhower defeated his Democratic rival even more soundly than he had in the 1952 race. On the domestic front Eisenhower left the basic structures of Roosevelt's New Deal programs in place. Although he wanted to avoid any more quagmires like the

Korean conflict, Eisenhower did act to counter the threat of communism around the world. For example, the administration worked to preserve South Vietnam from a take-over by the communist North Vietnam. (Vietnam had been divided at the seventeenth parallel after it gained its independence from France in 1954.) The United States joined with South Vietnam, Australia, and other Pacific Rim nations to form the Southeast Asia Treaty Organization, paralleling its anti-communist alliance in Europe, NATO.

Eisenhower made similar alliances with Turkey and Iran in 1959 to foster a global bulwark of anti-communist nations. Eisenhower also sought to ease tensions with the Soviet Union, holding meetings with Soviet premier Nikita Khrushchev in 1955, the first such talks between US and Soviet leaders since the end of World War II. But tensions resumed when the Soviets shot down an American spy plane in Russian airspace in 1960. The Eisenhower administration originally referred to the aircraft as a "weather reconnaissance" plane until the Soviets revealed that they had captured both the pilot and parts of the plane's wreckage and could prove that the United States was flying missions to spy on Soviet defenses.

A different kind of Cold War embarrassment had transpired in 1957, when the Soviet Union successfully launched the first space satellite, which they called Sputnik. When they deployed Sputnik II a month later, the satellite also contained a passenger: a dog named Laika. Many Americans concluded that the Soviets had outpaced the United States in rocket and space technology and wondered what military threats the Russians might develop with this new access to space. Although the United States maintained a decisive edge in missile technology, the popular resonance of Sputnik sparked a sense of crisis. Perhaps the United States was falling behind in the Cold War. A number of leading political voices called for massive increases in defense spending and for efforts to match Soviet innovations in space. One senator warned that unless the United States changed their approach, "the Soviets will move from superiority to supremacy." In 1958, Congress founded the National Aeronautics and Space Administration (NASA) to lead the US space program.

Conservative critics believed that, starting with Franklin Roosevelt, the US government had become bloated with ineffective domestic spending programs while failing to seriously confront the Soviets and the communist menace. Arizona Republican senator Barry Goldwater spoke for many in his 1960 book *The Conscience of a Conservative* when he argued that the US government had gotten away from the original purposes the nation's founders intended. "The root evil," Goldwater said, "is that the government is engaged in activities in which it has no legitimate business." He called for the federal government to curtail its involvement in "programs that are outside its constitutional mandate—from social welfare programs, education, public power, agriculture, public housing, [to] urban renewal." In other words, the national government needed to terminate the signature programs of the New Deal era. While Goldwater agreed with the justice of the civil rights cause, he did not believe the national government should have the power to meddle in local and state matters, including segregation in schools.

Goldwater further warned that even if conservatives succeeded in scaling back the national government and maximizing freedom, there was still a way they could become "slaves." "We can do this by losing the Cold War to the Soviet Union," he wrote. He did not doubt the loyalty of the Truman and Eisenhower administrations in opposing communism. But Goldwater did question whether they had the determination to defeat communism. The communists were at war with the United States, Goldwater insisted. It was time for the United States to stop seeking peace at any cost and to pursue victory instead. This meant establishing "military superiority," and risking open war when necessary.

Vice President Richard Nixon became the Republican standard-bearer in 1960, hoping to continue the legacy of the Eisenhower administration. But he was defeated by Massachusetts Democratic senator John Kennedy. Eisenhower left office in 1961 still framing the Cold War in stark terms. "We face a hostile ideology," he told Americans, "global in scope, atheistic in character, ruthless in purpose, and insidious in method. Unhappily the danger it poses promises to be of indefinite duration." But Eisenhower also warned about the ever-growing military and its vast network of supporting businesses. "This conjunction of an immense military establishment and a large arms industry is new in the American experience," warned the former general. "The total influence—economic, political, even spiritual—is felt in every city, every state house, every office of the federal government." He worried that while the military buildup was necessary to combat communist power, the "military-industrial complex" might itself become a great threat to freedom. He asked Americans to be vigilant against the rise of "misplaced power" and an American government dominated by military interests.

As America passed into the 1960s, it had enjoyed arguably the greatest time of sustained economic growth in national history. That growth undergirded the abundant resources of many Americans (though not all of them) and the rise of new outlets for consumption, not least television and rock-and-roll music. But even in the 1950s, there were signs of political, social, and spiritual anxiety: the fear of communism, the rise of conservatism and modern evangelical Christianity, and the coming of the early civil rights movement. Prosperity could not ultimately address those sources of American restlessness, a fact that the great social upheavals of the 1960s would demonstrate.

■ SELECTED BIBLIOGRAPHY ■

Altschuler, Glenn C. *All Shook Up: How Rock 'n' Roll Changed America*. New York: Oxford University Press, 2003.

Dittmer, John. *Local People: The Struggle for Civil Rights in Mississippi*. Urbana: University of Illinois Press, 1994.

Dudziak, Mary L. *Cold War Civil Rights: Race and the Image of American Democracy*. Princeton, NJ: Princeton University Press, 2000.

Garrow, David J. *Bearing the Cross: Martin Luther King, Jr., and the Southern Christian Leadership Conference*. New York: William Morrow, 1986.

Herzog, Jonathan P. *The Spiritual-Industrial Complex: America's Religious Battle against Communism in the Early Cold War*. New York: Oxford University Press, 2011.

Jackson, Kenneth T. *Crabgrass Frontier: The Suburbanization of the United States*. New York: Oxford University Press, 1985.

Kirk, Russell. *The Conservative Mind: From Burke to Santayana*. Chicago: H. Regnery, 1953.

Lahr, Angela M. *Millennial Dreams and Apocalyptic Nightmares: The Cold War Origins of Political Evangelicalism*. New York: Oxford University Press, 2007.

Patterson, James T. *Brown v. Board of Education: A Civil Rights Milestone and Its Troubled Legacy*. New York: Oxford University Press, 2002.

———. *Grand Expectations: The United States, 1945–1974*. New York: Oxford University Press, 1996.

Turner, John G. *Bill Bright and Campus Crusade for Christ: The Renewal of Evangelicalism in Postwar America*. Chapel Hill: University of North Carolina Press, 2008.

Wacker, Grant. *America's Pastor: Billy Graham and the Shaping of a Nation*. Cambridge, MA: Harvard University Press, 2014.

26

Civil Rights
and the Great Society

When President John F. Kennedy spoke of a "new frontier" in his acceptance speech at the 1960 Democratic National Convention, it seemed that the nation was preparing to turn a page. Eight years of mainstream Republican politics were about to be replaced with the administration of the fresh-faced, forty-three-year-old Democrat. But Kennedy was also a firm cold warrior. "We shall pay any price, bear any burden, meet any hardship, support any friend, oppose any foe to assure the survival and success of liberty," he declared in his 1961 inaugural address. One of the most resonant moments of Kennedy's presidency came when he visited West Berlin in 1963, declaring in solidarity, "*Ich bin ein Berliner.*" The city had become a democratic island in the midst of communist East Germany. Two years earlier East Germans with Soviet support had erected the Berlin Wall to keep its residents from fleeing to freedom on the western side.

The "*Ich bin ein Berliner*" speech was an important symbol of Kennedy's opposition to communist power, but the greatest international challenge of his presidency had come in 1962, with the Cuban missile crisis. In 1961, Kennedy's administration had tentatively backed an attempt by anti-communist Cuban exiles to overthrow Cuba's communist regime, headed by Fidel Castro. But Castro's forces had destroyed the invading force at the Bay of Pigs in southern Cuba in April 1961. The Bay of Pigs fiasco had convinced the Soviets to begin an escalation of defenses in Cuba to ward off any future American or American-backed attempts to dislodge Castro. This precipitated the US-Soviet clash over Cuba, which one historian has called the "most frightening military crisis in world history." This was the moment the Cold War came the closest to going hot, with the possibility of unfathomable destruction if Russia or the United States had used nuclear weapons.

By mid-1962, the Soviet Union was installing nuclear missiles and launchers in Cuba. The weapons easily could have reached the US mainland. (The United States likewise had missiles in position to hit Cuba.) US intelligence underestimated how formidable the Soviet presence on Cuba was. For example, the Soviets had a military force of 42,000 on the island, twice what American officials believed. Kennedy insisted that the Soviets not put nuclear missiles in Cuba, and Soviet premier Nikita Khrushchev denied that they had. American spy planes revealed otherwise. Kennedy and his advisors debated a range of strategies but settled on enforcing a blockade (technically, a "quarantine") of Cuba, preventing the Soviets from bringing more military equipment to the island. The world watched breathlessly as Soviet ships moved toward the island. But at the last minute, the ships turned around, as the Soviets decided not to provoke the ultimate confrontation.

But nuclear missiles remained in Cuba, and Kennedy demanded that these be removed or the United States would launch a strike to eliminate them. Tensions reached their highest point in late October 1962 when the Soviets shot down an American U-2 spy plane over Cuba. Khrushchev finally agreed to remove the missiles, however, if the United States would commit to not invading Cuba. (Kennedy also secretly let the Russians know that he would remove US missiles from Turkey.) Khrushchev had overplayed his hand, as he was unwilling to face the consequences of placing nuclear missiles in Cuba, perhaps hoping Kennedy would not respond decisively. The outcome of the Cuban missile crisis undoubtedly contributed to Khrushchev's removal as Soviet premier in 1964. Kennedy, likewise, has been criticized for letting the Cuban situation get out of control and for failing to make clear to the Soviets early on that the United States would not tolerate nuclear missiles in Cuba. Some military leaders and Cuban exiles also fumed that Kennedy had missed multiple opportunities to invade Cuba and remove Castro, allowing Castro's oppressive government to stay in place. Whatever else we might say about Kennedy's and Khrushchev's roles, however, the great Cold War powers had come to the brink of nuclear war, and thankfully they had backed away.

The Kennedy Presidency

Although Kennedy continued America's commitment to countering the communist threat, his presidency undoubtedly represented a new era of American politics. Kennedy was from a prominent family of Catholics in Massachusetts, and the nature of his faith became a major issue in the 1960 election. Some critics suggested that a Catholic was necessarily divided in political loyalties between the United States and the Vatican, the seat of power of the Roman Catholic Church. Kennedy vociferously denied that he would be a tool of the pope. Speaking before a Houston ministerial association, he said he believed in an "absolute" separation of church and state. "I am not the Catholic candidate for president. I am the Democratic Party's candidate for president, who happens also to be a Catholic. I do not speak for my church on public matters—and the church does not speak for me," Kennedy declared.

Kennedy's explanations were enough to help hold together Franklin Roosevelt's Democratic coalition of the urban North, African Americans, and the white South. He defeated Richard Nixon of California, Eisenhower's vice president. The staunch segregationist Harry Byrd of Virginia did draw away some electoral votes from Kennedy in the Deep South, but Byrd did not attempt a coordinated campaign, so his outcome did not match that of Strom Thurmond's "Dixiecrat" candidacy of 1948. Helped by his vice-presidential nominee, Texas senator Lyndon Johnson, Kennedy won most of the South. He also won parts of the Midwest and much of the Northeast. He won the Electoral College by more than 80 votes, but out of almost 69 million cast, Kennedy only garnered 100,000 more popular votes than Nixon.

Kennedy was an ideal candidate for the new era of televised politics. In September 1960, Kennedy and Nixon met in the first televised presidential debate in American history. Kennedy seemed relaxed and nimble during debate, while Nixon was visibly uncomfortable. Although Nixon performed better in subsequent debates, a negative public impression about Nixon had already formed. From 1960 forward, presidential candidates had to cultivate an image that would translate well on live television and, more recently, on the internet.

Much of Kennedy's presidency was devoted to countering Soviet ambitions in foreign affairs, military buildup, and the space race. Kennedy called on NASA to land a man on the moon by the end of the 1960s, but the Soviets still seemed to have the edge in space exploration. Just as they had put Sputnik in orbit as the first space satellite, the Soviets also flew the first manned space mission in 1961. But in 1962, the United States sent the former Marine pilot and future senator John Glenn on a successful mission to orbit the earth. Many in America saw Glenn's Mercury Project mission as the moment America caught up with Russia in exploring the heavens. During Richard Nixon's first term, the Apollo missions would fulfill Kennedy's vision of a moon landing. In late 1968, Apollo 8 astronauts read from Genesis 1 during the national telecast of their moon orbit. Then, on July 20, 1969, astronaut Neil Armstrong, commander of the Apollo 11 mission, became the first person to walk on the moon. Armstrong said

Figure 26.1. Astronaut John H. Glenn Jr. dons his silver Mercury pressure suit in preparation for launch of Mercury Atlas 6 rocket, January 20, 1962.

that stepping onto the surface of the moon was "one small step for man, one giant leap for mankind."

Like Truman and Eisenhower, Kennedy was committed to stopping the growth of communist influence. This desire played out most obviously in the Cuban missile crisis. But it also led the United States to seek to protect South Vietnam from communist takeover. During his tenure Kennedy oversaw the expansion of US military personnel in Vietnam from 1,000 to almost 17,000. For a time Kennedy's administration sought to work with the corrupt and unpopular South Vietnamese leader Ngo Dinh Diem. But when a coup removed Diem in 1963, US officials did nothing to stop it or to save Diem's life. Kennedy seemed to believe he could not turn the civil war in Vietnam in favor of the anti-communists in South Vietnam without a major influx of hundreds of thousands of American troops. He was hesitant to do this, especially without a reliable partner in South Vietnam. But he was also convinced the United States should not abandon South Vietnam to communist power. By the end of his presidency, it was unclear which direction Kennedy would have taken in Vietnam, whether withdrawal or escalation. Johnson, Kennedy's successor, would choose escalation.

Civil Rights

Kennedy was conflicted about how aggressively to move on civil rights issues as well. He was sympathetic to the civil rights movement, but he also did not wish to alienate white southern Democrats, on whom his political fortunes in the South depended. But civil rights protestors persisted in their attacks on Jim Crow segregation. By 1961, the

Supreme Court had repeatedly ruled against segregation on buses and bus terminals, yet many bus stations remained segregated and closed to blacks. Believing they had the law and a rising tide of public opinion on their side, activists decided to launch the "Freedom Rides" in 1961. Freedom riders insisted on gaining access to segregated bus terminal facilities. Leaders affiliated with groups including the Congress of Racial Equality informed the Kennedy administration that the rides were going to happen, hoping to secure some federal protection from the violence that was likely to ensue. The administration took little action, however, permitting vicious attacks on the riders— both blacks and whites—by white adversaries in places such as Anniston, Alabama. In Birmingham dozens of men affiliated with the Ku Klux Klan assaulted the freedom riders with chains and pipes. The activists had to call off the rest of the trip, fearing for their lives. But hundreds more activists followed in their wake, finally prompting the Interstate Commerce Commission to order an end to segregation in the bus stations.

The Kennedy administration tended to react to events in the civil rights movement rather than taking the initiative. The administration's hesitancy opened the door for more episodes, such as the clash over integrating the University of Mississippi in 1962. An African American Air Force veteran named James Meredith sought to become the first black student at the university, but Mississippi governor Ross Barnett vowed to stop it from happening. He called the defense of segregation a "righteous cause" and promised that Mississippi whites would not "drink from the cup of genocide." Barnett vowed to keep order at the university as Meredith prepared to enroll, but then he allowed Mississippi state police to withdraw when white rioters clashed with federal marshals on the campus in Oxford. Hundreds were injured, and two people died in the

Figure 26.2. *Integration at Ole Miss[issippi] Univ[ersity] / MST,* by Marion S. Trikosko, October 1, 1962. Photograph shows James Meredith walking on the campus of the University of Mississippi, accompanied by US marshals.

ensuing violence before attorney general Robert Kennedy sent in thousands more federal personnel to keep the peace and protect Meredith. Meredith, guarded by federal officials, managed to stay at the university and graduated in 1963 (he had come in with significant transfer credit).

In 1963, Martin Luther King and other leaders targeted Birmingham, Alabama, for the next great campaign against segregation. Birmingham had a reputation as having the most entrenched system of segregation and white supremacy in the nation. King guessed that when the campaign began, hostile whites led by Birmingham police commissioner Bull Connor would try to silence the protestors through violence. This would draw more sympathy to the civil rights movement from a national audience. Early in the Birmingham campaign, King was arrested and wrote his "Letter from Birmingham Jail," the most influential essay of his career. Addressing his "fellow clergymen" who were asking civil rights activists to moderate their approach, King explained why the activists could wait no longer for change. They had been waiting since the founding of the American colonies for an end to racial oppression, he said. The champions of civil rights were "standing up for what is best in the American dream and for the most sacred values in our Judeo-Christian heritage, thereby bringing our nation back to those great wells of democracy which were dug deep by the founding fathers in their formulation of the Constitution and the Declaration of Independence," he argued. They were not extremists, King said, unless you considered figures such as Jesus, Thomas Jefferson, and Abraham Lincoln as extremists too.

The civil rights activists ratcheted up the pressure in Birmingham when they sent 1,000 students and young children on a march into the city. Bull Connor arrested most of them and ordered the leaders not to send anyone else marching into the city. When the protestors disobeyed Connor's order, Connor snapped and turned the city's police and firefighters against the marchers. Using clubs, attack dogs, and high-pressure hoses, the city forces brutalized many of the marchers, including some children. Many of the marchers, including prominent Baptist pastor Fred Shuttlesworth, were knocked unconscious by blasts from the water cannons. Some of the protesters were so incensed by Connor's tactics that they gave up on nonviolence and began retaliating, though with far less force (generally they threw rocks and bottles at the police).

Much of the violence in Birmingham was shown on national television. It embarrassed many who were watching, including President Kennedy. Kennedy determined that it was time for him to throw his weight behind a new civil rights bill to prohibit segregation in public facilities and to ban discrimination on the basis of race, religion, or sex. Civil rights activists knew that to receive this kind of presidential backing represented a major milestone. But their joy was dampened the night Kennedy announced

Figure 26.3. In this May 4, 1963, photo, police lead a group of black schoolchildren to jail after their arrest for protesting against racial discrimination near city hall in Birmingham, Alabama.

his support for the bill when World War II veteran and NAACP worker Medgar Evers was shot in the back outside his home in Jackson, Mississippi. The murderer, Byron De La Beckwith, was not convicted of the crime until the 1990s, as all-white juries originally deadlocked in trials in 1963. Evers was buried in Arlington National Cemetery outside of Washington, DC.

Civil rights leaders were mixed in their view of Kennedy's proposed law, with some fearing it would become a meaningless gesture without real legal authority. Bayard Rustin of the Southern Christian Leadership Conference and A. Philip Randolph, a longtime labor and civil rights activist, organized the August 1963 March on Washington to promote the adoption of a far-reaching civil rights bill. They originally envisioned the march as including a sit-in at the Capitol, but the Kennedy administration worked feverishly to moderate the event's tone and aims. By August 28, it had become a short march, concluding with a number of speakers at the Lincoln Memorial. Critics such as the Nation of Islam leader Malcolm X called it the "Farce on Washington." Nevertheless, the March on Washington drew a titanic crowd of some 250,000 people to the national mall. Popular singers including Bob Dylan, Joan Baez, and Mahalia Jackson participated. But

Martin Luther King gave the most memorable address in his iconic "I Have a Dream" speech." Filled with allusions to the Bible and to America's founding, it reads, in part:

> I have a dream that one day this nation will rise up and live out the true meaning of its creed, "We hold these truths to be self-evident, that all men are created equal." I have a dream that one day on the red hills of Georgia, sons of former slaves and the sons of former slave owners will be able to sit down together at the table of brotherhood. I have a dream that one day even the state of Mississippi, a state sweltering with the heat of injustice, sweltering with the heat of oppression, will be transformed into an oasis of freedom and justice.
>
> I have a dream that my four little children will one day live in a nation where they will not be judged by the color of their skin but by the content of their character. . . .
>
> I have a dream that one day every valley shall be exalted, and every hill and mountain shall be made low. The rough places will be made plain, and the crooked places will be made straight; "and the glory of the Lord shall be revealed, and all flesh shall see it together" [Isa 40:4–5]. . . .
>
> . . . When we allow freedom to ring, when we let it ring from every village and every hamlet, from every state and every city, we will be able to speed up that day when all of God's children, black men and white men, Jews and Gentiles, Protestants and Catholics, will be able to join hands and sing in the words of the old Negro spiritual: "Free at last! Free at last! Thank God Almighty, we are free at last."*

As moving as King's speech was, it did not break the logjam in Congress over the proposed civil rights legislation. Three weeks after the March on Washington, in a brutal reminder of the enduring racial hostility in the South, an explosion devastated the Sixteenth Street Baptist Church in Birmingham on a September Sunday morning. The blast killed four girls ranging in age from eleven to fourteen. Federal investigators identified four members of the Ku Klux Klan as those who had planted the dynamite, but no prosecutions went forward until years later.

The Kennedy Assassination

Anticipating a tough reelection campaign in 1964, President Kennedy and his wife, Jacqueline, made a visit to Texas in November 1963. On November 22, the Kennedys

---

*Reprinted by arrangement with The Heirs to the Estate of Martin Luther King Jr., c/o Writers House as agent for the proprietor New York, NY. Copyright © 1963 Dr. Martin Luther King, Jr. © renewed 1991 Coretta Scott King.

took a ride in an open-air motorcade through Dallas. As their car passed the Texas School Book Depository building, the Kennedys and their entourage came under fire. President Kennedy suffered a fatal shot to the head. A man named Abraham Zapruder took the most complete video footage of the assassination, having brought a home movie camera to film Kennedy's visit but hardly expecting to document an assassination. The gruesome scene captured in the Zapruder film has become one of the most studied and controversial pieces of video in American history.

Dallas police quickly arrested Lee Harvey Oswald, who worked at the book depository, and charged him with killing Kennedy. Just days later Oswald himself was shot to death by a Dallas nightclub owner named Jack Ruby when Oswald was being moved by police. (News cameras caught the killing of Oswald happening live.) The circumstances and gravity of Kennedy's killing spawned an industry devoted to studying the assassination and proposing theories about how it happened and who was involved. President Lyndon Johnson appointed a commission led by Chief Justice Earl Warren to investigate. The Warren Commission determined that Oswald was the lone shooter and that he was not part of a larger conspiracy. Oswald was an unstable person with communist sympathies who had once lived in the Soviet Union for almost three years. Although US officials were generally content with the Warren Commission report, others have suggested that Oswald may not have been the only gunman or that he may have been part of a plot by the Soviets, Cubans, or organized crime members to kill Kennedy.

Kennedy had served as president for fewer than three years, so his accomplishments were necessarily limited. But the assassination and the remarkable dignity shown by Jacqueline Kennedy in the days following his death enshrined his status as an American martyr. Lyndon Johnson became the new president, sworn in on the presidential airplane *Air Force One* as it went back to Washington. Johnson believed the national government should honor Kennedy's memory by fulfilling his legislative agenda, including in the area of civil rights. Echoing Lincoln's Gettysburg Address, Johnson told Congress, "Let us here highly resolve that John Fitzgerald Kennedy did not live or die in vain."

Johnson, Poverty, and Civil Rights

Kennedy had picked Lyndon Johnson as his vice president for regional balance on the presidential ticket and because of Johnson's remarkable skills in dealing with Congress. Johnson grew up in rural Texas, was almost a decade older than Kennedy, and had little of Kennedy's polish. But Johnson was a master of the legislative process in Congress and had an unparalleled gift for persuading congressmen and senators to support his proposals. That gift of persuasion did not entirely translate to the presidency; nevertheless,

Johnson would oversee far more dramatic legislative change than Kennedy had. One of Johnson's first moves was to drive through an $11 billion income tax cut that Kennedy had proposed, which boosted consumer spending and helped create a million new jobs per year.

Johnson also moved forward with another Kennedy initiative that Johnson called the "War on Poverty." A little more than 20 percent of the nation lived below what experts designated the "poverty line." The American poor did not make enough money to meet basic needs for themselves and their families. (Critics observed that many of those designated as "poor" certainly had more affluence than the abject poor of the Great Depression era.) Johnson was convinced, along with other political liberals, that the right government programs could better the lot of the poor. Instead of making people permanently dependent on government, liberals believed, the best kinds of "welfare" programs would empower the poor to improve their job status and income and to ascend out of poverty. Conservatives were wary, believing top-down government programs inevitably became bloated and often did as much damage as good. Conservatives supposed that if anyone could help the poor, it was the poor themselves, as well as "mediating institutions" on the local level: families, schools, and churches. National government bureaucrats could never understand how to be of real assistance. In spite of these criticisms, Congress passed the $1 billion Economic Opportunity Act of 1964, which created the Office of Economic Opportunity and a host of job training and community development programs. Much of the bill's funding went to pay program administrators.

Getting the long-stalled Civil Rights Act passed would be difficult. Johnson knew that many of his fellow southern Democrats would stridently oppose the measure and seek to kill it by filibustering in the Senate. (Filibusters entailed endless talk and discussion about the bill, which senators could only end by a vote for cloture, which at the time required a two-thirds majority.) In 1957, South Carolina's Strom Thurmond had set the record for the longest filibuster by a single senator, speaking for more than twenty-four hours in opposition to another civil rights measure. But Johnson wielded his great powers of persuasion to bring enough Republicans on board, and Congress passed the Civil Rights Act of 1964.

The law prohibited racial discrimination by businesses that served the public such as restaurants, theaters, and hotels, and it directed states and towns to repeal remaining Jim Crow laws related to segregation. In what would become a common move by the federal government, the act warned that any school or other institution that received federal dollars could risk a loss of funding if they maintained any discriminatory policies. It also banned employment discrimination on the basis of race and color as well as sex or religion. The Civil Rights Act was a landmark measure, although it left many areas unaddressed such as voting rights. It also did not propose any substantive solutions to "de facto" segregation, meaning segregation that depended on local practice and custom rather than documented laws or policies ("de jure" segregation). De facto segregation was pervasive in many parts of American society outside the South. Segregationist policies were often more blatant in the South, but in some other areas of the country, they were just as entrenched.

The 1964 Election

Johnson wanted to secure a major victory in the 1964 presidential election, which would give him a mandate for his legislative agenda. His War on Poverty had fueled a backlash in the conservative movement, opening the door for Senator Barry Goldwater of Arizona to win the Republican nomination. Goldwater defeated Republican opponents coming from the establishment/Eisenhower segment of the party. Goldwater was an articulate and remarkably frank defender of conservative orthodoxy, but he was unwilling to moderate his rhetoric to score political points, so he was an ideal opponent for Johnson to defeat by a large margin. Knowing that many had accused him of political extremism, Goldwater gladly embraced the label. "Extremism in the defense of liberty is no vice," he told the Republican National Convention, and "moderation in pursuit of justice is no virtue." Johnson trounced Goldwater in the Electoral College, 486 votes to 52. Johnson also won 61 percent of the popular vote nationally.

Goldwater's losing candidacy was of enormous consequence, however, because it was an early indicator of massive shifts happening in regional political alliances. First, the Arizona senator's nomination signaled that leadership in the Republican Party was moving toward the West and Southwest. Most of the party's presidential nominees for the next four decades would hail from places such as Arizona, California, and Texas. One of those future nominees, Ronald Reagan of California, gave a major speech on Goldwater's behalf in the fall of 1964, explaining his tough stance on communism and opposition to top-down government programs and high taxes.

Citing the Bible, the American Founders, and Abraham Lincoln, Reagan explained why America could never cut a peace deal with the Soviets or leave the people of Cuba and Eastern Europe to languish under oppression. "Should Moses have told the children of Israel to live in slavery under the pharaohs?" Reagan asked. "Should Christ have refused the cross? Should the patriots at Concord Bridge have thrown down their guns and refused to fire the shot heard 'round the world? . . . You and I have a rendezvous with destiny. We will preserve for our children this, the last best hope of man on earth, or we will sentence them to take the last step into a thousand years of darkness."

Barry Goldwater's candidacy also signaled the end of the "solid South" for Democrats. Even though Johnson was a Texas Democrat, his support for government expansion and for the Civil Rights Act alienated many white southerners, who began defecting to the Republican Party and to Goldwater. Goldwater's only regional pocket of support was in the Deep South, where he won the states from Louisiana to South Carolina. Leading southern Democrats also shifted to the Republican Party: Strom Thurmond of South Carolina, for example, switched his affiliation to the Republicans during Goldwater's campaign. Democrats retained a number of key offices in the South and could still win some southern states in presidential contests. But the long-term trend was toward a new "solid South," this time in the Republican column.

The Great Society

In May 1964, as part of his reelection campaign, Johnson had explained his vision for the "Great Society" in America. "The Great Society rests on abundance and liberty for all," Johnson declared. "It demands an end to poverty and racial injustice, to which we are totally committed in our time. But that is just the beginning. The Great Society is a place where every child can find knowledge to enrich his mind and to enlarge his talents. It is a place where leisure is a welcome chance to build and reflect, not a feared cause of boredom and restlessness. It is a place where the city of man serves not only the needs of the body and the demands of commerce but the desire for beauty and the hunger for community." Spurred on by his overwhelming electoral victory in November 1964, Johnson set out to pass arguably the most ambitious legislative program since the presidency of Franklin Roosevelt. One of his measures vastly increased federal dollars for education, as Johnson and his supporters saw well-funded schools as a key to getting kids out of poverty. Critics argued that all the federal funding in the world could not change the factors that made for the best education: motivated teachers teaching safe and healthy kids who were part of supportive family and social networks.

Johnson also wanted to expand the "safety net" for older Americans, a process begun in the 1930s with the creation of Social Security. Half of Americans sixty-five and older in 1965 had no health insurance, and serious illnesses or injuries could easily bring financial ruin to the uninsured. Of course, older people were more likely to develop serious long-term ailments, so it was difficult for many of them to afford health insurance. Relying almost exclusively on Democratic votes, Johnson passed the Medicare program, which increased Social Security taxes to cover hospital stays for the elderly and offered subsidized health insurance to help cover other types of medical expenses for older Americans.

Medicare has become a fixture of old-age medical care in America. But the rising percentage of Americans over the age of sixty-five and rising costs of medical services have combined to make Medicare enormously expensive. In recent years Medicare expenses alone (not including the "Medicaid" program for low-income Americans) represented about 14 percent of all federal expenditures. Critics have noted that widespread insurance coverage has fed the rapid rise in medical costs. Doctors and patients have little incentive to keep costs down when patients are covering only a fraction of those costs "out of pocket." Battles over the 2010 Affordable Care Act suggested that Americans were still grappling with the tension between expanding health insurance coverage and the skyrocketing costs associated with doing so.

Democrats also pushed through immigration reform. At first glance the Immigration and Nationality Act of 1965 seemed to be of lesser short-term consequence than the other pillars of the Great Society. But this law would have transformative effects on the demographics of American society. The law was originally intended to even out the countries of origin of immigrants coming from Europe and to allow more people to come from southern and eastern Europe in particular. It abolished the previous national quota approach, which critics viewed as outdated and racist because of the preferences the United States had previously given to prospective immigrants from northern and western Europe. The 1965 law put the focus of immigration on people who had relatives in the United States and people with certain job skills. But the immigration law had many unintended consequences, and it set the stage for a new wave of immigrants from non-European nations. Unauthorized immigrants from Mexico and Central America continued to be an issue. But Mexico also became one of the top sources of legal immigrants to the United States, along with Latin American nations such as the Dominican Republic and Cuba and Asian nations such as Korea, the Philippines, Taiwan, and India. China produced the largest number of Asian immigrants after 1965. (The 1882 Chinese Exclusion Act had been repealed during World War II.) By the time of the 2010 US Census, the number of Chinese Americans was approaching 4 million.

The Johnson administration also saw major new initiatives related to environmental regulation. Spurred by the book *Silent Spring* (1962) by marine biologist Rachel Carson, many Americans had become concerned about the damaging effects of mass American industry, farming, and transportation on the natural world. (Carson was especially focused on the threat posed by indiscriminate use of toxic pesticides in agricultural businesses.) The landmark 1963 Clean Air Act encouraged states and towns to control air pollution. Congress added a number of major amendments to the Clean Air Act over several decades, accounting for new threats and technological advances such as the ability to control pollutant emissions from automobiles. Congress also passed measures in the mid-1960s intended to encourage clean water and to stop the pollution of rivers, lakes, and oceans.

Likewise, the Wilderness Act of 1964 set aside millions of acres of land the government protected from development, believing it was important to maintain large tracts that are "untrammeled by man." Over time the National Wilderness Preservation System has designated more than 100 million acres in America as protected wilderness. Critics of the wilderness system (and of the associated power of the president to designate areas as national monuments) say it hurts economic opportunity in the affected areas by cutting them off from even modest development. In 1970, Richard Nixon authorized the creation of the Environmental Protection Agency, which would become the most influential environmental regulatory unit of the federal government.

Freedom Summer and the Voting Rights Act

Civil rights reform continued to be one of the most difficult and controversial parts of Johnson's Great Society initiatives. The Civil Rights Act of 1964 was a major success, but activists believed they still had a long way to go to secure adequate education and voting rights for nonwhites. Led by the civil rights umbrella organization called the Council of Federated Organizations (including members from the Southern Christian Leadership Conference, the Student Nonviolent Coordinating Committee, and others), civil rights workers launched "Freedom Summer" in 1964 in Mississippi. They sought to register black voters and to set up "Freedom Schools" for African American children. The schools, meeting outside of the public school system—often in church basements—focused on civics and humanities education and inculcated the ideals of the civil rights movement. Freedom Summer led to another reaction among white supremacists, with Klansmen murdering three more civil rights workers near Philadelphia, Mississippi.

The Council of Federated Organizations also worked to establish an alternative Democratic Party in Mississippi, the Mississippi Freedom Democratic Party (MFDP), to challenge the power of the white-dominated official Democratic Party in the state. The MFDP believed they had a real chance at some kind of recognition from the national Democratic Party in light of Johnson's leadership on the Civil Rights Act. But Johnson saw the MFDP as troublemakers and tried to fend off any kind of formal participation by them at the party's 1964 national convention in Atlantic City, New Jersey.

The controversy over the MFDP set the stage for the eloquent appeals for civil rights of Fannie Lou Hamer, who came from a poor sharecropping family in Ruleville.

For her efforts at registering people to vote and speaking up for civil rights, Hamer was beaten and tortured by policemen and prisoners at a jail in Winona, Mississippi. A person of deep Christian faith, Hamer shared Bible verses with the jailer's wife after the beating and asked the jailer himself, "[Do you] ever wonder how you'll feel when the time comes [that] you'll have to meet God?" The police who oversaw her torture were tried in court, but an all-white jury exonerated them. Hamer pressed on, working for the Student Nonviolent Coordinating Committee for ten dollars a week. During the day Hamer would try to get sharecroppers to register to vote; at night she and other activists would meet in church rallies, singing gospel music and urging one another to keep going.

In August 1964, Hamer testified before the Democratic Convention on behalf of having the MFDP recognized. Her testimony and others were carried live on national television, and President Johnson was so concerned about the damage the MFDP was doing that he interrupted the coverage of Hamer with a press conference of his own on an unrelated topic. Hamer told the convention, "If the Freedom Democratic Party is not seated now, I question America."* The MFDP brought a total of sixty-eight delegates and alternates to the convention, but Democratic officials proved unwilling to give them anything more than token representation. The MFDP ended up getting no delegates seated at all.

In spite of the disappointment at the Democratic convention, civil rights activists kept working for reform, setting their sights in early 1965 on Selma, Alabama. Although that town of 29,000 had a majority of African Americans, fewer than 400 blacks were registered to vote in Selma. The white-run registration board would disqualify prospective voters for the most trivial errors in their applications. Civil rights leaders, recalling their experiences in Birmingham, expected Selma authorities to overreact and damage the segregationist cause. They were right. More than 3,000 demonstrators were jailed, including Martin Luther King and future congressman John Lewis. Selma police brutalized a number of protestors, beating them with nightsticks and shocking them with cattle prods.

In March 1965, King organized a protest march that would go from Selma to the Alabama state capital at Montgomery. As Lewis and other leaders led a crowd of 600 marchers toward the Edmund Pettis Bridge on the edge of Selma, Alabama police stood at the other end, telling them, "Go back to your church." When the protesters did not disperse, the police advanced, swinging their clubs. A policeman struck Lewis

---

* "Fannie Lou Hamer's Powerful Testimony | Freedom Summer," YouTube video, 3:40, June 23, 2014, https://www.youtube.com/watch?v=07PwNVCZCcY.

viciously, leaving him with a fractured skull. The police also unleashed tear gas on the crowd. Seventy marchers were ultimately hospitalized with injuries from the clash on "Bloody Sunday" at Selma. Federal officials belatedly allowed the march to go forward with protection two weeks later, with tens of thousands of supporters finally gathering at the Montgomery statehouse and singing "We Shall Overcome," a gospel song that had become one of the movement's anthems.

President Johnson was always attuned to political timing, and he knew Bloody Sunday had opened the door again to major civil rights reform. In August 1965, Johnson signed the Voting Rights Act, which Congress had passed with bipartisan support over the resistance of southern members. The act authorized the Justice Department to take action against discriminatory practices in voter registration and in voting itself. The act increased the number of African American adults registered to vote. In the six Deep South states of particular concern to the Justice Department, the percentage of eligible African Americans registered went up from less than a third to almost half in one year. The original promise of the Fifteenth Amendment to the Constitution, that of color-blind voting rights, was being fulfilled.

Figure 26.4. Participants, some carrying American flags, in the civil rights march from Selma to Montgomery, Alabama, in 1965. Photograph by Peter Pettus.

The Limitations of Civil Rights Reform

By 1965, the civil rights movement had an impressive list of successes to its credit, from *Brown v. Board of Education* to the Voting Rights Act. But some worried that the legal changes could not address the intractable social and economic inequality of African Americans, a status that had its roots in slavery and the tribulations of the Reconstruction era. The inadequacies of civil rights reform were cast into sharp relief the same month as the signing of the Voting Rights Act, when the largely African American neighborhood of Watts in Los Angeles exploded in riots. The violence in Watts led to dozens of deaths and tens of millions of dollars' worth of property damage from looting and arson. Where much of the civil rights movement had been animated by the principles of nonviolent resistance, the Watts rioters struck out against white motorists and businesses. This resulted in a harsh crackdown on black rioters by Los Angeles police, turning Watts into a veritable war zone. Similar episodes of violence and rioting spread to other American cities over the next few years.

Some observers suggested that the problems in black communities like Watts had less to do with a lack of political rights and more to do with a breakdown of family and social support networks. Assistant secretary of labor and future US senator Daniel Patrick Moynihan made this argument in his controversial 1965 report "The Negro Family: The Case for National Action." Moynihan contended rampant divorce, out-of-wedlock pregnancies, and dependence on government welfare programs had been toxic to African American families. Moynihan said that the black family was trapped in a "tangle of pathology" that made it difficult for African American teenagers to break out of poverty. Moynihan asserted that if the federal government really wanted to bring about full equality for African Americans, it needed to do whatever it could to enhance the "stability and resources of the Negro American family." Moynihan, who soon joined the faculty at Harvard, seemed genuinely interested in helping African American families. But critics saw the report as smug and patronizing. Congress of Racial Equality leader James Farmer saw Moynihan as blaming the oppressed instead of the oppressor. "We are sick to death of being analyzed, mesmerized, bought, sold, and slobbered over, while the same evils that are the ingredients of our oppression go unattended."

Some disillusioned black critics questioned the goals of the civil rights movement itself. Returning to themes of the early twentieth-century debates between Booker T. Washington and W. E. B. Du Bois, some argued that blacks would be better off if they remained separate from whites. Among the most provocative advocates of this view was Nation of Islam leader Malcolm X. The Nation of Islam was a distinctly American version of the Muslim religion. The Nation of Islam had emerged in urban America during the Great Depression. Malcolm was born Malcolm Little and was the son of a Baptist pastor, but he rejected his parents' faith. While Malcolm was once serving jail time for burglary, his brother told him about the Nation of Islam. Malcolm converted to the Nation and changed his last name to X because he said his surname was a name imposed on his ancestors by slave owners.

Malcolm argued that blacks should build their own strong institutions and largely avoid cooperation with whites, whom they could not trust. He generated great controversy when he said President Kennedy's assassination was a matter of "chickens coming home to roost." He fell out with the Nation of Islam's leader, Elijah Muhammad, but Malcolm also condemned Martin Luther King, calling him a "chump" and a "fool" for his focus on integration. Malcolm broke with the Nation of Islam in 1964, and after going on a traditional Muslim pilgrimage to Mecca, he converted to a more orthodox form of Sunni Islam. In 1965, Malcolm was assassinated, likely by enemies from the Nation of Islam. Some have speculated that US officials may have played a role in Malcolm's death.

Malcolm's book *The Autobiography of Malcolm X* (1965), which he wrote with Alex Haley, was one of the most compelling spiritual biographies in American history. It powerfully addressed the experience of African American alienation and the trials of Malcolm's relationship with the Nation of Islam. Malcolm and the Nation of Islam attracted some high-profile African American converts, including the most accomplished heavyweight boxer of the era, Cassius Clay. Clay changed his name to Muhammad Ali in 1964. Ali cited his commitment to the Nation of Islam in 1967 when he was drafted but refused to enlist in the army. He was stripped of his boxing title when he was convicted of draft evasion, but the Supreme Court overturned his conviction in 1971, arguing that Ali did not receive fair consideration for his claim of conscientious objector status. Like Malcolm X, Ali had gravitated toward a mainstream version of Sunni Islam by the early 1970s.

The Supreme Court, Individual Rights, and the Public Exercise of Religion

The school desegregation decision in *Brown v. Board of Education* heralded an aggressive era for the Supreme Court, which routinely sought to expand the scope of the First and Fourteenth Amendments and of other constitutional protections for individuals. Sometimes the aggressive decisions of Chief Justice Earl Warren's court were warmly received by a wide range of Americans, while other decisions caused controversies that persist in America today. Previous Supreme Courts had sometimes been profoundly traditional, even seeming to resist the plain implication of the Constitution on issues such as racial equality. Now the Supreme Court positioned itself as a leader on social change and individual rights in America. If legislators would not mandate cultural and legal advances, the Supreme Court might do so instead. For example, in cases such as *Miranda v. Arizona* (1966), the court came down on the side of the rights of people accused of crimes. In *Miranda*, a narrow majority of the justices mandated that a suspect must be advised of his or her legal rights before interrogation can proceed. They argued that the Fifth and Sixth Amendments protected the accused against self-incrimination and guaranteed them the right of representation and that law enforcement officials were obligated to tell the accused about those protections. The court in *Miranda* said police must inform alleged criminals that they have the right to remain silent, that any statements they make can be used against them in court, and that they have the right to consult with an attorney. This became known as the "Miranda warning," which became a fixture of many arrest scenes in movies and on TV. Dissenting justices argued that the *Miranda* requirement went far beyond what the Constitution said about the rights of the accused and that it would set the stage for innumerable criminals to be released on technicalities.

The Supreme Court also made a key decision on the freedom of the press in *New York Times v. Sullivan* (1964). This case was intertwined with the ongoing controversies related to civil rights, as a city commissioner in Montgomery, Alabama, sued the *New York Times* for running an advertisement that characterized the white backlash and police crackdowns against civil rights protestors in Montgomery as a "wave of terror." Under Alabama law this statement could be construed as libel because it damaged the reputation of a public official. Alabama courts found for the commissioner and awarded him $500,000 in damages, but the Supreme Court unanimously overturned the decision. They struck down Alabama's libel law, contending that it violated the First Amendment. Libel in the press required clear evidence of "actual malice," justices said, or knowledge that the statement in question was false, or at least "reckless disregard of whether it was false or not." This was a much higher standard for libel than Alabama's definition, and *New York Times v. Sullivan* helped foster America's no-holds-barred media environment when it comes to criticizing public officials.

Another of the court's crucial decisions during this era was *Griswold v. Connecticut* (1965), in which the court struck down a Connecticut state law against contraceptives, including drugs or devices intended to keep a woman from getting pregnant. Estelle Griswold, director of Planned Parenthood of Connecticut, had been charged with distributing contraceptives. The Supreme Court overturned Griswold's conviction and struck down the state's law against contraception. The justices based their ruling on the idea that people had a constitutional right to privacy, even though that right was not stipulated anywhere in the Constitution. Neither did the Constitution suggest that the Supreme Court must strike down state laws that restricted privacy. Nevertheless, Justice William O. Douglas argued that the court could infer the individual right to privacy from the "penumbras" of rights guaranteed in the First and Fourteenth Amendments, among others. The penumbras were "formed by emanations from those guarantees that help give them life and substance." The two justices who dissented in the case contended that since the right to privacy was not stated in the Constitution, it was beyond the power of the court to enforce such a right. While the immediate effects of *Griswold v. Connecticut* were somewhat limited, the decision was a critical precedent for future decisions related to morality, sexuality, and privacy. Most notably, the decision was foundational for *Roe v. Wade*, the 1973 decision legalizing abortion.

Many of the most transformative judicial decisions of the 1950s and 1960s indicated a growing concern by the court to interpret the Constitution as protecting minority groups from unfair practices or laws supported by majority groups. Along these lines some of the court's most controversial rulings of the early 1960s had to do with religion in public schools. In most parts of the country, there was broad-based support for religious teaching or Bible reading in schools. But small groups of dissenters argued that official promotion of religion violated their consciences and represented an "establishment of religion." The First Amendment had forbidden Congress from making any law respecting an establishment, but the courts increasingly applied such restrictions on Congress to states and towns. (The legal principle of expanding the applications of the amendment is called the "incorporation" of the First Amendment's guarantees.) At the time of the American founding, many states still had official tax-supported denominations, which was the original meaning of the term "establishment." Now courts decreed that even generic public religious expressions represented unconstitutional breaches of the "wall of separation" between church and state, a phrase taken from an 1802 letter written by Thomas Jefferson. The courts gave less weight in these types of cases to the First Amendment's guarantee of "free exercise of religion."

One of the Supreme Court's major decisions about religion in schools was *Engel v. Vitale* (1962), in which plaintiffs objected to a theistic (not explicitly Christian) school-day prayer sanctioned by public schools in New York. Although students could leave the room during the prayer or decline to participate, the court ruled that these protections were insufficient and that the prayer represented an establishment of religion. The decision did not intend to stifle student-initiated prayers or the silent prayers of any individuals at public schools. But the court determined that state officials could not compose prayers for students to recite.

The court followed up *Engel* with *Abington School District v. Schempp* (1963), which prohibited officially sanctioned Bible reading in public schools. Before *Abington*, it was common for American schools to have Bible readings as part of regular school-day activities. The majority of American states permitted such readings, and thirteen states required them. Typically teachers would read Bible passages without comment to avoid sectarian controversy. But since the Bible used was primarily the King James Version, groups that did not use or accept the authority of the King James, including Catholics, Jews, and others, sometimes felt excluded. At Abington High School in Pennsylvania, teachers actually used other holy texts besides the King James, including Catholic and Jewish versions of the Scriptures. But the Schempp family, who were Unitarians, protested that the Bible reading itself violated their consciences and represented an establishment of religion. (In a related case in Baltimore, an atheist family objected to Bible reading and a recitation of the Lord's Prayer.) The practice of official Bible readings in schools disappeared in most areas of the country after *Abington School District*, although courts have given latitude for student-led Bible clubs. Courts have also permitted some Bible-oriented school content as long as it approaches the Scriptures as history or literature, not as devotional material.

Many Christians lamented the effects of *Engel* and especially of *Abington School District*. Some said they could accept *Engel*'s ban on generically theistic prayer. Prohibiting Bible reading seemed like a severer blow. The president of the National Association of Evangelicals said *Abington* was helping create an "atmosphere of hostility to religion" in the schools. The government was supposed to be neutral between religion and irreligion, but the decision opened "the door for the full establishment of secularism as a negative form of religion." Numerous Catholic leaders also criticized the rulings in spite of some reservations Catholics once had about schools reading from Protestant Bibles. The Catholic archbishop of New York said the Supreme Court's decisions had struck "at the heart of the Godly tradition in which America's children have for so long been raised." Jewish and mainline denominational leaders generally supported the decisions. Many Southern Baptists, due to their denomination's historic antipathy toward any state collusion with religion, were content with the rulings, especially *Engel*. Some African American pastors regretted the court's actions in *Engel* and *Abington*, although Martin Luther King Jr. thought the prayer decision was correct.

"Who is to determine what prayer is spoken, and by whom?" he asked. Public schools were not in the best position to decide, he said.

Johnson and Vietnam

Johnson, Congress, and the Supreme Court initiated a host of transformative changes at home in America in the mid-1960s. Foreign policy, however, would prove Johnson's undoing. Naval altercations between US and communist North Vietnamese forces in August 1964 led Johnson to propose the Gulf of Tonkin resolution, under which Congress authorized the president "to take all necessary measures to repel any armed attack against the forces of the United States and to prevent further aggression" in the region. Although critics charged that Johnson had exaggerated the nature of the August 1964 clash in Vietnam, Congress overwhelmingly approved the resolution. It effectively allowed Johnson to take America to war in Vietnam without a formal declaration of war. In the short term the Gulf of Tonkin resolution undercut Barry Goldwater's assertion that the Democrats were weak on communism, boosting Johnson's landslide victory in the 1964 election.

Although Johnson was aware of the perils of sending large numbers of American troops into Vietnam, he began to escalate the American presence there in mid-1965. He hoped to save the floundering South Vietnamese government from the communist Viet Cong rebels, sending 50,000 Americans into South Vietnam and indicating he would send more if necessary. By the end of 1967, the number of US troops committed to Vietnam had expanded to 500,000. The Americans had massive advantages over the North Vietnamese and the Viet Cong, especially in air power. The American army dumped copious amounts of the defoliating chemical Agent Orange and the firebombing fuel napalm to clear out communists' cover and deprive them of food supplies. (Agent Orange was toxic and left many American soldiers and Vietnamese people with chronic health problems.) But years of bombardment of the communist forces availed little. The communist rebels were masters of guerrilla warfare and ambush attacks.

The American army in Vietnam was young. The average age of the GIs in Vietnam was only nineteen. Most of the American soldiers came from poor or working-class families, and Hispanics and African Americans were disproportionately represented in the army. Men who were in college could typically get student deferments, while those who went to work after high school often got drafted and sent to Vietnam. Future president Donald Trump, for example, got four student deferments and one medical exemption (for bone spurs in his feet). American soldiers felt pride in their call to serve. But many also became disenchanted with the lack of clear objectives in the war and suffered under the constant threat of land mines and Viet Cong ambushes. Relations between the South Vietnamese and American forces in the field were often tense, as Americans suspected that South Vietnamese "allies" were actually communist sympathizers.

American commanders too often measured success by the number of Vietnamese killed, or what became known as the "body count." This tempted soldiers to kill any Vietnamese person whether they were sure of their allegiances. If they encountered a Vietnamese person in the jungle at night, US soldiers assumed he or she was Viet Cong. One soldier expressed the frustration of many when he asked, "What am I doing here? We don't take any land. We don't give it back. We just mutilate bodies. What the f**** am I doing here?" Both sides committed atrocities against the other, culminating in episodes such as the US massacre of hundreds of unarmed Vietnamese civilians at My Lai in 1968.

Figure 26.5. A soldier of the First Infantry Division motions to a woman refugee to keep her children's heads down during a fight with Viet Cong who had attempted to ambush the unit during a move through an area crisscrossed with bamboo hedgerows, January 16, 1966. Photograph by the Department of Defense.

Protests at Home

The stalemate in Vietnam gave a focal point for unrest in America about concerns that erupted among students and other activists. (Ironically, many of these protesting students remained home from the war because of student deferments.) Protesters held anti-Vietnam rallies on campuses across the country and staged assemblies at the Pentagon and other military sites. In 1968, activists took control of a number of buildings at New York's Columbia University, shutting much of the school down for a week before police could regain control. The unrest fueled the expansion of a new "hippie" culture, rooted in the older "Beat" movement that had emerged in the 1950s. Hippie culture glamorized New Age religion and the use of drugs like marijuana and LSD, and it inspired new genres of popular rock and folk music.

Perhaps the signature moment of the hippie movement came at the Woodstock music festival in New York in 1969, advertised as "An Aquarian Exposition: 3 Days of Peace & Music." Some 400,000 people attended the Woodstock festival, hearing round-the-clock musical performances from headliner acts such as Joan Baez, the Grateful Dead, and the African American guitar impresario Jimi Hendrix. Many Americans found the hippie and protest culture distasteful and unpatriotic. The idealization of America's traditional small-town values was also expressed in popular music, such as in Merle Haggard's 1969 country music hit "Okie from Muskogee." That anthem opened with Haggard explaining that people in small-town Oklahoma didn't smoke marijuana or use LSD. "We don't burn our draft cards down on Main Street," he sang, "'Cause we like livin' right, and being free." As president, Richard Nixon used the term "silent majority" to describe those average Americans who did not join the protests or the countercultural hippie movement.

Frustrations over Vietnam and the slow progress of social change energized a radical and sometimes violent phase of the civil rights movement. Some blacks in northern and western cities felt left out of the movement, which had focused so much on the racist practices of southern cities. Blacks and other minorities outside the South suffered under many of the same disadvantages in terms of economic opportunity, residential segregation, and tensions with police. Martin Luther King Jr. tried to take his movement to Chicago in 1965 and 1966 but found it almost impossible to bring about reform in the city's segregated schools and neighborhoods. Chicago's segregation tended to depend on local practices and habits rather than overtly racist laws.

Increasing numbers of blacks adopted the black nationalist philosophy of Malcolm X, calling for violence against whites when necessary. The Student Nonviolent Coordinating Committee came under the leadership of Stokely Carmichael and repudiated its roots in King's philosophy of nonviolence. Urban riots continued after the violence in Watts in 1965, with forty-three people dying in clashes in Detroit in 1967. Many whites who had not yet joined in the flight to the suburbs gave up on the cities in the aftermath of these riots, speeding up the founding of new white-majority suburban towns, school districts, and churches. "White flight" increasingly left the "inner cities" of America economically impoverished, with disproportionately large African American and Hispanic populations.

Mexican Americans also became a more politically cohesive force in the 1960s, led especially by farmworker activist César Chávez. Even though Chávez was a third-generation US citizen, Chávez's family had endured segregation and discrimination while he was growing up in Arizona and California. In the early 1960s, Chávez quietly organized the National Farm Workers Association (NFWA) among California field workers. The soft-spoken Chávez was an appealing figure to many because he did not seem like a radical. He wanted to enlist the help of Catholic churches, which held such a dominant presence in Hispanic communities. Chávez asked for the presence of the church and its leaders "with us, beside us, as Christ among us."

Figure 26.6. *César Chávez, Migrant Workers Union Leader,* July 1972, by Cornelius M. Keyes.

In 1965, Chávez organized a boycott against grape producers to force them to recognize the NFWA. Although many workers suffered terrible financial hardship for their role in the union, Chávez and the NFWA finally broke through to a settlement with the grape producers in 1970. Poverty and language barriers had made Mexicans among the least unionized workers before the 1960s, but Chávez helped consolidate a new "Chicano" political and social identity. Chicano high school and college students began to demand representation of Hispanic figures in literature and history courses. Others insisted that schools accommodate Spanish-speaking elementary school students and that school districts work to hire more Hispanic teachers.

The 1960s helped spawn a reinvigorated women's movement as well. Books such as Betty Friedan's *The Feminine Mystique* (1963) detailed the dissatisfaction and even loathing some women felt for the conventional roles of wife, mother, and homemaker. Friedan shockingly claimed that the middle-class women "who 'adjust' as housewives, who grow up wanting to be 'just a housewife,' are in as much danger as the millions who walked to their own death in the concentration camps" of Nazi Germany. Many American women and men, of course, rejected such characterizations of American domestic life and traditional women's roles. Evangelical women such as Anita Bryant and Beverly LaHaye defended distinct male and female roles in marriage and family. Traditionalists insisted that women's desire for professional careers undermined God's plan for most women, which was to be mothers. Ella May Miller's *I Am a Woman* (1967), for example, said that "woman's primary role and greatest contribution is that of being a mother."

American women who did seek professional careers often encountered unequal pay or barriers to being hired and promoted because of their sex. Legislation sought to address these issues with the 1963 Equal Pay Act and a provision in the Civil Rights Act (1964) that prohibited employment discrimination on the basis of one's sex. In reality these congressional measures were difficult to enforce without aggressive legal action. This difficulty was part of the inspiration for Friedan and other women to found the National Organization for Women (NOW) in 1966. NOW positioned themselves as a civil rights organization and demanded employment equality as well as the legalization of contraception and abortion. Most states had laws restricting abortion. But liberal women's activists believed women and their doctors should have the right to "control their reproductive lives," including the right to terminate an unborn infant's life, as part of women's broader access to contraception.

1968: A Year of Turmoil

The year 1968 opened with the Viet Cong launching broad-based attacks on the South Vietnamese. The attacks began at Tet, the Buddhist new year, so the Viet Cong campaign became known as the Tet Offensive. Although the American and South Vietnamese forces were able to repulse most of the Viet Cong's assaults, the Tet Offensive brought American morale to a new low. Following the Tet Offensive, polling showed that only 32 percent of Americans approved of Johnson's handling of the conflict in Vietnam. The conflict in Vietnam showed no signs of coming to a conclusion soon, contrary to what some leaders had told Americans. Popular CBS anchor Walter Cronkite, viewed by many Americans as a trusted and impartial observer, reported from Vietnam in February 1968 and suggested it was time for the United States to accept that the Vietnam War was unwinnable. When it appeared that Johnson might face major challenges in the Democratic primaries for president in 1968, Johnson made two major decisions. First, he decided to scale back his bombing campaigns in Vietnam and to approach the North Vietnamese about peace negotiations. Then he announced that he would not seek reelection as president.

On April 4, 1968, Martin Luther King Jr. was killed by an assassin in Memphis, Tennessee, where King had gone to lead protests on behalf of poorly paid sanitation workers. In his last public sermon the day before his death, King spoke almost prophetically about what was to come. "We've got some difficult days ahead. But it doesn't matter with me now. Because I've been to the mountaintop. And I don't mind. Like anybody, I would like to live a long time. Longevity has its place. But I'm not concerned about that now, I just want to do God's will."* King was thirty-nine. In 1986, President Ronald Reagan would sign an act making King's birthday a national holiday.

After Johnson decided not to run for president again, President Kennedy's brother Robert, a US senator, emerged as one of the leading candidates for the Democratic nomination. Kennedy won the California Democratic presidential primary on June 5, but that night he was shot and killed by a deranged gunman named Sirhan Sirhan. Democrats were bitterly divided over the political contest that followed between the peace candidate, Senator Eugene McCarthy of Minnesota, and Johnson's vice president, Hubert Humphrey (also from Minnesota). Humphrey supported Johnson's measured approach to resolving the war in Vietnam. Humphrey won the Democratic Party nomination. But the Democrats' national convention in Chicago in 1968 was marred by anti-Vietnam and anti-Humphrey protests, including televised clashes between protestors and police. Alabama's former governor George Wallace, a firm proponent of segregation, also announced an independent bid for the presidency, once again threatening the Democrats' traditional dominance of the Deep South.

The Republicans, by contrast, easily unified around the candidacy of Richard Nixon in 1968. Nixon had lost the presidential election of 1960 but had worked to bolster his national support among Republicans in the intervening years. Nixon indicated that he planned to bring the war to an end as well, but he offered few specifics about what

---

*Reprinted by arrangement with The Heirs to the Estate of Martin Luther King Jr., c/o Writers House as agent for the proprietor New York, NY. Copyright © 1968 Dr. Martin Luther King, Jr. © renewed 1996 Coretta Scott King.

approach he would take. Johnson's decision in October 1968 to stop the bombing in North Vietnam did help Humphrey consolidate the support of antiwar Democrats, but in the end Nixon won the Electoral College handily. The popular margin was razor-thin, however, with Nixon winning 31.8 million votes to Humphrey's 31.2 million. Wallace won five Deep South states and almost 10 million votes nationally. Nixon dominated the upper South, the West, and much of the Midwest. His election signaled the end of the era of expanding domestic government programs that had run from the New Deal to the Great Society. Nixon's "silent majority" looked to him to restore order after the strategic disaster of Vietnam and to soothe the tumult of radicalization and protests the war had inspired. Some even hoped Nixon might restore the national hope and optimism that had prevailed at the time of John Kennedy's inauguration, just eight years earlier. But Vietnam and presidential scandal would mire the nation even deeper in cultural "malaise."

■ SELECTED BIBLIOGRAPHY ■

Branch, Taylor. *Parting the Waters: America in the King Years, 1954–63.* New York: Simon and Schuster, 1988.

Garcia, Matthew. *From the Jaws of Victory: The Triumph and Tragedy of Cesar Chavez and the Farm Worker Movement.* Berkeley: University of California Press, 2012.

Hale, Jon M. *The Freedom Schools: Student Activists in the Mississippi Civil Rights Movement.* New York: Columbia University Press, 2016.

Herring, George C. *America's Longest War: The United States and Vietnam, 1950–1975.* 5th ed. New York: McGraw-Hill Education, 2013.

Howard-Pitney, David, ed. *Martin Luther King, Jr., Malcolm X, and the Civil Rights Struggle of the 1950s and 1960s: A Brief History with Documents.* Boston: Bedford/St. Martin's, 2004.

Marsh, Charles. *God's Long Summer: Stories of Faith and Civil Rights.* Princeton, NJ: Princeton University Press, 1997.

Patterson, James T. *Grand Expectations: The United States, 1945–1974.* Repr. ed. New York: Oxford University Press, 1997.

Schäfer, Axel, ed. *American Evangelicals and the 1960s.* Madison: University of Wisconsin Press, 2013.

Williams, Daniel K. *Defenders of the Unborn: The Pro-Life Movement before* Roe v. Wade. New York: Oxford University Press, 2016.

Young, Neil J. *We Gather Together: The Religious Right and the Problem of Interfaith Politics.* New York: Oxford University Press, 2015.

27

Nixon, Watergate, and Carter

President Richard Nixon won by the smallest of margins in the 1968 election, but he utterly trounced Democratic senator George McGovern in 1972. Nixon secured almost 47 million votes to McGovern's 29 million. More important, McGovern lost the electoral votes of every state except Massachusetts. The landslide should have represented a mandate for Nixon and congressional Republicans to roll back the expansion of government under the New Deal and Great Society programs. But Nixon's insecurity and ambition destroyed his presidency. In 1972, agents affiliated with the Nixon administration broke into the Democratic Party offices at the Watergate hotel in Washington, DC. Nixon personally ordered administration officials to cover up his connection to the burglary.

Vice President Gerald Ford served out the rest of Nixon's term after the president's resignation over "Watergate," as the scandal became known. Ford was unable to emerge from the shadow of Nixon's disgrace, and voters chose Georgia Democratic governor Jimmy Carter as a fresh start in 1976. There was still growing sentiment against big government and massive entitlement programs, however. When Carter seemed unable to contend with the economic malaise that had settled over the nation in the 1970s, Republicans once again looked for a candidate who could champion smaller government and economic freedom. That champion would emerge in the person of former actor and California governor Ronald Reagan.

Nixon's Foreign Policy

When he was elected in 1968, Nixon remained convinced that communism represented a grave threat to America. But Nixon and many Republican leaders were chastened by the disaster of American involvement with Vietnam. Nixon and Henry Kissinger, his national security advisor, believed America needed to employ smarter diplomacy instead of jumping into any more communist-influenced civil wars overseas. Kissinger's German Jewish family had immigrated to the United States in the 1930s to escape Nazi persecution. Kissinger went on to become one of the nation's most respected foreign policy experts, consulting with Eisenhower, Kennedy, and Johnson before becoming the most influential foreign policy advisor for Nixon. Kissinger and Nixon crafted the principles behind the "Nixon Doctrine" as well as the policy of "détente" (a reduction of tension) with Russia and China.

In 1969, the president announced the Nixon Doctrine, based on the determination that the United States "cannot—and will not—conceive all the plans, design all the programs, execute all the decisions and undertake all the defense of the free nations of the world." Nixon and Kissinger remained committed to giving economic and military aid to freedom fighters around the globe. But the doctrine signaled America's reluctance to commit troops to combat the spread of communism as it had in Korea and Vietnam. Its sense of America's limitations stood in contrast to the Truman Doctrine of 1947, which indicated America's willingness to intervene militarily on behalf of anti-communist powers. Nixon also struck a different tone from President Kennedy, who had pledged in 1961 to "support any friend, [and] oppose any foe to assure the survival and success of liberty."

Nixon and Kissinger came to believe that playing China and the Soviet Union off of one another was the key to securing concessions from both. Russia remained America's great military rival. Neither the Soviets nor the Americans felt they could indefinitely sustain the nuclear arms buildup. The Soviets were also under major economic duress due to the cost of the arms race and the communists' failures of state ownership and central planning. Nixon decided a major show of American friendliness toward the Chinese would likely lead to greater flexibility from the Russians, who feared any kind of US–Chinese pact. So in 1972, Nixon took a much-publicized trip to the People's Republic of China, the first such visit for an American president. Although Nixon had earlier criticized Democratic officials for being soft on communist power, his China trip showed that Nixon realized he would have to deal with the global balance of power as it was rather than refusing to negotiate with communists.

If the China trip was designed to bring the Russians to the negotiating table, it worked. Three months after Nixon went to China, he made a visit to Moscow, Russia, also a first for an American president. Expressing a desire for a de-escalation of tensions, Nixon and the Russians signed treaties that committed both nations to pausing the development of inter-continental ballistic missiles (ICBMs) and of systems designed to counter the threat of ICBMs. ICBMs were the kind of missiles the United States and the Soviet Union would need to stage nuclear attacks on each other. Although the treaties signed by Nixon and his Soviet counterpart, Leonid Brezhnev, were more symbolic than substantive, just the fact that such negotiations were happening signaled a different tone to US–Soviet relations. Nixon and Kissinger had helped

Figure 27.1. *President and Mrs. Nixon Visit the Great Wall of China and the Ming Tombs, February 24, 1972, by Byron E. Schumaker.*

defuse some of the frightening tensions of the early 1960s and the Cuban missile crisis.

The great test of Nixon's foreign policy was how to deal with the war in Vietnam. A clean, satisfying end to the war would have been an unrealistic goal. In accord with the Nixon Doctrine, the president wanted to put more of the burden of fighting the war on the South Vietnamese themselves, with abundant economic and backup military support from the United States. Over his first term Nixon dramatically reduced the number of US combat troops in Vietnam while expanding American bombing. The enhanced bombing campaigns included secret missions into neighboring Cambodia, where many North Vietnamese troops hid. Over the course of four years, American planes would drop more than a million tons of bombs on Cambodia.

Many American troops remained proud of their service. One infantry soldier from Kentucky said he had given "110 percent" during his thirteen months in Vietnam, and he had "no regrets at all, and if I had to do it again tomorrow I wouldn't even hesitate."

Many soldiers privately or publicly questioned the rationale for their presence in Vietnam, of course. Some soldiers in Vietnam felt disillusioned or abandoned by the Nixon administration. The army reported hundreds of incidents of "fragging" of officers, or troops intentionally shooting their own leaders. Tens of thousands of soldiers in Vietnam reportedly suffered from the abuse of heroin and other drugs. Many troops joined antiwar movements when they came back from Vietnam. Future Massachusetts senator and Democratic presidential candidate John Kerry, who had served as a decorated naval officer in Vietnam, testified before a Senate committee in 1971. Kerry deplored the kinds of indiscriminate violence that had become routine in Vietnam. Veterans commonly told stories of how American soldiers had committed atrocities and brutalized Vietnamese people, "cut off limbs, blown up bodies, randomly shot at civilians, [and] razed villages in fashion reminiscent of Genghis Khan," Kerry said. Kerry's statements and his role in the war would come under scrutiny during his 2004 presidential campaign against President George W. Bush.

The ongoing combat and violence in Vietnam and Cambodia kept fueling the antiwar movement on college campuses. Clashes between protestors and police led to the 1970 shooting deaths of four students at Kent State University in Ohio and two at Jackson State College in Mississippi. Hundreds of other colleges saw significant protests in the early 1970s. But there was also a continuing sense that the protestors and radicals did not represent "Middle America." *Time* magazine even made "Middle Americans" their Man and Woman of the Year for 1969. *Time*'s story on Middle Americans opened with a scene of people praying defiantly in schools where the Supreme Court had banned such prayers. The evangelist Billy Graham and the comedian-actor Bob Hope headlined an "Honor America Day" rally on July 4, 1970, drawing hundreds of thousands of supporters to the nation's capital. "The vast majority of us still proudly sing, 'My country, 'tis of thee, sweet land of liberty,'" Graham assured his audience at the Lincoln Memorial.

The conflict in Vietnam lingered on, however, as did frustration over the war. Nixon and Kissinger had hoped to secure a peace agreement by the November 1972 election, but North Vietnam proved unwilling to concede to Nixon's demands. Nixon already realized he was going to defeat George McGovern, so he would not moderate his negotiating points. With reelection in hand, Nixon ordered a further escalation of bombing over Hanoi in December, dropping tens of thousands of tons of explosives over two weeks. The North Vietnamese capitulated, and in January 1973 they signed an end to hostilities with the United States. Nixon had promised the American people "peace with honor," and the United States now agreed to withdraw all remaining troops from South Vietnam if the North would release all prisoners of war. North Vietnam did release hundreds of prisoners, although many veterans insisted for decades that

the Vietnamese had not released all captives. Among the best known of the prison-
ers released in 1973 was future Arizona Republican senator and presidential candidate
John McCain, who was tortured by his captors and spent more than five years at the
"Hanoi Hilton" prison.

Fifty-eight thousand American soldiers had died in the Vietnam War, along with
hundreds of thousands of Vietnamese troops and countless civilians. The American
withdrawal of troops did not stop its bombing campaigns. But Congress became unwilling to keep supporting the South Vietnamese, cutting off funding for the bombings in
August 1973. Believing the president's powers to make war had gotten out of control
due to the secretive policies of the Johnson and Nixon administrations, Congress also
passed the War Powers Act in November 1973. This required the president to advise
Congress of the initiation of any military action within forty-eight hours. It also mandated that the president could not continue any such action for more than sixty days
without explicit congressional approval. Nixon believed the War Powers Act represented an unconstitutional intrusion on his power as commander in chief, so he vetoed
the measure. Congress overrode the veto.

The War Powers Act has reframed the relationship between Congress and the president on military matters. Congress has not declared war since World War II, but presidents have repeatedly gone to Congress to request authorization for the use of military
force. President George H. W. Bush received congressional approval to help force
Iraq to withdraw from Kuwait in 1991, and George W. Bush similarly got Congress to
authorize action against the perpetrators of the September 11, 2001, terrorist attacks.
Much more controversial was the 2002 congressional approval of George W. Bush's
use of force against Iraq, which led to the US invasion of Iraq in 2003.

In the end Congress's full withdrawal of American military support from Vietnam
left both Cambodia and South Vietnam vulnerable. In 1975, Cambodia's government fell to the communist Khmer Rouge party, which unleashed a genocide on the
Cambodian population. The Khmer Rouge government was responsible for almost 2
million deaths in three years. In 1975, the North Vietnamese finally conquered South
Vietnam, and Vietnam was unified under communist rule. The South Vietnamese capital at Saigon fell to the communists in April 1975. The US military frantically evacuated
remaining Americans from the city, as well as thousands of loyal South Vietnamese who
feared the retribution of the communists. With the collapse of South Vietnam, many
Americans wondered why the United States had gotten involved in the Vietnam War
in the first place.

As devastating as Vietnam was, Nixon and Kissinger did try to contain the spread
of communism elsewhere. For example, Nixon sought to have CIA operatives stop

the election of a communist as president of Chile, but the attempt failed, and Salvador Allende became Chile's leader anyway in 1970. The CIA continued to undermine Allende, however, and he was overthrown in a military coup in 1973.

Nixon also faced a major foreign policy and economic challenge in the Middle East, where longtime antagonism between Israel and Arab nations not only threatened the nation of Israel's existence but also jeopardized the global market in oil. Israel had scored a remarkable victory over Egypt, Jordan, and Syria in the Six-Day War in 1967. In 1973, however, Egypt and Syria launched a surprise invasion of Israel on Yom Kippur, the Jewish holy day. Although Israel was able to recover from the attacks and push Egyptian and Syrian forces back, the Yom Kippur War emboldened Arab resolve against Israel and its allies in the United States. Saudi Arabia and other Arab nations announced that they would cut off oil deliveries to the United States, and the Organization of Petroleum Exporting Countries (OPEC) followed up by vastly increasing the going price of oil. America's automobile-dependent society needed affordable oil and gasoline, so the embargo plus the price increases were painful for many consumers. Gas prices shot up, and many gas stations ran out of supplies. The Arab nations ended the embargo in 1974, but the episode revealed the difficulty the United States faced in trying to support Israel while also depending on the OPEC nations for much of its oil supply.

American Malaise

The oil crisis was just one sign the American economy had become weak and over-extended. Federal government spending soared during the 1960s and '70s due to the expansion of entitlement programs associated with the New Deal and the Great Society, as well as the phenomenal costs of the war in Vietnam. Nixon spoke about the need to curtail government spending, but like most American political leaders since the Great Society he declined to attempt serious entitlement reform to rein in the costs of programs such as Social Security and Medicare. The national debt grew from $427 billion in 1972 to over $1 trillion by 1982.

Nixon and Daniel Patrick Moynihan, a key domestic policy advisor, did try to enact welfare reform. They especially tried to change the Aid to Families with Dependent Children (AFDC) program, which gave government assistance to poor families with children at home. This program was part of Social Security, and the number of people receiving benefits through it rose from 3.1 million in 1960 to 6.1 million Americans in 1968. Critics argued that aspects of the program encouraged dependence on government payments and discouraged employment, which might make recipients ineligible to collect benefits. Some also suggested that since the program regarded single mothers as having the most urgent needs, AFDC discouraged marriage and incentivized unmarried women to have more children. Nixon cited these effects as evidence of welfare's "vicious cycle of dependency."

Moynihan attempted to replace AFDC with a Family Assistance Program, which he believed would eliminate the destructive aspects of AFDC. Moynihan proposed that the government guarantee a minimum income for poor families, whatever their employment status. But his program would have also mandated that unemployed heads of poor households would have to accept any job that came available to them. The proposal fell victim to critics on the left and right. Some said the payments were too low, while some conservatives saw the Family Assistance Program as just another expansion of government spending. Liberal critics also argued against the work requirement. In the end the failure of Moynihan's centrist reform in Congress showed just how difficult it was to change welfare and entitlement programs once they had been adopted.

Even after the oil embargo ended, prices for gas, heating oil, automobiles, and other staples of American life continued on a long-term rise. Suburbanization meant the use of automobiles had become a fixture of American life. Especially in the growing South and Southwest, air-conditioning was becoming a necessity in most new homes and businesses, sending energy consumption and prices even higher. Between 1973 and 1982, the price of a gallon of gas went from $0.37 to $1.28. Prices for everything from cars to bread went up significantly during the decade. Wage increases did not keep up with rising costs. By the mid-1970s, unemployment had reached almost 9 percent of the American workforce, the worst numbers since the Great Depression.

The Decline of Traditional Family Life and Mainline Religion

Rising prices and unemployment were troubling trends, but arguably the most transformative and damaging demographic changes of the era were happening at the family level. Divorce and births outside of marriage went up sharply starting in the mid-1960s. Marriage rates had been roughly equal between African Americans and whites until the 1960s, but during that decade African American marriages became less common, and the number of children born to black unmarried parents went up. Trends away from marriage among Hispanics and whites were less pronounced at first, but in recent decades similar family patterns (less marriage, more divorce, more children to unmarried parents) have emerged among poorer Americans of most ethnic groups. There were many reasons for these changes in marriage and parenting. Liberalization of divorce law was one factor. Beginning with a California bill signed by Ronald Reagan in 1969, "no fault" divorce became typical. Under no fault divorce law, spouses no longer had to convince a court that one or the other partner had committed some wrongdoing (such as adultery) in order to be granted a divorce. The introduction of more women into the ranks of wage earners also may have encouraged some women to contemplate breaking away from undesirable or abusive marriages because now they could financially cope without their husbands.

The early stages of growth in divorce and unmarried parenting had preceded no-fault divorce laws, however. Cultural trends were surely part of the explanation for the growing breakdown of traditional families. Rock-and-roll music, movies, and the youth culture of the 1960s increasingly glorified unrestrained sexuality and individual expression. For example, the controversial 1967 Oscar-winning film *The Graduate* featured actor Dustin Hoffman as a recent college graduate who is seduced by an older married woman, Mrs. Robinson (played by Anne Bancroft). Hoffman's character then falls in love with Mrs. Robinson's daughter and runs away with her from the church after the daughter had just been forced into an unhappy marriage ceremony. The folk duo Simon and Garfunkel scored a number-one hit with the song "Mrs. Robinson," taken from the movie's soundtrack, with its opening line assuring Mrs. Robinson, "Jesus loves you more than you will know." Sexually explicit films also became more common, and some even won mainstream accolades. Dustin Hoffman also appeared in 1969's *Midnight Cowboy*, which became the only X-rated film ever to win the Oscar for Best Picture.

Greater movement of the population, especially into urban areas, also may have changed patterns of marriage and family. Moving frequently took many Americans out of the restraining environments of dense family networks and small-town cultures, where divorce or sex before marriage might have caused more embarrassment. Even in traditional ethnic enclaves in the cities, there would have been a heavy price to pay for premarital sex or having children outside of marriage. One Jewish woman explained, "In East New York, the Jewish values were passed on from generation to generation. . . . A girl having an illegitimate child, or a girl getting a divorce, it was unheard of, you just didn't have it. You knew all on the block, the street was like a small town."

Another related factor in the decline of traditional family structures was the weakening of many traditional faith communities and denominations, which (as had East New York's Jewish community) gave structures of accountability and support that bolstered families. American Jews (save for those in the most conservative Jewish groups) became among the most likely to marry outside of their religion. This further destabilized a religion that was closely tied to Jewish ethnicity. American Protestant "mainline" denominations also saw a catastrophic pattern of decline that began in the mid-1960s. The mainline denominations included groups such as the United Methodist Church, the Presbyterian Church (USA), and the Episcopal Church. These denominations' leaders embraced more liberal theology than evangelical and fundamentalist churches had. Their leaders were also more likely to endorse the various reform and civil rights movements of the 1960s than were their conservative counterparts. John Hines, who served as presiding Episcopal bishop from 1965 to 1974, spoke for many mainline leaders when he declared that the church must serve as a "radical minister of change" in society. Mainline congregations tended to be more comfortable with trends in elite American culture too, while conservative churches often adopted a more adversarial role toward the dominant culture.

Whatever the reason for their decline, the mainline churches saw decades of membership losses, which began around the same time as the cultural upheavals of the mid-1960s. The total membership of the mainline churches reached its height in 1966, when they claimed about 28 million members. By 2003, their total membership stood at 20 million. The mainline churches still enjoyed a great deal of cultural influence, but they had lost their appeal for many in the rising generations. The number of American Catholics grew substantially after the 1960s, partly because of steady infusions of Catholic immigrants from Mexico and elsewhere. But Catholics also showed signs of weakness, with the number of American Catholics reporting weekly attendance at mass dropping almost by half between the 1970s and 2010s. The number of nuns serving in the United States dropped precipitously during that time, while the number of Catholic priests has been on a slow decline since the 1960s.

Conservative Protestant churches generally held steady during the period following the 1960s. The Southern Baptist Convention (SBC) was less affected by the liberalizing trends than the mainline churches, but it saw some advocates of liberal theology at its seminaries before the denomination's "Conservative Resurgence," which began in 1979. The Conservative Resurgence led to theological uniformity around conservative doctrine in the SBC. The Resurgence also spawned the formation of new moderate and liberal Baptist groups, such as the Cooperative Baptist Fellowship (1991), which is committed to the ordination of women as pastors. The SBC remained on a slow pattern of reported growth from about 11 million reported members in 1966 to a peak of 16.4 million in 2003. At that point the SBC entered a pattern of slow membership decline.

A number of smaller conservative denominations saw phenomenal growth after the 1960s. Some of this growth came as new denominations left the more liberal mainline churches. The Presbyterian Church in America (PCA), the nation's second-largest Presbyterian body, broke away from the mainline Presbyterian Church (USA) in 1973 over concerns about liberal theology and the ordination of women as pastors. Some southern PCA leaders were also bothered by the mainline denomination's support for civil rights for African Americans. The PCA grew from about 41,000 members in 1973 to more than 340,000 in 2010.

Pentecostal and charismatic churches and denominations, which emphasized the gifts of the Holy Spirit, including speaking in tongues, were among the fastest growing since the 1960s. Among the most remarkable examples are the Assemblies of God and the Church of God in Christ. The Assemblies of God went from a US membership of just under 600,000 in 1969 to more than 2 million in 1989. (The global growth of the Assemblies of God was even more explosive.) The Church of God in Christ, an African American Pentecostal denomination, is by some calculations the largest African American church and the largest Pentecostal group in the nation. It went from about 425,000 members in 1964 to 5.5 million by 2012.

Some signs of Christian strength in America appeared in parachurch and inter-denominational trends, such as in the Jesus movement. The "Jesus people" emerged in late 1960s California as both a complement to and a reaction against the excesses of the hippie movement of the same era. Jesus people paired traditional evangelical beliefs with hippie style, dress, and lingo, introducing such elements as rock-style music into church worship. The Jesus movement spurred greater interest in the fulfillment of biblical prophecy, inspired by books such as Hal Lindsey's *The Late Great Planet Earth*, one of the best-selling books of the era on any topic. The evangelist Billy Graham helped some of the trends of the Jesus movement become mainstream through events such as the Explo '72 festival in Dallas, sponsored by the parachurch ministry Campus Crusade for Christ. Organizers called Explo '72 the "Christian Woodstock." Hundreds of thousands of attendees listened to sermons by Graham and performances by musicians including the great country singer Johnny Cash, who became a fixture at Billy Graham crusades as well.

Civil Rights Campaigns in the 1970s

In the 1950s and early 1960s, the civil rights movement had focused largely on the struggles of ethnic minorities, especially African Americans in the South. This movement had not gotten everything it wanted, but it could point to great triumphs, such as *Brown v. Board of Education*, the Civil Rights Act (1964), and the Voting Rights Act (1965). After 1965, movements for civil rights went in different directions, lacking the cohesion of the campaign headed by Martin Luther King Jr. Some of the protests were redirected toward the war in Vietnam, while other ethnic groups took up their own causes. Some American women sought to turn equality between the sexes into the next great civil rights campaign. Small numbers of activists also began to call for legal rights for gays and lesbians. The net effect of these campaigns was to make the civil rights movements even more fractured and controversial than during the King era.

African American activism in the 1970s focused on two main issues: school busing and "affirmative action." Advocates of affirmative action urged employers to hire nonwhites, women, and people from other traditionally underrepresented groups to bring balance to fields typically dominated by white males. School busing became the next step in school desegregation across the nation, not just in the South. Many schools remained functionally segregated because schools drew heavily from their local neighborhoods. If those neighborhoods were overwhelmingly white, black, or Hispanic, then the neighborhood's public school would be also. The proposed solution was to redraw school district boundaries and sometimes to bus children away from their closest school to ensure schools had a mixed ethnic composition that reflected the entire racial makeup of a town or city.

Local school districts and many parents (including many nonwhites) had reservations about busing, worrying about sending their children on long bus trips to schools across town. A federal court order on busing resulted in the Supreme Court case of *Swann v. Charlotte-Mecklenburg Board of Education* (1971), in which the court, led by Chief Justice Warren Burger, unanimously approved a busing plan to desegregate the schools of Charlotte, North Carolina. Resentment about busing came to a head in Boston in 1974, where working-class whites expressed outrage over a federal order to bus students between the majority-black neighborhood of Roxbury and the Irish-dominated South Boston. Ten thousand protestors, including many working-class white women, descended on Boston City Hall in September 1974 to make clear their opposition to the busing plan. US senator Ted Kennedy, part of the Irish-American Kennedy political clan, tried to address the crowd in favor of busing. The crowd shouted him down, saying he was an embarrassment to the Irish and pelting him with tomatoes and eggs. The city's busing system still went forward, but many black students in South Boston faced harassment and insults.

Government policies also encouraged businesses and schools receiving taxpayer support to make special efforts to recruit and hire people of color and women. Critics argued that this type of policy, when based on racial or gender preferences, represented "reverse discrimination" and violated the Fourteenth Amendment's guarantee of "equal protection of the laws." The key early challenge to affirmative action in education came in the Supreme Court case of *Regents of the University of California v. Bakke* (1978). Allan Bakke, a white male applicant to the University of California–Davis medical school, had sued because he was denied admission in favor of minority candidates with lower academic qualifications. In a closely divided vote, the court ruled that the university's "quota" system, setting aside specific spots for minority candidates and closing those spots to whites, was unconstitutional. But the majority did agree that ethnic balance in education was a "compelling state interest" so that schools could use race as one factor in admissions. *Bakke*'s close decision left the door open to future challenges such as *Fisher v. University of Texas* (2016), in which a narrow majority once again confirmed that schools may take race into account as a factor in admissions.

Women's Rights and Gay Activism

Women's rights activists in the 1970s focused on equal pay and job opportunities, as well as the legalization of abortion. All states had put laws against abortion on the books during the nineteenth century, as scientists and doctors began to realize that the unborn infant or "fetus" was clearly alive long before the mother could feel it move. Although many American women continued to seek or cause illicit abortions, there was widespread agreement until the mid-twentieth century that abortion was barbaric and jeopardized the mother's health. Some states had made exceptions in rare cases where the pregnancy was causing life-threatening medical complications for the mother.

In the 1960s, some women's rights activists argued for extending abortion exceptions to women who were victims of rape or incest or in cases of serious deformity or other major medical problems in the unborn baby. By the late 1960s, groups such as the National Organization for Women were asserting that abortion was a constitutional right. There was a broad tradition of pro-life activism dating back to the nineteenth-century laws against abortion. As demands for abortion rights became louder in the 1960s, a more active pro-life movement also emerged. Leaders in the Catholic Church were among the most visible pro-life advocates, insisting that God had made all life and that Christians should defend the most vulnerable people in society, from unborn children to the elderly. Although the women's rights movement has become identified with the abortion agenda, some feminists still regarded abortion as bad for women (and for unborn children, both female and male). For example, in 1972, a group of women activists organized Feminists for Life.

About a dozen states had started to liberalize their abortion laws by the late 1960s. Neither political party took a clear position on abortion. Richard Nixon had hesitantly approved liberalizing abortion laws during his first term as president but then changed his mind and became more pro-life during the 1972 presidential campaign. His rival, Senator George McGovern, opposed efforts by activists to insert proabortion language into the Democratic Party platform. At this time the pro-life movement had deeper roots in the Democratic Party than the Republican Party, especially because of the Democrats' traditional Catholic constituency.

The Supreme Court decision in *Roe v. Wade* (1973) represented a dramatic shift in the debate over abortion. In *Roe* the court affirmed an almost unlimited right to abortion, at least in the first and second trimesters of a pregnancy. *Roe* emerged out of a lawsuit regarding a Texas woman, Norma McCorvey, who argued that she should have been allowed to have an abortion after suffering a gang rape assault. (McCorvey later admitted that the rape had not happened. She also became a Christian and a pro-life activist, repudiating the landmark decision she helped to create.) Writing for a 7–2 majority, Justice Harry Blackmun ruled that women had a right to abortion, building on the 1965 decision *Griswold v. Connecticut* and its invocation of the "right to privacy." Pro-life attorneys argued that abortion violated an unborn baby's right to life under the Fourteenth Amendment, which says that no state could "deprive any person of life, liberty, or property, without due process of law." But Blackmun wrote that "the word 'person,' as used in the Fourteenth Amendment, does not include the unborn."

Justice Byron White wrote one of the dissenting opinions in *Roe*, arguing that the court had intruded on a heated moral controversy best left to the states and that the right to abortion was not supported by the Constitution. "I find nothing in the language or history of the Constitution to support the Court's judgment," White wrote.

> The Court simply fashions and announces a new constitutional right for pregnant mothers and, with scarcely any reason or authority for its action, invests that right with sufficient substance to override most existing state abortion statutes. . . . As an exercise of raw judicial power, the Court perhaps has authority to do what it does today; but, in my view, its judgment is an improvident and extravagant exercise of the power of judicial review that the Constitution extends to this Court. The Court apparently values the convenience of the pregnant mother more than the continued existence and development of the life or potential life that she carries.

The decision in *Roe* fueled the development of a much larger pro-life movement, which sought to overturn *Roe* by constitutional amendment or by a reversal at the Supreme Court. By 1976, much of the energy of the pro-life movement began to funnel into the Republican Party, which adopted an official pro-life position, while Democrats adopted a plank in their party platform affirming *Roe*'s principles. Evangelical Christian leaders became more vocal in their pro-life advocacy after *Roe* as well, with books such as *Whatever Happened to the Human Race?* (1979) by future surgeon general C. Everett

Koop and the influential Christian apologist Francis Schaeffer. Beginning in 1974, pro-life activists gathered each January in the March for Life in Washington, DC, an event that has typically drawn tens of thousands and sometimes hundreds of thousands of marchers.

Women still struggled to achieve equal access and fair treatment in workplaces and education, though gender (or racial) discrimination was often difficult to prove. One statutory reform with the most far-reaching consequences was the 1972 passage of Title IX of the Higher Education Act, which mandated that schools and colleges that received federal funds had to offer equal opportunities and activities to female and male students. The most visible consequence of this was a large expansion in funding for women's high school and college athletics, which had only received a tiny fraction of universities' athletic budgets before Title IX. (Title IX did not specifically mention sports, but this became one easily quantifiable way to test whether schools were offering equal opportunities and benefits to male and female students.) In the 2010s, Title IX investigations became increasingly focused on allegations of sexual assault on college campuses and on charges that schools were improperly handling accusations of those assaults.

The biggest statutory goal of the women's rights movement in the 1970s, however, was the Equal Rights Amendment (ERA). The Civil Rights Act of 1964 had

Figure 27.2. *Pro-Life at White House*, January 22, 1979, by Marion S. Trikosko.

banned employment discrimination on the basis of sex, but women's rights activists believed equality between the sexes needed a firmer constitutional basis. The proposed amendment said that "equality of rights under the law shall not be denied or abridged by the United States or by any State on account of sex." (In more recent decades the term "gender" became preferred by many activists and academics over "sex." The proponents of "gender" emphasized that many, if not all, ideas about male and female attributes have changed over time. "Sex" tended to imply fixed biological categories of male or female persons.) Congress passed the ERA in 1972 and sent it out to the states for ratification. Although twenty-eight states ratified the amendment within a year, the ERA bogged down in the southern states and the mountain West. It ultimately failed to reach the required three-fourths of the states' approval. Critics argued that the ERA was unnecessary, that it would spawn hosts of frivolous lawsuits, and that it implied there were no real differences between women and men or mothers and fathers.

Among the most effective opponents of the ERA was Catholic conservative activist Phyllis Schlafly. Her organization STOP ERA, which later became the Eagle Forum, drew tens of thousands of members. Schlafly argued that it was harmful to women to ban any legislative recognition of their particular needs. For example, Schlafly contended that the ERA would overturn state laws that required husbands to provide support for their wives and minor children, even if the husband no longer lived with them. Schlafly and other ERA opponents contended that women had natural biological roles as mothers that attached them to home and children. "You can't make the having of babies equally shared," she observed. The law should "reflect the natural differences and the role assigned by God, in that women have babies and men don't have babies." The ERA effectively denied the realities of those biological roles, Schlafly argued. She also contended that the law could not change the fact that men were better suited than women for jobs requiring more physical strength. She forecast that if women's rights activists got their way, women would be introduced into combat roles in the military, a controversial notion at the time. By the 2010s, however, women in America did have voluntary access to all combat positions in the military, although the lack of a draft had not yet raised the question of compelling women to fight.

The new emphasis on equality between men and women helped spur a gay rights movement. Its advocates argued that people in homosexual relationships should have the same legal rights as heterosexual couples. Homosexual activity was not new in American society, of course. But biblical prohibitions against homosexual acts and the longstanding cultural tradition of heterosexual marriage as the cornerstone of American society made homosexuality a largely taboo topic among Americans until the 1960s. The era's array of challenges to traditional views on gender and sexuality translated easily into claims that homosexual relationships were just as legitimate as heterosexual ones.

The catalyst for the gay rights movement was a riot at the Stonewall Inn in New York City in June 1969. Police raided this gay bar, but patrons and other onlookers resisted, jeering and throwing bottles at the police. The next night thousands of protestors and the police clashed in the streets of Greenwich Village, the heart of the city's bohemian and gay subcultures. The Stonewall riots prompted the formation of new gay and lesbian advocacy groups. The fact that practicing homosexuals only represented a small fraction of Americans presented a problem for the movement. Thus, gay activists sought to get gays and lesbians to "come out of the closet" and identify publicly as homosexuals. The movement saw incremental successes starting in the 1970s. In 1974, the American Psychiatric Association removed homosexuality from its list of mental disorders. States began repealing laws prohibiting homosexual sex acts, or "sodomy."

Before the Supreme Court's 2015 *Obergefell* decision mandating that the states recognize homosexual marriages, the gay rights movement's greatest legal success was the Supreme Court case of *Lawrence v. Texas* (2003). It overturned state laws against consensual homosexual sex acts. As in many cases since the 1960s, the court's 6–3 ruling in *Lawrence* was based heavily on the concept of "substantive due process" under the Fourteenth Amendment. Under this principle the court majority argued that they were bound to protect a number of rights, such as privacy, that were not mentioned in the Constitution. These also included rights that the framers of the Constitution would never have envisioned, such as a right to homosexual sex. Critics contended that the Supreme Court was absorbing too much power in a quest to reshape American society according to progressive ideals. In his dissent in *Lawrence*, Justice Antonin Scalia denounced the court's ruling in overturning Texas's law against sodomy: "What Texas has chosen to do is well within the range of traditional democratic action, and its hand should not be stayed through the invention of a brand-new 'constitutional right' by a Court that is impatient of democratic change."

Watergate and the Ford Presidency

As Americans faced dire economic and cultural challenges, President Nixon's administration was spiraling into the Watergate scandal. President Nixon may not have known about his campaign operatives' bizarre plan to wiretap the offices of the Democratic Party at the Watergate Hotel, but he definitely ordered administration officials to cover up the break-in and its connection to his administration. He probably could have survived if he had admitted what happened and fired all those involved, but Nixon's inclination instead was to entrench and hide evidence.

Exploiting leaks from a high-ranking FBI source they code-named "Deep Throat," *Washington Post* reporters Carl Bernstein and Bob Woodward revealed the Nixon administration's complicity in Watergate, including figures such as White House special counsel Charles Colson, who had helped hire the wiretappers. (Colson would serve jail time for obstruction of justice in the scandal but experienced a dramatic Christian conversion in 1973 and went on to become one of the most articulate evangelical leaders of the next four decades.) Senate investigations and the appointment of an independent counsel in 1973 began to pull the noose tighter and tighter around Nixon. He desperately forced a number of coconspirators out of his administration, but it became ever clearer that Nixon himself had helped cover up the break-in.

Nixon's vice president, Spiro Agnew, was forced to resign due to an unrelated financial scandal in late 1973. Representative Gerald Ford of Michigan took Agnew's place as vice president. Pressure against Nixon began to crest when he also fell under suspicion of financial improprieties and tax evasion, prompting his unforgettable statement "I am not a crook." Investigators also discovered that Nixon routinely had made secret tapes of conversations in the Oval Office. Nixon resisted releasing the tapes, and when he did give up some tapes and transcripts, they contained omissions, including an eighteen-minute deleted portion of a conversation between the president and chief of staff H. R. Haldeman that occurred just days after the break-in. The Supreme Court ordered Nixon to release all the tapes, but a bipartisan majority of the House Judiciary Committee had already voted to begin impeachment proceedings against the president. Although Nixon remained defiant, top Republican leaders realized he could not survive impeachment and a Senate trial for removal. They finally convinced him to resign, and Gerald Ford became president on August 9, 1974. Ford proclaimed that "our long national nightmare is over."

President Ford was a welcome relief compared to the scandal-ridden Nixon, but his presidency never fully escaped the shadow of Watergate. Especially after Ford pardoned Nixon a month after taking office, many Americans viewed Ford as part of the same corrupt Republican machine that had produced Nixon. During his short time in office, Ford made little headway on the nation's besetting economic problems or foreign policy challenges. Cynicism about politicians was at an all-time high, and Congress adopted several measures designed to restrain the presidency and to ensure transparency in government. In addition to the War Powers Act of 1973, they passed the Privacy Act (1974), which protected citizens from the secret collection or misuse of personal information about them by the government. In 1975–76, a committee headed by Democratic senator Frank Church led investigations of the Central Intelligence Agency. The Church Committee reports led to heightened constraints on the work of US intelligence operatives overseas. The committee revealed the CIA's complicity in coup and assassination attempts in a number of foreign nations, leading President Ford to issue an order forbidding any peacetime killings of foreign leaders.

Democrats had already made major gains in Congress in 1974, but President Ford's reelection prospects grew even dimmer as Saigon fell to the North Vietnamese and the unemployment rate exceeded 9 percent. Perceptions that Ford was soft on communism led to the emergence of Ronald Reagan as a challenger for the Republican presidential nomination in 1976. Reagan said that Ford had "shown neither the vision nor the leadership necessary to halt and reverse the diplomatic and military decline of the United States." Although Ford maintained enough support within the Republican establishment to narrowly win the nomination, Reagan scored some major victories in state primaries, especially in the South and West.

Ford's weakness and the lingering stigma of Watergate made Democrats realize that 1976 was their time to recapture the White House. Many Democratic contenders entered the fray, but former Georgia governor Jimmy Carter emerged as the nominee. Carter, a Naval Academy graduate who had served in the navy's nuclear submarine program, was politically moderate. Carter was wealthy, but he played up his humble roots in a rural Georgia peanut farming family. Although Carter was equivocal on moral issues such as abortion, he emphasized his Baptist faith and sent reporters scrambling to find out what he meant when he described himself as "born again." (Along with Carter's testimony, Charles Colson's successful 1976 memoir, *Born Again*, made that biblical term much more familiar in America.) Some secular observers found Carter's faith perplexing, especially when he told *Playboy* magazine that he had often looked lustfully at women other than his wife and "committed adultery in my heart." Still, Carter's homespun religious style made him appear to be the ethical opposite of Richard Nixon. In the end Carter defeated Ford in a close election by holding together enough of the old Roosevelt/Kennedy coalition of southern and northeastern states.

The Carter Administration

As president, Carter faced similar challenges as Ford had on foreign policy and economic issues. If anything, Carter showed even less decisiveness or political conviction and became increasingly frustrated with the malaise that marked the nation's post-Vietnam mood. Among the most formidable challenges were rampantly rising prices and inflation, especially in the energy sector, even as economic growth sputtered. (Economists call this demoralizing situation "stagflation.") America's move to the suburbs, its dependence on big cars, and the unpredictability of OPEC had made prices for gasoline and other commodities intolerably high. But the Carter administration seemed unsure of what to do to bring relief other than to urge Americans to conserve their resources. He also promoted nuclear power as a key to increasing Americans' energy independence. A near meltdown at the Three Mile Island nuclear plant in Pennsylvania in 1979 soured the media and public opinion against this energy source, in spite of nuclear energy's apparent efficiency and minimal pollution as compared to options such as coal-fueled plants.

Carter originally scored some foreign policy victories, especially when he helped broker a 1978 peace deal between Israel and Egypt. As part of the Camp David Accords, Israel agreed to withdraw from the Sinai Peninsula, which it had captured from Egypt during the 1967 Six-Day War. But other developments in the Middle East and central Asia would exceed the Carter administration's diplomatic capacities. Carter initially made some progress on "détente" in US-Russian relations. But the Soviets' naked aggression in invading Afghanistan in 1979 forced Carter to take a tougher stance against the USSR. Most of Carter's moves had only symbolic value, however, including his decision to have US athletes boycott the 1980 Summer Olympics in Moscow. In early 1980, the Russians did participate in the Winter Olympics in Lake Placid, New York, before the announcement of the US boycott of the summer games. The winter games saw the United States defeat the heavily favored Russians in hockey, a stunning victory that became known as the "Miracle on Ice."

Developments in Iran undermined Carter's presidency as the 1980 election approached. Since the 1950s, the United States had backed the authoritarian pro-Western government of Mohammed Reza Pahlavi, the shah of Iran. Successive administrations saw the shah's government as essential to stopping the spread of Soviet influence in central Asia. Democratic Iranian reformers as well as reactionary Shi'a Muslims loathed the shah's government and resented the United States for helping him maintain power. (Shi'a Muslims represent a small fraction of the world's Muslims; the majority of Muslims are Sunni. But in Iran, the Shi'as have a strong majority.) Followers of the Ayatollah Ruhollah Khomeini overthrew the shah in early 1979. When Carter allowed the shah to move to the United States, radical Muslims took over the US embassy in Tehran and took dozens of American hostages. Khomeini's regime demanded that the United States return the shah to Iran and make restitution for large stores of money he had supposedly deposited in America.

Carter and his advisers seemed paralyzed by the Iranian hostage crisis, and months went by before they attempted a rescue of the hostages. In the meantime the crisis was the lead story on virtually every national news show. When Carter finally authorized a rescue attempt, it was impossibly complicated and led to a disaster when an American helicopter and cargo plane collided. Eight American soldiers died, and the mission was aborted. Iran came under heavier pressure to negotiate when Iraq and its new leader, Saddam Hussein, invaded Iran in September 1980. The Iranians finally agreed to release the hostages when the United States released billions of dollars' worth of Iranian assets to them. But in a clear attempt to humiliate Carter, the Iranians did not release the fifty-two remaining captives until the inauguration of Ronald Reagan as the new president in 1981.

The 1980 Election

Carter's inability to address his economic and foreign-policy challenges eroded his support, even among many Democrats. Massachusetts senator Ted Kennedy ran against Carter and won a number of Democratic presidential primaries. Having captured the hearts of many Republican voters in 1976, Ronald Reagan emerged as the Republican standard-bearer. Reagan relentlessly hammered Carter's ineptitude, his weakness on communism,

Figure 27.3. Iran Hostage Crisis student demonstration, Washington, DC.

and the dreadful state of the American economy. Many traditional Democrats, especially blue-collar Democrats hurt by rampant inflation and unemployment, switched over to vote Republican. One Wisconsin housewife who had typically voted Democrat in the past explained that "inflation is eating us up, welfare is a mess, we don't have any power in this country—why shouldn't we switch? . . . Carter can't decide anything. Reagan would return us to this country's true meaning." The third-party liberal Republican John Anderson, who gained more than 5 million votes in November 1980, probably damaged Carter more than he did Reagan.

In the end Reagan defeated Carter in a landslide, winning forty-four states and 51 percent of the vote. Carter held on to Georgia, but most of the rest of the South went for Reagan. The New Deal coalition was badly shaken, as the Democrats only retained a strong majority of African American voters. A majority of working-class whites supported Reagan. Although Carter's credentials as a practicing evangelical Christian were clearer than Reagan's, Reagan had many evangelical friends and knew just how to speak to an evangelical audience. School prayer and the pro-life cause were major themes of his campaign, and 1980 represented the beginning of a great separation between the two major parties on the question of abortion rights.

Reagan attracted the support of a number of key white evangelical ministers, most notably Jerry Falwell, pastor of Thomas Road Baptist Church in Lynchburg, Virginia. In 1979 Falwell founded the Moral Majority, a religious advocacy group seeking to "return America to moral sanity." Catholic conservatives such as Phyllis Schlafly and her organization, Eagle Forum, also backed Reagan and helped get the Republican Party to commit formally to the pro-life cause and to oppose the Equal Rights Amendment.

In his inaugural address Reagan set the tone for a presidency committed to reducing the size and intrusiveness of government bureaucracy. "These United States are confronted with an economic affliction of great proportions," he said. "We suffer from the longest and one of the worst sustained inflations in our national history. . . . In this present crisis, government is not the solution to our problem; government is the problem."* Reagan and a rejuvenated Republican Party would seek to reduce taxes and spending on social programs even as they escalated defense spending in hopes of defeating Soviet power and ambitions. Reagan's inauguration represented the triumph of the modern conservative movement and a surprising comeback for the party just six years after the humiliated Nixon had resigned. Reagan's America would see even greater flourishing of consumer capitalism and cultural conservatism, as well as the last days of Soviet communism.

---

*"President Reagan 1981 Inaugural Address," YouTube video, 20:48, January 14, 2009, https://www.youtube.com/watch?v=hpPt7xGx4Xo.

■ SELECTED BIBLIOGRAPHY ■

Critchlow, Donald T. *Phyllis Schlafly and Grassroots Conservatism: A Woman's Crusade.* Princeton, NJ: Princeton University Press, 2005.

Dochuk, Darren. *From Bible Belt to Sunbelt: Plain-Folk Religion, Grassroots Politics, and the Rise of Evangelical Conservatism.* New York: W. W. Norton, 2010.

Garthoff, Raymond L. *Détente and Confrontation: American-Soviet Relations from Nixon to Reagan.* Rev. ed. Washington, DC: Brookings Institution Press, 1994.

Hull, N. E. H., and Peter Charles Hoffer. *Roe v. Wade: The Abortion Rights Controversy in American History.* 2nd ed. Lawrence: University Press of Kansas, 2010.

Jenkins, Philip. *Decade of Nightmares: The End of the Sixties and the Making of Eighties America.* New York: Oxford University Press, 2008.

McGirr, Lisa. *Suburban Warriors: The Origins of the New American Right.* Upd. ed. Princeton, NJ: Princeton University Press, 2015.

Miller, Steven P. *The Age of Evangelicalism: America's Born-Again Years.* New York: Oxford University Press, 2014.

Patterson, James T. *Restless Giant: The United States from Watergate to Bush v. Gore.* New York: Oxford University Press, 2005.

Thomas, Evan. *Being Nixon: A Man Divided.* New York: Random House, 2015.

Zelizer, Julian. *Jimmy Carter.* New York: Times Books, 2010.

28

Reagan's America

Since the colonial era, America had been part of a global economy—just think of the British-shipped tea, grown in China and India, that had helped cause the American Revolution. Or how the South dominated the world's trade in cotton before the Civil War. But the 1980s marked a distinct escalation in globalization for America and the world. The American automobile market, once dominated by Detroit-based companies such as Ford and Chevrolet, had already seen a growing presence of foreign competitors, including Volkswagen (Germany), by the 1970s. In the 1980s, Japanese-based Toyota and Honda threatened to displace the Detroit carmakers at the top of the industry.

"Buy American" sentiment was common during the 1980s, as American automakers struggled to keep up with the increasingly popular Japanese models. The notorious assault and killing of Chinese immigrant Vincent Chin in Detroit in 1982 was said to have been provoked by resentment against growing Asian power in the auto industry. One of Chin's assailants was a supervisor at a Chrysler plant. American politicians accused the Japanese of unfair trade practices, but Japanese companies blunted those charges by setting up more Japanese-owned factories in the United States. By 1988, more than 300,000 American citizens worked for Japanese businesses in US-based offices and factories. In a watershed moment in 1989, the Honda Accord became the best-selling car in America, the first foreign model to achieve that rank.

In technological fields the United States was also bringing products to market that would change the global economy as well as everyday life around the world. The Cold War had accelerated the use of computers in weapons and space flight systems, but in "Silicon Valley" in California, some entrepreneurs dreamed of introducing personal computers to the consumer market. Among these were Steve Wozniak and Steve Jobs, who founded Apple Computer in 1976, and in 1977 they introduced the Apple II computer. Unlike previous home computer kits, which only hard-core electronics enthusiasts could build, the Apple II was designed to be accessible to anyone. About 2 million Apple IIs eventually sold. In 1981, International Business Machines entered the market with the IBM PC, which eventually became the most common computer model used in American businesses. IBM PCs and their numerous "clones" would generally use the operating system made dominant by Microsoft, founded by Bill Gates and Paul Allen in 1975. Later, Steve Jobs helped design the Apple Macintosh, or "Mac," which put Apple computers into even more homes and schools.

Jobs left Apple in 1985 but would return as CEO in 1997 and went on to play a major role in the development of the smartphone, a combination of computer and cellular phone technology. Older phone technologies had depended on landlines, but the cell phone concept allowed users to take their phones with them wherever they went. Wireless phones were first approved for commercial use in the United States in 1982,

Figure 28.1. Apple IIc, 2012.

but their early functionality was low and expense was high. International companies such as Finland's Nokia produced affordable cell phones in the 1990s. In the 2000s, a Canadian company successfully introduced the BlackBerry, one of the first smartphones, with a small physical keyboard on the phone for email and text messaging.

In 2007, Jobs and Apple introduced the iPhone, with touch screen technology and a suite of "apps" that grew exponentially over time.* The iPhone and related technologies dramatically transformed the global personal electronics and phone markets and turned Apple into the largest company in the world. Parts of the iPhone were designed in places from the United States to Germany and Japan, but for its first ten years, most of the phones were manufactured in China. Globalization meant alluring products at affordable prices, but the associated decline of America's manufacturing sector presented one of the most difficult economic and political problems of the post-1960s era in American history.

Reagan's Presidency

Ronald Reagan became president in 1981, presiding over a nation in considerable economic distress. Reagan believed the key to revitalization was supply-side economics, or "Reaganomics." This philosophy included the idea that a booming private sector, not government spending, was essential to true economic health. Reagan helped push through tax cuts as well as tens of billions of dollars in government spending cuts in areas such as social welfare, job training, and transportation. Reagan sought to encourage more private-sector competition through actions such as the 1982 settlement that resulted in the breakup of the American Telephone and Telegraph company and its monopoly over much of the telecommunications business. Although the nation went into a deep recession in 1981–82 and the federal budget deficit went up sharply, the rest of Reagan's tenure was generally marked by economic growth, increasing employment, and reduced inflation.

Reagan's presidency had barely gotten started when he was nearly assassinated. In March 1981, a mentally unstable man named John Hinckley Jr. opened fire on Reagan outside a Washington, DC, hotel. Several in Reagan's entourage were wounded, including Reagan himself, who took a shot to his left lung. Reagan was bleeding badly and was saved only by a two-hour operation. Ironically the attempt on his life made Reagan more popular than ever, as he projected courage and good cheer throughout the ordeal. He

---

* "Steve Jobs Introduces iPhone in 2007," YouTube video, 10:19, October 8, 2011, https://www.youtube.com/watch?v=MnrJzXM7a6o.

parlayed his injuries into political capital that helped him pass his budget and tax cuts. As he lobbied Congress, Reagan successfully wooed conservative southern Democrats, whose votes he needed to pass legislation in the House of Representatives.

The high drama of Reagan's first year continued in August 1981, as he faced down the air traffic controllers' union, which threatened to strike in order to obtain better hours and pay. During his film career, Reagan had served a number of terms as the head of the actors' union, the Screen Actors Guild. Union workers had typically voted Democratic, but many of them had warmed to Reagan's candidacy in 1980. But in his standoff with the air traffic controllers, he showed a steely resolve that delighted many business leaders and conservatives and dismayed union representatives. Believing the controllers' walkout would cripple America's transportation system and freeze many business activities, Reagan also noted that as federal employees, the air traffic controllers could not legally go on strike. The president gave the controllers an ultimatum: return to work within two days or be fired. When only a minority of controllers returned to work by the deadline, he fired the rest, which was more than 11,000 workers. The action wrecked the controllers' union and put the rest of America's unions on notice that they should not trifle with Reagan. The number of strikes afterwards dropped to some of the lowest levels since the beginning of the American labor movement.

Although Reagan wanted to curtail domestic government spending, he wanted to increase military spending. He felt that America had become paralyzed by the failure in Vietnam and that it still needed to confront the threat of Soviet communism with robust military power. The Republicans called their military philosophy "peace through strength," or the idea that only by maintaining a formidable military could America challenge and forestall the aggressive acts of nations opposed to US interests. Critics argued that military buildup only made war more likely. When Reagan won congressional approval for a new class of nuclear weapons, hundreds of thousands of protestors joined a rally in New York's Central Park in 1982, calling for a freeze in the development of nuclear arms.

Reagan's Foreign Policy

Reagan embodied the Cold War conviction that Soviet power represented a grave threat to the United States and that the Soviets were looking to expand their sphere of influence around the world in countries such as Afghanistan, Nicaragua, and the West African nation of Angola. Addressing a meeting of evangelical Christian leaders in 1983, Reagan called the Soviet Union an "evil empire" and the "focus of evil in the modern world." He also positioned more missiles at US outposts in Europe, countering the Soviets' missile installations that threatened America's European allies in NATO.

Reagan boosted investment and research into the Strategic Defense Initiative (SDI), a futuristic program that would have employed satellite-based laser beams to destroy incoming Soviet missiles. Critics mocked SDI as "Star Wars," a term derived from the wildly successful space film of 1977. But without an effective missile defense system, the Reagan administration contended, the United States would simply have to accept the nightmare scenario of a nuclear attack leading to the mutually assured destruction of much of America and the Soviet Union.

Reagan's tough stance toward the Soviet Union helped promote diplomatic breakthroughs with the communist nation in his second term. This was partly due to major changes in Soviet leadership. Longtime American rival Leonid Brezhnev died in 1982. After the quick deaths of two successors to Brezhnev, Mikhail Gorbachev finally became Soviet premier in 1985. The reform-minded Gorbachev would take the USSR into a new era of "glasnost," or domestic freedoms and openness to the West. Gorbachev feared that his brittle, impoverished nation was going to collapse without serious change. Gorbachev also realized that Reagan's aggressive military buildup could destroy an already-weakened Russian economy if the Soviets tried to keep up with the Americans' pace in programs such as SDI.

Negotiations between Gorbachev and Reagan began in 1985, and in 1986 they met at a summit in Reykjavík, Iceland. The summit produced wildly ambitious talks about the Russians and Americans eliminating their entire stockpile of nuclear weapons. No firm deal was struck, though. Reykjavík did set the stage for a significant agreement in Washington in 1987, in which Reagan and Gorbachev agreed to draw down the intermediate-range nuclear missiles the nations had stationed in Europe. The Intermediate-Range Nuclear Forces Treaty, or INF Treaty, represented the first time during the Cold War the two sides had agreed to eliminate any nuclear weapons rather than just limit additional ones. Although some critics suggested that Reagan was going soft on communism, the Senate overwhelmingly approved the INF Treaty in 1988.

The INF Treaty left a great deal of unfinished business in US-Soviet relations as well as in the status of communism in Eastern Europe. The full collapse of the Soviet Union and of the communist regimes in Europe would transpire under Reagan's successor, his vice president, George H. W. Bush. But even as he negotiated with Gorbachev about nuclear weapons, Reagan called for freedom and democracy in the Soviet bloc. One of Reagan's most famous speeches came in West Berlin in June 1987. Standing in front of the Brandenburg Gate, one of the most recognizable symbols of the wall that divided Berlin into its democratic and communist sections, Reagan called on the Soviet premier to allow freedom to come to East Germany and to reunite Berlin. "Mr. Gorbachev, open this gate!" the president proclaimed. "Mr. Gorbachev, tear down this wall!"

Similar to the policy of "containment" from the post–World War II era, the Reagan administration was determined to halt the global spread of Soviet power, especially in the Western Hemisphere. This concern came to a head in Nicaragua, where the revolutionary Sandinista government had received aid from the Carter administration. Reagan and his secretary of state, Alexander Haig, saw the Sandinistas as a conduit for communist power in Central America. The Sandinistas took assistance from the Soviets and Cubans even as they accepted American aid. So Haig stopped payments to the Sandinistas in 1981, which led them to align more firmly with the Soviet bloc. Reagan decided to put US support behind the Nicaraguan "Contras," anti-communist revolutionaries trying to overthrow the Sandinistas. Congress was reluctant to give direct assistance to the Contras, however, fearing a repeat of the quagmire in Vietnam. The Central Intelligence Agency began funneling covert assistance to the Contras, but the wary Congress banned any unit of the American government from doling out assistance in Central America.

National Security Council (NSC) officials under Reagan remained resolved to help the Contras, however, and concocted secret plans to do so. Among these plans were illicit arms sales to Iran, which they hoped would simultaneously help them gain the release of American hostages in Lebanon and give them a funding source for the Contras. None of these plans worked well, and they came to light during Reagan's second term in 1986, when an American plane carrying assistance for the Contras was shot down over Nicaragua. When one of the American crew members was captured, the story behind the American arms sales to Iran and funding for the Contras emerged in the international media. John Poindexter, head of the NSC, resigned, and Oliver North, the architect of the funding scheme, was fired. The "Iran-Contra Affair" damaged Reagan's image, although he successfully deflected charges that he must have known about the elaborate NSC plans.

Turmoil in the Middle East and the threat of terrorism took on a new prominence during Reagan's first term. Middle Eastern and North African political organizations and government-backed entities increasingly turned to terrorist acts in hopes of wearing down the resolve of enemy states. In spite of widespread antagonism against Israel by its Arab neighbors, Reagan was determined to support Israel in its struggle with the Palestinians of the West Bank and Gaza Strip. The Palestinian Liberation Organization (PLO), then based in Lebanon, launched attacks on Israelis. Israel responded by invading Lebanon in 1982, ultimately driving out the PLO from its haven there. The United States also stationed Marines in Beirut, Lebanon, as part of an international peacekeeping force. In early 1983, terrorists associated with Iran killed sixty-three people in an explosion at the US embassy in Beirut. Terrorists also detonated truck bombs at the

Marine barracks in Beirut later in 1983, killing 241 American troops and dozens of French soldiers. A group calling itself "Islamic Jihad" claimed responsibility for the bombings, but the attacks clearly had the support of elements within Iran. Not wishing to start a new war when it was difficult to discern who had ordered the bombings, Reagan took no major actions against Lebanon or Iran in response to the Beirut barracks bombings. In 1984, Reagan withdrew the remaining peacekeeping forces from Lebanon.

Reagan sought to act more decisively against other state sponsors of terrorism when possible. When Israelis and the PLO continued to clash in the PLO's new haven in Tunisia in 1985, terrorists representing the PLO-affiliated Palestine Liberation Front hijacked an Italian cruise ship, the *Achille Lauro*. When Israel refused to comply with the terrorists' demands that they release Palestinian prisoners held in Israel, the terrorists on the ship executed a wheelchair-bound American Jew named Leon Klinghoffer, dumping his body into the sea. Negotiators agreed to give the terrorists safe passage in Egypt, but when the terrorists attempted to leave Egypt by plane, US jets forced the plane to land in Italy. Klinghoffer's killers were convicted of conspiracy and murder in Italian courts. The *Achille Lauro* incident badly damaged the PLO's international reputation. Its chairman, Yasir Arafat, subsequently issued a statement repudiating terrorism. The PLO maintained that it had the right to resist Israeli occupation of Palestinian territory, however. Palestinians would continue to employ tactics Israeli and American officials regarded as terrorism.

The United States repeatedly clashed in the 1980s with Libya and its leader, Muammar Gaddafi, over Libya's involvement with terrorist attacks. In 1986, Libyan agents blew up a West Berlin disco known to be a popular hangout for US soldiers. The bombing killed three and injured hundreds, and two of the dead were US servicemen. President Reagan ordered retaliatory strikes in Libya, including the bombing of Gaddafi's home. Gaddafi escaped unharmed, but he claimed the strike had killed his young daughter. Terrorists were also behind the destruction of Pan American Airways flight 103 in 1988, in which 259 passengers and crew died in a midair explosion over Lockerbie, Scotland. Among the dead were 189 Americans. After lengthy investigations, Gaddafi took responsibility for the bombing in 2003.

A Renewal of Conservatism

The 1980s saw a renewal of religious and political conservatism. Reagan helped inspire that renewal, but he was also a product of its success. The cultural changes of the 1960s and '70s, including the challenges to traditional gender roles and the legalization of

abortion, certainly sparked the conservative revitalization. Many conservatives and people of traditional faith saw America as a culture in decline and wanted to return to the
great resources of the Judeo-Christian tradition and Western civilization as bulwarks
against that decline. The Moral Majority, led by Jerry Falwell, was among the most visible organizations of traditional religion in politics, but the conservative renaissance of
the era was far more varied and vital than the Moral Majority.

The conservative trend was not restricted to politics, either. Conservative
Catholicism received a generation-defining boost from the papacy of John Paul II, who
became pope in 1978. John Paul II (Karol Wojtyla), a native of Poland, was the first
non-Italian pope for almost half a millennium. The worldwide influence of Catholicism
had been drifting for some time, in spite of modernizing innovations introduced by the
Second Vatican Council of the 1960s. But John Paul II's winsome defense of Catholic
orthodox teaching on moral issues such as the value of human life in all of its stages as
well as his courageous opposition to communism in Poland and Eastern Europe energized many of the Catholic faithful and drew legions of young people into the church.

Although many Protestants still had concerns about problems in Catholic theology,
John Paul II also had longtime connections with evangelical Christians and employed
an evangelical style in his ministry. When the pope held a mass at Los Angeles Coliseum,
a Hispanic minister named Isaac Canales was struck by the Protestant emphases in the
service. "It could've been a Billy Graham crusade," Canales said. He noted that the
attendees sang distinctively Protestant hymns and the focus was on "Jesus rather than
on the Virgin of Guadalupe." Catholics in the Americas, including in the United States,
continued to lose large numbers of parishioners to Pentecostal and evangelical congregations, however.

Among Protestants, the most remarkable conservative renewal movement of the
1980s and 1990s came in the Southern Baptist Convention (SBC). Whereas the other
large Protestant denominations (including northern Baptists) had gone through the
fundamentalist-modernist controversy of the early 1900s, the SBC had passed through
that period fairly untroubled by arguments over social issues or theological innovations. This was partly because of the relative isolation of SBC churches within southern culture, which retained a heavy veneer of nominal Christian commitment into the
1970s. Official agencies of the SBC showed signs of cultural liberalism, however, and
were slow to take a stand against *Roe v. Wade* and the legalization of abortion. Even
as late as 1979, the SBC could not garner enough support to pass a resolution calling for a pro-life constitutional amendment. But that year theological conservatives
began a campaign known as the Conservative Resurgence, during which conservatives
would take the reins of the denomination's top offices and seminaries and marginalize

moderate and liberal leaders. The SBC conservatives prioritized uniformity on issues such as abortion, the inerrancy of Scripture, traditional marriage roles, and restricting the senior pastoral office to men alone.

American Baptist (or northern Baptist) churches became formally committed to ordaining women as senior pastors in 1989. The practice had become more common in the SBC as well, especially during the 1970s and the era of the Equal Rights Amendment. But conservatives insisted the Bible taught that God intended for men to occupy positions of spiritual leadership in the church and in families. The energized conservative movement in the SBC passed a resolution against women's ordination at the denomination's annual meeting in 1984, precipitating a mass showdown at the 1985 convention in Dallas for control of the SBC. Forty-five thousand Southern Baptist messengers attended the meeting, far beyond the previous attendance record. The moderates' preferred candidate for convention president was no liberal, but he believed liberals and conservatives could coexist in the governing boards and seminaries. The conservatives insisted there could be no compromise with those who doubted any part of the Bible as the Word of God. Dallas pastor W. A. Criswell predicted that "whether we continue to live or ultimately die lies in our dedication to the infallible Word of God." When a telegram went public in which Billy Graham (a longtime member of Criswell's church) seemed to endorse the traditionalist candidate, Pastor Charles Stanley of Atlanta, conservatives reelected Stanley as SBC president with 55 percent of the vote.

The 1985 convention represented the beginning of the end for the liberal-to-moderate faction in the SBC. Conservatives ensured that new and existing faculty members at SBC seminaries affirmed the inerrancy of the Bible, that they affirmed the historicity of events such as Adam's and Eve's immediate creation by God, and that they did not present the miraculous events of the Scripture as myths or metaphors. Investigations suggested a significant presence of theologically liberal professors at half or more of the SBC seminaries. The flagship Southern Baptist Theological Seminary in Louisville, Kentucky, became the biggest flashpoint for conservatives trying to restore full theological orthodoxy at all SBC institutions. The appointment of Albert Mohler as president of Southern Seminary in 1993 led to a nearly wholesale turnover in faculty and administration. Mohler's presidency, and similar developments at other SBC schools, ensured far more theological and cultural uniformity and conservatism within the SBC.

Cultural and political issues such as abortion brought together Christians from across traditional denominational lines. Jerry Falwell presented the Moral Majority as an ecumenical organization, although it was dominated by evangelical Protestants and drew limited support from groups such as Roman Catholics. Nevertheless, traditionalist Protestants, Catholics, and even Jews often found themselves having more in common culturally with one another than with liberals in their own denomination or faith tradition. This sense of conservative commonality led to the founding of publications such as *First Things* (1990) by Father Richard John Neuhaus, a convert to Roman Catholicism and former Lutheran minister. *First Things* offered a platform to an extraordinary range of Christian and Jewish academics and clergy, with common concern for a traditionalist cultural witness, the Judeo-Christian intellectual tradition, and the primacy of theological orthodoxy. *First Things* coordinated the "Evangelicals and Catholics Together" statement of 1994, which admitted enduring differences between the two traditions yet affirmed a common commitment to basic principles of Christian theology, religious liberty, and the right to life. Neuhaus and the evangelical leader Charles Colson of Prison Fellowship were the key organizers and signatories of the document.[*]

The 1980s also saw a renewal of conservative thought in legal circles. Many judges and law professors felt that American courts had become shadow legislatures, imposing their opinions and preferences on American society rather than rigorously adhering to the law and the Constitution. The Federalist Society, one of the most influential conservative legal associations in America, began in 1982 with a mission to encourage judicial restraint and the principle that it is the "duty of the judiciary to say what the law is, not what it should be." President Reagan's Supreme Court nominees had a mixed record on judicial restraint and cultural issues such as abortion, however. Reagan's first appointee, Sandra Day O'Connor, was the first woman member of the Supreme Court. But religious conservatives were dismayed by her selection as she lacked clear pro-life credentials, and she went on to become a reliable vote in favor of abortion rights. In 1986, Reagan named conservative William Rehnquist, a Nixon appointee, to replace the retiring chief justice Warren Burger. Reagan tried to appoint the formidable conservative judge Robert Bork in 1987, but the Senate rejected Bork's nomination after contentious confirmation hearings. Reagan then nominated Anthony Kennedy, who represented the court's "swing vote" between liberal and conservative members for three decades before his retirement in 2018. On cultural issues such as abortion and sexuality, Kennedy typically adhered to the liberal activist position.

---

[*] *First Things*, "Evangelicals and Catholics Together: The Christian Mission in the Third Millennium," May 1994, https://www.firstthings.com/article/1994/05/evangelicals-catholics-together-the-christian-mission-in-the-third-millennium.

Ideologically, Reagan's most significant Supreme Court appointment was Antonin Scalia, who joined the court in 1986. Scalia served for thirty years on the court until his death in 2016. During that time he became the most influential conservative legal voice in the nation. Scalia explained that the proper way of "interpreting the Constitution is to begin with the text, and to give that text the meaning that it bore when it was adopted by the people." Scalia became best known for his biting dissents in cases such as *Planned Parenthood v. Casey* (1992), the most important abortion decision since *Roe v. Wade*. In it the Court affirmed the "essential holding" in *Roe* that access to abortion was a constitutional right. Rejecting this idea, Scalia suggested that the Supreme Court's liberal majority was

Figure 28.2. Antonin Scalia, Associate Justice of the Supreme Court of the United States, August 11, 2005.

"systematically eliminating checks upon its own power." Characterizing the majority opinion as "standardless" and a "verbal shell game," Scalia insisted that what really motivated the justices were "raw judicial policy choices concerning what is 'appropriate' abortion legislation."

Society and Culture in 1980s America

Conservatives pointed to what they saw as the suffering and turmoil the cultural changes of the 1960s had unleashed. In addition to ongoing evidence of the breakdown of traditional family structures, the appearance of a newly public gay rights movement was followed by the AIDS epidemic. In the early 1980s, the American medical community diagnosed a deadly sickness called "acquired immune deficiency syndrome" (AIDS), which left patients vulnerable to infections and certain types of cancer. AIDS could be transmitted through a variety of means, including blood transfusions, needle sharing in drug use, and most any type of sexual activity. But in the 1980s, the most common victims were men engaging in homosexual acts. By 1990, some 100,000 people had died in America due to AIDS. Some Christians speculated that AIDS was divine wrath against homosexuals. But when Magic Johnson of the Los Angeles Lakers announced that he had been diagnosed with AIDS in 1991, it changed public perception of the disease. Johnson, one of the greatest basketball stars of the 1980s, said he had never engaged in homosexual acts. He admitted that he likely contracted the disease from one of a number of sexual encounters he'd had with women other than his wife. Treatment for AIDS improved significantly over time, meaning that people like Johnson with access to good care could live active lives for many years after an AIDS diagnosis. A cure for the disease remained elusive, however.

African Americans had made a great deal of legal progress by the time Ronald Reagan came into office. But social and economic problems remained intractable, and informal kinds of discrimination against blacks and other ethnic minorities have remained common into the present day. Certain blacks began ascending to positions of major political power: New York City and Chicago both elected their first African American mayors during the 1980s. The Reverend Jesse Jackson won several Democratic primaries for president in 1984 before losing the nomination to Walter Mondale. But for impoverished African Americans, the prospects for advancement looked bleaker than ever in the 1980s. The disintegration of African American families continued, and the majority of poor black children lived in families headed by a single mother.

The aspirations and frustrations endemic to black culture helped produce rap music, one of the most distinctive musical forms in modern America. Rap was part of a broader hip-hop culture of art, music, and dance, first emerging from African American communities in New York City in the 1970s. Rap featured rhythmic speech over musical tracks. The first commercially successfully rap song was the Sugarhill Gang's "Rapper's Delight" (1979). Rap musicians routinely focused on edgy themes of sex and violence, drawing criticism even from certain black leaders. With relentless profanity and misogynist talk about women, N.W.A.'s 1988 album, *Straight Outta Compton*, raged against police violence toward blacks and represented the "gangsta" culture of south-central Los Angeles.

African Americans maintained a strong position in mainstream pop music too. Michael Jackson, the son of working-class African American parents from Gary, Indiana, became the most popular pop singer of the 1980s. Tens of millions of listeners worldwide bought Michael Jackson's 1983 album, *Thriller*, making it one of the best-selling American albums and best-selling albums globally of all time. The cable television station MTV, launched in 1981, greatly facilitated Jackson's ascent as one of the country's most popular singers. Jackson's popularity and charitable work earned him a visit to the Reagan White House in 1984. With the rise of MTV, video became just as essential to a musician's success as audio. The advent of cable television also signaled a new proliferation of media outlets, which would slowly challenge the dominance of the major television networks ABC, NBC, and CBS. The cable channels offered increasingly specialized programming as well. The all-sports network ESPN, for example, debuted on cable television in 1979.

Televised sports had taken on their contemporary format by the 1970s, pioneered by shows such as ABC's hugely successful *Monday Night Football*, which started in 1970. With flamboyant announcers, slow-motion replays, and multiple cameras, *Monday Night Football* turned football watching at home into an entertainment event. Televised football now had appeal beyond hard-core fans and served as a revenue-generating event on its own, not just as an enticement to get people to pay to go to games. Sunday afternoon NFL games followed suit, all leading up to the season-ending ratings bonanza of the Super Bowl. By the mid-2010s, the Super Bowl was routinely drawing an average television audience of well over 100 million people. Many sporting events retained massive in-stadium attendance numbers too, with devoted fans showing up to watch sports from NASCAR auto racing to college football. Football games at schools such as Michigan, Penn State, and Tennessee routinely drew more than 100,000 fans.

Some combat-themed sports chose to adopt "pay-per-view" instead of broadcast television, requiring fans to pay to get direct access to live events. One of the first major boxing matches to be distributed as a pay-per-view event was the 1975 "Thrilla in Manila" fight between Muhammad Ali and Joe Frazier. By the 1980s, headline boxing matches were routinely available only by pay-per-view. The best fights still generated enormous revenue, but boxing faded as a dominant national sport because it only reached a niche audience willing to pay to see top-billed events. Professional wrestling, led by the World Wrestling Federation (later World Wrestling Entertainment, or WWE), also pioneered the televising of arena events, bringing wrestling out of its former setting of small television studios. But the WWE still reserved their top matches for pay-per-view. "Wrestlemania" became the WWE's preeminent annual event, and in the 1980s Hulk Hogan became the WWE's top-billing star and the most recognizable wrestler in the world. Hogan headlined the early Wrestlemanias, including his match against André the Giant at Wrestlemania III, held in Detroit in 1987. That event showed that pro wrestling could produce both huge ticket and pay-per-view sales. The paid attendance at the Pontiac Silverdome in 1987 was more than 93,000 and the pay-per-view revenue exceeded $10 million, which was a pay-per-view record at the time. Wrestlemania has remained popular, with the 2016 attendance at "Wrestlemania 32" exceeding 100,000 people.

Perhaps the most celebrated athlete of the 1980s and 1990s was basketball's Michael Jordan, who paralleled Michael Jackson's celebrity in music. After growing up in Wilmington, North Carolina, Jordan starred for the University of North Carolina before joining the National Basketball Association's Chicago Bulls. Jordan's spectacular athleticism made him a fan favorite even before the Bulls began routinely winning NBA championships in the early 1990s. Jordan would show the lucrative potential for basketball players promoting sporting goods when he signed a major endorsement deal with the shoe company Nike in 1984. It was an agreement that would result in phenomenal profits for Jordan, Nike, and the NBA. Nike developed the "Air Jordan" line of shoes, marketed most effectively by the mid-1980s commercials directed by and starring the movie director Spike Lee. Lee's character Mars Blackmon was determined to find out the secret of Jordan's basketball talent, concluding, "It's gotta be the shoes!"[*] Jordan went on to become one of the wealthiest African Americans in the country, at a net worth of more than $1 billion.

Hispanic Americans also found success in sports, especially in baseball, which was popular in many countries throughout the Americas. Hispanic baseball greats included the Panamanian-born Rod Carew and the Puerto Rican Roberto Clemente, who played his whole career for the Pittsburgh Pirates. Clemente was the first Latin American baseball player elected to the sport's national Hall of Fame. Boston Red Sox great Ted Williams grew up in California with a Mexican mother, but he did not emphasize that part of his heritage. Latin America has produced legions of soccer stars, but those players have often gravitated toward Europe's more lucrative professional soccer leagues. Soccer has become a popular sport to play in the United States, but it has not been as central to the American sports industry as football or other pastimes.

Hispanics and Immigration

The growing Hispanic presence in sports such as baseball suggested their growing numbers in American society generally. Hispanics continued to come to the United States in large numbers, with distinctive pockets of ethnic Latino communities emerging across the nation—Puerto Ricans and Dominicans in New York City, Cubans and Puerto Ricans in south Florida, and Mexicans in regions of the Southwest from California to Texas. The Hispanic population continued to swell through the 1980s with large numbers of immigrants and a higher birth rate than average American families. The 2000

---

[*] "Retro Michael Jordan and Spike Lee Commercial," YouTube video, 0:30, August 15, 2006, https://www.youtube.com/watch?v=Abr_LU822rQ.

census revealed that Hispanics had become the nation's largest ethnic minority group, surpassing African Americans.

In the 1980s, there was growing political concern to do something about the millions of "undocumented" or "illegal" immigrants living in the United States, most of them from Latin America. The 1986 Simpson-Mazzoli Act, or the Immigration Reform and Control Act, sought to impose "comprehensive" immigration reform by giving long-term undocumented immigrants a legal status and by attempting to discourage traffickers who brought illegal immigrants across the US border. Any undocumented immigrant of "good moral character" who had been living in the United States since 1982 could establish a legal residency status by paying a fee and agreeing to learn English. The law resulted in about 2.7 million immigrants receiving "green cards" as permanent US residents. Critics called the program "amnesty," but it represented the largest legalization of undocumented immigrants in American history and was signed by President Reagan. Millions of other undocumented immigrants were not covered by the Simpson-Mazzoli program, however, so they lingered in uncertainty. Moreover, the law's enforcement measures, designed to discourage more illegal immigration, did not work well. By the 2010s, the number of illegal immigrants in the US rose to more than 11 million.

Hispanic immigration of any sort was normally fueled by a desire to reunite families or for adult men to earn money for families back home. But immigration could also happen in bursts prompted by political developments in Latin America. One of the most dramatic influxes came during the 1980 Mariel Boatlift from Cuba, which produced a flood of 125,000 Cuban immigrants to Florida in five months. Cuba's communist dictator, Fidel Castro, had permitted Cubans wishing to leave the island to do so, but the Cuban government also actively sought to remove "subversives" from the island. These could include democratic activists, the mentally ill, homosexuals, and a host of others. Earlier Cuban immigrants to Florida had tended to be light skinned and middle class, while the Mariel immigrants tended to be dark skinned (with more African ancestry) and poor. Miami's longstanding Cuban population was determined to distinguish themselves from the new *marielito* population.

Republican Electoral Triumphs

The US economy in 1983–84 was growing again after the early Reagan recession and the malaise of the 1970s. In 1984, Reagan faced Minnesota's Walter Mondale, who had been Jimmy Carter's vice president. Although Mondale could count on much of the Democratic base, and he made some inroads in recovering the white working-class vote, he had little chance against the popular Reagan. Reagan's campaign produced the "Morning in America" TV advertisement, which observers regard as one of the most effective ads in American political history.* Reagan staked his campaign on the idea that America was better off in 1984 than it had been at the end of Carter's presidency. Mondale reminded voters that the national debt was rising quickly and honestly admitted that he would support tax increases if he were elected. Mondale named Democratic congresswoman Geraldine Ferraro as his vice-presidential nominee, the first woman candidate on a major party's presidential ticket in American history.

In November 1984, Reagan won reelection in a landslide over Mondale, taking the Electoral College 525 to 13. Reagan received almost 59 percent of the popular vote. Although Republicans held the majority in the Senate until 1986, Democrats still controlled the House, forcing Reagan to look for bipartisan support for his agenda. Democratic soul-searching led some southern Democrats to conclude that the party had swerved too far to the left with the nomination of Mondale and that the party needed to bolster its moderate credentials and appeal to white southerners. This desire resulted in the formation of the Democratic Leadership Council (DLC) in 1985. One of the rising stars of the DLC was Arkansas governor Bill Clinton, who would end the Republicans' streak of presidential victories in 1992.

Reagan's second term was marked by more struggles, especially because of episodes such as the Iran-Contra Affair. Yet Reagan remained generally popular, not least because of his uncanny ability for rallying Americans (and even people around the world) through his outstanding speeches. This was displayed in Berlin when he called on Mikhail Gorbachev to "tear down this wall." Most poignantly, Reagan comforted a grieving nation when the space shuttle *Challenger* exploded just after liftoff on January 28, 1986. The disaster killed all seven crew members, including Christa McAuliffe, a New Hampshire schoolteacher whom NASA had chosen to go on the mission to bring renewed attention to the space program. Many American schoolchildren were watching the launch live. Reagan had been scheduled to give the State of the Union Address that evening, but instead he gave a tribute to the *Challenger* astronauts. The memorial was composed by Reagan's speechwriter Peggy Noonan, who wrote a number of the most important speeches of Reagan and George H. W. Bush. After reassuring American schoolchildren, Reagan concluded his address by quoting the poet

---

* "Ronald Reagan TV Ad: 'It's Morning in America Again'," YouTube video, 0:59, November 12, 2006, https://www.youtube.com/watch?v=EU-IBF8nwSY.

John Magee. Americans would never forget the *Challenger* crew, remembering how they "waved goodbye and 'slipped the surly bonds of earth' to 'touch the face of God.'"

Investigations into the *Challenger* explosion blamed a faulty fuel tank seal for the explosion. In 2003, the space shuttle *Columbia* also broke apart on reentry, signaling the beginning of the end of NASA's shuttle program. In recent years the United States has increasingly depended on private space transportation companies such as SpaceX to perform missions, including resupplying the International Space Station, a joint venture of the United States, Russia, and other nations.

After Reagan's two terms as president, Vice President George H. W. Bush of Texas was his clear successor. Bush was one of the best-qualified presidential candidates ever: he had served with distinction as a pilot in the Pacific during World War II, as a successful oil businessman in Texas, as a US representative, as ambassador to the United Nations, as head of the Central Intelligence Agency, and finally as vice president. Christian conservatives were lukewarm toward the moderate Bush, however, and

Figure 28.3. Sharon Christa McAuliffe received a preview of microgravity during a special flight aboard NASA's KC-135 "zero gravity" aircraft. A special parabolic pattern flown by the aircraft provides short periods of weightlessness. McAuliffe represented the Teacher in Space Project aboard the STS 51-L/*Challenger* when it exploded during takeoff on January 28, 1986, and claimed the lives of the crew members.

in the primaries they tended to support New York congressman Jack Kemp or the religious broadcaster Pat Robertson, who ran an energetic campaign as the first candidate produced directly by the Christian Right. Robertson's campaign attracted millions of supporters, but his charismatic theology turned away some Christians who did not like Robertson's emphases on divine "words of knowledge" and prayers for miraculous healings on his *700 Club* TV show.

Bush came out on top in the Republican primaries, partly through cultivating his ties to Christian leaders such as Billy Graham and Jerry Falwell. The Reverend Jesse Jackson once again made a strong showing in the Democratic primaries but lost eventually to the Democrats' nominee, Massachusetts governor Michael Dukakis. Dukakis was the son of Greek immigrants and had a reputation as a capable administrator with left-wing social beliefs. Dukakis established and then squandered a large lead in the polls over Bush. Once again television ads played a major role in the campaign, as Bush ads lampooned a Democratic photo op that had Dukakis looking a bit ridiculous as he rode around in a tank, grinning underneath his oversized helmet.[*] The ad suggested that there was a big difference between the reality of Dukakis's opposition to Reagan's defense buildup and the image of his feeble attempt to show himself as a martial leader. Racially charged ads by Republican groups made much of a prison furlough program in Massachusetts that had given a weekend pass to an African American man named William "Willie" Horton, who had been convicted of first-degree murder. On his weekend furlough, Horton had raped a woman and stabbed her fiancé. These kinds of ads convinced many voters that Dukakis was out of touch and hopelessly liberal.[†]

Bush's popularity paled in comparison to Reagan's among the Republican base. But Bush undoubtedly profited from Reagan's legacy in a strong economy and foreign policy achievements, and he ran a hard-edged general election campaign. Bush trounced Dukakis in November 1988, winning 426 electoral votes to Dukakis's 111. Bush would have to deal with a Democratic majority in the House and Senate, however. His desire to compromise with the Democrats on taxes—which he had promised never to raise—ensured that George H. W. Bush would become a one-term president. In the short term, however, Bush's election seemed the natural extension of Reagan's America.

[*] "Commercial—Bush 1988 Election Ad," YouTube video, 0:30, August 4, 2011, https://www.youtube.com/watch?v=9LyYD166ync.

[†] "Willie Horton 1988 Attack Ad," YouTube video, 0:32, November 3, 2008, https://www.youtube.com/watch?v=Io9KMSSEZ0Y.

■ SELECTED BIBLIOGRAPHY ■

Brands, H. W. *Reagan: The Life*. New York: Doubleday, 2015.

Busch, Andrew E. *Reagan's Victory: The Presidential Election of 1980 and the Rise of the Right*. Lawrence: University Press of Kansas, 2005.

Collins, Robert. *Transforming America: Politics and Culture during the Reagan Years*. New York: Columbia University Press, 2009.

Hankins, Barry, and Thomas S. Kidd. *Baptists in America: A History*. New York: Oxford University Press, 2015.

Halberstam, David. *Playing for Keeps: Michael Jordan and the World He Made*. New York: Random House, 1999.

Harvey, Paul, and Philip Goff, eds. *The Columbia Documentary History of Religion in America Since 1945*. New York: Columbia University Press, 2005.

Himmelfarb, Gertrude. *One Nation, Two Cultures: A Searching Examination of American Society in the Aftermath of Our Cultural Revolution*. Upd. ed. New York: Vintage, 2001.

Patterson, James T. *Restless Giant: The United States from Watergate to* Bush v. Gore. New York: Oxford University Press, 2005.

Scalia, Antonin, and Amy Gutmann. *A Matter of Interpretation: Federal Courts and the Law*. Princeton, NJ: Princeton University Press, 1997.

Wilson, James Graham. *The Triumph of Improvisation: Gorbachev's Adaptability, Reagan's Engagement, and the End of the Cold War*. Ithaca, NY: Cornell University Press, 2014.

29

George H. W. Bush, Bill Clinton, and a Changing America

As we approach the contemporary American era, it becomes more difficult for historians to assign relative significance to recent events. Some episodes that seemed enormously important at the time do not end up having much lingering influence. There is no doubt, however, that the coming of the internet has been one of the most far-reaching changes in the history of American technology and culture. Beginning in the early 1990s, the advent of the internet, email, and e-commerce dramatically changed American business and everyday life for American citizens. The idea of linking large-storage computers began in the Defense Department during the Cold War era as a way to improve American military capabilities. By the 1990s, however, people recognized the potential in linking America's vast network of home computers (and eventually mobile devices) together, initially for email messaging. Websites of companies, politicians, and countless other entities could also put information and products at Americans' fingertips.

The changes wrought by the internet were so profound and ubiquitous that it can be difficult to remember what it was like in the deeply "analog" world of the 1980s: no email, no search engines, no text messaging, no smartphones. Consider the everyday experience of college students before the internet: they used to go to a building for registration, stand in line, and physically sign up for classes. They could only talk to their professors in person or on the (landline) phone. There was no way to share documents online or via email. A professor might keep a computer file of attendance and assignment grades before the internet, but she or he could not post such records on a website. Students received grades when they were physically posted on a written list or (in the case of final grades) via the postal service. Most college courses in America remain somewhat "analog," in the sense that a professor still holds class meetings and gives lectures to students who are physically present. But many have speculated that the future will belong to online education, in which students and professors might never be in the same room. All information in such courses proceeds back and forth over the internet.

These changes were just beginning in the early 1990s. When Bill Clinton became president in 1993, there were about 50 websites in the world. By 1995, that number had shot up to 18,000. By 2006, there were more than 100 million websites, and by 2015, there were more than 1 billion. Internet-related business proved to be lucrative and fast growing for high-tech companies and for their investors. By 2017, the four largest companies by stock market capitalization in America were either profoundly connected to internet-related products and services (as in the case of Apple and Microsoft) or utterly dependent on the internet (e.g., Amazon and Alphabet, the parent company of Google). But the changes wrought by globalization and internet technology further destabilized more traditional segments of the American economy, such as manufacturing. They also increased the vast wealth gap between rich and poor Americans. By the year 2000, the wealthiest 1 percent of American households controlled 40 percent of the nation's wealth. In the decades since, concern about the power of "the 1 percent" has become a constant refrain in American politics among liberal politicians and Republican populists alike.

The Presidency of George H. W. Bush

The internet revolution was just on the horizon when George H. W. Bush became president in 1989. Bush continued to emphasize that the national government could not be the answer to all of America's problems—indeed, it was just as likely to be the source of the nation's problems. In his 1988 Republican Convention speech (cowritten by Peggy Noonan), Bush spoke of the nation's mediating institutions—service organizations that stood between the individual and the national government—as a "thousand points of light," a phrase he repeated in his inaugural address. Bush wanted to highlight the oft-forgotten work of charities and service organizations, who were commonly more effective than federal bureaucracies at helping Americans in need.

Bush also wanted to cut the size of government and of the national debt. Although Reagan had also expressed concern about the nation's debt, it had ballooned over the 1980s. Bush believed he could not enact serious debt reduction without giving in to demands for tax increases from congressional Democrats. So in addition to spending cuts, Bush agreed to increase the top marginal tax rate from 28 to 31.5 percent and to increase the gas tax (which Reagan had done as well). But Bush had promised Republicans in 1988 that when Congress came to him pleading for tax hikes, he would tell them, "Read my lips: no new taxes."

Bush's move reflected his pragmatic desire to get the budget deficit under control, but going back on his tax pledge proved damaging. The deficit deal was accompanied by a sharp downturn in the American economy starting in 1990. That downturn reduced government tax revenues and forced the national debt even higher. Tax-averse congressional Republicans, led by future Speaker of the House Newt Gingrich of Georgia, saw the tax deal as a betrayal. It widened the rift in the Republican Party over the validity of political compromise with Democrats.

Bush also showed an openness to some new government regulations, most significantly the Americans with Disabilities Act (1990). The law was a milestone in the equal treatment and accommodation of people with disabilities, requiring businesses and public places to make reasonable additions and adjustments to their facilities (such as wheelchair ramps and automatic doors) to improve access. Critics said the Americans with Disabilities Act would create costly bureaucratic regulations, especially for small businesses. The law has unquestionably generated an entirely new class of lawsuits against businesses, schools, and other organizations for disability discrimination. But over time the law also made it easier for people with disabilities to work in and get access to public facilities.

Bush and the Supreme Court

As with all presidents since Nixon, Bush had to contend with the highly politicized question of Supreme Court appointments. The possibility of overturning *Roe v. Wade*'s legalization of abortion was a preeminent concern. In 1989, the Court majority, including new justice Anthony Kennedy, upheld a Missouri law that prohibited abortions in state-funded clinics and hospitals. That decision, *Webster v. Reproductive Health Services*, seemed like a possible first step toward overturning *Roe*. The Court's decision in *Planned Parenthood v. Casey* (1992) somewhat alleviated the proabortion bloc's fears, however. In 1990 and 1991, Bush had the opportunity to fill two Supreme Court vacancies. His first choice, David Souter, was uncontroversial among most Democrats, but

Souter was not preferred by some conservatives. In spite of being opposed by groups such as the National Organization for Women, Souter easily received Senate confirmation and went on to become one of the most reliable liberal votes on the court. Even though they were appointees of Bush and Reagan, Souter, Kennedy, and Sandra Day O'Connor cast decisive votes in the 1992 *Planned Parenthood* decision upholding the basic principles of *Roe v. Wade*.

Souter had not emerged as a liberal justice yet when Bush made his next appointment to the Supreme Court in 1991. Bush chose the conservative African American judge Clarence Thomas to replace the retiring Thurgood Marshall, a stalwart liberal and a hero of the civil rights movement. Civil rights advocacy groups such as the NAACP opposed Thomas's nomination, as Thomas had a record of opposing affirmative action policies, which were intended to alleviate employment and educational discrimination. Thomas's confirmation hearings turned lurid and acrimonious due to the testimony of Anita Hill, an African American professor at the University of Oklahoma. Hill charged Thomas with sexually harassing her when they worked together at the Equal Employment Opportunity Commission during the 1980s. Thomas vehemently denied Hill's charges, saying the controversy was a "circus" and a "national disgrace." He further stated, "From my standpoint, as a black American, it is a high-tech lynching for uppity blacks who in any way deign to think for themselves, to do for themselves, to have different ideas." There was no clear way to corroborate or refute Hill's charges against Thomas. In the end the Senate narrowly confirmed Thomas by a vote of 52 to 48. Thomas went on to become a quieter voice of conservatism on the court than Antonin Scalia. But from conservatives' perspective, Thomas turned out far better than Souter.

Race, Violence, and Entertainment

Thomas's talk of a "high-tech lynching" spoke to the way racial tensions and suspicions still played a powerful role in America in the 1990s. Technology was often a factor in exposing and stoking racial animosity, whether in the twenty-four-hour news cycle of cable television networks or new technologies that allowed people to capture videos of police assaults on blacks and other minority suspects. A home video of the police beating of Los Angeles–area motorist Rodney King brought volcanic racial resentments to the surface in California in 1991. King had been speeding and then led police on a chase. When they finally stopped him, King resisted arrest. Several white police officers stunned King and then mercilessly beat him with batons as he lay on the ground. The video was the key to the sensation that King's beating and the subsequent trial of the white officers caused. Beatings of defenseless blacks by white authorities had a long history in America, of course, but until the age of video cameras, such beatings were not usually captured and replayed publicly.*

In 1992, a jury with no African American members failed to convict any of the officers who had beaten King. This verdict set off horrific rioting in Los Angeles, which left fifty-five people dead, thousands injured, and caused about a billion dollars' worth of property damage. Video also captured appalling random violence by rioters against a white driver and a Latino driver. The Latino driver, a Guatemalan immigrant named Fidel Lopez, was attacked by a group of blacks, his head bashed by a stereo speaker, his left ear nearly cut off, and his body doused with gasoline, likely with the plan of setting him on fire. An African American pastor named Bennie Newton saved Lopez's life when he flung himself on Lopez and told his assailants that if they killed Lopez, they would have to kill him too. The Los Angeles riots were the most damaging in American history since the Civil War's draft riots.

Cable television coverage also fed the furor and racial tensions over the murder trial of former NFL football star O. J. Simpson in 1995. When police issued a warrant for Simpson's arrest on suspicion of murdering his former wife and a friend of hers (both of them white), Simpson and a friend led the police on a fifty-mile low-speed chase through Los Angeles. Perhaps 100 million Americans watched the pursuit of Simpson as news helicopters covered the scene. Simpson's nine-month murder trial drew unprecedented media coverage, overshadowing all other American news stories of the year. Deals for books and similar products by the key participants netted them hundreds of millions of dollars in royalties. Unlike most minority Americans, Simpson was able to hire a formidable legal defense team, who convinced the majority-black jury that Simpson was innocent. Polls indicated that a majority of whites strongly suspected Simpson had gotten away with murder, while African Americans tended to see him as innocent. A majority-white jury in an untelevised civil trial later ordered that Simpson pay $33 million to the families of the deceased.

---

* "3/7/91: Video of Rodney King Beaten by Police Released," video, 0:30, https://abcnews.go.com/Archives/video/march-1991-rodney-king-videotape-9758031. The beating of Rodney King was the first of a series of notorious episodes, some of them videotaped by bystanders or police dashboard cameras, of violence by police against blacks in recent decades. In a 2014 episode in Ferguson, Missouri, a white police officer shot at the unarmed Michael Brown twelve times, killing Brown. Protestors, believing Brown was trying to surrender when the officer shot him, chanted, "Hands up, don't shoot." The shooting unleashed a week of riots in Ferguson (a suburb of St. Louis) and other cities, but subsequent investigations exonerated the officer who shot Brown of any criminal actions.

The nonstop media coverage of the Simpson trial suggested a broader coarsening of American culture, a trend that bothered critics on both the left and the right. The trend away from the wholesome (if often unrealistic) media culture of the 1950s accelerated in the 1990s. Profanity, explicit sexual content, and lurid behavior all became more central components of America's vast entertainment industry. The brilliant but edgy sitcom *Seinfeld*, one of the most popular shows of the 1990s, routinely focused on the relational dysfunctions and sexual escapades of its characters. Sexual content became standard fare in network programming in the evenings. Cable TV programming gradually adopted more explicit sexual scenes and extreme violence that fell into the TV-14 or TV-MA ratings under the new "parental guidelines" adopted by the entertainment industry in the mid-1990s. The pornography industry was approaching revenues exceeding $10 billion annually by the early 2000s, with the internet vastly expanding the reach of pornographic images and videos. Religious and conservative critics argued that pornography was addictive and that it utterly violated biblical standards for sexuality and marriage. Some feminists argued that pornography was based on the denigration and sexual abuse of women.

President Bush and Foreign Policy

Although he only served one term as president, Bush helped the nation navigate one of the greatest flowerings of democracy in world history, from 1989 to 1991. Following on the negotiations between President Reagan and Mikhail Gorbachev, and Gorbachev's pursuit of "glasnost," the Soviet empire in Eastern Europe began to crumble. The oppressive communist governments of Poland, Czechoslovakia, and other nations fell one by one. Most spectacularly, in late 1989 the East German government announced that it was opening the Berlin Wall and that it would allow East Germans free access to West Germany. Jubilant citizens of West and East Berlin used sledgehammers and other tools to dismantle sections of the wall, and millions of Germans passed into the other section of the country, a simple journey that under communism was impossible for most Germans. When President Bush realized the Soviets were going to allow the wall to come down, he knew the Soviet empire was coming to an end.

Democratic government spread fast in Eastern Europe, but authoritarian rule was more difficult to displace in Russia. Bush and Gorbachev continued the nations' reduction of nuclear arms with the signing of the START I treaty in mid-1991. Hard-line Soviets were angry with Gorbachev, however, for moderating Russia's stance toward the United States and for allowing the Russian satellite nations to fall to the democratic reformers. Communist opponents briefly arrested Gorbachev in 1991, but the new Russian Republic leader, Boris Yeltsin, insisted on his release. Russian communists' attempt at a reactionary coup withered, and Gorbachev was freed. Almost immediately, the Soviet republics decided to dissolve the USSR, and Gorbachev resigned as Soviet premier. Yeltsin went on to attempt to institute democratic and free-market reforms. But economic problems and personal health struggles debilitated Yeltsin's presidency. When Yeltsin abruptly resigned as Russian president at the end of 1999, he was replaced by his prime minister, the former Russian secret police officer Vladimir Putin. Putin would go on to consolidate power over a corrupt, authoritarian government. A number of Putin's political opponents were jailed or died under mysterious circumstances. Putin has maintained a volatile relationship with American presidents. Government-sponsored Russian "hackers" were widely suspected of spreading bogus news stories in the United States during the 2016 election and trying to undermine Americans' confidence in the democratic system.

President Bush also expressed support for pro-democracy protestors in China beginning in May 1989, but their protests ended when communist authorities ruthlessly dispersed the protestors from Beijing's Tiananmen Square on June 4, 1989. Hundreds of unarmed Chinese protestors were killed. When the crackdown began, Chinese officials demanded that all Western news coverage of the protests cease. Americans watching CBS News even witnessed the spectacle of Chinese officials forcing the crew of anchorman Dan Rather to literally unplug its satellite feed so it could no longer broadcast from the site of the protests. Western photographers captured unforgettable images of a lone protestor standing in front of a column of Chinese tanks in spite of Chinese security forces' attempts to confiscate all journalists' film of the crackdown. The Bush administration took little enduring action against the Chinese other than to denounce the violence against the protesters. But Tiananmen Square showed the world the harsh realities behind continuing communist control of China.

Bush remained engaged in Latin America, which also saw a surge of successful democratic movements. The Sandinista regime in Nicaragua fell in a free election in 1990, ending the need for the anticommunist "Contra" rebellion there. In Panama, Reagan's CIA had supported the military dictator Manuel Noriega as a bulwark against the Sandinistas and Central American communism. But as the Sandinistas started to lose power, the myriad problems with Noriega's regime became more conspicuous. Not only was Noriega corrupt and abusive, but he oversaw a lucrative trade in drugs. Noriega invalidated a legitimate presidential election in 1989 and had his thugs rough up the candidate who had won. Under a treaty signed by the Carter administration, the Panama Canal was slated to come under Panamanian (instead of American) control in 1999. Bush could not countenance the idea of that vital trade link being held by a corrupt and hostile regime. When a marine was killed in Panama in late 1989 and Panamanian soldiers attacked and harassed other US personnel, the Bush administration decided to remove Noriega.

Just before Christmas 1989, the United States launched Operation Just Cause, sending tens of thousands of American paratroopers and special forces into Panama to secure the canal and to capture Noriega. Noriega barricaded himself in Panama City, but after a two-week siege he surrendered. The United States flew him to Miami and put him in jail, charging him with a variety of crimes, including cocaine trafficking. Noriega was eventually extradited to Panama, where he died in 2017. Post-Noriega Panama maintained free elections and saw successive transfers of power to opposition parties.

Iraq, the Gulf War, and Operation Desert Storm

The greatest foreign policy test during the Bush administration was Iraq's invasion of Kuwait in 1990. At the head of a multinational coalition, the Bush administration would take the leading role in expelling the forces of Iraqi dictator Saddam Hussein from Kuwait. Saddam had a long track record of committing atrocities against his own people and against Iranians during the Iran-Iraq War of the 1980s. Saddam's regime had no qualms about the indiscriminate use of chemical weapons against their enemies. The Reagan administration viewed Iran as a bigger threat in the Middle East than Iraq, so the United States sided with Iraq in its conflict with the Iranians. Saddam seems to have believed the United States would not act decisively when he ordered the invasion of Kuwait, an oil-rich nation on Iraq's southeastern border.

Some in the Bush administration, including Colin Powell, the chairman of the Joint Chiefs of Staff (the highest position in the American military), were worried that Kuwait could turn into another Vietnam-style quagmire if America intervened. Powell advocated a position that became known as the "Powell Doctrine": America should only go into overseas conflicts as a last resort, but when they did, they should bring such massive force that it would ensure quick, decisive victory. Bush met Saddam's unprovoked invasion of Kuwait with the vow "This will not stand." Although Bush was clearly concerned about maintaining a reliable supply of oil from the Middle East, he insisted that the main point of intervention was putting a stop to Iraq's brazen takeover of a sovereign nation. The president began working to assemble a large coalition of nations—thirty-four in all, including a number of Arab and Muslim states—that would assist in expelling Iraq from Kuwait. Liberal critics in the United States cried, "No blood for oil" and called for an end to American overseas escapades. But over the opposition of a majority of Democrats, Congress narrowly authorized military action against Iraq in early 1991.

When Saddam failed to respond to a United Nations resolution deadline for Iraq to leave Kuwait, the American-led coalition launched an overwhelming aerial assault on Saddam's occupying forces on January 16, 1991. Following the Powell Doctrine, the bombing decimated the Iraqi army and Iraq's power grid, leading to heavy defections from Saddam's army. Cable news channel CNN followed the fighting in real time, showing vivid images of Iraqi "Scud" missiles streaking toward targets in Israel and Saudi Arabia, which the coalition forces used as a major staging ground. American general Norman Schwarzkopf then launched the second phase of the war in Kuwait, Operation Desert Storm. Almost a million coalition troops, including some 700,000 US forces, were involved in the planning and execution of the ground assault to liberate Kuwait. The actual ground force commanded by Schwarzkopf totaled about 400,000 troops. They quickly routed Iraqi forces in Kuwait, taking about 100 hours in late February to break Iraq's hold in the nation. About 148 American soldiers died during the Gulf War.

Figure 29.1. US military personnel arrive at a base camp during Operation Desert Shield. US Army photo by Staff Sergeant Lee Corkran. 1991.

Some Republicans wanted Bush to follow up the expulsion of the Iraqis from Kuwait with an invasion of Iraq itself, which they hoped would result in the deposing of Saddam Hussein. Bush and his defense secretary, Dick Cheney, argued that they had fulfilled their mission of liberating Kuwait and that was enough. Invading and controlling Iraq, a far larger nation, really did present risks of quagmire, as President Bush's son George W. Bush would discover in the 2000s. Bush instead preferred to leave Saddam in place, with significant new military and economic sanctions against Iraq. Saddam did face uprisings in the south and north of Iraq, from Shi'a Muslims (Saddam was a Sunni Muslim) and from ethnic Kurds. In spite of a "no fly" zone the coalition had imposed in those areas, these uprisings were crushed by Saddam's forces. Bush chose not to intervene further, leaving in place the Saddam regime as well as seething resentments toward both Saddam and the United States. America also left a significant military presence in a number of Gulf nations, including Saudi Arabia. Terrorists affiliated with groups such as al-Qaeda would routinely cite their desire to expel American forces from Saudi Arabia, the home of Islam's holiest sites. In the short term the successful conclusion to the Gulf War made Bush enormously popular, with many suggesting that the war signaled an end to America's "Vietnam syndrome."

Moving to America, Moving to the Sunbelt

By the 1990s, America was returning to immigration patterns reminiscent of a century before. Because of the changes wrought by the 1965 Immigration and Nationality Act, as well as the continuing flow of legal and illegal immigrants from Latin America, America once again became heavily populated by new immigrants. By 2010, 38 million people lived in the United States who had been born outside the country. This represented 12 percent of the population. Certain states, including Texas, New York, Illinois, Florida, and California, took in disproportionately high numbers of those immigrants. Most of the new immigrants came from Asia or Latin America.

The 1986 Simpson-Mazzoli Act had tried to create a comprehensive solution to giving illegal immigrants—mostly from Mexico—a legal status and stopping the future flow of undocumented immigrants, but it did not succeed. The lure of better employment prospects kept bringing immigrants across the southern border, and certain sectors of the economy, including many construction companies, factories, farms, hotels, restaurants, and other businesses, were willing to employ such workers without confirming their immigration status. Undocumented workers often spoke little English and feared deportation. They were easily subject to mistreatment and poor pay, at least by typical standards in the United States. Hundreds of immigrants also died each year along the border, often when they were abandoned by "coyotes" who had promised to get them across the US border.

Although immigrants from Latin America were the largest cohort, Asian Americans had become America's fastest-growing ethnic group by 2000. Chinese-background people were the largest segment of the Asian immigrants, followed by people of Filipino, Japanese, and Indian heritage. Some recent Asian immigrants, such as the Vietnamese who fled their country in the 1960s and '70s, struggled to find good-paying work. But overall the average Asian immigrant family has done well in the United States according to metrics of education and income. Asians were disproportionately well represented in professions such as engineering and medicine, and by 2010 the average income of Asian American families was almost 30 percent higher than the national average.

Asian Americans, Africans, and other ethnic groups have added to the remarkable diversity of many American cities. By the 2010 census, Houston was America's most ethnically diverse city. In the mid-twentieth century Houston became one of the great centers of the American energy sector. Its traditional mix of white, Latino, and African American residents shifted in the 1970s with a major influx of Vietnamese immigrants. In the 1980s, higher numbers of new Latino immigrants came to the city looking for employment opportunities. Many of these Latino immigrants were there legally, but a significant number were undocumented. During the same period much of the white population of the city flowed out to the suburbs. Between 1970 and 2010, Houston's white majority turned into a strong Hispanic plurality of 44 percent, with whites at 26 percent, African Americans at 23 percent, and Asians at 6 percent. The city also has significant populations of Africans and Middle Easterners. At Wisdom High School in southwest Houston, a student's classmates included boys and girls whose families were from Mexico, Cuba, Uganda, Ethiopia, Afghanistan, and other nations. Many American cities could point to similar signs of diversity. Los Angeles's Catholic archdiocese reported that by the 1990s you could find services spoken in forty-two different languages in its city parishes.

The increasingly visible presence of immigrants became a source of concern for a number of critics. They said that controlled, legal immigration remained a healthful part of American life, but America's lack of border enforcement caused a host of social and economic problems and jeopardized American cultural integrity. The rising number of authorized and unauthorized immigrants willing to take low-paying jobs caused disruptions in the labor market for blue-collar American workers, leading to lower wages and higher unemployment. Many also feared the operations and endemic violence of Mexican gangs would spill over into America's streets. Conservative writer Pat Buchanan, who ran against George H. W. Bush for the Republican nomination in 1992, visited the US–Mexico border during the campaign and said he was "calling attention to a national disgrace," namely, "the failure of the national government of the United States to protect the borders of the United States from an illegal invasion that involves at least a million aliens a year. As a consequence of that, we have social problems and economic problems. And drug problems." The presidential nominees of the Republicans and Democrats typically took a more moderate stance on the problem of immigration than did Buchanan. (President Donald Trump, however, would make opposition to illegal immigration and building a more secure border wall cornerstones of his 2016 campaign.)

Within the United States a population shift toward the "Sunbelt" continued into the late twentieth century. The majority of the American population by the 1990s lived in the broad southern swath of the United States running from the Carolinas in the east to California in the west. There are many explanations for the swelling numbers living in the Sunbelt. One was that much of the tide of new immigrants flowed into the Sunbelt. Another key development was the widespread use of air-conditioning in homes and businesses, which made it easier to endure the broiling Sunbelt summers, at least for those who could afford it. Jobs were another factor. Southern and western politicians had done a great deal to attract military bases and defense industries to the Sunbelt starting in the 1940s. California became the center of the high-tech world, while Texas was home to much of the energy sector.

More generally, people and businesses came to view the Sunbelt as an attractive place to live, with (generally) favorable weather and an encouraging business climate. Many Sunbelt states offered tax incentives for companies looking to move, and many had lower taxes overall for individuals too. States including Florida, Texas, and Nevada had no state income taxes for individuals, although they made up the difference with higher sales taxes and other sources of revenue. Much of the Sunbelt, especially the Deep South, still struggled with poverty, but the new southern suburban centers of growth sought to project fresh new images with "good schools and a cultural environment that [attracts] high-level technical people," one business writer explained. The decision to relocate a company, an American businessman noted, could hinge on a simple "walk around town to look at the parks to see if the grass is cut, at the schools to see what shape they're in, at the churches and the homes themselves to see if they're painted and well kept."

Cities and metropolitan areas from across the Sunbelt saw enormous post–World War II growth. Charlotte, North Carolina, went from about 100,000 people in 1940 to 731,000 in 2010. In the 1990s alone, Phoenix, Arizona, grew by a million residents. During the 2010s, Phoenix surpassed Philadelphia as the fifth-largest city in the nation.

A number of northern states and cities saw their population plateau or drop during the post–World War II era. Between 1950 and 2000, Philadelphia's population dropped from more than 2 million to just over 1.5 million. Between 1950 and 2010, Detroit's population declined from 1.85 million to just over 700,000. Shifting state populations also affected a state's number of representatives in Congress. Between 1950 and 2000, Texas added ten members of the House of Representatives, while Florida added seventeen, and California added twenty-three. New York lost fourteen members, and Pennsylvania lost eleven during that period. Previous congressional districts were merged into geographically larger ones to account for the northern states' dwindling percentage of the American population.

Poverty and Culture

The 1980s and 1990s saw a long period of growth for American businesses and the incomes of many American families. But that growth also masked deeper problems in America related to the concentrations of wealth and poverty and the continuing breakdown of major segments of American society. Increasingly, America was divided not just by race but by class. Single-parent households and out-of-wedlock births became more common across America but especially among people with lower incomes and education levels. Overall, between 1965 and 1990, the percentage of babies born to unmarried mothers went up from 3 to 18 percent for whites and from 24 to 64 percent for African Americans. The reasons for the decline in traditional marriage and family arrangements are complex. One obvious factor is that the widespread use of contraceptives and abortion beginning in the 1960s and 1970s helped dissociate sexual activity from childbearing. Many more women could reasonably expect to be sexually active but to have children at a time of their choosing. A number of feminists also insisted that women should not define themselves by their marital status and deplored the restrictions placed on women by traditional marital roles.

At the same time, much of American society lost the stigma associated with a woman getting pregnant outside of marriage. Before the 1970s, men who got their girlfriends pregnant often faced family and social pressure to marry them, resulting in what Americans called "shotgun weddings." As one San Francisco man explained in the late 1960s, "If a girl gets pregnant, you married her. There was no choice. So I married her." In the 1970s and 1980s, media representations of single mothers became much more prominent and affirming. The "single mom" was now a cultural icon of courage and perseverance. Sitcoms such as *One Day at a Time* and *Who's the Boss?* depicted divorced mothers making their way in the world without a husband. During the 1992 campaign, vice president Dan Quayle caused controversy by criticizing the TV show *Murphy Brown*, in which actress Candace Bergen played a divorced woman who had a baby outside of marriage. "Bearing babies irresponsibly is simply wrong," Quayle insisted. The cast of *Murphy Brown* brought the controversy into the show itself, with the title character addressing the vice president, who, she said, should "recognize that, whether by choice or circumstance, families come in all shapes and sizes."

Many people in traditional religious groups continued to believe in a God-ordained pattern of committed marriage and child-rearing only within marriage. Certain ethnic groups (including many Asian Americans) maintained stronger taboos against child-bearing outside of marriage. But one of the strongest indicators for having children within marriage was education and income level. By 2011, 57 percent of women without a high school diploma were unmarried when they gave birth, while just under 9 percent of women with at least a bachelor's degree were unmarried when they gave birth. Among the states Mormon-dominated Utah had by far the fewest out-of-wedlock births at under 15 percent. Some of the places with the worst poverty rates in the country—such as Washington, DC; Louisiana; Mississippi; and New Mexico—hovered around 50 percent out-of-wedlock births. During the era many liberal American elites professed not to believe in any universal standards of monogamy, marriage, and child-bearing. But whether liberal or conservative, Americans in elite educational and income circles remained among the most likely to observe traditional practices.

These trends in marriage and childbearing undoubtedly fed into cycles of endemic poverty, especially for American Indians and African Americans. (Both groups had out-of-wedlock birth rates well above 60 percent by 2011.) Individual African Americans routinely attained the highest levels of achievement in American society by the 1990s, when Colin Powell became chairman of the Joint Chiefs of Staff (and later secretary of state), and Condoleezza Rice served as provost of Stanford University, national security adviser, and secretary of state. Barack Obama achieved the highest office possible in 2008, as the first African American president. But for many African Americans and for many poorer Americans of all ethnicities, such opportunities seemed far out of reach.

A "get tough on crime" trend that began in the 1970s fell hardest on the poor and ethnic minorities, especially Hispanic and African American men. A surge in crime during the 1970s resulted in requirements for higher minimum sentences and laws such as California's "three strikes and you're out" rule. These types of laws could result in minimum sentences of twenty-five years to life in prison for thrice-convicted felons, regardless of the severity of the crimes. The "war on drugs" netted innumerable convicts involved at some level of traffic in illicit drugs such as marijuana and cocaine. The increased vigilance, often backed by politicians of all races, certainly reduced crime rates by the 1990s. But it also created a phenomenal increase in the number of incarcerated Americans. The number of the imprisoned grew fivefold between 1970 and 2000 to more than 2 million people. More than half of those in federal prisons were there on drug-related convictions.

Hispanics and especially blacks were overrepresented in America's prison population by the time of the 2010 census. Whites represented 64 percent of the total US population but only 39 percent of the prison population. Conversely, Hispanics made up 16 percent of the total population but 19 percent of those imprisoned, while African Americans were 13 percent of the total population but 40 percent of the prison population. About a quarter of inmates in federal facilities were not US citizens, many of them Mexicans. Experts have debated the extent to which these numbers reflect the actual pervasiveness of criminal activity among these groups and how much they reflect entrenched patterns of racism in policing and the criminal justice system. Whatever the case, by 2010 blacks were five times more likely to be in jail than whites in the United States.

The Clinton Presidency

A struggling economy made George H. W. Bush a vulnerable incumbent president in 1992. His weakness was exacerbated when independent challenger Ross Perot, a billionaire Texas businessman, entered the contest and eroded some of Bush's voter base. Perot especially harped on Bush's North American Free Trade Agreement (NAFTA) with Canada and Mexico, contending that it would decimate American jobs. In a presidential debate Perot insisted that when NAFTA went into effect (as it did in 1994), American workers would hear a "giant sucking sound going south" as more American jobs went to Mexico. Although Perot did not win, he did take 19 percent of the popular vote. His populist, no-nonsense, business-oriented style was a predecessor to that of President Donald Trump.

The real political threat to Bush in 1992 emerged in the person of popular Arkansas Democratic governor William Jefferson (Bill) Clinton. Clinton's background was a true rags-to-riches story. His father died before Clinton was born in 1946 in Hope, Arkansas. Clinton's stepfather was an alcoholic and was sometimes abusive to his mother. Clinton, however, went on to become a Rhodes Scholar at Oxford. Then at Yale Law School Clinton met his future wife, Hillary Rodham, who would become among the most powerful first ladies and the 2016 Democratic nominee for the presidency. Clinton, who grew up in the evangelical milieu of the South, spoke with easy familiarity in the language of faith and the Bible. He had a knack for making people feel as if he understood their struggles. Republican critics highlighted ever-present rumors that Clinton was an adulterer and a womanizer. Such rumors might have derailed earlier presidential candidates. But changing American mores about sexuality and marriage, Bill Clinton's charm, and Hillary Rodham Clinton's steadfast support assuaged the potential damage of his indiscretions. In November 1992, Clinton won 370 electoral votes to Bush's 168. Clinton cut into the Republicans' hold on the South, and he dominated the far West, Northeast, and Great Lakes regions.

Clinton projected moderation on issues such as welfare policy. But on social issues he was reliably liberal. His nominees for the Supreme Court in 1993–94, Ruth Bader Ginsburg and Stephen Breyer, became staunch members of the court's liberal bloc. Clinton quickly permitted greater public access to abortion and allowed medical researchers to use "fetal tissue" (the bodies of aborted infants) in experiments. Clinton also announced that he intended to lift the prohibition on gays in the military. Many military leaders and service members protested, arguing that the presence of gays would disrupt the integrity and harmony of units. Clinton was forced to accept a compromise, the "don't ask, don't tell" policy. In other words, leaders were not to investigate the sexual practices of soldiers, and soldiers would not be discharged if they did not voluntarily reveal that they were active homosexuals. "Don't ask, don't tell" was

Figure 29.2. Bill Clinton and Hillary Rodham Clinton, April 23, 1993.

repealed under President Obama in 2010, allowing gays and lesbians to serve openly in the military.

There were still limits to the social liberalism of any major politician in the 1990s, however. As Clinton turned more moderate in the mid-1990s, he promoted the Defense of Marriage Act (1996), which stipulated that marriage was a union of one man and one woman. Supporters of the Defense of Marriage Act had grown concerned that courts and state legislatures would start recognizing gay unions as marriages. The Defense of Marriage Act sought to protect the states from having to give official sanction to such marriages performed in other states. In the 5–4 decision in *US v. Windsor* in 2013, the Supreme Court struck down the Defense of Marriage Act as a violation of the due process rights of people wishing to enter a same-sex marriage.

The key legislative initiative of Clinton's first year was comprehensive health insurance reform. Clinton entrusted this project to Hillary Rodham Clinton, who assembled large groups of scholars and other health-care experts to devise a massive system that they hoped would eventually provide health insurance coverage to most Americans. Hillary Clinton's process reflected American liberals' confidence in experts to design effective top-down solutions to complex economic problems. The resulting proposal for the health-care plan ("Hillarycare") weighed in at 1,342 pages. Conservatives warned that the plan would cause major hardships for small businesses, lead to rising unemployment, and create a vast new federal bureaucracy. The Clintons had secured little support in Congress for the plan, even among Democrats, and they were forced to abandon Hillarycare in 1994. Its failure, the continuing shadows of scandal over the Clintons, and the fierce Republican opposition led by Georgia Republican congressman Newt Gingrich, led to devastating losses for the Democrats in the 1994 midterm elections. Republicans now controlled both houses of Congress, setting up a protracted series of policy and legal battles with Clinton.

Clinton charted a more moderate path on reducing the budget deficit and proposing reforms to welfare programs. By raising taxes on businesses and the wealthiest Americans and by cutting federal spending, Clinton narrowly secured a deal in 1993 that put the government on track to balance its budget by the late 1990s. As the 1996 election loomed, Clinton sought to bolster his moderate credentials further, declaring in his state of the union address that "the era of big government is over." Working with the Republican majority in Congress, Clinton in 1996 signed a welfare-reform bill designed to reduce the number of families receiving government assistance, partly by instituting work requirements and a maximum number of years families could keep receiving welfare. Liberals saw the law as cruel. Senator Patrick Moynihan, once a great champion of welfare reform, called it the "most brutal act of social policy since Reconstruction."

Experts have debated whether this welfare reform fundamentally hurt poor American families or freed more of them from dependence on government aid. There is no question, however, that it caused a major reduction in the number of Americans receiving cash welfare payments, dropping from more than 12 million people in 1996 to 5.3 million in 2001.[*]

Welfare reform and a strong economy gave Clinton advantages going into his 1996 race against Robert (Bob) Dole, a longtime moderate Republican senator from Kansas. A World War II hero, the seventy-three-year-old Dole was one of the oldest major party nominees ever. Many Republican voters were dissatisfied with Dole, who survived a primary challenge from conservative writer Pat Buchanan. Ross Perot ran again, and though he did not fare as well as in 1992, he still got almost 8 million votes. This was roughly the margin by which Clinton defeated Dole. In spite of Perot's presence in the race, Clinton won more than 49 percent of the overall vote. He received 55 percent of women's votes, suggesting the opening of a "gender gap" in American voting patterns. Dole did slightly better than Clinton among white and male voters overall, but Clinton's strong showing among women, African Americans, and Hispanics proved decisive.

Clinton and Terrorism

Foreign affairs were not a major focus of Bill Clinton's presidency, but the United States still wrestled with the implications of developments overseas. The Clinton administration had to grapple with the looming threat of Islamic terrorism, especially the threat posed by the al-Qaeda network led by the radical Saudi-born jihadist Osama bin Laden. Saudi Arabia expelled bin Laden in 1996, and he took refuge in Afghanistan with the blessing of the Taliban, the Islamist regime that had taken over much of Afghanistan after the withdrawal of Soviet forces in the late 1980s. Al-Qaeda, the Taliban, and similar reactionary Muslim groups were sworn enemies of the societies of Western Europe and North America, which they saw as degenerate Christian "crusader" states. They also hated the United States for its cooperation with Saudi Arabia during the Gulf War and for its steadfast defense of Israel.

By the 1990s, Americans had often seen terrorism just as an overseas threat. This changed in 1993 when Muslim terrorists exploded a truck bomb in a parking garage

---

[*] "Clinton Says Era of Big Government Is 'Over' in 1996 State of the Union," video, 0:59, January 22, 2014, https://www.washingtonpost.com/video/politics/clinton-says-era -of-big-government-is-over-in-1996-state-of-the-union/2014/01/22/da7c0cb4-83b6-11e3 -8099-9181471f7aaf_video.html.

under the World Trade Center in New York City, killing six and wounding more than a thousand people. The leader of the bomb plot, a Pakistani named Ramzi Yousef, had family connections to al-Qaeda. He escaped arrest in the United States and was involved in several other major terrorist schemes before being captured by Pakistani and American intelligence officials in Pakistan in 1995. Even though the 1993 bombing did not take down the World Trade Center or cause massive numbers of deaths, the Trade Center towers became an alluring target for future terrorist plots.

When a truck bomb devastated the Murrah Federal Building in Oklahoma City in 1995, many suspected that it was also the work of foreign jihadists. But that terror attack was committed by white American citizens Timothy McVeigh and Terry Nichols. With 168 killed and 800 injured, Oklahoma City was the deadliest terror attack in American history before September 11, 2001. The attackers claimed to be angry over federal overreach and violence against American citizens, such as had occurred in the disastrous siege of the Branch Davidian sect's compound outside of Waco, Texas. The bombers planned the Oklahoma City attack for the second anniversary of the end of the Branch Davidian siege, which had left seventy-six people dead in 1993.

Al-Qaeda stepped up its attacks on American interests overseas in the late 1990s. In 1998, terrorists launched simultaneous bomb attacks on US embassies in Kenya and Tanzania. The bombings killed more than 300 people. Although most of the dead were Africans, twelve Americans died in the Africa attacks too. In response to the bombings, the Clinton administration launched missile strikes on suspected al-Qaeda-affiliated sites in Sudan and Afghanistan. Then in late 2000, as a new presidential election approached, al-Qaeda attackers sailed a boat with explosives alongside the USS *Cole*, docked in a port in Yemen. The explosion resulted in the deaths of seventeen American sailors. Attacks like those on the African embassies and the *Cole* were carried out by suicide bombers, which made them even more worrisome. Terrorist groups had long used remote bombings to commit violence, but al-Qaeda and similar jihadist groups were raising up zealots willing to die in the act. Some of the Muslim bombers believed they would receive rewards in the afterlife for dying as a jihadist "martyr." The Clinton administration directed some increased resources toward countering the terrorist threat, but the lumbering intelligence bureaucracy, split between the FBI, the CIA, the National Security Agency, and other units, did not work well together. They were not especially good at tracking and sharing terrorist communications, which increasingly depended on satellites, cell phones, and the internet.

Clinton generally preferred not to get America involved in overseas conflicts, but certain developments made it nearly impossible for the United States to remain passive. Early in his presidency Clinton took action in Somalia, where gunmen associated with a local warlord had murdered two dozen United Nations peacekeepers in mid-1993. Clinton sent in American special forces to capture the warlord, hoping to restore order to the lawless Somali capital of Mogadishu. But Somali rebels shot down two Black Hawk helicopters, resulting in a battle in the streets of Mogadishu that left eighteen Americans dead and eighty-four wounded. One of the dead soldiers was shown on international television being dragged about the streets of Mogadishu by celebrating Somalis. Conservative critics wondered how the president had allowed American troops to get into such a volatile situation without sufficient backup, while liberals cited the memory of Vietnam as they warned against getting bogged down in another no-win foreign conflict. The sting of the battle in Mogadishu certainly influenced the Clinton administration's inaction when genocidal violence broke out in Rwanda in 1994. Some 800,000 Rwandans died during the genocide in a paroxysm of tribal violence. The Clinton administration advised the UN and other Western powers not to intervene.

More genocidal violence—though not at the same scale or intensity as Rwanda—broke out in Bosnia and Croatia in 1992, and the United States also did little to respond. Between 1992 and 1995, some 200,000 Bosnian Muslims were killed, with many others raped and forced from their homes. When a related conflict broke out in the Serbian territory of Kosovo in 1998, the Clinton administration was more open to intervention to prevent the kind of bloodletting seen in Bosnia and Rwanda. At the urging of the United States, NATO warplanes began bombing Serbia in March 1999, targeting the forces of Serbian president Slobodan Milošević. After several months of bombings, Milošević reluctantly accepted a peace agreement. NATO losses were minimal in a campaign that studiously avoided putting "boots on the ground," and no NATO pilots died in the conflict.

The Clinton Scandal and Impeachment

Dating back to his time as Arkansas governor, rumors of illicit relationships and shady financial dealings had dogged Bill Clinton. In 1994, Judge Kenneth Starr was appointed as an independent counsel to investigate accusations of the Clintons' financial malfeasance in real estate investments in Arkansas. Starr's probe broadened in early 1998 when he began looking into accusations of sexual harassment made by Paula Jones of Arkansas. More sensationally, Starr investigated a long-running series of sexual encounters between Clinton and a White House intern named Monica Lewinsky. The allegations about his affair with Lewinsky first broke on the Drudge Report, one of a new breed of internet-based news and scandal websites. The mainstream media hesitated to repeat the charges about the Lewinsky affair, but they finally became national news in January 1998.

The lurid details of Clinton's relationship with Lewinsky—with many of their liaisons transpiring in the White House itself—guaranteed that the affair would receive nonstop media coverage. It was a perfect storm of a political and sex scandal for America's increasingly coarsened media culture. It also seemed like a possible opportunity for the Republicans in Congress to remove Clinton from office. Clinton ratcheted up the pressure himself when he held a press conference a week after the revelations broke and proclaimed, "I did not have sexual relations with that woman." Hillary Clinton defended her husband, accusing independent counsel Starr of being a tool of a "vast right-wing conspiracy."

Unfortunately for Bill Clinton, one of Lewinsky's coworkers secretly taped conversations with Lewinsky about the details of the affair. When Starr granted Lewinsky immunity from prosecution for perjury, she also testified about her relationship with Clinton before a federal grand jury. Starr ultimately produced a lengthy report on the affair and on Clinton's apparent attempts to cover it up, including lying under oath about it. Liberal critics attacked Starr for being obsessed with the details of Clinton and Lewinsky's encounters, and media outlets painted Starr as an overzealous prude. But many Americans were disgusted with Clinton's lack of personal discipline and his seeming efforts to obstruct justice in the case.

Congressional Republicans believed the charges against Clinton were serious enough to merit impeachment proceedings. But impeachment proceeded under chaotic conditions: House Speaker Newt Gingrich resigned under pressure from Republican members after Republicans performed poorly in the November 1998 midterm elections. (Gingrich was also carrying on a long-term affair with a much younger woman at the time.) Gingrich's designated replacement, Robert Livingston of Louisiana, also had to resign because of an extramarital affair. The Republicans' efforts at impeachment had already suffered embarrassing setbacks, but they pressed forward. On narrow party-line votes in the House, they impeached Clinton on charges of perjury and obstruction of justice. Those votes sent the case to the Senate for trial and a vote on removing the president.

There was never any question of the outcome in the Senate because Republicans could not hope to get the two-thirds majority required for removal when they only held fifty-five Senate seats. In the end a number of Republicans joined Democrats in voting against removal. The closest the Republicans got to removing Clinton was a 50 to 50 vote on the obstruction-of-justice charge. Like President Andrew Johnson before him (but with a more comfortable margin), Clinton had survived his impeachment trial. Average Americans were just tired of the whole ordeal. Both the Republicans and President Clinton had paid a considerable price for the impeachment proceedings,

Figure 29.3. Rainbow PUSH Coalition anti-impeachment rally in support of President Bill Clinton at the US Capitol, December 17, 1998, by Elvert Barnes Protest Photography.

though Clinton's approval ratings remained surprisingly high through the end of his presidency. Once the trial was over, the Clintons redirected their focus to Hillary's political ambitions. She was elected as a senator from New York in 2000. The nation had gone through remarkable political turmoil and technological change during the 1990s. Both trends were only to accelerate in the 2000s.

■ SELECTED BIBLIOGRAPHY ■

Alexander, Michelle. *The New Jim Crow: Mass Incarceration in the Age of Colorblindness.* Upd. ed. New York: New Press, 2012.

Engel, Jeffrey A. *When the World Seemed New: George H. W. Bush and the End of the Cold War.* New York: Houghton Mifflin Harcourt, 2017.

Gibbs, Jewelle Taylor. *Race and Justice: Rodney King and O. J. Simpson in a House Divided.* Hoboken, NJ: Jossey-Bass, 1996.

Gormley, Ken. *The Death of American Virtue: Clinton vs. Starr.* New York: Crown, 2010.

Halberstam, David. *War in a Time of Peace: Bush, Clinton, and the Generals*. New York: Scribner, 2001.

Iber, Jorge, et. al. *Latinos in U.S. Sport: A History of Isolation, Cultural Identity, and Acceptance*. Champaign, IL: Human Kinetics, 2011.

Mejia, Brittny. "How Houston Has Become the Most Diverse Place in America." *Los Angeles Times*, May 9, 2017. http://www.latimes.com/nation/la-na-houston-diversity-2017-htmlstory.html.

Mize, Ronald L., and Grace Peña Delgado. *Latino Immigrants in the United States*. Malden, MA: Polity, 2012.

Naftali, Timothy. *George H. W. Bush*. New York: Times Books, 2007.

Shermer, Elizabeth Tandy. *Sunbelt Capitalism: Phoenix and the Transformation of American Politics*. Repr. ed. Philadelphia: University of Pennsylvania Press, 2013.

Troy, Gil. *The Age of Clinton: America in the 1990s*. New York: Thomas Dunne Books, 2015.

30

The Age of Terrorism

Between the year 2000 and the present, America saw swift technological changes and deep political turmoil. This was a time of cultural fragmentation, heightened individual expression, and the eclipse of the ideal of the traditional nuclear family. In economics the financial crash and deep recession that began at the close of 2007 represented the most severe crisis since the Great Depression. The terrorist attack of September 11, 2001, was the deadliest foreign assault ever on American soil, exceeding the death toll of Pearl Harbor in 1941. September 11 alerted a generation of Americans to the grave threat posed by jihadist terror. Finally, this period saw three extraordinarily important presidential elections: 2000, in which George W. Bush was chosen in one of the closest and most divisive contests in national history; 2008, in which Americans elected their first black president, Barack Obama; and 2016, when an Electoral College majority gave the presidency to Donald Trump, one of the most controversial and unconventional presidents America has ever known.

The 2000 Election and George W. Bush

The 2000 election was, in many ways, a referendum on Bill Clinton's presidency. In spite of his wearying scandals and impeachment trial, Clinton remained popular. The economy seemed to be doing well, at least until mid-2000. Clinton's vice president, Albert Gore Jr. of Tennessee, was the heir apparent and sailed through the Democratic primaries with relative ease. Gore was unhappy with Clinton because of his affair with

Monica Lewinsky, however, and worried that Clinton would be a liability to him. Gore and Clinton rarely appeared together during the campaign.

George W. Bush, the governor of Texas and son of the forty-first president, won the Republican nomination over a strong challenge from Arizona senator John McCain. Although Bush was the choice of much of the Republican establishment and had degrees from Harvard and Yale, he emphasized his business and political experience in Texas to cast himself as an outsider to Washington, DC, culture. Bush also had deep ties to the evangelical community, as he had experienced Christian conversion in the mid-1980s after having struggled with alcohol abuse. The evangelist Billy Graham had counseled Bush at the time of his conversion. Bush said in one of the 2000 presidential debates that Jesus was his favorite philosopher because Jesus had changed his heart. Bush cast himself as a "compassionate conservative," one who was attuned to the struggles of the poor and who wished to find empowering solutions to help them. Bush took a strong pro-life stance in the campaign, in contrast to Gore's support for legalized abortion. Neither candidate was asked much about terrorism.

The candidates were evenly matched, and the amazing results in November 2000 reflected it. Gore won the popular vote nationally by about 500,000 votes. The result of the Electoral College was difficult to determine because of an unclear outcome in Florida, one of the largest states. The uncertainty in Florida set the stage for one of the most excruciating political controversies in American history. Gore had dominated the Northeast, far West, and upper Midwest, with Bush capturing most of the South and the mountain West. The results confirmed the continuing role of the "gender gap," with the majority of women favoring Gore and the majority of men selecting Bush. Traditional Democratic constituencies such as African Americans went heavily for Gore, but Bush cut into the Democrats' usual lead among Hispanics. On the evening of the election, most news outlets initially reported that Florida, with its 25 electoral votes, had gone for Gore. But in the wee hours of the next morning, the consensus switched and gave Florida to Bush, which would mean Bush won the presidency.

For more than a month, the razor-thin margin of votes in Florida became the focus of unprecedented scrutiny. Ostensible voting errors on ballots led election officials to conduct recounts with magnifying glasses, as they sought to discern the actual intent of voters. Americans learned the term "hanging chads," or still-attached bits of paper on punch-out ballots. Inconclusive judgments by county and state officials led finally to arguments before the US Supreme Court in December 2000. In a 5–4 ruling in *Bush v. Gore*, the court majority put an end to competing recount rulings and processes. They affirmed Florida's certification of Bush as the winner in Florida by a mere 537 votes. Liberal critics and Gore supporters saw the court's ruling as a partisan power grab.

Nevertheless, with Florida in hand Bush won the Electoral College with 271 votes, the bare majority necessary.

Bush's Domestic Policy

Tax cuts were the key to President Bush's early domestic policy. Bush was also concerned about the budget deficit and national debt, but he contended that tax cuts would stimulate the economy. The attendant revenues from a growing economy, Republicans said, would make up for the government income lost by lower tax rates. In 2001, Congress approved a remarkable $1.35 trillion reduction in tax rates over a decade, and in 2003 they approved another tax cut of $350 billion. Bush inherited a faltering economy, however, partly due to the bursting of a speculative bubble in technology and other stocks. Investors lost billions of dollars when overnight sensations in e-commerce, including Pets.com, went bust starting in 2000. Corrupt accounting practices wrecked the giant Texas energy company Enron in 2001, with its stock price plummeting from almost

Figure 30.1. *Election Protest*, by Elvert Barnes Protest Photography. Presidential Election 2000. Protest at the US Supreme Court on Maryland Avenue, Washington DC, on Monday, December 11, 2000.

$100 to less than $1. Because of the tax cuts, the enormous ongoing costs of the military and of entitlement programs such as Social Security, and the economic turmoil of the early 2000s, annual government budget deficits began to grow once again.

As part of his "compassionate conservative" agenda, Bush worked with a bipartisan majority in Congress, including Senator Ted Kennedy, to pass the No Child Left Behind Act (2001). No Child Left Behind was one of the boldest and most controversial federal policies ever adopted related to precollege education. Bush wanted to establish a system that required standardized testing in core subjects to hold schools accountable for educating children. The law also sought to address the lagging performance of many poor and minority students and to force schools to find solutions to address the "achievement gap" between such students and their more affluent peers. In exchange for standardized testing, Democrats won major increases in federal funding to schools. Critics argued that No Child Left Behind took power away from local school districts and gave the federal government a more intrusive role in education. Many also contended that No Child Left Behind forced teachers to focus obsessively on "teaching to the test" lest they face punitive action for low scores. By 2015, No Child Left Behind had come under so much bipartisan criticism that Congress overhauled it in favor of a state-based system of enforcement.

The September 11, 2001, Terrorist Attacks

Given his experience as a governor, Bush came into his role as president with more interest in domestic than foreign policy. The appalling terrorist attacks on New York and Washington, DC, of September 11, 2001, permanently changed the focus of his presidency. On that day nineteen Muslim terrorists affiliated with Osama bin Laden's al-Qaeda network launched a coordinated plot to murder thousands of people. They hijacked commercial airplanes and flew them on suicide missions into the two towers of New York's World Trade Center and into the Pentagon in Washington, DC. A fourth plane crashed in rural Pennsylvania after passengers attempted to stop the hijackers. All told, the attacks killed almost 3,000 people, making it one of the deadliest days in American history. The worst casualty rates came at the World Trade Center towers, which both collapsed due to the explosions and intense fires that followed. More than 400 police officers and firefighters, who had rushed into the buildings to save people, died when the towers collapsed. Three days later President Bush visited the smoldering ruins of "Ground Zero" in New York. When recovery workers shouted to the president that they could not hear him, it sparked perhaps the most poignant moment of Bush's presidency. Speaking through a bullhorn, the president declared, "I can hear you. The

Figure 30.2. Firefighters amid smoking rubble following the September 11, 2001, terrorist attack on the World Trade Center, New York City.

rest of the world hears you. And the people who knocked these buildings down will hear [from] all of us soon."*

The Reverend Billy Graham addressed a "National Day of Prayer and Remembrance" at the National Cathedral in Washington, DC, on September 14. Then on September 20, President Bush spoke before a joint session of Congress. He vowed to hunt down Osama bin Laden and the other leaders of al-Qaeda and demanded that the Taliban regime in Afghanistan stop giving shelter to al-Qaeda. He told Americans that "freedom and fear, justice and cruelty, have always been at war, and we know that God is not neutral between them." Partnering with the Afghan Northern Alliance, which had already been fighting the Taliban, US military and intelligence forces began operations against the Taliban in October 2001. By the end of the year, the Taliban was out of power in the Afghan capital of Kabul. Tracking down Osama bin Laden would prove more difficult. US intelligence found bin Laden a decade later, hiding in a compound in Pakistan. US Navy SEALs attacked the compound and killed bin Laden in May 2011, under orders from President Barack Obama.

---

* "George W. Bush—9/11 Bullhorn Speech," YouTube video, 2:02, https://www.youtube.com/watch?v=x7OCgMPX2mE.

The reaction to the 9/11 attacks brought significant changes at home in the United States. The government created a consolidated Department of Homeland Security (DHS) to coordinate efforts of various departments involved in policing US borders and points of entry. It also created a new Transportation Security Administration (TSA) as part of the DHS. The TSA replaced private contractors who had previously run security for air travelers, as the federal government hoped to ensure uniform and rigorous screening at all airports. New regulations also required airplanes to have secure, reinforced cockpit doors.

More controversially, Congress overwhelmingly passed the PATRIOT Act in October 2001. This act gave the federal government broad new powers to fight the threat of terrorism by monitoring communications. It lowered standards for authorities to gain search warrants and detain suspects. The Justice Department detained hundreds of citizens and noncitizens, many of them of Arab and/or Muslim background, on suspicion of terrorism. Critics argued that many of these detentions were unconstitutional, haphazard, and based on weak evidence. As the "War on Terror" expanded into Afghanistan and Iraq, US officials also gathered many captives from overseas at the US naval base at Guantánamo Bay, Cuba, holding many foreign "enemy combatants" there in a state of indefinite detention.

By the mid-2000s, it became clear that intelligence departments, led by the National Security Agency (NSA), were conducting widespread surveillance of foreign communications and tracking international calls to or from the United States. Again critics argued that these programs represented an overreaction and a violation of American legal norms. They contended that the heightened surveillance jeopardized Americans' constitutional protections, such as the prohibition on "unreasonable searches and seizures" in the Fourth Amendment. Some of the most extreme aspects of the post-9/11 anti-terrorist programs, including large-scale indiscriminate detentions of people in the United States, were scaled back after 2001. But former NSA contractor Edward Snowden leaked thousands of pages of NSA documents to the media in 2013, and the documents suggested that the NSA was continuing to run a remarkable global surveillance program of phone records, internet communications, and more. Snowden, charged with espionage in the United States, took refuge in Russia.

The Iraq War

The 9/11 attacks also changed the Bush administration's approach to foreign policy. Bush had previously expressed reservations about "nation building" and excessive foreign intervention. Now he put the world on notice that his administration would not tolerate state sponsors of terrorism. Having already invaded Afghanistan to displace the Taliban, Bush declared in his 2002 State of the Union address that Iraq, Iran, and North Korea represented an "axis of evil" and a threat to the safety of free nations. Adopting the philosophy of his secretary of state, Colin Powell, Bush believed the United States should maintain such overwhelming military strength that it would guarantee quick victory in any conflict it entered. Moreover, "neoconservative" figures in the Bush administration, including Vice President Dick Cheney, argued that the threat of terrorism required the United States to act overseas to lessen the chance of 9/11-style attacks at home. Removing the despotic regimes like those in the "axis of evil" could set the stage for a flowering of global democracy, the neoconservatives believed.

The Bush administration implemented the neoconservative vision in Iraq, where the Gulf War in the early 1990s had left Saddam Hussein in power. In his 2002 State of the Union address, Bush also said the United States was obligated to "prevent regimes that sponsor terror from threatening America or our friends and allies with weapons of mass destruction." Iraq had a long history of using poison gas against its enemies. Administration officials worried that Saddam might pass chemical, biological, or (worst of all) nuclear weapons to terrorists, who would employ them in the United States. Iraq denied that it had stockpiles of weapons of mass destruction (WMD). Iraq had previously not cooperated with international inspectors who could verify the presence or absence of WMD. When the threat of invasion loomed, Iraqis allowed inspectors back in. The new inspections turned up little evidence of WMD, but the United States insisted that Saddam was toying with United Nations representatives and hiding the weapons.

The UN Security Council would not authorize the use of force against Iraq, but the United States decided to launch an invasion anyway. Britain, Australia, and Poland joined in the effort, but it was a much smaller coalition than that which George H. W. Bush had assembled to expel Iraq from Kuwait two decades earlier. The initial invasion in March 2003 easily swept aside Iraqi forces on the way to Baghdad, and soon Saddam Hussein was deposed and went into hiding. (American troops discovered and captured Saddam in late 2003, and he was executed by Iraqi authorities three years later.) America and its allies never found substantial stockpiles of WMD, however. Critics argued that the Bush administration had exaggerated, if not falsified, evidence for Saddam's alleged WMD stockpiles. But the administration argued that deposing the ruthless Saddam was worth the effort. In May 2003, Bush gave a celebratory speech on board the USS *Abraham Lincoln* underneath a banner that read, "Mission Accomplished."

Bush acknowledged that there was still much work to do in Iraq, but few realized what a perilous situation existed in the power vacuum of post-Saddam Iraq. Iraqis

AMERICAN HISTORY, VOLUME 2

conducted a brutal guerrilla insurgency against the occupying forces and against the newly installed American-backed Iraqi government. Meanwhile, decades of pent-up frustration against Saddam's dictatorial government spawned civil war in Iraq, fought largely between Sunni and Shiʻa Muslims. Iraq descended into murderous chaos, and it became clear that US planners had no clear strategy to manage the occupation. Finally, in 2007–8, Bush's commanders devised a "surge" of US troops to get parts of Iraq under control. The domestic political situation there also stabilized.

By the time President Obama began the mass withdrawal of troops in 2010, more than 4,000 American soldiers had died in Iraq. Many of the dead and the maimed had fallen victim to "improvised explosive devices" that insurgents used to kill and demoralize US forces. Obama's withdrawal was fraught with danger too, as the absence of US power gave rise to a new terrorist menace called the Islamic State in Iraq and Syria (ISIS). ISIS exploited a civil war that broke out in neighboring Syria in 2011. By 2015, ISIS controlled large swaths of territory between Damascus and Baghdad. Its jihadist members killed, tortured, and enslaved untold numbers of Syrian and Iraqi Christians and members of other religious minorities. ISIS's brutal rule caused a mass exodus of hundreds of thousands of refugees from the region.

ISIS, al-Qaeda, and other terrorist organizations struggled to carry out more spectacular attacks in the United States after 9/11. Ongoing terrorist acts in the United States were often carried out by "lone wolf" perpetrators inspired or radicalized by jihadist leaders overseas, sometimes via Islamist websites. A 2016 nightclub shooting in Orlando, Florida, in which a heavily armed Afghan-background American citizen murdered fifty people, was the most lethal terrorist incident since 9/11. The shooter professed allegiance to ISIS.

The 2004 Election and the Great Recession

The turmoil in Iraq was the key issue in the 2004 presidential election. Democrats nominated Senator John Kerry of Massachusetts, a Vietnam War veteran and critic of Bush's Iraq policy. Many Americans were frustrated with the war in Iraq, which seemed headed for a Vietnam-style quagmire. But many also preferred to let the Bush administration and the military finish what it had started in Iraq rather than to endorse a precipitous withdrawal. The 2004 election harked back to the vitriol of Vietnam-era elections such as 1968. By 2004, internet sites and cable news channels were feeding America's political furor. Critics saw Kerry as indecisive and elitist, and in November 2004 Bush defeated Kerry for reelection. Unlike in 2000, Bush won the popular vote as well as the Electoral College. Bush dominated the Plains states, the mountain West, and the South. Kerry controlled much of the Northeast, upper Midwest, and far West. Bush won by small majorities in "swing states" such as Virginia, Florida, and Ohio.

Bush presided over an economy that was innovative yet fragile. In spite of the dot-com bust of the early 2000s, new internet-based companies continued to proliferate. Some of the survivors of the bust, such as Google and Amazon, grew into internet behemoths. Major new players were also emerging, especially in the world of "social media," sites that combined personal connection to online "friends" with news and marketing. Facebook was founded in 2004, Twitter in 2006, and Instagram in 2010. New products related to the online economy kept appearing as well. Most important, Apple introduced the iPhone in 2007. Within a decade smartphones were pervasive globally. Estimates suggested that by 2017 there were more than 700 million global users of the iPhone alone.

There were also major signs of innovation in some traditional sectors due to other new technologies. For example, many American politicians in the 2000s made a major issue of America's dependence on foreign oil. They called for increased drilling and exploration, even in environmentally sensitive areas. But drastic improvements in the technique of hydraulic fracturing, or "fracking," revolutionized the American oil industry by the early 2010s. (Critics suggested that there were serious environmental and geological risks created by fracking.) Between 2000 and 2016, the amount of oil produced in the United States by fracking shot up from 2 percent to 50 percent. In 2015, the United States allowed crude oil exports to resume after a forty-year ban on oil exports that had begun during the energy crisis of the mid-1970s. Fracking in domestic wells meant America was reemerging as one of the leading global forces in oil production.

Innovation, enhanced automation, and the processes of globalization fueled nearly unprecedented growth and prosperity from the 1980s to the 2000s, but they also introduced volatility and disruption into the economy. The domestic manufacturing sector was hurt badly by American companies' use of factories and workers overseas. Dependence on overseas manufacturing workers, especially in places such as China, made consumer products less expensive. But it resulted in a collapse in the number of traditional factory jobs in America. Even though the US population was growing at a steady pace from the late 1970s to the late 2000s, the number of Americans employed in manufacturing dropped from 20 million to about 12 million during that period. Many new jobs were created in the "service economy" and the technology sector. Some of these were good-paying jobs. Many of those in the service sector, however, were low-paying positions with little security, benefits, or union protections. These included jobs in which employees serve or interact with customers, such as workers in restaurants or "big box" stores. Hispanics, African Americans, and people with less than a college education struggled disproportionately with unemployment, job instability, and poverty.

By the mid-2000s, serious structural weaknesses in the economy were emerging. The Federal Reserve Bank established low interest rates in the early 2000s as a response to the dot-com bust. Low interest rates are good for people and businesses borrowing money but not good for those saving money. The Bush tax cuts combined with the low interest rates made the economy unusually fluid. The financial environment made it easier for people with poor credit records to borrow money for purchases of homes and other expensive items. Financial institutions and companies also created complex products by which banks and other institutions could invest in "subprime" mortgages. These and other shadowy "derivatives" took on an outsized, speculative role in global investing markets. Many areas of the country saw an unsustainable spike in housing prices as more and more buyers could get cheap loans. A thriving market developed in housing speculation as individuals and companies "flipped" houses, buying them cheap, doing some improvements, and selling them at a vast profit just months later.

The first signs of the Great Recession appeared in 2005–6 as housing prices started to plummet. Homeowners found themselves owing more on mortgages than their houses were worth. Speculators wound up with surplus houses they could no longer sell. Homeowners defaulted on loans they could not afford to pay off. In some cities streets were lined with foreclosed and bargain-sale homes. Just months before, many of these houses would have commanded steep prices. Financial institutions that had made major investments in derivatives and the housing sector took huge losses. The venerable New York investment firm Bear Stearns collapsed in 2008. Likewise, Lehman Brothers was forced to declare bankruptcy, the largest company to do so in American history. Major companies from insurers to automakers faced similar prospects. Some argued that the government should just let the free market do its devastating work: market processes would naturally weed out weak and irresponsible companies. But Bush and Obama administration officials believed the government needed to intervene in order to blunt the effects of the recession. They hoped to avert a return to the conditions of the Great Depression era. In the end the federal government spent more than $1 trillion to prop up the financial markets and to bail out major companies, including the massive insurance company American International Group in 2008 and General Motors, which declared bankruptcy in 2009.

Barack Obama's Presidency

The Great Recession was the central issue of the 2008 presidential campaign. Republicans nominated Arizona senator and Vietnam War hero John McCain. New York senator and former first lady Hillary Clinton was the choice of many Democrats, but she was ultimately defeated in the Democratic primaries by Illinois senator Barack Obama. Obama had emerged as a rising star for the Democrats due to his scintillating keynote speech at the 2004 Democratic National Convention.* Though he had relatively little political experience, Obama was a compelling orator and inspired many younger voters and people outside the Democratic establishment to support him. Obama's race was a conspicuous issue in the election. As the son of a white American mother and an African father, he would become the first African American major party nominee and the first black president in American history. Obama's candidacy drew out many new voters, and total voter turnout in 2008 was one of the highest in American history. Obama handily defeated McCain, more than doubling McCain's total Electoral College votes. Obama won in typical Democratic strongholds but also in swing states, such as Florida and Ohio.

Obama initially enjoyed majorities in both houses of Congress, and he moved forward with legislation designed to alleviate the financial crisis and to bring reform to the broken banking system. The signature legislative accomplishment of his presidency came in 2010 with the Affordable Care Act (ACA), or "Obamacare," as it was popularly known. This law sought to expand health insurance coverage for tens of millions of Americans who were too well-off to qualify for Medicaid or too young to qualify for Medicare, but who did not receive health insurance through their employers. The problem was that many of these people were young and healthy and did not wish to purchase health insurance, but the profitability of insurance depends on having many healthy people in the system who do not require extensive health care. So the ACA instituted a requirement that uninsured people buy health insurance or pay a fine. The ACA narrowly passed through Congress, depending almost exclusively on Democratic votes. The ACA faced numerous legal challenges. But in a 2012 ruling, a 5–4 majority headed by Chief Justice John Roberts (a 2005 George W. Bush appointee) affirmed the constitutionality of the law, including the mandate that individuals purchase health insurance.

The ACA was controversial in the first place because critics said it represented an unwarranted federal intrusion into the health care and insurance sectors. But its implementation raised even more controversial issues related to religious liberty and sexuality. In 2011, President Obama's Department of Health and Human Services (HHS) issued regulations mandating that employers offer insurance coverage for contraceptives and abortion-inducing drugs. Churches that objected were exempted from this policy, but

---

* "2004 Barack Obama Keynote Speech," YouTube video, 16:51, https://www.youtube.com/watch?v=_fMNIofUw2I.

Figure 30.3. President Barack Obama and First Lady Michelle Obama prepare to participate in a memorial service November 10, 2009, at Fort Hood, Texas. The ceremony was to honor the victims of the November 5 shooting rampage that left thirteen dead and thirty-eight wounded.

other religious nonprofits were not. The regulations also failed to contemplate how the policy might affect closely held private companies owned by people opposed to contraception or abortion. A number of ministries, charities, religious schools, and businesses brought legal challenges against the HHS Mandate. One of them resulted in the Supreme Court case of *Burwell v. Hobby Lobby Stores* (2014). In this 5–4 decision, the court majority ruled that the HHS Mandate violated the 1993 Religious Freedom Restoration Act, which prohibited the "Government [from] substantially burden[ing] a person's exercise of religion" unless doing so represented a "compelling government interest." The court decided that even private, closely held corporations like the Christian-owned craft store chain Hobby Lobby could claim religious liberty rights. Controversy over the HHS Mandate also focused on attempts by the Little Sisters of the Poor, a Catholic charitable order of nuns, to gain an exemption from the requirement that they provide coverage for contraception.

The Obama years saw a number of these kinds of controversies associated with the "culture wars." Liberal judges and lawyers attempted to limit the scope of religious liberty to "freedom of worship" alone. Arguably the most important Supreme Court religious liberty decision during these years was *Hosanna-Tabor v. Equal Employment Opportunity Commission* (2012). Unlike many close culture war decisions, *Hosanna-Tabor* resulted in a unanimous ruling in favor of the right of churches and church schools to make their own hiring decisions. Longtime legal precedent had suggested that "ministerial" positions under religious employers were not subject to antidiscrimination laws because of the religious liberty and antiestablishment provisions of the First Amendment to the Constitution. Under the "ministerial exemption," congregations are free to hire and fire according to their own convictions rather than being subject to federal regulations. The Obama Department of Justice argued that the ministerial exemption, if it should even exist, should only apply to employees whose duties were "exclusively religious," meaning clergy. But the Court—including Obama nominees Sonia Sotomayor and Elena Kagan—affirmed a broader view of the ministerial exemption, asserting it also applied to teachers at church schools. *Hosanna-Tabor* signaled that while traditional religious convictions were becoming increasingly contested in American culture, the Supreme Court was inclined to maintain a robust understanding of religious liberty as it applied to the internal affairs of churches and their schools.

The Obama years also saw a heightened pace of change with regard to the legal status of homosexual couples and the definition of marriage. As we have seen, the institution of marriage and child-rearing within marriage had started to fade as cultural norms in America by the 2000s. Until the Supreme Court decision of *Lawrence v. Texas*, many states still had laws prohibiting homosexual acts. But in 2004, the Massachusetts Supreme Court granted homosexual couples the right to be married. This began a decade-long effort to change the traditional understanding of marriage as being a union between one man and one woman. Gay activists insisted that legal equality for homosexuals was the next major front in America's quest for full civil rights. In the early stages of the gay rights movement, many observers believed marriage laws would never change to include homosexual couples. Some gay activists were not even sure marriage was the right focus for their movement. By the time of Barack Obama's election, prominent politicians in both parties still opposed the legal recognition of "gay marriage." Obama himself professed to be opposed to legalizing gay marriages in the 2008 election, although advisors have since said that President Obama was not being candid about his actual views. By 2012, he acknowledged that he supported recognition of gay marriage.

In 2010, President Obama signed a law overturning President Clinton's "don't ask, don't tell" policy with regard to homosexuals in the military. In response to the surging trend toward gay marriage, many states had passed laws defining marriage as a union between one man and one woman. Likewise, the Defense of Marriage Act (1996), with the same definition of marriage, remained on the federal books. These laws set up an inevitable clash at the Supreme Court. Many observers wanted states to be able to decide for themselves, through their own legislatures, about their policy on gay marriage. But homosexual activists insisted that the Supreme Court must strike down the federal and state laws against gay marriage and impose a uniform rule on all states. That is what the Supreme Court did, beginning with its 2013 decision *US v. Windsor*, in which a narrow majority struck down the Defense of Marriage Act. The deciding vote was cast by Reagan appointee Anthony Kennedy, who also sided with the court's liberal majority in key abortion cases.

It was no surprise to conservative critics when the same five-vote majority, led by Kennedy, overturned state laws prohibiting gay marriage in the 2015 decision *Obergefell v. Hodges*. They argued that such laws violated the due process and equal protection clauses of the Fourteenth Amendment. In his dissent in *Obergefell*, the conservative stalwart Antonin Scalia (who would pass away in 2016) called the ruling a threat to American democracy because it was "the furthest extension in fact—and the furthest extension one can even imagine—of the Court's claimed power to create 'liberties' that the Constitution and its Amendments neglect to mention." Some county clerks initially refused to comply with the Supreme Court's edict to start issuing marriage licenses to homosexual couples. But by the end of President Obama's second term, officials were granting such licenses even in the most conservative areas of the country. In certain instances homosexual couples also sued devout florists and bakers for discrimination when they would not provide services to the couples' wedding ceremony.

Many conservative Christians responded to these developments in much the same way Jerry Falwell and the founders of the Moral Majority had done in the 1970s and 1980s: they sought to influence the political process and to get Republicans elected who would nominate traditionalist judges. But since George W. Bush, the Republicans had not nominated a presidential candidate who had clear evangelical credentials. White evangelical voters tended to coalesce around Republican candidates, however, regardless of the candidate's personal beliefs. This was the case in 2012, when nominee Mitt Romney was a Mormon, and in 2016, when candidate Donald Trump said little about his own faith. Trump welcomed evangelicals' support, but he had a long history of extramarital affairs and seemed to many observers to be functionally secular.

Other conservative Christians argued that while politics was important, Christians should focus more on the work of the kingdom of God by strengthening churches and maintaining biblical theology. These Protestant renewal movements centered around organizations and ministries such as The Gospel Coalition and Desiring God, the latter headed by Minnesota Baptist pastor John Piper. These alliances often attracted like-minded churches and pastors through books, conferences, and an active internet presence. Their leaders were devoted to the value of missions, traditional Reformed theology, and biblical views on the family and culture.

Mainline denominations have continued their decades-long pattern of decline since 2000. The Roman Catholic Church, still America's largest religious organization, was damaged by a series of priestly sexual abuse scandals that emerged in the early 2000s. But the continuing flow of immigration from Latin America, Asia, and Africa kept adding new adherents to many evangelical and Catholic churches. Some immigrants brought their own denominations with them to America. For example, the Redeemed Christian Church of God, a Nigerian-based Pentecostal denomination, developed an aggressive church-planting presence in the United States and opened a major denominational camp in north Texas. American-based denominations also helped feed the globalizing trend. For example, the Anglican Church in North America (ACNA) broke away from the liberal US Episcopal Church and Anglican Church of Canada in 2009 and began aligning with traditionalist Anglican provinces in Africa and South America. One of ACNA's greatest concerns was the mainline Episcopal Church's affirmation of gay marriage and openly homosexual clergy.

The 2012 Presidential Election

The furor over the Great Recession bailouts and "Obamacare" helped spawn the "Tea Party" movement. Leaders of this populist surge criticized the entire Washington political establishment, but they tended to support combative, fiscally conservative Republican candidates. The energy of the Tea Party was largely absorbed into the Republican Party. Partly because of Tea Party unrest over Obama's policies, the Democrats suffered terrible losses in the 2010 elections, including losing the majority in the House of Representatives. President Obama seemed vulnerable to Republican challenge in 2012. That year the Republicans nominated Mitt Romney, a wealthy businessman and former Massachusetts governor. As the campaign came to a head, Romney was secretly taped making comments to a Republican fund-raising dinner, in which he spoke of the "47 percent who are with [Obama], who are dependent upon government," who pay no income taxes and who simply support whatever politician promises to keep their entitlements in place. Critics said that this kind of talk revealed Romney as an out-of-touch elitist. The video hurt Romney among working-class voters in swing states. In the November 2012 election, President Obama defeated Romney 332 to 206 in the Electoral College, with Obama winning critical states such as Ohio, Florida, and Virginia.

Even though President Obama sought to end combat operations in Iraq, his administration kept pursuing the War on Terror, in some ways as vigorously as George W. Bush had. President Obama vowed to close down the controversial Guantánamo Bay prison in Cuba, but dozens of prisoners remained there when he left office. The military increasingly used unmanned drones for surveillance and military strikes. One of the most controversial of these strikes came in 2011, when the United States killed the al-Qaeda preacher and recruiter Anwar al-Awlaki in Yemen. Al-Awlaki was born in New Mexico, and accordingly was a US citizen. Critics said the United States had crossed a line by assassinating one of its own citizens, but others said al-Awlaki was a combatant in the War on Terror.

Al-Qaeda militants also overran the US embassy in Benghazi, Libya, in 2012, killing the US ambassador there and several other Americans. Obama administration officials, including Secretary of State Hillary Clinton, seemingly tried to obscure the fact that the Benghazi attack was a planned al-Qaeda operation. They insisted that the assault was a spontaneous convulsion of violence by Libyan Muslims. Benghazi turned into a minor scandal for Obama's second term. It also left questions that dogged Hillary Clinton into her run for president in 2016. During his second term the Obama administration and John Kerry, Clinton's successor as secretary of state, also worked feverishly to secure an agreement with Iran on its nuclear program. The resulting deal, announced in 2015, lifted sanctions against Iran in exchange for promises that Iran would not continue to pursue the development of nuclear weapons. In 2018, President Donald Trump announced that the United States was withdrawing from the agreement with Iran.

Donald Trump and the 2016 Election

Faced with a Republican Congress for much of his presidency, President Obama did not have an extensive record of legislative achievements by the end of his tenure. Yet he remained generally popular. By 2016, the economy had regained stability, if not vigor, since the Great Recession. It was assumed that Hillary Clinton would become the Democratic standard-bearer after her narrow loss to Obama in the 2008 primaries. However, Clinton did face a major challenge from the socialist senator Bernie Sanders of Vermont, who ferociously criticized Clinton for her connections to Wall Street banking interests and for her relatively hawkish views on foreign policy. Democratic primary procedures gave disproportionate weight to "superdelegates," usually party insiders, who gave Clinton the nomination in spite of Sanders's enthusiastic support among many younger Democratic voters.

The Republican primaries saw a vast field of conventional candidates face off against Donald Trump, a New York businessman and television reality show star. Trump surged to early leads in polls, but many experts did not take him seriously. Trump had virtually no political experience, and he struggled to articulate the specifics of his approach to various policy issues. Trump tapped into deep populist sentiments and frustrations with the Obama presidency, however. He reviled the American political establishment as incompetent, corrupt bunglers, promising voters that if he was elected, he would "drain the swamp" of Washington, DC, and "make America great again."

Trump also adopted an aggressive stance against undocumented immigrants from Mexico and Central America. "They're bringing drugs. They're bringing crime. They're rapists," Trump said in a campaign speech. He vowed to build a new security wall along the length of the US-Mexico border. He also assured voters that he would stop the flow of immigrants and refugees from Muslim-majority countries in the Middle East and North Africa. Many Democrats were delighted when Trump improbably won the Republican nomination, assuming he would be easier to defeat than some of the more conventional Republican candidates. Most Republican officials and conservative publications kept their distance from Trump during the primaries, worrying that his bombastic style could never prevail in a general election. Some feared that Trump would fatally damage the Republican brand. Many conservative Christians also viewed Trump warily at first because of his checkered personal history and his seeming lack of interest in issues of importance to social conservatives. But by the November 2016 election, the majority of white Christians had consolidated around Trump, and Trump cultivated connections with some prominent evangelical and Pentecostal leaders.

Many observers regarded the general election campaign of 2016 as one of the nastiest—and least substantive—in the history of American politics. Trump and the Republicans constantly called for further scrutiny of Clinton's actions as secretary of state, including the Benghazi scandal. They also pushed for investigation into Clinton's use of a private email server while she served in the Obama administration, which opened her to possible charges of mishandling classified information. Hackers or leakers compromised Democratic operatives' emails and publicized a series of communications that proved embarrassing to the Clinton campaign. Trump also faced a series of controversies and revelations about statements he made that were denigrating to women. In a 2005 video that surfaced a month before the election, Trump bragged about his sexual exploits in extraordinarily lewd terms, seeming to suggest that he had sexually harassed or even assaulted women. Some Republicans assumed the video would end Trump's candidacy and called for him to step down.

Trump did not step down, and until Election Day 2016 most observers believed Clinton would win. But Trump in fact won a convincing victory in the Electoral College, with broad-based national support and stunning victories in traditionally Democratic states such as Wisconsin, Michigan, and Pennsylvania. Clinton won the national popular vote, however, buoyed by large Democratic margins in a number of cities and in large states such as California and New York. This outcome, harking back to Al Gore's loss to George W. Bush in 2000, made critics call once again for an end to the Electoral College. For the second time in sixteen years, the Electoral College had awarded the presidency to a candidate who did not win the popular vote nationally. The "gender gap" continued to be a major factor in the election, with a majority of women supporting Clinton and a majority of men favoring Trump. White working-class northern men were arguably the key demographic component of Trump's victory, with Clinton seriously underperforming President Obama's results with that group. Critics argued that many of these white male supporters were animated by an ugly streak of nativism and a loathing of women such as Clinton. But Trump had found a way to appeal to legions of white male voters with promises to bring blue-collar manufacturing jobs back to the United States.

Trump was inaugurated in early 2017, putting Republicans in control of the presidency and Congress. Trump had promised to reverse many of the policies of the Obama administration, including the Affordable Care Act. But divisions among Republicans, some dating to the Tea Party movement and some spawned by controversies over Trump himself, made concerted Republican action difficult. Trump became the subject of an unusual level of animosity in the mainstream news media, even for a Republican president. There was virtually no "honeymoon" period for President Trump in 2017. He immediately had to contend with constant reports of chaos in his cabinet and accusations that his campaign had colluded with Russian operatives during the 2016 election.

One reason Clinton had been expected to win was that her campaign raised almost twice as much money as Trump's. But Trump ran a new kind of campaign that depended little on paid publicity. People thronged to his rallies, where Trump fed on the crowd's energy. Clinton often seemed stilted and tired at her campaign stops. Trump was unusually adept at turning even negative media coverage to his advantage, seeming always to foil Clinton's attempts to control the "media narrative." Trump also used social media—especially Twitter—more actively than any previous candidate or president. He took to social media to lambaste opponents, the media, and even people within his own administration and party. Trump's aides were sometimes caught off guard by his tweets, especially when they announced policies the campaign or administration had not yet fully worked out. But social media allowed Trump to enhance his maverick image, bypassing the conventional media to communicate in real time with his supporters. Trump's tweets became a part of the daily news. In this sense Trump was a president for a new era. He employed novel forms of media and communication to express the anxieties of many Americans about terrorism, immigration, globalization, and other factors that seemed to be changing the United States so quickly.

■ SELECTED BIBLIOGRAPHY ■

Allen, Jonathan, and Amie Parnes. *Shattered: Inside Hillary Clinton's Doomed Campaign.* New York: Broadway Books, 2017.

Batchelor, Bob. *The 2000s.* Westport, CT: Greenwood, 2008.

Bernstein, Carl. *A Woman in Charge: The Life of Hillary Rodham Clinton.* New York: Vintage, 2007.

Hansen, Collin. *Young, Restless, Reformed: A Journalist's Journey with the New Calvinists.* Wheaton, IL: Crossway, 2008.

Jenkins, Philip. *A History of the United States.* 5th ed. New York: Palgrave, 2017.

Levin, Yuval. *The Fractured Republic: Renewing America's Social Contract in the Age of Individualism.* New York: Basic Books, 2016.

Lewis, Michael. *The Big Short: Inside the Doomsday Machine.* Repr. ed. New York: W. W. Norton, 2010.

Moscowitz, Leigh. *The Battle over Marriage: Gay Rights Activism through the Media.* Urbana: University of Illinois Press, 2013.

Remnick, David. *The Bridge: The Life and Rise of Barack Obama.* New York: Vintage, 2010.

Wright, Lawrence. *The Looming Tower: Al-Qaeda and the Road to 9/11.* New York: Vintage, 2006.

ILLUSTRATION CREDITS

Figure 16.1. Photograph by Solomon D. Butcher (Solomon Devore), 1886. Library of Congress, Prints and Photographs Division. Public Domain. Library of Congress Digital Collections.

Figure 16.2. Photographer: Andrew J. Russell. Publisher: Union Pacific Railroad Company. The Miriam and Ira D. Wallach Division of Art, Prints and Photographs: Photography Collection, New York Public Library.

Figure 16.3. Photo by Charles F. Lummis. Library of Congress, Prints and Photographs Division. Public Domain. Library of Congress Digital Collections.

Figure 16.4. Photograph by Northwestern Photo Co. (Trager & Kuhn) Chadron, NE, ca. 1891 January 17. South Dakota. Library of Congress, Prints and Photographs Division. Public Domain. Library of Congress Digital Collections.

Figure 16.5. St. Paul, MN: The Ingersoll View Company, ca. 1905. Library of Congress, Prints and Photographs Division. Public Domain. Library of Congress Digital Collections.

Figure 16.6. Photo by Bain News Service, NYC, 1909. Library of Congress, Prints and Photographs Division. Public Domain. Library of Congress Digital Collections.

Figure 16.7. Lithograph by L. Prang, Boston. Library of Congress, Prints and Photographs Division. Public Domain. Library of Congress Digital Collections.

Figure 16.8. Photograph by Lewis Wickes Hine, March 1912. Library of Congress, Prints and Photographs Division. Public Domain. Library of Congress Digital Collections.

Figure 16.9. Bain News Service, 1917. Library of Congress, Prints and Photographs Division. Public Domain. Library of Congress Digital Collections.

Figure 17.1. Photograph by Richard Kyle Fox, July 15, 1899. Exhibited: "The Great American Hall of Wonders: Art, Science, and Invention in the Nineteenth Century" at the Smithsonian American Art Museum, Washington, DC, July 2011–January 2012. Library of Congress, Prints and Photographs Division. Public Domain. Library of Congress Digital Collections.

Figure 17.2. Oil on canvas. Amon Carter Museum of American Art, Fort Worth, Texas, Amon G. Carter Collection. Photograph of original painting by Wikimedia user. Public Domain. Wikimedia Commons.

Figure 17.3. Created by "The Strobridge Lith. Co., Cinti, NY & London" [1889]. Library of Congress, Prints and Photographs Division. Public Domain. Library of Congress Digital Collections.

Figure 17.4. Goodwin & Co., 1887–1890. Library of Congress, Prints and Photographs Division, Forms part of: Baseball cards from the Benjamin K. Edwards Collection. Public Domain. Library of Congress Digital Collections.

Figure 17.5. Chromolithograph by Edward Windsor Kemble. New York: Wm. M. Clarke, ca. 1883. Library of Congress, Prints and Photographs Division. Public Domain. Library of Congress Digital Collections.

Figure 17.6. Photograph by Elmer Chickering, c1910 January 27. Library of Congress, Prints and Photographs Division. Public Domain. Library of Congress Digital Collections.

Figure 17.7. Chicago: E. W. Kelley, publisher, ca. 1911 October 2. Library of Congress, Prints and Photographs Division. Library of Congress Digital Collections.

Figure 17.8. Photograph by E. L. Wolven, ca. 1913. Library of Congress, Prints and Photographs Division. Library of Congress Digital Collections.

Figure 17.9. Copy of original photo by J. E. Purdy. Published by Bain News Service [n.d.]. Library of Congress, Prints and Photographs Division. Library of Congress Digital Collections.

Figure 17.10. The Metropolitan Museum of Art, New York. Gift of Mrs. Frank B. Porter, 1922. PD-US. Wikimedia Commons.

Figure 17.11. Library of Congress, Prints and Photographs Division. Library of Congress Digital Collections.

Figure 18.1. Artist: Frank Beard. In *Judge* 6, no. 154 (September 27, 1884): cover. Library of Congress, Prints and Photographs Division. Library of Congress Digital Collections.

Figure 18.2. In *Puck* magazine, May 18, 1904, centerfold. Library of Congress, Prints and Photographs Division. Library of Congress Digital Collections.

Figure 18.3. Chicago: James Lee Co., 1907. From the New York Public Library, Schomburg Center for Research in Black Culture, Photographs and Prints Division. The New York Public Library Digital Collections.

Figure 18.4. New York, NY: Strohmeyer & Wyman, ca. 1899. Library of Congress, Prints and Photographs Division. Library of Congress Digital Collections.

Figure 18.5. New York: Underwood & Underwood, publishers, ca. 1906 November 30. Library of Congress, Prints and Photographs Division. Library of Congress Digital Collections.

Figure 19.1. Library of Congress, Prints and Photographs Division, National Photo Company Collection. Library of Congress Digital Collections.

Figure 19.2. Photograph by C. M. Bell, between February 1894 and February 1901. Gift: American Genetic Association, 1975. Library of Congress, Prints and Photographs Division. Library of Congress Digital Collections.

Figure 19.3. Unicorn drops patent for medicine. (S. W. Chandler & Co. Lith., 204 Washington St., Boston. Copyright by F. W. Thayer. Library of Congress, Prints and Photographs Division. Library of Congress Digital Collections.)

Figure 19.4. Library of Congress, Prints and Photographs Division. Library of Congress Digital Collections.

Figure 19.5. Photograph by John C. H. Grabill, 1888. Library of Congress, Prints and Photographs Division. Library of Congress Digital Collections.

Figure 19.6. Library of Congress, Prints and Photographs Division, National Photo Company Collection. Library of Congress Digital Collections.

Figure 20.1. Bain News Service, between 1910 and 1923. Library of Congress, Prints and Photographs Division. Library of Congress Digital Collections.

Figure 20.2. Harris & Ewing, 1917. Gift; Harris & Ewing. 1955. Library of Congress, Prints and Photographs Division. Library of Congress Digital Collections.

Figure 20.3. Library of Congress, Prints and Photographs Division. Library of Congress Digital Collections.

Figure 21.1. Library of Congress, Prints and Photographs Division. Library of Congress Digital Collections.

Figure 21.2. Signed, lower left: Russell / Patterson. Bequest and gift; Caroline and Erwin Swann; 1977. Library of Congress, Prints and Photographs Division. Library of Congress Digital Collections.

Figure 21.3. Library of Congress Digital Collections.

Figure 21.4. Photograph by F. C. Quimby, c1921. Library of Congress, Prints and Photographs Division. Library of Congress Digital Collections.

Figure 21.5. Library of Congress Prints and Photographs Division Washington, DC 20540.

Figure 21.6. Library of Congress, Prints and Photographs Division, National Photo Company Collection. Library of Congress Digital Collections.

Figure 21.7. Library of Congress, Prints and Photographs Division, National Photo Company Collection. Library of Congress Digital Collections.

Figure 21.8. Library of Congress, Prints and Photographs Division, George Grantham Bain Collection. Library of Congress Digital Collections.

Figure 21.9. Photograph by Harris & Ewing, 1928. Gift; Harris & Ewing, Inc. 1955. Library of Congress, Prints and Photographs Division. Library of Congress Digital Collections.

Figure 22.1. Library of Congress, Prints and Photographs Division. Library of Congress Digital Collections.

Figure 22.2. Photograph by Arthur Rothstein, April 1936. Transfer: United States. Farm Security Administration/Office of War Information. Overseas Picture Division. Washington Division, 1944. Library of Congress, Prints and Photographs Division. Library of Congress Digital Collections.

Figure 22.3. Transfer; United States. Farm Security Administration/Office of War Information. Overseas Picture Division. Washington Division, 1944. Library of Congress, Prints and Photographs Division. Library of Congress Digital Collections.

Figure 22.4. Photograph by Underwood & Underwood. Library of Congress, Prints and Photographs Division. Library of Congress Digital Collections.

Figure 22.5. Photograph by Jack Delano, May 1941. Transfer; United States. Farm Security Administration/Office of War Information. Overseas Picture Division. Washington Division, 1944. Library of Congress, Prints and Photographs Division. Library of Congress Digital Collections.

Figure 22.6. Photograph by Harris & Ewing, January 1935. Gift; Harris & Ewing, Inc. 1955. Library of Congress, Prints and Photographs Division. Library of Congress Digital Collections.

Figure 22.7. From Portraits of African American ex-slaves from the U.S. Works Progress Administration, Federal Writers' Project slave narratives collections. Library of Congress, Prints and Photographs Division. Library of Congress Digital Collections.

Figure 22.8. Photograph by Harris & Ewing, ca. 1938. Gift: Harris & Ewing, Inc. 1955. Library of Congress, Prints and Photographs Division. Library of Congress Digital Collections.

Figure 23.1. Photo by Al. Aumuller, October 1, 1940. Library of Congress Prints and Photographs Division Washington, DC 20540.

Figure 23.2. U.S. Government Printing Office, 1943. Library of Congress Prints and Photographs Division Washington, DC 20540.

Figure 23.3. Library of Congress Prints and Photographs Division Washington, DC 20540.

Figure 23.4. Official U.S. Navy Photograph 80-G-411123, U.S. National Archives Wikimedia Commons, Public Domain.

Figure 23.5. Library of Congress Prints and Photographs Division Washington, DC 20540.

Figure 23.6. Library of Congress.

Figure 23.7. Library of Congress Prints and Photographs Division Washington, DC 20540.

Figure 23.8. National Archives; Wikimedia Commons, Public Domain.

Figure 23.9. By Ed Westcott/Department of Energy Oak Ridge. Wikimedia Commons, Public Domain.

Figure 24.1. Photo by Corporal Peter McDonald, USMC. Public domain. Wikimedia Commons.

Figure 24.2. Library of Congress Serial and Government Publications Division Washington, DC 20540.

Figure 25.1. Library of Congress Prints and Photographs Division Washington, DC 20540.

Figure 25.2. Photo courtesy of the National Archives, September 20, 2007. Wikimedia Commons, public domain.

Figure 26.1. Source: NASA Commons on Flickr. This image was catalogued by Johnson Space Center of the United States National Aeronautics and Space Administration (NASA) under Photo ID: GPN-2000-001027 AND Alternate ID: S64-36910. Wikimedia Commons, public domain.

Figure 26.2. Library of Congress Prints and Photographs Division Washington, DC 20540.

Figure 26.3. AP Photo/Bill Hudson.

Figure 26.4. Library of Congress Prints and Photographs Division Washington, DC 20540.

Figure 26.5. Department of the Army. Office of the Chief Signal Officer (National Archives Archeological Site, Still Picture Records Section, Special Media Archives Services Division (NWCS-S). Wikimedia Commons, public domain.

Figure 26.6. National Archives Archeological Site, Still Picture Records Section, Special Media Archives Services Division (NWCS-S). Wikimedia Commons, public domain.

Figure 27.1. Richard Nixon Presidential Library and Museum. Available in the holdings of the National Archives and Records Administration, cataloged under the National Archives Identifier (NAID) 194421.

Figure 27.2. Library of Congress Prints and Photographs Division Washington, DC 20540.

Figure 27.3. *U.S. News & World Report Magazine* Photograph Collection. Contact sheet available for reference purposes. 1979. This image is available from the United States Library of Congress's Prints and Photographs division under the digital ID ppmsca.09800. Wikimedia Commons, public domain.

Figure 28.1. This file is licensed under the Creative Commons Attribution-Share Alike 3.0 Unported, 2.5 Generic, 2.0 Generic and 1.0 Generic license. Wikimedia Commons.

Figure 28.2. The Oyez Project; author: Collection of the Supreme Court of the United States. Wikipedia Commons, public domain.

Figure 28.3. Photo by NASA (Wikimedia Commons, public domain.

Figure 29.1. U.S. Army photo by Staff Sgt. Lee Corkran. 1991. Public domain.)

Figure 29.2. Library of Congress Prints and Photographs Division Washington, DC 20540.

Figure 29.3. Wikimedia Commons.

Figure 30.1. Wikimedia Commons.

Figure 30.2. Retrieved from the Library of Congress. The 250 color slides made at the World Trade Towers in New York City on September 11, 2001, received from the New York District Attorney's office from an unattributed photographer, are in the public domain. Privacy and publicity rights may apply. These slides were received from the New York District Attorney's office with the photographer relinquishing any and all copyright and right of attribution. Therefore, the photographer's name will not be associated with these photographs. Wikimedia Commons, public domain.

Figure 30.3. By MC1 Chad J. McNeeley, USN. Permission, http://defenseimagery.mil/imagery.html#guid=035f32e6b4df3d6e0f51ab7c55bb8e42e0d17df0. This file is a work of a sailor or employee of the U.S. Navy, taken or made as part of that person's official duties. As a work of the U.S. federal government, the image is in the public domain in the United States. Wikimedia Commons.

INDEX